Latin American Economic Outlook 2024

FINANCING SUSTAINABLE DEVELOPMENT

This work is published under the responsibility of the Secretary-General of the OECD, the President of the Corporación Andina de Fomento (CAF) and the President of the European Commission. The opinions expressed and arguments employed herein do not necessarily reflect the official views of the Member countries of the OECD, the members of its Development Centre, those of the Corporación Andina de Fomento (CAF), or of the European Union and its Member States, or the Member States of the United Nations.

The names of countries and territories and representation used in this joint publication follow the practice of the OECD.

This document, as well as any data and map included herein, are without prejudice to the status of or sovereignty over any territory, to the delimitation of international frontiers and boundaries and to the name of any territory, city or area.

Please cite this publication as:
OECD et al. (2024), *Latin American Economic Outlook 2024: Financing Sustainable Development*, OECD Publishing, Paris, https://doi.org/10.1787/c437947f-en.

ISBN 978-92-64-81213-0 (print)
ISBN 978-92-64-57271-3 (PDF)
ISBN 978-92-64-83786-7 (HTML)

Latin American Economic Outlook
ISSN 2072-5159 (print)
ISSN 2072-5140 (online)

CAF Reference Number: CAF-513i-2024

ECLAC Reference Number: LC/TS.2024/125

European Union
ISBN 978-92-68-22577-6 (PDF)
Catalogue number: MN-01-24-008-EN-N (PDF)
ISBN 978-92-68-22578-3 (print)
Catalogue number: MN-01-24-008-EN-C (print)

Photo credits: Cover design by Aida Buendía using images from © Shutterstock.com

Corrigenda to OECD publications may be found at: https://www.oecd.org/en/publications/support/corrigenda.html.

Foreword

Since 2007, each edition of the annual *Latin American Economic Outlook* (LEO) analyses one of the multiple challenges faced by the Latin America and the Caribbean (LAC) region in its transition towards sustainable and inclusive development, comparing LAC's performance against its peers, suggesting policy recommendations and providing examples for policy learning.

The LEO benefits from the expertise and inputs of several institutions. In 2011, the United Nations Economic Commission for Latin America and the Caribbean joined the OECD as co-author, as did the Development Bank of Latin America and the Caribbean in 2013, and the European Commission in 2018.

This 17th LEO, *Financing Sustainable Development*, maps and analyses the region's various sources of financing in a context of tight fiscal space, unpacking the options for funding development agendas better at national, regional and international levels. It provides policy recommendations for governments to improve tax collection, fiscal expenditure and the management of public debt. It stresses the strategic role of the private sector and how further developing financial markets can help channel more private investment towards development goals. Finally, the report underscores the necessity for stronger international partnerships to accelerate the mobilisation of international resources towards the region's sustainable development.

Acknowledgements

Partners of this report are the United Nations Economic Commission for Latin America and the Caribbean (ECLAC), the Development Bank of Latin America and the Caribbean (CAF), the European Commission (EC) and the Development Centre of the Organisation for Economic Co-operation and Development (OECD). This report is supported by the Directorate-General for International Partnerships of the European Commission (INTPA).

The contribution of the OECD Development Centre to this report was led and managed by Sebastián Nieto-Parra, Head of the Centre's Latin America and the Caribbean (LAC) Unit. Co-ordination was led by Olivia Cuq and René Orozco, Policy Analyst and Economist respectively at the same Unit, under the guidance of Ragnheiður Elín Árnadóttir, Director of the OECD Development Centre, and Federico Bonaglia, Deputy Director of the OECD Development Centre. ECLAC's contribution was led by Marco Llinás, Director of the Production, Productivity and Management Division, Daniel Titelman, Director of the Economic Development Division and Sebastián Rovira, Economic Affairs Officer in Charge of the Innovation and New Technologies Unit, under the guidance of José Manuel Salazar-Xirinachs, Executive Secretary of ECLAC. The contribution from CAF was led by Veronica Frisancho Robles, Chief Economist, Ignacio Corlazzoli, Responsible for Resource Mobilisation and Global Partnerships Management, and Reinier Schliesser, Senior Economist - Acting Director, Unit of Macroeconomic Studies, under the guidance of Sergio Díaz-Granados, Executive President of CAF. The European Commission contribution was led by Diana Montero Melis, Deputy Head of Unit at the Directorate-General for International Partnerships of the European Commission (INTPA) and Marc Vothknecht (INTPA), under the guidance of Olivier Luyckx, former Head of Unit - South America and Regional Operations, Felice Zaccheo, Head of Unit - Regional Programmes for Latin America and the Caribbean, and Felix Fernández-Shaw, Director for Latin America and the Caribbean and Relations with all Overseas Countries and Territories (INTPA).

The report benefited from the research, drafting and fruitful collaboration among various authors, including María Carolina Arcila (OECD), Els Berghmans (EC), Carl Bernadac (AFD), Marie-Pierre Bourzai (AFD), Laura Buchet (OECD), Adriana Caicedo (OECD), Regina Casillas Rodríguez (OECD), Luis Cecchi (OECD), Chiara Cirignaco (EC), Olivia Cuq (OECD), Rita Da Costa (OECD), Victoria de la Puente (OECD), Jimena Durán (CAF), Sofia Faurie (OECD), Alessandro Ferrario (EC), Eleonore Fignolet (EC), Sonia García Lorenzana (OECD), Martín Grandes (OECD), Laura Gutiérrez Cadena (OECD), Rodolfo Lazarich (EC), Martina Lejtreger (OECD), Oswaldo López (CAF), Carlos Maldonado (ECLAC), Xavier Mancero (ECLAC), Thomas Manfredi (OECD), Diana Mejía (CAF), Nathalia Montoya González (OECD), Mariana Navarro (OECD), Sebastián Nieto Parra (OECD), Esteban Pérez (ECLAC), René Orozco (OECD), Noel Pérez (ECLAC), Zoe Pigasse (OECD), Ramón Pineda (ECLAC), Claudia Robles (ECLAC), Callum Ryan (OECD), Daniel Titelman (ECLAC), Manuel Toledo (CAF), Francisco Villarreal (ECLAC), María José Zambrano (AFD) and Juan Vázquez Zamora (OECD). Rosario Hernando Cruz (OECD) provided invaluable administrative support throughout the elaboration of the report.

A group of OECD experts and colleagues have been particularly active and supportive during the production process, providing views, inputs and comments. We would like to highlight the support of Michael Abendschein, Jens Arnold, Julia Benn, Marisa Berbegal, Bert Brys, Magdalena Burtscher, Aida Caldera, Pietrangelo De Biase, Gabriel Di Paolantonio, Luisa Dressler, Charlotte Dubald, Abdoulaye

Fabregas, Camilo Gamba, Paula Garda, Jason Gagnon, Pilar Garrido, Antonio Gomes, Alberto Gonzalez, Andrea Grifoni, Paul Horrocks, Felix Hugger, Raphaela Hyee, Kentaro Kato, Fatos Koc, Horacio Levy, Mario López Roldán, Alejandra Medina, Chiara Monticone, Pierce O'Reilly, Lorenzo Pavone, Sarah Perret, Cécilia Piemonte, Luca Policino, Monika Queisser, Emma Raiteri, Claudia Ramirez, Yannic Rehm, Katherine Scrivens, Daniela Sena, Micheal Sicsic, Joseph Stead, Yung Tang, and John-David Tochon.

The content of the report was enriched by constructive feedback received during an informal consultation meeting with the LAC countries and members of the OECD Development Centre Governing Board on 21 February 2024; a virtual Experts' Meeting on 16 and 17 April 2024; and a private-sector consultation meeting that took place on 11 April 2024. In addition to the LAC delegates to the Governing Board of the OECD Development Centre, we are particularly grateful to the experts, academics, private-sector representatives and other public servants who joined us during the Experts' Meeting, the private-sector consultation meeting and informal meetings: Alberto Arenas (ECLAC), Nour Barnat (UNCTAD), Romy Calderón (ALIDE), Javier Carbajal Galarza (ALIDE), Anderson Caputo (IDB), Andrea Costafreda (Oxfam), Joana Conde (EIB), Eric David (French delegation to the OECD), Francisco Duque (Financial Superintendency, Colombia), Alejandra del Mar Dussán Zuluaga (IDB), Andrés Felipe Espejo Rivera (ECLAC), Ernesto Espíndola (ECLAC), Almudena Fernández (UNDP), Juan Huitzilihuitl Flores Zendejas (University of Geneva), Sebastián García Andrade (Central Bank of Colombia), Chris Garroway (UN), Martin Grandes (Universidad de Buenos Aires), Felipe Andrés Guerra Cuadrado (Financial Superintendency, Colombia), Petra Kynclova (UNCTAD), Eirini Koutra (EIB), Kristin Lang (EIB), José Ignacio López (ANIF), Juan Martínez (IDB), Baptiste Mesa (AFD), María Luisa Montero Marinho (ECLAC), Natalia Moreno Rigollot (Telefónica), Hugo Ñopo (The World Bank), José Antonio Ocampo (Columbia University), Anu Peltola (UNCTAD), Javier Pérez (Central Bank of Spain), Fazia Pusterla (IDB), Andrea Repetto (Pontificia Universidad Católica de Chile), Nuria Rodríguez Aller (COFIDES), José Antonio Sanahuja (Universidad Complutense de Madrid), Isabel Fernández Sarabia (EIB), Ricardo Santos (EIB), Paola Subacchi (Sciences Po), Luciana Trindade de Aguiar (UNDP), Andrea Trujillo (Financial Superintendency, Colombia), Oscar Valencia (IDB), Ana Valero (Telefónica), Marta Vegas (Telefónica), Guido Zack (Fundar) and Nancy Eugenia Zamudio Gómez (Central Bank of Colombia).

The country notes benefited from constructive inputs, scrutiny and verification by delegations to the OECD from Chile, Colombia, Costa Rica and Mexico, as well as the embassies in France of Argentina, Brazil, Dominican Republic, Ecuador, El Salvador, Guatemala, Panama, Paraguay, Peru and Uruguay. OECD delegations and embassies also co-ordinated the relevant inputs from different national ministries and governmental areas. The OECD Development Centre also expresses its sincere gratitude to the Agence française de développement (AFD), the Departamento Nacional de Planeación (DNP) of Colombia, the European Union, the Spanish Ministry of Foreign Affairs, the Swiss Agency for Development and Co-operation, Telefónica, and Universidad del Rosario for their support of the Latin American Economic Outlook report.

Finally, many thanks go to the Publications and Communications Division of the OECD Development Centre, in particular Aida Buendia, Delphine Grandrieux, Elizabeth Nash, Henri-Bernard Solignac-Lecomte and Felix Zimmermann, for their steadfast patience and expedient work on the production of this report and associated materials. The authors also sincerely appreciate the editing and proofreading activities undertaken by Mary Bortin and Jill Gaston; the co-ordination of the Spanish translation by Alejandro Barranco, Julia Gregory and Alexander Summerfield; the Spanish editing and proofreading services by Liliana Tafur and the infographics design by Milagros Gastaldi.

Editorial

The *Latin American Economic Outlook 2024: Financing Sustainable Development* is the product of longstanding co-operation between the OECD, the United Nations Economic Commission for Latin America and the Caribbean, the Development Bank of Latin America and the Caribbean, and the European Commission.

This 17th edition focuses on how Latin American and Caribbean (LAC) countries can mobilise resources to tackle socio-economic challenges and promote economic development, energy transitions and growth, in line with the Sustainable Development Goals. It offers policy recommendations to increase spending efficiency, optimise budget allocation, improve access to finance, and boost productivity.

The Outlook highlights that countries can improve public spending, tax collection, and the way they raise and manage public debt. Better targeted spending towards households and businesses most in need would enhance value for money, and citizens' and businesses' trust in government. Optimising the tax administration and tax revenues would improve the state's capacity to strengthen institutions, enable the provision of better public services, minimise distortions to entrepreneurship, and promote equality of opportunities.

Financial systems with more depth, efficiency and better access can provide citizens and businesses in LAC countries with opportunities to increase investments. Countries in the region have made significant progress in improving depth and access to finance. Domestic credit to the private sector rose from 22% of GDP in 2000 to 50% of GDP in 2022. Account ownership nearly doubled from 29% in 2011 to 57% in 2021 for people aged 15 or above.

To maintain this positive trajectory, the Outlook recommends investing in digital innovation and digital literacy, and expanding market finance. Digital banks and payments have increased in importance, while financial literacy remains limited. Market capitalisation is at 36% of GDP, compared with 65% in OECD countries, with large companies accounting for a large share of it. Expanding fixed-income and equity markets, including venture capital and private equity, would boost innovation and productivity. Innovative financial instruments, such as green, social, sustainability and sustainability-linked bonds, catastrophe bonds, and debt-for-nature swaps, could mobilise additional resources, though further progress in the regulation and the supervision of these tools will be necessary.

Renewed regional and international partnerships will be important to mobilise greater resources in LAC. This includes the EU-LAC Global Gateway Investment Agenda, which aims to mobilise EUR 45 billion investment in LAC by 2027. Better alignment among national, regional, and multilateral development banks and other capital market actors is key to achieve this.

In the coming months, the LAC region has an opportunity to bring its perspective to the international debate on the transformation of the international financial architecture, including through the follow-up to the Paris Pact for People and the Planet, and at the Finance in Common Summit and the United Nation's Fourth International Conference on Financing for Development.

We stand ready to work together to support the region's efforts, and trust that this report provides a solid basis for the ambitious policy dialogue that is needed at national, regional and international levels.

Mathias Cormann

Secretary-General, OECD

Sergio Díaz-Granados

Executive President, CAF – Development Bank of Latin America and the Caribbean

José Manuel Salazar-Xirinachs

Executive Secretary, ECLAC

Jutta Urpilainen

European Commissioner for International Partnerships

Table of contents

Foreword 3

Acknowledgements 4

Editorial 6

Executive summary 12

Abbreviation and acronyms 14

Overview 17

1 Structural socio-economic challenges and financing conditions 33
- Introduction 35
- Weak growth in LAC points to the need to address structural challenges 36
- Persistent challenges are more difficult to address when there is limited room for demand-side policies 41
- Fiscal space remains limited while the region undergoes fiscal consolidation 43
- Social conditions and poverty: A multi-dimensional perspective 47
- The role of public and private financing in closing development gaps 57
- Policy recommendations 66
- Notes 68
- References 69

2 Public finance for development 79
- Introduction 81
- Trends in public spending in LAC 81
- Towards greater equity, efficiency and simplicity of taxation systems 85
- Rethinking debt management and strengthening fiscal frameworks 98
- A strengthened fiscal pact to sustain long-term revenue mobilisation 105
- Policy recommendations 108
- Notes 110
- References 111

3 Rallying financial market resources for development 119
- Introduction 121
- The functioning of the banking system in LAC 121
- Challenges and opportunities for greater financial inclusion 129
- Boosting financing through public development finance institutions 140

Deepening capital markets in LAC 145
Policy recommendations 161
Notes 163
References 164

4 International finance and partnerships to catalyse international resources 175
Introduction 177
Navigating a challenging international financial context 178
Unlocking the potential of international financial flows 184
Scaling up debt tools for financing the sustainable development agenda 198
Policy recommendations 208
References 211

5 Country notes 223
Reader's guide 225
Argentina 232
Brazil 234
Chile 236
Colombia 238
Costa Rica 240
Dominican Republic 242
Ecuador 244
El Salvador 246
Guatemala 248
Mexico 250
Panama 252
Paraguay 254
Peru 256
Uruguay 258

FIGURES

Figure 1. Labour productivity in LAC as a percentage of OECD labour productivity per hour worked, 1990-2023 17
Figure 2. Distribution of the LAC population, by household informality status, latest available year 18
Figure 3. Average tax structure as a % of total tax revenues in the LAC region and the OECD, 2022 20
Figure 4. Debt service-to-tax revenues ratio in LAC, 2012 and 2022 21
Figure 5. Domestic credit to the private sector as percentage of GDP and financial depth in LAC, 2022 22
Figure 6. Access to homeownership loans by the degree of households' informality in selected LAC countries 23
Figure 7. Concentration of equity markets in LAC, 2019 and 2024 24
Figure 8. Currency composition and average maturity of corporate bonds issued by country group, 2015-23 25
Figure 9. Annual venture capital investment in LAC, 2016-23 26
Figure 10. Distribution of financing types and financial instruments targeting green, digital and gender dimensions offered to MSMEs by DFIs in LAC, 2023 27
Figure 11. Components of external financing flows to the LAC region, 2011-22 28
Figure 12. International GSSS bond issuance in LAC by type, as a % of total and by issuer, 2014-23 29
Figure 1.1. Labour productivity in LAC as a percentage of OECD labour productivity per hour worked, 1990-2023 36
Figure 1.2. Total factor productivity (TFP) in LAC and OECD, 1950-2023 (1950 = 100) 37
Figure 1.3. Growth accounting (growth decomposition) in LAC, 1950-2023 38
Figure 1.4. Potential GDP per capita growth in LAC and in advanced economies 39
Figure 1.5. Sectoral labour productivity (PPP adjusted) in LAC relative to OECD, 2017 40
Figure 1.6. Monthly inflation in LAC economies under different inflation regimes 41

Figure 1.7. Total portfolio flows, May 2022-May 2024 (equity and debt) 42
Figure 1.8. FDI inflows in LAC as a % total world FDI, 1990-2023 43
Figure 1.9. Overall and primary fiscal balance in central governments in LAC as a % of GDP, 2010-23 44
Figure 1.10. Changes in tax-to-GDP ratio in LAC countries by main tax heading, 2022 45
Figure 1.11. Public debt dynamics in LAC, % of GDP 46
Figure 1.12. Monetary poverty rates in selected Latin American countries, 2001-22 47
Figure 1.13. Impact of inflation on the most vulnerable people in LAC 48
Figure 1.14. Distribution of the LAC population, by household informality status, latest available year 51
Figure 1.15. Poverty rates of workers in LAC by informality status 52
Figure 1.16. Income inequalities in LAC countries, 2002-22 53
Figure 1.17. SDG targets by their likelihood of achievement in LAC by 2030 58
Figure 1.18. Public and private spending on social protection programmes in LAC, 2018 62
Figure 1.19. Private vs. public investment as a share of total investment in LAC and OECD, 2019 63
Figure 1.20. Investment in infrastructure by subsector in selected LAC countries, 2021 64
Figure 1.21. Share of R&D investment by funding source in LAC and other territories, 2011-20 65
Figure 2.1. Central government total expenditure as % of GDP, by function and by country 82
Figure 2.2. Government spending on education per student, 2000-18, vs. PISA maths scores, 2022 84
Figure 2.3. Fossil fuel subsidies as a proportion of GDP (%) 85
Figure 2.4. Tax-to-GDP ratios and Equivalent Fiscal Pressure in the LAC region 86
Figure 2.5. Average tax structure in the LAC region and the OECD, 2022 87
Figure 2.6. Corporate effective tax rates in LAC, 2021 89
Figure 2.7. EATRs under standard tax treatment and investment tax incentives in the corresponding sector 91
Figure 2.8. Recurrent taxes on immovable property in LAC 92
Figure 2.9. Environmentally related tax revenues in LAC countries, by main tax base, 2022 95
Figure 2.10. Public debt by legislation and currency as % of GDP, 2021 99
Figure 2.11. Public debt by remaining maturity as % of GDP, 2021 100
Figure 2.12. External public debt stock by creditor (public and private), 2022 101
Figure 2.13. Number of positive and negative sovereign credit rating actions by country, 2023 102
Figure 2.14. Debt service-to-tax revenues ratio in LAC, 2012 and 2022 103
Figure 2.15. Ratio of LAC central government interest payments to expenditure in key fields, 2010-23 average 104
Figure 2.16. Motivation to pay taxes vs. satisfaction with public services in LAC 106
Figure 3.1. Domestic credit to the private sector as percentage of GDP, and financial depth in LAC, 2022 122
Figure 3.2. Access to formal saving and borrowing mechanisms in LAC, 2021 123
Figure 3.3. Reasons declared by adults in LAC for not having a bank account, 2021 124
Figure 3.4. Financial inclusion in LAC by firm size, 2009-20 125
Figure 3.5. Interest rate spreads between loans to SMEs and to large firms, 2020-22 126
Figure 3.6. Banking system profitability in selected LAC countries, 2021 127
Figure 3.7. Banking system soundness indicators in LAC, 2022 128
Figure 3.8. Credit quality in LAC, 2022 129
Figure 3.9. Access to homeownership loans in selected LAC countries, poorest and richest quintiles 131
Figure 3.10. Access to homeownership loans by the degree of households' informality in selected LAC countries 132
Figure 3.11. Informality and financial inclusion, 2021: Partial correlations 133
Figure 3.12. Growth of digital payments and neobanking in LAC 135
Figure 3.13. Fintech users and markets served by digital banks in LAC 136
Figure 3.14. Understanding of interest rates and inflation in LAC, 2023 138
Figure 3.15. Institutional mandate of DFIs and financing types offered to MSMEs in LAC, 2023 142
Figure 3.16. Evolution of guarantee funds and coverage of SMEs by guarantee schemes in LAC 143
Figure 3.17. PDBs' climate strategy and main obstacles to climate financing 144
Figure 3.18. Market capitalisation and stock turnover ratio in LAC, 2022 or latest year available 146
Figure 3.19. Concentration of equity markets in LAC, 2019 and 2024 147
Figure 3.20. Newly listed and delisted companies in LAC, 2000-23 148
Figure 3.21. Ownership concentration and public equity holdings by type of investor, 2023 148
Figure 3.22. Investment by type of asset in LAC, Q3 2023 149
Figure 3.23. Average venture capital deal size by region and annual venture capital investment in LAC, 2016-23 150
Figure 3.24. VC investment by industry vertical in LAC (2016-23) and by region (2023) 151
Figure 3.25. Domestic vs. non-domestic venture capital investors in LAC, 2016-23 151
Figure 3.26. Domestic corporate and public bond issuance in LAC, 2015-23 152
Figure 3.27. Domestic corporate bond issuers in LAC and average amount issued, 2015-23 153

Figure 3.28. Currency composition of non-financial corporate bonds issued by country group 2015-23 154
Figure 3.29. Average maturity of corporate bonds issued by country group and sector, 2015-23 155
Figure 3.30. Share by country in MILA total traded volume, 2012-18 156
Figure 3.31. Market capitalisation and number of issuers of nuam exchange by country, August 2024 157
Figure 3.32. LAC public and corporate international bond issuance, 2019-23 158
Figure 3.33. LAC public and corporate international bond issuance by country, 2023 159
Figure 3.34. CEMBI spread (basis points) year change by region, 2023 160
Figure 3.35. Number of issuers of American Depositary Receipts in LAC by country, March 2024 161
Figure 4.1. Cumulative share of multilateral financing commitments in LAC, 2022 183
Figure 4.2. ODA as a share of GNI, average per region and income group, 2000-22 185
Figure 4.3. China's development finance to LAC, 2005-23 188
Figure 4.4. Components of external financing flows to the LAC region, 2011-22 188
Figure 4.5. Mobilised private finance by official development interventions per region, 2012-22 190
Figure 4.6. Mobilised private finance by official development interventions to LAC by sector, 2022 191
Figure 4.7. Mobilised private finance by official development interventions to LAC, 2020-22 192
Figure 4.8. TOSSD disbursements from the EU institutions to LAC 2019-22 194
Figure 4.9. Remittances to LAC countries as a share of GDP, 2003-22 196
Figure 4.10. Sectors receiving philanthropic financing in LAC vs. other regions, 2017-22 198
Figure 4.11. International bond issuance in LAC: GSSS by type and as percentage of total, 2014-23 199
Figure 4.12. LAC's GSSS and conventional bond issuance, by type of issuer, 2020-23 202

INFOGRAPHICS

Infographic 1.1. To finance the development priorities, larger sources of funding are needed in LAC 34
Infographic 2.1. LAC needs to improve tax collection, spending and debt management 80
Infographic 3.1. Financial markets can mobilise additional resources from the private sector in LAC 120
Infographic 4.1. International financing and partnerships can catalyse more foreign resources in LAC 176

TABLES

Table 2.1. Carbon taxes, ETS and carbon credit markets in LAC 96
Table 4.1. The priorities of selected LAC countries on financing for development 179
Table 4.2. Overview of taxonomy initiatives in selected LAC countries 207

BOXES

Box 1.1. Measuring multi-dimensional poverty 49
Box 1.2. Measuring the financing gap for sustainable development 59
Box 1.3. Key policy messages 67
Box 2.1. OECD recommendations on budgetary governance 83
Box 2.2. The new global minimum corporate tax rate can significantly impact LAC tax incentives 91
Box 2.3. OECD recommendations on citizen participation 107
Box 2.4. Key policy messages 109
Box 3.1. OECD Recommendation on Financial Literacy 139
Box 3.2. Finance in Common 141
Box 3.3. How are PDBs in LAC supporting the climate transition? 144
Box 3.4. Key policy messages 162
Box 4.1. Total Official Support for Sustainable Development 186
Box 4.2. Unlocking strategic investments: The example of the Latin America and the Caribbean Investment Facility (LACIF) 195
Box 4.3. The EU's Global Green Bond Initiative (GGBI) 200
Box 4.4. Key policy messages 209

Executive summary

Latin American and Caribbean (LAC) countries need vast financial resources to achieve sustainable development. For instance, the spending gap for the Sustainable Development Goals currently is estimated to average USD 99 billion per year. Mobilising these resources requires a co-ordinated strategy by public and private sectors at national, regional and international levels.

LAC faces a considerable financing gap, aggravated by the socio-economic context

The socio-economic context hinders efforts to mobilise more domestic revenue. Economic growth has been modest due in part to long-term structural challenges such as low productivity. In 2023, average labour productivity in LAC amounted to 33% of that of the OECD, down from 40% in 1990. Poverty remains high in LAC, representing 26.8% of the region's total population in 2024, while extreme poverty continues to affect one in ten people in the region. High inflation has exacerbated the poverty situation, as for people in extreme poverty, the price of the basket of goods consumed was 20% higher in 2023 than in 2021, a difference much greater than the 13.1% increase recorded in the general price levels of the region. More than half of employees in LAC remain in informal jobs, with low pay, limited social insurance and heightened vulnerabilities for women and youth.

There is little space for demand-side policies to support aggregate demand. Many countries are maintaining a tight monetary framework to keep inflation expectations anchored and undergoing a fiscal consolidation phase, after fiscal space decreased significantly following the pandemic.

LAC countries will need to improve the way they collect taxes, spend, and manage public debt

LAC tax revenues averaged 21.5% of GDP in 2022, below the OECD's 34.0%, constraining governments' ability to finance development agendas. The region's tax structures are characterised by high reliance on indirect taxes (48% of total taxes, mostly VAT), which tend to be more regressive than direct taxes. Policies should focus on increasing revenues from personal income tax, rationalising tax expenditures, exploring additional revenue sources such as recurrent taxes on immovable property, health and environmentally related taxes, fostering a tax-paying culture, and improving tax administration. The effectiveness of spending should also be improved: expenditure tends to be short-term and pro-cyclical, decreasing during downturns (especially capital investments) and increasing during upswings (especially current spending).

Improving debt management can help free up revenue for development. Public debt levels in the region remained high in 2023, though heterogenous – ranging from less than 40% of GDP to more than 100% – with a high cost of debt servicing. While OECD countries reduced their debt service from 6.4% of tax revenue in 2012 to 4.8% in 2022, in LAC it increased from 9.8% to 12.2%. Over the past decade, interest payments have surpassed core government expenditures. In some countries, debt service has exceeded the spending on education and been up to two times that on healthcare and on capital investment.

Deeper and more innovative financial markets can help mobilise more private resources

A well-developed financial system, providing fundamental services such as loans, savings products and insurance, can help individuals and businesses smooth consumption, invest in physical and human capital, and promote entrepreneurship. Here, policies should focus on improving three dimensions: i) financial systems lack *depth*, with domestic credit to the private sector reaching 50% of GDP in 2022, below the 80% in other regions; ii) *access* is constrained, particularly for the most vulnerable, with account ownership standing at 57% in 2021, below the OECD average of 94%. There are significant disparities in access to credit between formal and informal households. For example, in some cases, access to housing loans for informal households can be up to six times lower compared to formal households; iii) *efficiency* is low, with banks exhibiting high net interest margins of 5% in 2021, exceeding the OECD average of 1.7%.

Capital markets – equity and debt – in LAC remain small, heterogeneous and concentrated. Policies should aim to diversify funding sources, enhance financial stability and support long-term investments. In 2022, equity market capitalisation reached 35.9% of GDP, below OECD levels (64.7%). Most LAC markets are more concentrated than that of Korea, except for Brazil and Chile, which are among the least concentrated in the region; however, all of them still have higher concentration levels than the New York Stock Exchange. Meanwhile, in 2023, the outstanding amount of corporate bonds in LAC represented around 2% of the global total. Regional debt markets are focused on the public sector, accounting for 81% of local issuances over 2015-2023. In the same period, firms in LAC issued bonds mainly in foreign currency (58% of corporate issues), which exposes them to exchange rate risk, but with longer maturities than those in emerging markets (9.3 years vs. 5.2 years on average). Policies should aim to boost the participation of institutional investors, modernise regulations, enhance financial literacy, and deepen regional financial integration.

Development Finance Institutions (DFIs) can channel more resources towards development goals, addressing financial market depth issues, redistributing risks, and fostering inclusive markets. Their deep local market knowledge and strong connections with private and public sectors are key to developing projects and facilitating capital flows. 34% of DFIs have a specific mandate to support the financial inclusion of micro-, small and medium-sized enterprises through instruments like guarantee schemes and loans, but only 19% of the financial instruments they propose address the green transition, gender equality and digital transformation or innovation.

A unified regional agenda can bring LAC's perspective to global financing challenges, in co-ordination with international partners

The Fourth International Conference on Financing for Development in 2025 is an opportunity for the region to adopt a strategic approach. The conference will enable the design of reforms to promote development financing in key areas, such as improving liquidity, measuring risk, mobilising private finance, and enhancing co-ordination among development providers. A unified regional agenda can not only bring forward LAC's perspective on international financing challenges, but also trigger discussions on innovative risk-sharing tools, blended finance, and improved regulations to strengthen LAC's financial landscape.

International co-operation will be key to scaling up additional resources, such as the funds pledged by the Global Gateway Initiative or debt instruments. Financing instruments such as green, social, sustainability, and sustainability-linked (GSSS) bonds, catastrophe bonds, debt-for-nature swaps, and natural disaster clauses can mobilise public and private investment where needs are greatest. Enhanced regulation and supervision through consolidated sustainable finance frameworks will be essential to ensure the effectiveness of these instruments and mitigate risks.

Abbreviation and acronyms

AAAA	Addis Ababa Action Agenda
ADB	Asian Development Bank
AFD	French Development Agency (*Agence Française de Développement*)
ADR	American Depositary Receipt
AECID	Spanish Agency for International Development Co-operation
AI	Artificial intelligence
ALIDE	Latin American Association of Development Financing Institutions
ALMPs	Active Labour Market Policies
APEC	Asia-Pacific Economic Cooperation
AR	Autoregressive
ASEAN	Association of Southeast Asian Nations
B2C	Business-to-Consumer
BIICC	Climate Change Indicator Indexed Bond
BIS	Bank for International Settlements
BNCR	Banco Nacional de Costa Rica
BROU	Banco República Oriental del Uruguay
CABEI	Central American Bank for Economic Integration
CAF	Development Bank of Latin America (*Corporación Andina de Fomento*)
CAT	Catastrophe bonds
CBI	Citizen by Investment programme
CEESEG	Central and Eastern Europe Stock Exchange Group
CEMBI	Corporate Emerging Markets Bond Index
CIT	Corporate income tax
CIVs	Collective investment vehicles
CMIM	Chiang Mai Initiative Multilateralisation
CPI	Consumer Price Index
CRA	Credit Rating Agencies
DAC	Development Assistance Committee
DFIs	Development finance institutions
DFNS	Debt-for-nature swap
DSSI	Debt Service Suspension Initiative
EAP	East Asia and the Pacific
EATR	Effective average tax rate
ECLAC	United Nations Economic Commission for Latin America and the Caribbean
EFP	Equivalent Fiscal Pressure
EFSD+	European Fund for Sustainable Development Plus
EIB	European Investment Bank
EMBIG	Emerging Markets Bond Index Global
EMTR	Effective marginal tax rate

ERTR	Environmentally related tax revenues
ESG	Environmental, Social, and Governance
ETR	Effective tax rate
ETS	Emissions trading systems
EU	European Union
FfD4	Fourth International Conference on Financing for Development
FDI	Foreign Direct Investment
FTA	Free Trade Agreement
G20	Group of 20
GDP	Gross domestic product
GEMs	Global Emerging Markets
GGBI	Global Green Bond Initiative
GGIA	Global Gateway Investment Agenda
GHG	Greenhouse gas
GMT	Global minimum effective corporate tax rate
GNI	Gross national income
GPGs	Global public goods
GSSS	Green, social, sustainability, and sustainability-linked bonds
HEI	Higher Education Institutions
HHI	Herfindahl-Hirschman Index
HP	Hodrick-Prescott
IBRD	International Bank for Reconstruction and Development
ICMA	International Capital Market Association
ICTs	Information and Communication Technologies
IDB	Inter-American Development Bank
IEA	International Energy Agency
IFAD	International Fund for Agricultural Development
IIF	Institute of International Finance
ILO	International Labour Organization
IMF	International Monetary Fund
IPO	Initial Public Offering
ITID	OECD Investment Tax Incentives Database
KPI	Key performance indicators
LAC	Latin America and the Caribbean
LACIF	Latin America and the Caribbean Investment Facility
MDB	Multilateral Development Bank
MENA	Middle East and North Africa
Mercosur	Common Market of the South (*Mercado Común del Sur*)
MILA	Latin American Integrated Market
MNEs	Multinational enterprises
MSCI	Morgan Stanley Capital International
MSMEs	Micro, small and medium-sized enterprises
MTFFS	Medium-Term Fiscal Frameworks
MXN	Mexican pesos
NAFTA	North American Free Trade Agreement
NDC	Nationally Determined Contributions
NDPs	National Development Plans
NFIS	National Financial Inclusion Strategy
NGO	Non-governmental organisations
NIM	Net Interest Margin
NPL	Non-Performing Loan

NYSE	New York Stock Exchange
ODA	Official Development Assistance
OECD	Organisation for Economic Co-operation and Development
OPHI	Oxford Poverty and Human Development Initiative
PAYG	Pay-As-You-Go
PHC	Primary Health Care
PPPs	Public-Private Partnerships
PDBs	Public Development Banks
PISA	Programme for International Student Assessment
PIT	Personal income tax
Q3	Third Quarter
R&D	Research and Development
ROA	Return on Assets
SBIE	Substance-Based Income Exclusion
SDGs	Sustainable Development Goals
SDR	Special Drawing Rights
SIDS	Small Island Developing States
SLBs	Sustainability-linked bonds
SMEs	Small and Medium-sized Enterprises
SOCX	Social Expenditure Database
SPO	Secondary Public Offering
SPVs	Special purpose vehicles
SSA	Sub-Saharan Africa
SSC	South-South co-operation
SSBs	Sugary-sweetened beverages
SSC	Social security contributions
STR	Statutory tax rate
STT	Standard tax treatment
TFP	Total Factor Productivity
TFT	Time for Trade
TOSSD	Total Official Support for Sustainable Development
UN	United Nations
UNCTAD	United Nations Conference on Trade and Development
UNESCO	United Nations Educational, Scientific and Cultural Organization
UNICEF	United Nations International Children's Emergency Fund
USD	United States dollar
VAT	Value Added Tax
VC	Venture Capital
WFP	World Food Programme
WHO	World Health Organization
WTO	World Trade Organization

Overview

The Latin America and Caribbean (LAC) region requires additional financial resources to tackle its significant socio-economic challenges and fulfil the development agendas. For instance, the spending gap for the main development priorities is currently estimated to average USD 99 billion per year (UNCTAD, 2023[1]). Mobilising the needed resources will require a co-ordinated strategy that includes the public and private sectors as well as innovative financing mechanisms and close co-ordination with international partners.

The current socio-economic context makes it increasingly challenging to mobilise the necessary resources for LAC

Low productivity growth continues to affect long-term economic growth in the region. Economic activity in LAC has slowed since 2023 due to cyclical dynamics and ongoing long-term structural challenges. In 2023, average labour productivity in LAC amounted to 33% of that of the OECD, below the 40% of 1990 (Figure 1). Low productivity growth affects most sectors of the economy, and much of the gap in labour productivity with advanced economies can be attributed to differences in total factor productivity.

Figure 1. Labour productivity in LAC as a percentage of OECD labour productivity per hour worked, 1990-2023

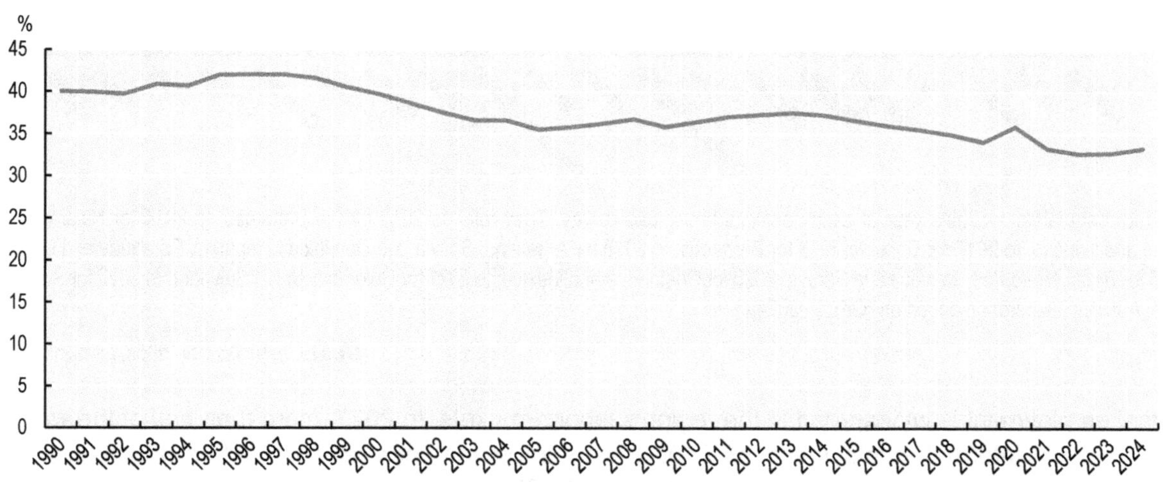

Note: LAC refers to a simple average that includes Argentina, Bolivia, Brazil, Chile, Colombia, Costa Rica, the Dominican Republic, Ecuador, Guatemala, Jamaica, Mexico, Paraguay, Peru, Trinidad and Tobago, Uruguay, and Venezuela. For the OECD, it is a simple average that includes its 38 member countries.
Source: Authors' elaboration based on (The Conference Board, 2024[2]).

StatLink https://stat.link/j5w6r4

The current context leaves little space for monetary and fiscal policies to support economic growth. Many LAC economies have maintained a tight monetary stance to keep inflation expectations anchored. As in the rest of the world, inflation in the region is converging towards the levels prior to the COVID-19 pandemic; after topping in the middle of 2022, inflation started to decrease in the second half of 2023 in most LAC countries. Monetary policy has been fundamental in taming headline inflation and keeping its expectations in check. Going forward, monetary authorities should continue to be cautious.

The economies of the region are undergoing a fiscal consolidation phase, as LAC's fiscal space has decreased significantly since the pandemic. As a result of macroeconomic dynamics and the ongoing fiscal consolidation efforts, the ratio of debt to gross domestic product (GDP) has begun to converge toward pre-pandemic levels. However, debt dynamics and fiscal accounts should continue to be closely monitored, and a credible fiscal framework should play a fundamental role.

The socio-economic conditions are also complex, with persistent poverty and inflation. Although it has declined in recent decades, poverty remains high in LAC, accounting for 26.8% of the region's total population in 2024, while extreme poverty has remained relatively stable, affecting one in ten people in the region (ECLAC, 2024[3]). High and persistent inflation has aggravated the living conditions of Latin Americans and Caribbeans, especially the most vulnerable.[1]

Figure 2. Distribution of the LAC population, by household informality status, latest available year

Percentages of the population

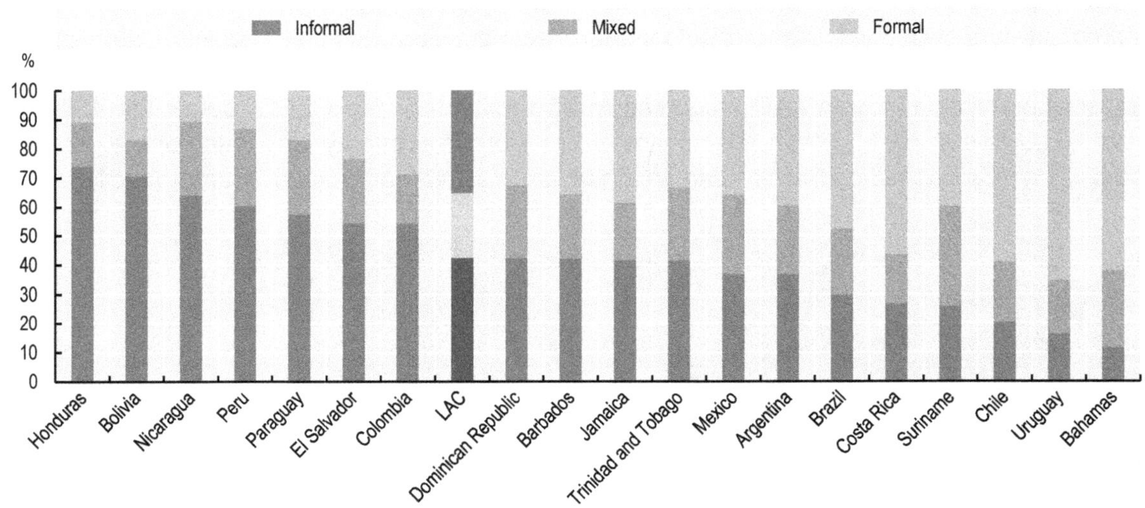

Note: Data from latest available year of each country's household survey. They refer to 2013 for the Bahamas; to 2014 for Nicaragua and Trinidad and Tobago; to 2017 for Chile; to 2016 for Barbados; to 2018 for Argentina, Bolivia, the Dominican Republic, Paraguay and Uruguay; to 2019 for Brazil, Honduras, Jamaica and Peru; to 2020 for Costa Rica and Mexico; to 2021 for Colombia and El Salvador; to 2022 for Suriname.
Source: Authors' elaboration based on (OECD, 2024[4]).

StatLink https://stat.link/es7wtu

Informal employment is widespread in the region's labour markets. In 2022, more than half of the workers in LAC were in informal employment (55.7%), a slight improvement over 2010, when 59.4% of people employed were informal. Informality affects both men (55.9%) and women (55.4%), but in countries where overall informality is particularly high, women are much more likely than men to hold an informal job (ILO, 2024[5]). Informality affects the living standards not only of workers but also of the dependents living in the same household. Across LAC in recent years, 64.9% of people lived in households where at least one of the principal earners held an informal job, 42.5% in households depending entirely on informal employment and 22.4% in mixed households with earners holding formal and informal jobs. People living in households where all earners were formal workers represented 25.1% of the population, although heterogeneity is high across the region (Figure 2).

The mobilisation of public and private financing is essential to close development gaps in LAC. Persistent inequalities, vulnerability to climate change, and recent socio-economic disruptions demand a co-ordinated investment strategy focused on priority sectors aligned with productive development policies (ECLAC, 2024[6]). National Development Plans (NDPs) provide frameworks for effective resource allocation, supporting high-impact sectors critical for the region's resilience and fostering synergies between the public and private sectors. In this context, the social contract serves as a foundation for mobilising public and private resources by fostering inclusive and participatory governance that builds trust, strengthens fiscal systems, and aligns the interests of diverse stakeholders with long-term sustainable development goals (OECD et al., 2021[7]). The private sector's involvement, through innovative financing models, introduces scalability, innovation, and competitiveness, while supporting national development agendas. Despite existing fiscal constraints, aligning both public and private resources with sustainable development goals allows for transformative economic change in priority sectors, enabling structural shifts essential for the region's solid and long-term growth.

To achieve their development agendas LAC countries will need to improve the way they spend resources, collect taxes and manage public debt

Optimising budget allocation and increasing spending efficiency can free up additional resources. To finance their development agendas, governments must reallocate and implement strategic budgets that prioritise key sectors. For example, oil remains the most subsidised fossil fuel in LAC, sometimes benefiting high-income households and carbon-intensive industries. Improved budget design and co-ordinated budget implementation, together with data availability, can ensure that each development priority is adequately funded, at both the national and local levels.

Tax revenues in LAC are currently insufficient to meet its development objectives. Tax revenues allow governments to fund essential public services, infrastructure and social welfare programmes. However, in 2022, LAC's tax revenues amounted to just 21.5% of GDP, ranging from 10.6% in Guyana to 33.3% of GDP in Brazil, below the OECD average of 34.0% (OECD et al., 2024[8]). The region's tax structure does little to mitigate inequality, as it remains heavily dependent on indirect taxes, which accounted for 48% of total taxes in 2022 (32% in the OECD), with value-added tax a prominent amount. Personal income tax and social security contributions accounted for only 26.7% of LAC's total tax revenues in 2022, compared to 48.4% in OECD countries. Conversely, corporate income tax contributed more in LAC (16% of total taxes) than in OECD countries (12%) (Figure 3) (OECD et al., 2024[8]).

LAC has an array of tax policy options that would help increase revenues and positively impact development agendas. Expanding recurrent taxes on immovable property, which averaged 0.4% of GDP in LAC in 2022 compared to 1% in OECD countries, can raise revenues and promote wealth redistribution. Simplifying the tax process, ensuring efficient administration, and promoting fairness are crucial for improving tax collection and progressivity. Health taxes on tobacco, alcohol, and sugary drinks can generate funds while reducing health risks and their long-term costs. Environmentally related taxes in LAC, averaging 0.9% of GDP compared to 1.8% in OECD countries, rely heavily on fuel taxes and energy subsidies. Expanding carbon taxes, carbon emissions trading systems and carbon credits could generate revenues and reduce emissions, provided protections for vulnerable populations are addressed. Additionally, reassessing high effective corporate tax rates and optimising incentives to pay taxes can help support investment and entrepreneurship. Currently, the effective average tax rate for a given investment project is 23.9%, compared to 21.9% in OECD countries and 17.1% in 25 emerging economies (Hanappi et al., 2023[9]).

Figure 3. Average tax structure as a % of total tax revenues in the LAC region and the OECD, 2022

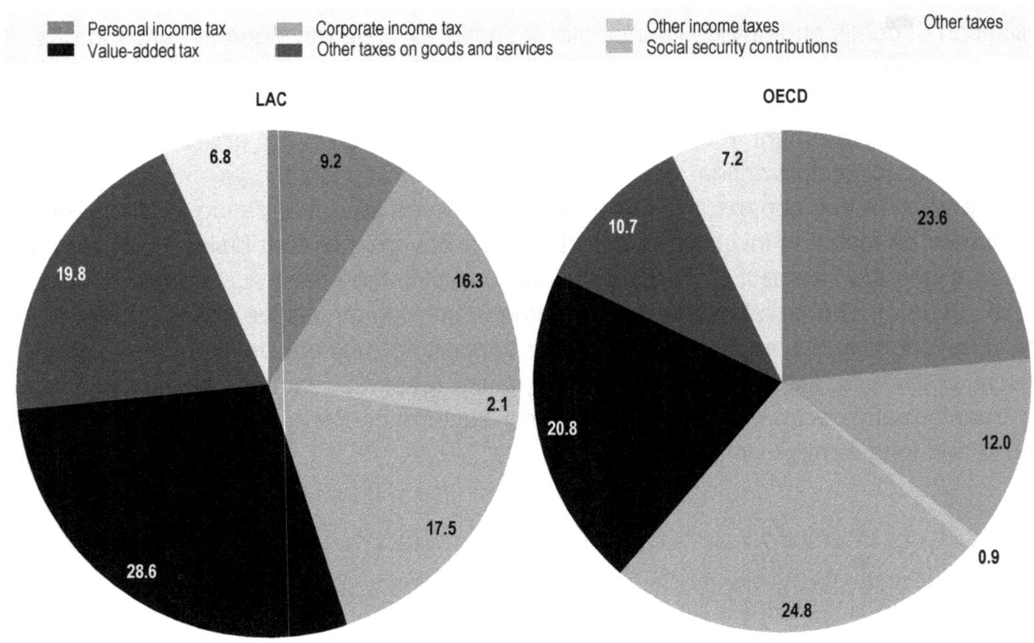

Note: The LAC average excludes Venezuela due to data issues. Ecuador is excluded from the LAC average for PIT and CIT revenues due to data quality issues. The OECD average represents the unweighted average of the 38 OECD member countries, which include Chile, Colombia, Costa Rica and Mexico.
Source: (OECD et al., 2024[8]).

StatLink https://stat.link/xr8b45

Improving public debt management can help free up revenues for development purposes. In 2021, public debt levels across central governments in the region varied widely, ranging from 23% to 140% of GDP with heterogeneous aspects of debt composition, including the currency of issuance, legislative frameworks and maturity profiles. In some cases, debt in domestic currency represented 66% to 95% of total debt, while in others, non-domestic currency issuances made up 70% to 90% of the total. Rising debt levels together with high interest rates have had an impact on debt service costs, constraining the fiscal space for development-oriented investments. In 2022, the debt service-to-tax revenue ratio in the region reached 12.2%, up from 9.8% in 2012 and above the OECD average of 4.8% (Figure 4). Over the past decade, interest payments on debt have surpassed core government expenditures in several countries, with debt service exceeding the spending on education and reaching two times that on healthcare and capital investment.

Figure 4. Debt service-to-tax revenues ratio in LAC, 2012 and 2022

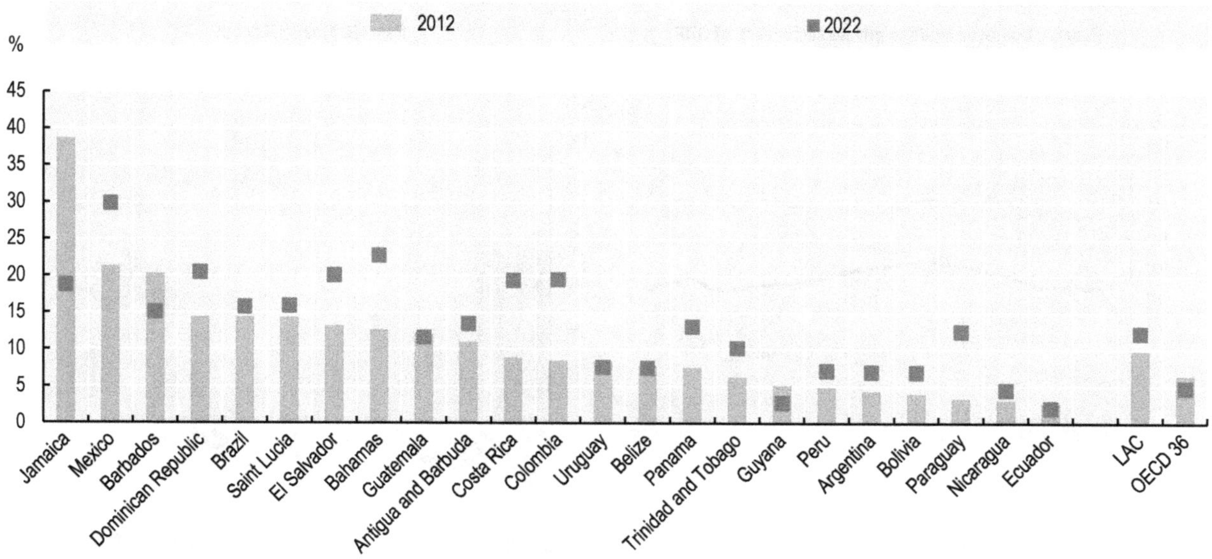

Source: Authors' elaboration based (OECD et al., 2024[8]) and (IMF, 2023[10]).

StatLink https://stat.link/50tebv

Well-developed and inclusive financial markets are essential for channelling private resources towards development

Financial markets are critical for economic growth and development. They provide individuals and businesses with access to essential services, such as loans, savings and insurance, and enable them to increase investment in physical and human capital and to smooth consumption.

Financial systems in LAC are lagging behind, as they lack access, depth and efficiency. Financial depth in LAC is low, with domestic credit to the private sector reaching 50% of GDP in 2022, lagging behind other regions where it exceeds 80% (Figure 5, Panel A). Similarly, bank deposits as a percentage of GDP stood at 55.1% for LAC in 2021, compared to 99.3% for OECD countries (Figure 5, Panel B). Although access to financial services has improved, with account ownership rising from 29.6% in 2011 to 57.2% in 2021, it remains below the OECD average of 93.7%. Efficiency in the banking sector is limited, as it exhibits a net interest margin of 5.0%, above the OECD average of 1.7%. While this indicates profitability, it also signals costly credit due to various factors that vary between countries, such as high market concentration, high risks, and inadequate regulatory frameworks.

Figure 5. Domestic credit to the private sector as percentage of GDP and financial depth in LAC, 2022

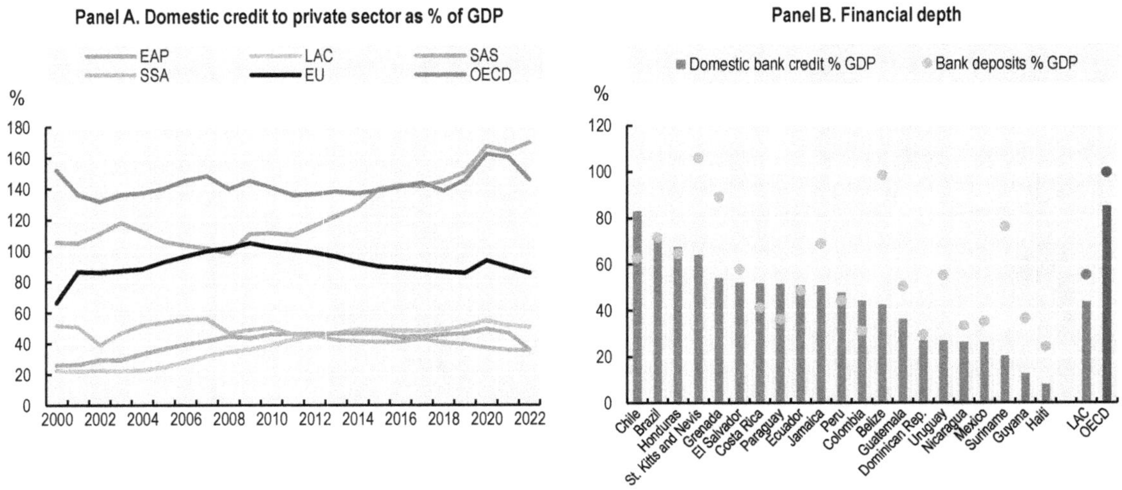

Note: Figures for bank deposits as a percentage of GDP correspond to 2021 due to data availability. EAP = East Asia and the Pacific, SAS = South Asia, SSA = Sub-Saharan Africa, EU = European Union and GDP = gross domestic product.
Source: Authors' elaboration based on (World Bank, 2024[11]), *World Development Indicators*.

StatLink https://stat.link/eapqt0

Inclusion is a fundamental aspect of a well-developed financial market; however, despite progress, significant gaps in financial inclusion persist in LAC. The region's countries have made considerable progress in increasing access to financing, but the financial system excludes some vulnerable groups. For instance, households with informally employed members typically have worse access to financial products (Figure 6). The gap between formal and informal households varies considerably across countries. In Mexico, the disparity is the largest, with only 2.3% of informal households having access to homeownership loans, compared to 14.9% of formal households. In Chile, 6.4% of informal households have 6.4% access to homeownership loans, while formal households reach 15.6%. In countries with smaller gaps, such as the Dominican Republic, access remains very limited for formal, informal and mixed households.

To enhance financial inclusion, digital innovation and financial literacy can provide ways forward. Digital innovation is reshaping financial inclusion in LAC by overcoming traditional banking barriers, offering non-traditional solutions and expanding access. Between 2014 and 2021, the proportion of individuals aged 15 and older who made or received a digital payment rose from 35.9% to an average of 49% in LAC. Additionally, 69% of digital banks' clients in the region consist of previously unbanked and underbanked individuals and small and medium-sized enterprises, illustrating the sector's capacity to effectively reach underserved populations. Improving financial inclusion depends on advancing financial literacy. Financial literacy empowers informed decision-making and helps prevent pitfalls like over-indebtedness (OECD, 2023[12]). Financial literacy remains limited in LAC, with significant gender disparities. On average, 27% of men and only 18% of women understand what interest rates mean in nine selected countries, while 50% of men and 44% of women understand what inflation means.

Figure 6. Access to homeownership loans by the degree of households' informality in selected LAC countries

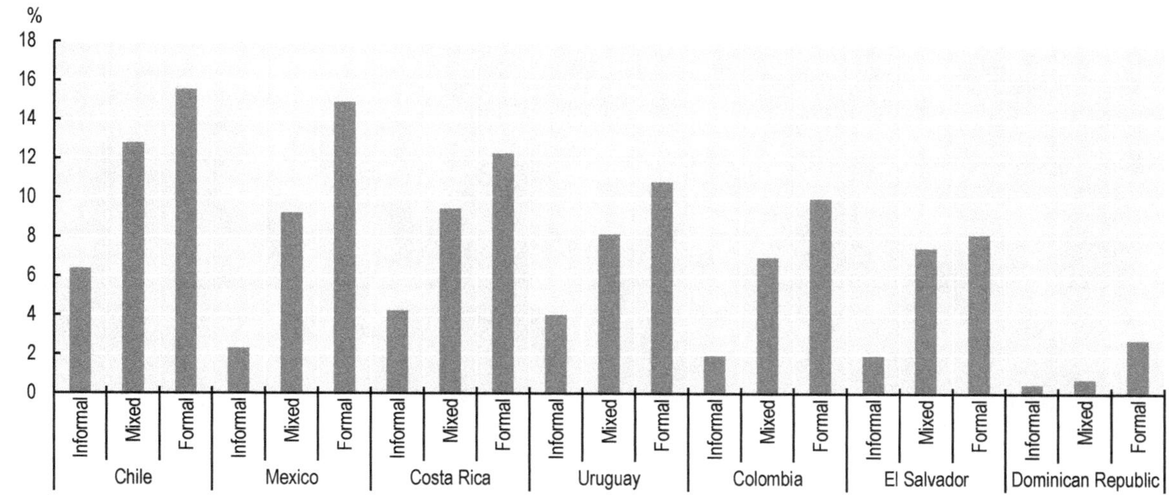

Note: The figure is based on data from household surveys conducted in the selected countries. The surveys included a question about the respondent's current housing status, with answers typically classified into three categories: homeowner, homeowner with a mortgage or tenant. The figure represents the percentage of individuals who indicated they are homeowners currently paying a mortgage, whether financed through a public or private financial institution. The data presented span multiple years across the eight LAC countries (2017-21), with certain datasets collected during the COVID-19 pandemic, which may have introduced variations in standard data collection methodologies. The data for Chile are from 2017, Colombia 2021, Costa Rica 2021, the Dominican Republic 2018, El Salvador 2021, Mexico 2020 and Uruguay 2018.
Source: Authors' calculations based on (OECD, 2021[13]) and national household surveys.

StatLink https://stat.link/a2c9y7

Capital markets are still a largely untapped resource to finance investments

Capital markets, composed of equity and debt markets, offer firms and governments access to diverse funding sources. Equity and corporate domestic bond markets allow for the rise of long-term capital, provide saving opportunities for households, and support capital formation, investment diversification and risk management.

In LAC, equity markets are reduced, lack liquidity and remain concentrated. In 2022, on average, market capitalisation in the region stood at 35.9% of GDP compared to 64.7% for OECD countries. Moreover, the stock turnover ratio indicates low levels of market liquidity, averaging 24% compared to 53.8% in OECD countries. In the region, the activity of equity markets is concentrated in both offerings and ownership and consists mostly of secondary public offerings. The Herfindahl-Hirschman Index for market capitalisation shows significant heterogeneity across the region in terms of concentration (Figure 7, Panel A). Most LAC markets are more concentrated than those of Korea, the exceptions being Brazil and Chile, which are among the least concentrated in the region; however, all LAC markets still have higher concentration levels than the New York Stock Exchange. Company ownership in LAC is considered highly concentrated, with the top 1% of shareholders owning, on average, 46% of a company's total holdings, while in other regions it averages 31% (Figure 7, Panel B).

LAC's equity markets have shrunk in the last two decades due to a negative trend of net listings as companies migrate to advanced markets, and access to medium-sized and small companies is limited. Regional financial integration can reverse these trends by increasing efficiency, lowering transaction costs for investors, improving liquidity conditions and reducing risks. Regional integration of securities markets is being pursued in LAC through the regional holding company nuam exchange which aims at the full integration of the stock exchanges of Colombia, Lima and Santiago.

Figure 7. Concentration of equity markets in LAC, 2019 and 2024

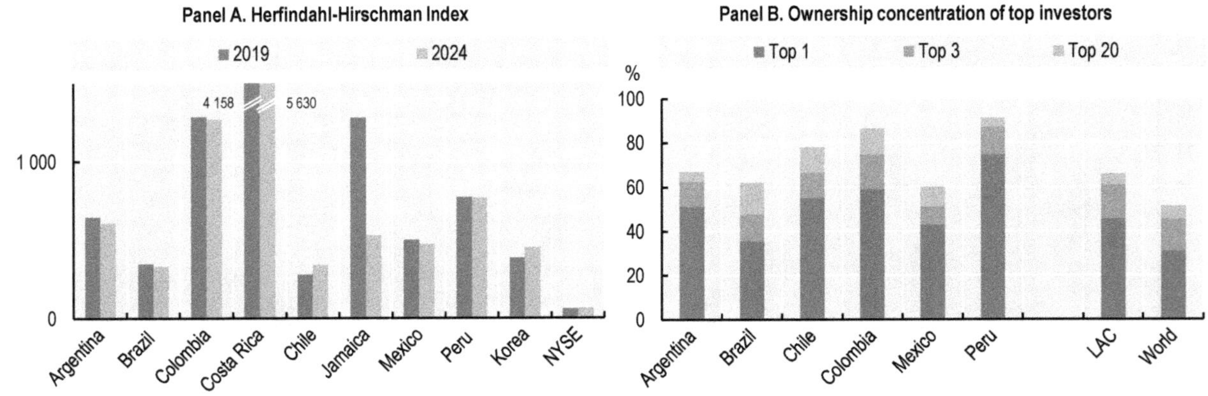

Note: A market is considered highly concentrated if the Herfindahl-Hirschman Index exceeds 1 800 points and moderately concentrated if it is between 1 000 and 1 800 points. The exchanges analysed were Bolsa de Comercio de Buenos Aires in Argentina, BM&F Bovespa SA Bolsa de Valores Mercadorias e Futuros in Brazil, Bolsa de Santiago in Chile, Bolsa de Valores de Colombia, Costa Rica Stock Exchange, Jamaica Stock Exchange, Bolsa Mexicana de Valores S.A. de C.V., Bolsa de Valores de Lima S.A. in Peru, Korea Exchange and New York Stock Exchange (NYSE). Data were extracted on 12 June 2024.

Source: Panel A: Authors' calculation based on (London Stock Exchange Group, 2024[14]). Panel B: Authors' elaboration based on (OECD, 2024[15]).

StatLink https://stat.link/knlz8h

In LAC, private bond market issuances remain largely underdeveloped despite their progress in recent years. In 2023, the outstanding amount of corporate bonds in the region accounted for around 2% of the global total. Market activity remains mainly concentrated in the public sector (81% of LAC's local issuances between 2015 and 2023) and largely in Brazil and Mexico. For the non-financial corporate sector, there is space to improve currency composition. Between 2015 and 2023, on average in LAC, 58% of the amount issued by non-financial firms was denominated in foreign currencies (Figure 8, Panel A), which could expose them to exchange rate risk. However, firms in LAC also issue bonds with a profile of longer maturities compared to those in emerging markets. Between 2015 and 2023, on average, firms issued bonds with a maturity of 9.3 years, compared to a 5.2-year maturity in emerging markets (Figure 8, Panel B).

Figure 8. Currency composition and average maturity of corporate bonds issued by country group, 2015-23

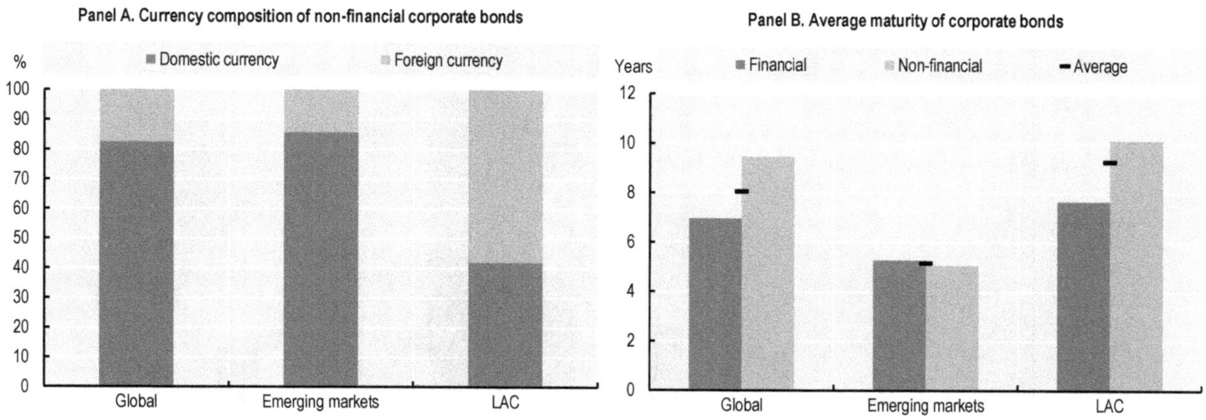

Note: The figure covers bonds issued during the period from 1 January 2015 to 31 December 2023. It includes bonds with an original maturity greater than one year and issues greater than USD 1 million. Countries included in the LAC group are Argentina, Bahamas, Barbados, Bolivia, Brazil, Chile, Colombia, Costa Rica, the Dominican Republic, Ecuador, El Salvador, Guatemala, Honduras, Jamaica, Mexico, Panama, Paraguay, Peru, Trinidad and Tobago, and Uruguay. Panel A: Bonds are of the amount issued in USD. Panel B: Average maturity by year is weighted by issued amount. Average maturity over a period of years is computed as the simple average of the yearly average maturity.
Source: Authors' elaboration based on (OECD, 2024[15]).

StatLink https://stat.link/am7yxp

LAC companies can also access private markets by privately selling stock, with venture capital (VC) being the most commonly used financing option in the region. Venture capital represents a key opportunity for companies that face difficulties in accessing equity and bond markets. However, recent VC dynamics in LAC have slowed down. In 2016, VC funding reached USD 1.1 billion across 249 deals, and in 2021, it peaked at USD 25.1 billion across 859 deals, driven by post-COVID incentives and high demand. By 2023, however, VC funding had declined to USD 5.4 billion, falling below pre-pandemic levels (Figure 9). Compared to other global regions, most of the VC funding in LAC is directed towards mobile apps and fintech, while the region lags in sectors like manufacturing and e-commerce.

Figure 9. Annual venture capital investment in LAC, 2016-23

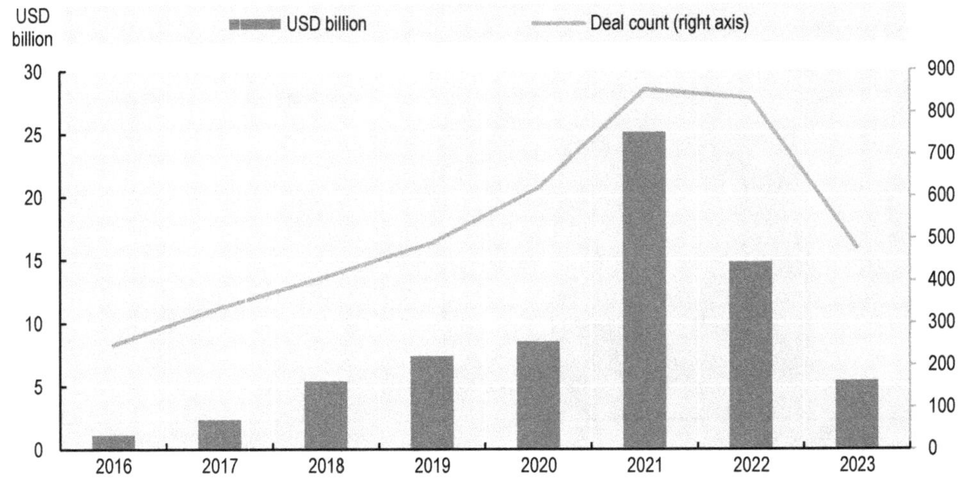

Note: Due to missing information on deal size in some instances, values of deal size were imputed based on the average size by groups of target region, by year and vertical activities (a more specific dimension of a company's activities that provides a view about niche markets spanning multiple industries, such as fintech, healthtech, and e-commerce).
Source: Authors' elaboration based on (Preqin, 2024[16]).

StatLink https://stat.link/evqscw

Development finance institutions play a vital role in strengthening LAC's financial markets

Development finance institutions (DFIs), mostly represented by national and subnational public development banks, are crucial in providing innovative financial services, technical and digital support, and expanded access for firms to financial markets. A 2023 analysis of 38 national and subnational public DFIs in 13 LAC countries underscores their key role in financing micro, small and medium-sized enterprises (MSMEs). Of 473 financial instruments mapped, 42% target both MSMEs and large companies, 39% focus solely on MSMEs, 7% target public institutions, and 4% are for large companies. DFIs offer MSMEs a range of financial instruments that address various needs, including day-to-day operations (34%) and investment financing (45%) (Figure 10, Panel A). DFIs also help MSMEs contribute to green, digital and gender goals. Nevertheless, currently only 19% of the instruments address at least one of the three cross-cutting challenges: 51% support the green transition, 29% target gender equality, and 20% focus on digital transformation and innovation (Figure 10, Panel B).

Figure 10. Distribution of financing types and financial instruments targeting green, digital and gender dimensions offered to MSMEs by DFIs in LAC, 2023

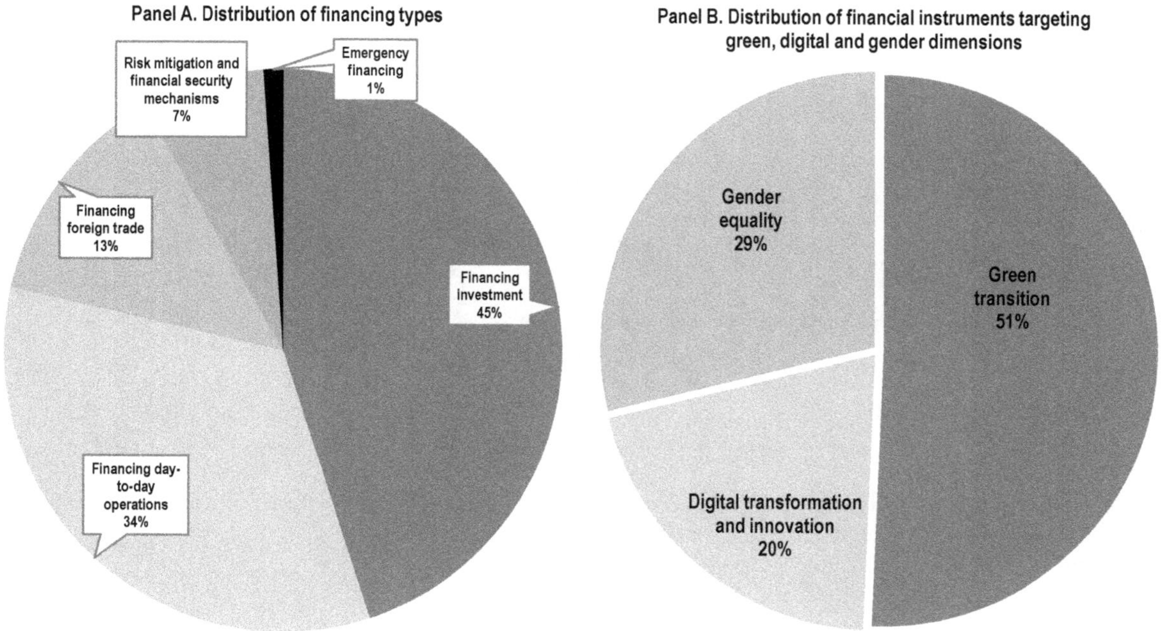

Note: Panel B: Distribution is only concentrated in 19% of the DFIs' financial instruments that had one or more services targeting a green, digital or gender dimension.
Source: Authors' elaboration based on public data (annual and sustainability reports) accessed in 2023 from 38 public DFIs in 13 LAC countries: Argentina, Brazil, Chile, Colombia, Costa Rica, the Dominican Republic, El Salvador, Guatemala, Mexico, Panama, Paraguay, Peru and Uruguay.

StatLink https://stat.link/85sdto

International financing and partnerships can help increase resources

In the face of a changing context for international financing, LAC countries could benefit from sharing an agenda for development priorities and their financing. International financing is evolving as it adapts to a multiplicity of global challenges as well as to the rise of new actors, with emerging economies and non-traditional creditors playing more important roles in financing for development. Both the Paris Pact for People and the Planet (4P) and the Fourth International Conference on Financing for Development in 2025 constitute key opportunities to assess the strategic priorities of LAC. A shared agenda on addressing the challenges of today's international financing context – such as access to liquidity, risk perceptions and access to concessional finance, as well as the fragmentation and co-ordination of development providers – is needed for the region to realise its development opportunities and increase financial flows for sustainable development.

LAC countries need to seize the opportunities available in private-sector finance to unlock different international financial flows. Private investors are the single most important external creditor for LAC governments, and their share has grown over time (ECLAC, 2023[17]) (Figure 11). In addition, the region is well positioned for mobilising greater private-sector finance through official development interventions. In 2022, LAC had the highest level of private mobilised finance for development of any region, with an overall amount of USD 21.2 billion, a 16-fold increase over the 2012 level (OECD Data Explorer, 2024[18]). While the levels of official development assistance have been reduced, the challenges facing the LAC region have increased, stressing the need for other financial flows to be better integrated through a sustainable development framework.

Figure 11. Components of external financing flows to the LAC region, 2011-22

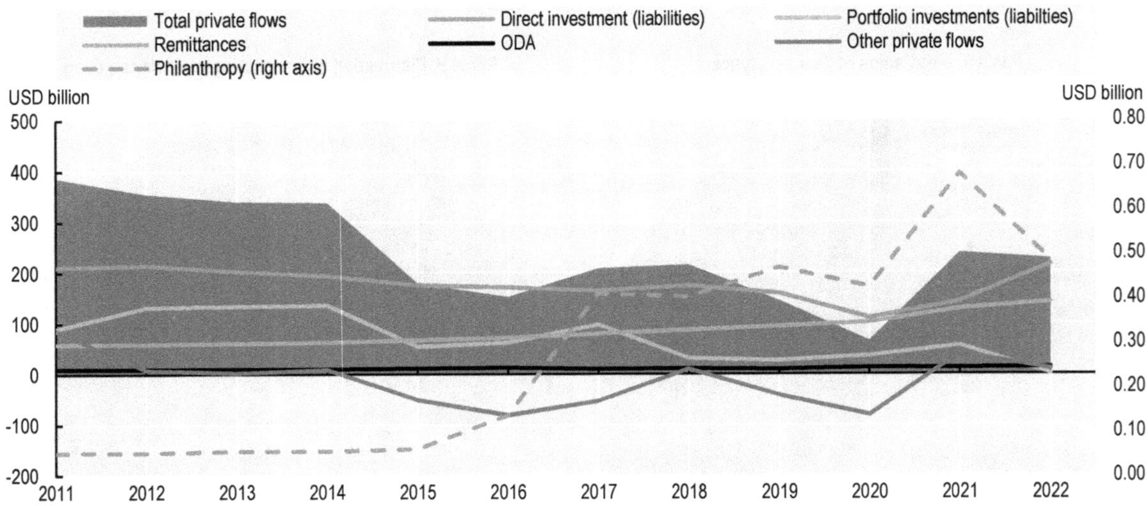

Note: Total private flows include direct investments (liabilities), portfolio investments, and other private flows such as capital accounts, financial derivatives and other investments (liabilities).
Source: Authors' elaboration based on (OECD, 2024[19]); (IMF, 2024[20]).

StatLink https://stat.link/6bhg1p

Development co-operation can help reduce barriers to international financial flows as well as perceived risks. Development co-operation can allow access to "de-risking instruments" that aim to share risks among multilateral, public and private actors, such as blended finance or guarantees offered at concessional or competitive terms to unlock private finance (OECD et al., 2023[21]). LAC development partners such as the European Union (EU) are pursuing initiatives that drive the mobilisation of financing through the use of such tools. With the Global Gateway Strategy, the EU has put forward a holistic approach to international partnerships with integrated financing structures that bring together investment, trade and co-operation actors. The EU-LAC Global Gateway Investment Agenda promotes a 360-degree approach, mobilising quality investments that create local added value and promote growth, jobs and social cohesion.

Remittances and philanthropy are other international financial flows that benefit LAC. Given the region's high outward migration level, remittances constitute a significant and relatively stable source of finance for LAC (IMF, 2017[22]). However, there is a disparity in remittances inflows, as the majority are concentrated in a few LAC countries, with the top six recipients with regard to the size of countries – El Salvador, Guatemala, Haiti, Honduras, Jamaica and Nicaragua – receiving significantly higher amounts than the rest (World Bank, 2024[23]). Philanthropic flows provide LAC with substantive funding for sectors often overlooked by the private sector. There are largely two groups of countries that benefit from the bulk of the international philanthropic financing: i) Brazil, Colombia, El Salvador and Mexico, which each received USD 90-100 million per year from philanthropic foundations; and ii) Ecuador, Guatemala, Haiti and Peru, which each received USD 10-20 million per year (OECD, 2023[24]). Philanthropic foundations can also play a role in boosting collaboration across providers of international co-operation, given their unique convening power as a non-state actor and their focused mission objectives.

Green, social, sustainability and sustainability-linked (GSSS) bonds continue to be an attractive financing mechanism, and international co-operation will be key in scaling up such debt securities for financing the sustainable development agenda. GSSS bonds increased from 9.3% of total LAC bond issuance in international markets in 2020 to almost 35% in 2023 (ECLAC, 2024[25]). The gradual shift from conventional bonds towards sustainable debt securities indicates a growing investor appetite for sustainable projects. Between 2014 and 2023, the GSSS international bond market in LAC reached a cumulative value of

USD 131 billion (Figure 12, Panel A). In 2023, sovereign issuances accounted for the largest share of GSSS issuances at 74%, followed by corporate issuances at 18%, and supranational and quasi-sovereign issuances at 9% (Figure 12, Panel B). To scale up GSSS bonds in the region and overcome barriers hindering market development, international financial co-operation is crucial. This includes the establishment of harmonised frameworks and reliable monitoring and supervision mechanisms to prevent greenwashing and SDG washing (OECD, 2024[26]).

Figure 12. International GSSS bond issuance in LAC by type, as a % of total and by issuer, 2014-23

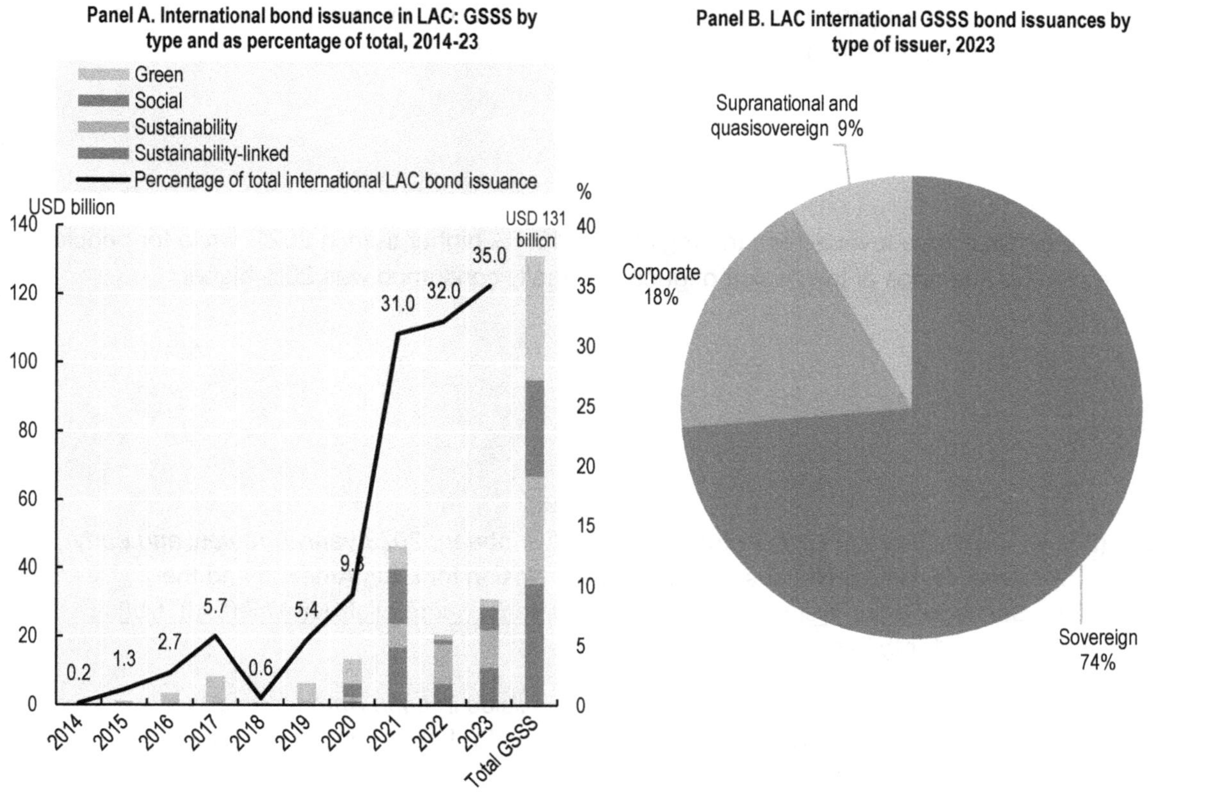

Note: Panel A: GSSS refers to green, social, sustainability and sustainability-linked bonds. Total sustainability bonds include blue bond issuance. Panel B: Quasi-sovereign issuers are defined as companies with full or partial government ownership or control. Supranational issuers are defined as entities formed by two or more central governments to promote economic development for the member countries.
Source: Authors' elaboration based on (OECD et al., 2023[21]); (ECLAC, 2024[25]).

StatLink https://stat.link/ioanjy

Scaling up other debt tools such as catastrophe bonds, debt-for-nature swaps and natural disaster clauses will also be essential to mobilise resources. Catastrophe bonds can increase external borrowing by enhancing governments' borrowing capacity and transferring financial risk to investors. Examples from Jamaica and Mexico show a market appetite for these instruments among highly exposed countries. For biodiverse and highly indebted countries, nature or climate or nature swaps can also be effective, particularly as complements to debt restructurings. Debt-for-nature swaps have been employed in the region, with new proposals emerging, particularly among Caribbean countries that have low credit ratings and limited market access (OECD/IDB, 2024[27]). Natural disaster clauses can allow countries in LAC to capitalise interest and defer principal payments on bonds after major natural disasters, linking repayment capacity to risk exposure. These clauses align debt servicing obligations with a country's ability to recover from disasters.

Countries in LAC are focusing on improving sustainable finance frameworks by harmonising standards and expanding definitions of sustainable finance. Interoperable standards and common taxonomies are necessary for regulating, monitoring and verifying the issuance of GSSS bonds and other sustainable financial instruments. While overarching principles and guidelines provide valuable advice, it is essential for issuers of GSSS bonds at the national level to establish clearer, more binding standards and taxonomies. By December 2023, 14 LAC countries had launched nearly 180 initiatives, aimed at developing their sustainable finance frameworks. Green and sustainable taxonomies have increasingly been adopted in the region since 2022, with publications in Argentina, Chile, Colombia, the Dominican Republic, Mexico and Panama and ongoing development in Brazil, Costa Rica and Peru. The interoperability and harmonisation of frameworks across the region are crucial, as each taxonomy determines environmental priorities based on its unique context.

Notes

[1] In 2023, the general price level across the region was 13.1% higher than in 2021, while for people living in extreme poverty, the price of the basket of goods normally consumed was 20% higher.

References

ECLAC (2024), *Capital flows to Latin America and the Caribbean: 2023 year-in-review and early 2024 developments*, United Nations Economic Commission for Latin America and the Caribbean, Santiago, https://repositorio.cepal.org/server/api/core/bitstreams/ce02481f-b84e-409d-8ccd-30ae1c14efb1/content. [25]

ECLAC (2024), *Panorama of Productive Development Policies in Latin America and the Caribbean, 2024*, United Nations Economic Commission for Latin America and the Caribbean, Santiago, https://repositorio.cepal.org/server/api/core/bitstreams/ef207540-b0d4-4cc9-8248-63b3ebac878d/content. [6]

ECLAC (2024), *Social Panorama of Latin America and the Caribbean, 2024*, United Nations Economic Commission for Latin America and the Caribbean, Santiago, https://repositorio.cepal.org/items/e1403b62-ae38-461c-af18-00c8ed1610b3. [3]

ECLAC (2023), *Public Debt and Development Distress in Latin America and the Caribbean*, United Nations Economic Commission for Latin America and the Caribbean, https://repositorio.cepal.org/server/api/core/bitstreams/d84a5041-0a2c-4b8e-9b01-d91b187477ce/content. [17]

Hanappi, T. et al. (2023), "Corporate Effective Tax Rates in Latin America and the Caribbean", *IDB Technical Note*, No. IDB-TN-2782, https://doi.org/10.18235/0005168. [9]

ILO (2024), *ILOSTAT*, https://ilostat.ilo.org/data/. [5]

IMF (2024), *Balance of Payments and International Investment Position Statistics (BOP/IIP)*, International Monetary Fund, Washington, DC, https://data.imf.org/?sk=7a51304b-6426-40c0-83dd-ca473ca1fd52. [20]

IMF (2023), *World Economic Outlook Database: October 2023 Edition*, International Monetary Fund, Washington, DC, https://www.imf.org/en/Publications/WEO/weo-database/2023/October. [10]

IMF (2017), *Regional Economic Outlook: Tale of Two Adjustments: Ch.5 Migration and Remittances in Latin America and the Caribbean: Macroeconomic Stabilizers and Engines of Growth?*, International Monetary Fund, Washington, DC, https://www.imf.org/en/Publications/REO/WH/Issues/2017/05/10/wreo0517?intcid=OBanner. [22]

London Stock Exchange Group (2024), *DataStream (Database).* [14]

OECD (2024), *Capital Market Series dataset.* [15]

OECD (2024), *Key indicators of Informality based on Individuals and their Households (KIIbIH)*, https://shorturl.at/IZXI5. [4]

OECD (2024), *Official Development Assistance (ODA): Disbursements*, OECD, Paris, https://data-explorer.oecd.org/vis?fs[0]=Topic%2C0%7CDevelopment%23DEV%23&pg=0&fc=Topic&bp=true&snb=10&df[ds]=dsDisseminateFinalDMZ&df[id]=DSD_DAC2%40DF_DAC2A&df[ag]=OECD.DCD.FSD&df[vs]=1.0&lc=en. [19]

OECD (2024), "The surge of Green, Social, Sustainability and Sustainability-linked (GSSS) bonds in Latin America and the Caribbean: Facts and policy implications", *OECD Development Policy Papers*, No. 56, OECD Publishing, Paris, https://doi.org/10.1787/f1c893a3-en. [26]

OECD (2023), "Creditor Reporting System: Private philanthropy for development (Edition 2023)", *OECD International Development Statistics* (database), https://doi.org/10.1787/dd620077-en (accessed on 28 November 2024). [24]

OECD (2023), "OECD/INFE 2023 International Survey of Adult Financial Literacy", *OECD Business and Finance Policy Papers*, No. 39, OECD Publishing, Paris, https://doi.org/10.1787/56003a32-en. [12]

OECD (2021), *Key Indicators of Informality based on Individuals and their Household (KIIbIH) database*, OECD Publishing, Paris, https://www.oecd.org/dev/key-indicators-informality-individuals-household-kiibih.htm. [13]

OECD Data Explorer (2024), *Mobilised Private Finance for Development*, OECD, Paris, https://data-explorer.oecd.org (accessed on 9 July 2024). [18]

OECD et al. (2024), *Revenue Statistics in Latin America and the Caribbean 2024*, OECD Publishing, Paris, https://doi.org/10.1787/33e226ae-en. [8]

OECD et al. (2023), *Latin American Economic Outlook 2023: Investing in Sustainable Development*, OECD Publishing, Paris, https://doi.org/10.1787/8c93ff6e-en. [21]

OECD et al. (2021), *Latin American Economic Outlook 2021: Working Together for a Better Recovery*, OECD Publishing, Paris, https://doi.org/10.1787/5fedabe5-en. [7]

OECD/IDB (2024), *Caribbean Development Dynamics 2025*, OECD Publishing, Paris, https://doi.org/10.1787/a8e79405-en. [27]

Preqin (2024), *Preqin (Database)*, https://www.preqin.com/. [16]

The Conference Board (2024), *Total Economy Database*, The Conference Board, https://www.conference-board.org/data/economydatabase. [2]

UNCTAD (2023), *The Costs of Achieving the SDGs*, United Nations Conference on Trade and Development, Geneva, https://unctad.org/sdg-costing/about. [1]

World Bank (2024), *World Bank Indicators: Personal Remittances, Received (% of GDP) - Latin America & Caribbean*, World Bank, Washington, DC, https://data.worldbank.org/indicator/BX.TRF.PWKR.DT.GD.ZS?end=2022&locations=ZJ&start=2003. [23]

World Bank (2024), *World Development Indicators (Database)*, World Bank, Washington, DC. [11]

1 Structural socio-economic challenges and financing conditions

This chapter examines the need to address sustainable development in Latin America and the Caribbean (LAC) in light of the region's subdued economic activity. It analyses the region's low productivity growth as a structural drag on the economy. This chapter also looks at current macroeconomic trends in LAC countries with a focus on monetary conditions and fiscal space. The chapter then turns to social conditions and poverty, with a focus on social protection and health systems and the challenges they face in the context of pervasive labour informality. It considers how to finance the investment agenda needed to achieve higher sustainable growth and create quality jobs and highlights the need to improve the coverage of social programmes to better protect the most vulnerable. Finally, the chapter calls for co-ordinated policy planning that strategically integrates public and private actors to help close the financing gap of sustainable development.

Infographic 1.1. To finance the development priorities, larger sources of funding are needed in LAC

The spending gap to finance sustainable development in LAC amounts to

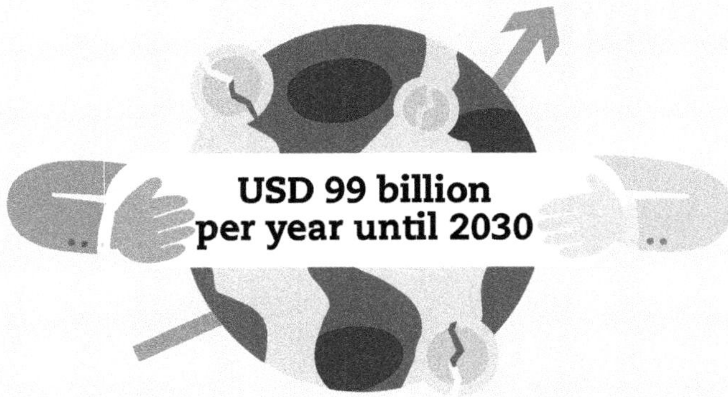

In 2024, 10.4% of citizens lived in extreme poverty, and inflation hit them 2.9 percentage points harder than the rest of the population in 2023

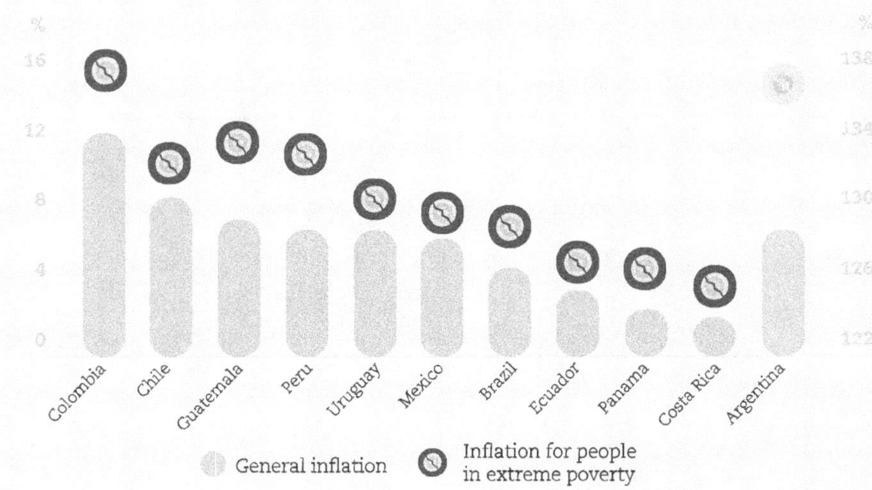

Structural challenges limit the region's development

Labour productivity in the region amounted to 33% of the OECD average in 2023

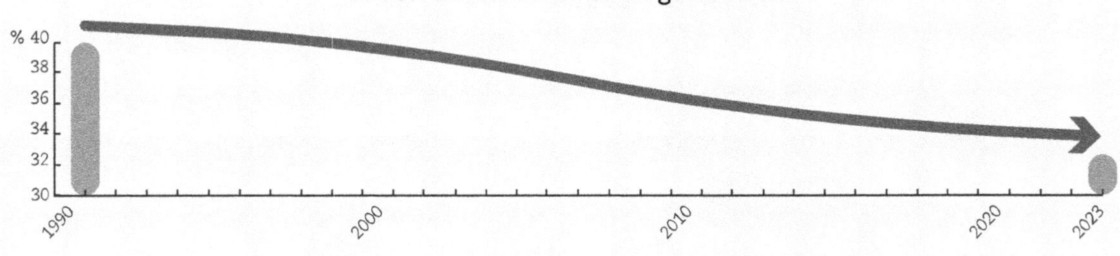

Introduction

Latin America and the Caribbean (LAC) is a vast and diverse region. Its economies exhibit a wide range of characteristics, with countries facing distinct challenges based on several factors including their economic structure, trade dynamics, reliance on commodities, and energy potential. While the countries of LAC face distinct challenges based on their unique circumstances, they also share many common trends, such as vulnerability to external economic shocks, the need to transition to a green economy, persistent inequality, and governance issues. To overcome these challenges and capitalise on new opportunities, co-ordinated efforts at the national, regional, and global levels will be essential to mobilise the needed resources.

Tackling LAC's challenges demands co-ordinated and effective policy planning as well as effective financing with the strategic integration of public and private actors. Given fiscal constraints, there is a pressing need for innovative and efficient financing mechanisms and partnerships among government, the private sector, and international actors. While public sector financing remains crucial for addressing social challenges, the creation of appropriate incentives and frameworks is essential to attract private-sector investment towards market-driven development objectives. Policy strategies must transcend sectoral boundaries to tackle interconnected social, economic, and environmental challenges. This collaborative approach aims to mobilise resources efficiently, enhance infrastructure resilience and foster inclusive growth.

These efforts must be undertaken at a time when economic activity in LAC has been subdued due to cyclical dynamics and pending structural challenges. Low productivity growth continues to affect long-term economic growth in the region, working as a significant drag on potential per capita growth rates. In 2023, average labour productivity in LAC amounted to 33% of that of the OECD, a figure that decreased from 40% in 1990. Much of the gap in labour productivity between LAC and high-income economies can be attributed to differences in total factor productivity. Low productivity growth in LAC is pervasive – it affects most sectors of the economy, especially those where the private sector plays a leading role, such as trade, manufacturing, and services.

Most LAC economies have reacted to their different economic contexts with adequate monetary and fiscal instruments, although the space for demand policies is limited. In terms of monetary policy, authorities in countries that have adopted an inflation-targeting regime have maintained a tight monetary stance to keep inflation expectations anchored. At the same time, high domestic interest rates have averted financial risks derived from higher international interest rates that could stimulate capital flight. In terms of fiscal policy, the region is undergoing a consolidation phase, as the fiscal space available in the region has decreased significantly since the COVID-19 pandemic. With higher debt stocks and higher interest rates, debt service as a proportion of tax revenues has increased considerably. Together with the need to improve primary fiscal results to reduce, or at least contain, debt-to-GDP ratios, this has resulted in the need to reduce primary spending in some LAC countries, thus subtracting from aggregate demand at a time of activity slowdown.

Long-standing poverty and informal employment remain significant socio-economic challenges in LAC. Although poverty has declined in recent decades, poverty remains high in LAC, accounting for 26.8% of the region's total population in 2024, while extreme poverty has remained relatively stable, affecting one in ten people in the region. Multi-dimensional poverty – which includes non-monetary factors such as education, health, housing and sanitation conditions – persists in the region, and climate change further threatens the most vulnerable populations. Although employment rates have increased slightly, more than half of those employed in LAC remain in informal jobs, with low pay, limited social insurance, and heightened vulnerabilities for women and youth. Informal work is especially widespread in rural areas and sectors like agriculture and construction. Effective policies that incorporate multi-dimensional poverty indices and target informal work are essential for providing targeted social benefits, enhancing formal employment, and reducing inequality in the region.

This chapter examines the region's low economic growth, highlighting structural challenges in light of the region's subdued potential growth and low productivity performance. In addition, the chapter analyses the current monetary and fiscal policy space as well as the status of the region's external accounts. It then turns to social conditions in LAC, with a focus on informality and the role that social security systems could play in reducing the region's social vulnerabilities. Finally, it stresses the need to formulate a clear roadmap for development with a clear financing agenda and concludes with main policy messages.

Weak growth in LAC points to the need to address structural challenges

The LAC region has been slowing economically since 2022. While this trend is the result of cyclical dynamics, long-term structural factors continue to persist in most LAC countries. It is amplified by the domestic macroeconomic policy mix in the majority of LAC countries, which face insufficient fiscal space and persistently high inflation rates.

Low productivity growth is a major structural challenge in the region

A key structural challenge in LAC is low productivity growth. Low productivity growth is a key factor in the region's poor economic performance and in its inability to catch up with developed economies. Average labour productivity per hour worked in the region amounted to 33% of the OECD average in 2023, and the gap has widened since 1990, when the LAC average stood at 40% (Figure 1.1). Low productivity growth in LAC is associated with several factors, including low levels of innovation and adoption of new technologies, low levels of investment in physical and human capital, high informality, and suboptimal allocation of resources (OECD et al., 2019[1]). Allocation of resources is suboptimal when established firms are favoured over innovative startups or when capital is channelled towards politically connected enterprises rather than those with higher growth potential (IDB, 2024[2]).

Figure 1.1. Labour productivity in LAC as a percentage of OECD labour productivity per hour worked, 1990-2023

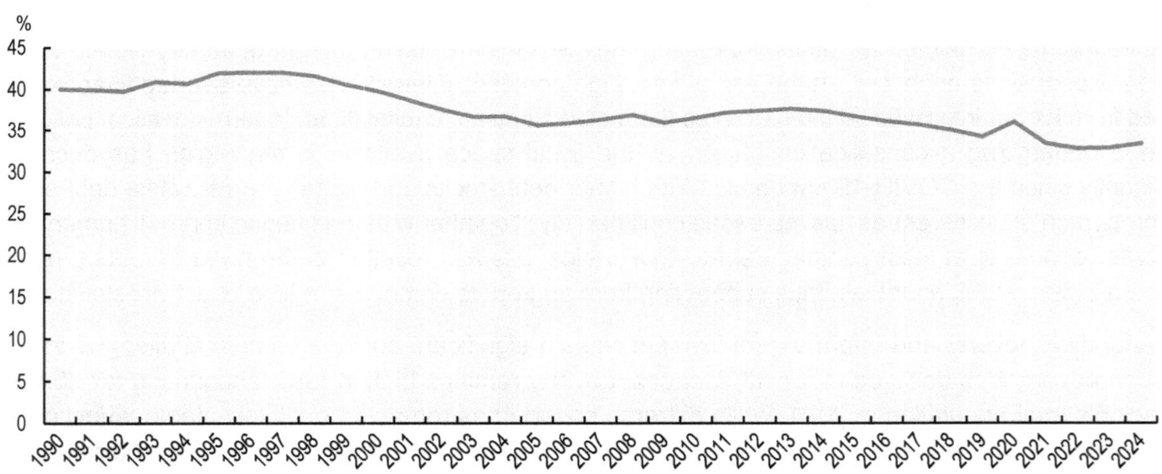

Note: LAC refers to a simple average that includes Argentina, Bolivia, Brazil, Chile, Colombia, Costa Rica, the Dominican Republic, Ecuador, Guatemala, Jamaica, Mexico, Paraguay, Peru, Trinidad and Tobago, Uruguay, and Venezuela. For the OECD, it is a simple average that includes its 38 member countries.
Source: Authors' calculations based on (The Conference Board, 2024[3]).

StatLink https://stat.link/j5w6r4

Low labour productivity in LAC is mainly due to the low productive efficiency of the region's economies. Poor productive efficiency can be attributed to decades of lacklustre growth in total factor productivity (TFP), a measure of how efficiently the economy uses its inputs (such as capital and labour) to produce goods and services. For instance, labour productivity in LAC is 70% relative to the United States on average. About 80% of the gap can be attributed to differences in TFP, which in LAC is about a third of that in the United States on average (differences in human capital account for most of the rest of the gap).[1] TFP in LAC has been below TFP in OECD countries since 1950 (Figure 1.2). From 1950 to 1975, TFP grew on average at about 1.1% per year in LAC, less than half of the 2.4% observed in OECD countries, and the region's performance has worsened since then. From 1975 to 2023, TFP decreased at an average annual rate of 0.08% in LAC, whereas in the OECD, it barely grew on average at 0.05%.

Figure 1.2. Total factor productivity (TFP) in LAC and OECD, 1950-2023 (1950 = 100)

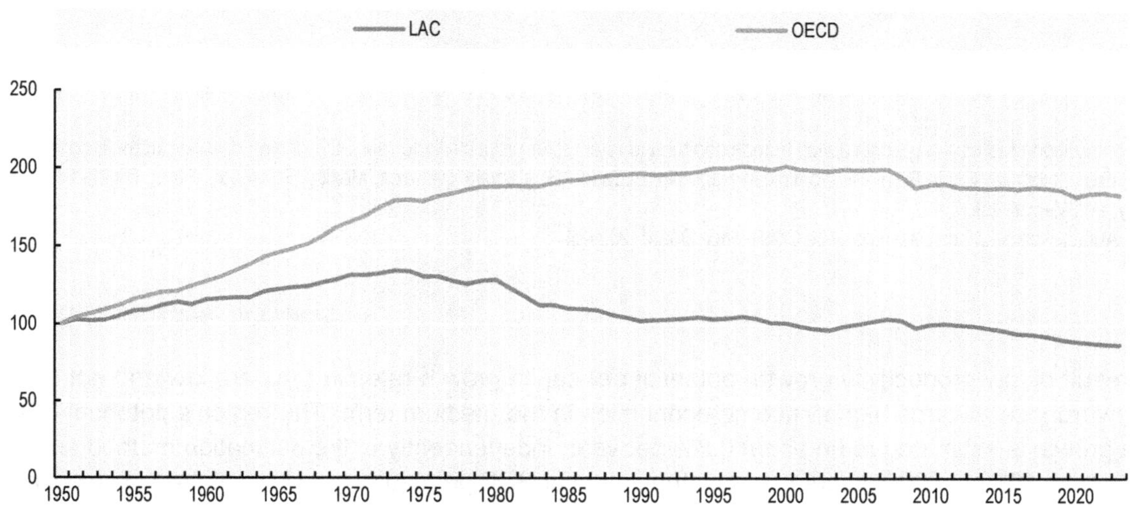

Note: LAC refers to a simple average that includes Argentina, Bolivia, Brazil, Chile, Colombia, Costa Rica, the Dominican Republic, Ecuador, Guatemala, Jamaica, Mexico, Paraguay, Peru, Trinidad and Tobago, Uruguay, and Venezuela. For the OECD, the simple average includes Australia, Austria, Belgium, Canada, Denmark, Finland, France, Iceland, Ireland, Israel, Italy, Japan, Luxembourg, the Netherlands, New Zealand, Norway, Portugal, Spain, Sweden, Switzerland, Türkiye, the United Kingdom and the United States.
Source: Authors' calculations based on (The Conference Board, 2024[3]).

StatLink https://stat.link/lf3mga

Capital per worker levels are also low in the region. On average, the level of capital per worker in LAC is about a quarter that of the United States. However, this difference is explained ultimately by the lower levels of TFP in LAC, as weak capital relative to workers is in part the result of the inefficient production structure of LAC economies. Thus, lower TFP has a direct negative effect on output and labour productivity as well as a compounded adverse effect through capital accumulation. As a result, capital stock relative to gross domestic product (GDP) in LAC, on average, is similar to the ratio observed in the United States.

The evolution of productivity in the region has been a significant drag on economic growth, especially since the 1980s (Figure 1.3). During the period 1950-70, TFP growth contributed about a quarter of the region's real GDP growth, which averaged 5.3% per year. In the 1970s, however, TFP not only did not contribute to economic growth but actually held it back slightly. Since 1980, TFP has significantly hindered economic growth, particularly in the 1980s and again since 2011. As a result, over the period 1980-2023, GDP in LAC grew at an average rate of 2.1% annually, slightly lower than the 2.3% observed in OECD countries.

Figure 1.3. Growth accounting (growth decomposition) in LAC, 1950-2023

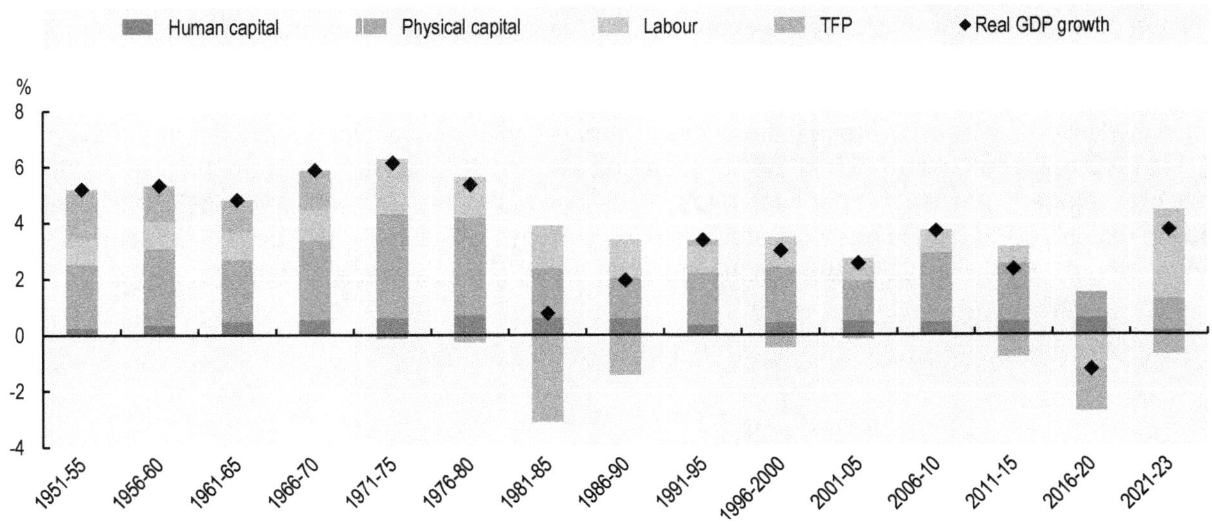

Note: Contribution of labour, physical capital, human capital and total factor productivity to real GDP growth. LAC includes Argentina, Bolivia, Brazil, Chile, Colombia, Costa Rica, the Dominican Republic, Ecuador, Guatemala, Jamaica, Mexico, Paraguay, Peru, Trinidad and Tobago, Uruguay, and Venezuela.
Source: Authors' calculations based on (The Conference Board, 2024[3]).

StatLink https://stat.link/rb3pxz

As a result of low productivity growth, potential per capita growth rates in LAC are low and not sufficient for convergence towards higher-income economies in the medium term. The region's potential GDP per capita growth is estimated to be about 0.8% per year, independently of the estimation method and based on data from 1980 to 2023. In comparison, the potential GDP per capita growth of high-income economies is estimated at around 1.7% annually (Figure 1.4).

Figure 1.4. Potential GDP per capita growth in LAC and in advanced economies

As estimated by different methods since 1980

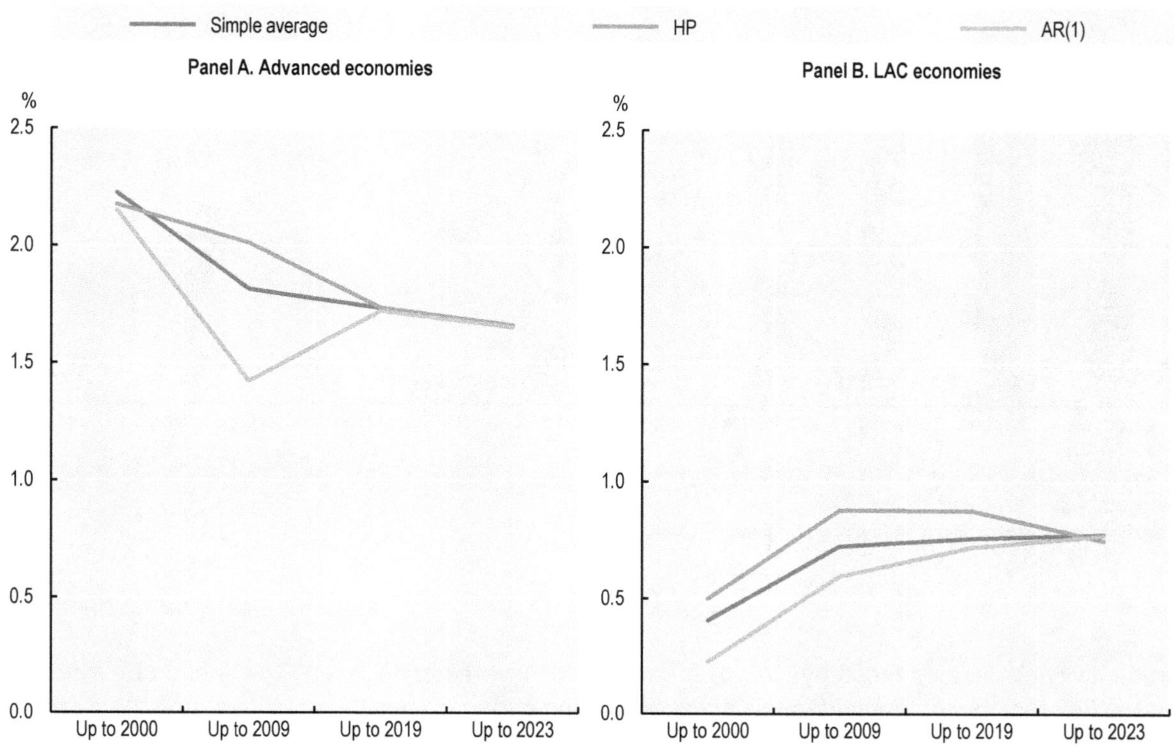

Note: Average growth is a simple average over the period analysed. HP = the Hodrick-Prescott filter, which was used as an alternative model due to its resilience to short-term shocks to create a smoothed curve (lambda equal to 100). AR(1) refers to an autoregressive model of order 1. The AR model uses GDP per capita growth data. The LAC series refers to 33 economies, while the term "advanced economies" includes 41 economies as listed in the IMF's World Economic Outlook database.
Source: Authors' calculations based on 1980-2023 data from (IMF, 2023[4]).

StatLink https://stat.link/khbpis

Low productivity growth in LAC affects most sectors of the economy (Figure 1.5). Labour productivity is lower than in the OECD on average in all sectors except the government and utilities. More specifically, the average relative sectoral productivity in LAC is 66% of that of the OECD. The labour productivity of key sectors such as trade, manufacturing, and other services – which employ a significant fraction of workers (23%, 10% and 11% respectively) – amounts to 33%, 39% and 42% of that of the OECD. Agriculture, which accounts for 15% of total employment, also presents a significant gap, with labour productivity of 55% relative to the OECD.

Figure 1.5. Sectoral labour productivity (PPP adjusted) in LAC relative to OECD, 2017

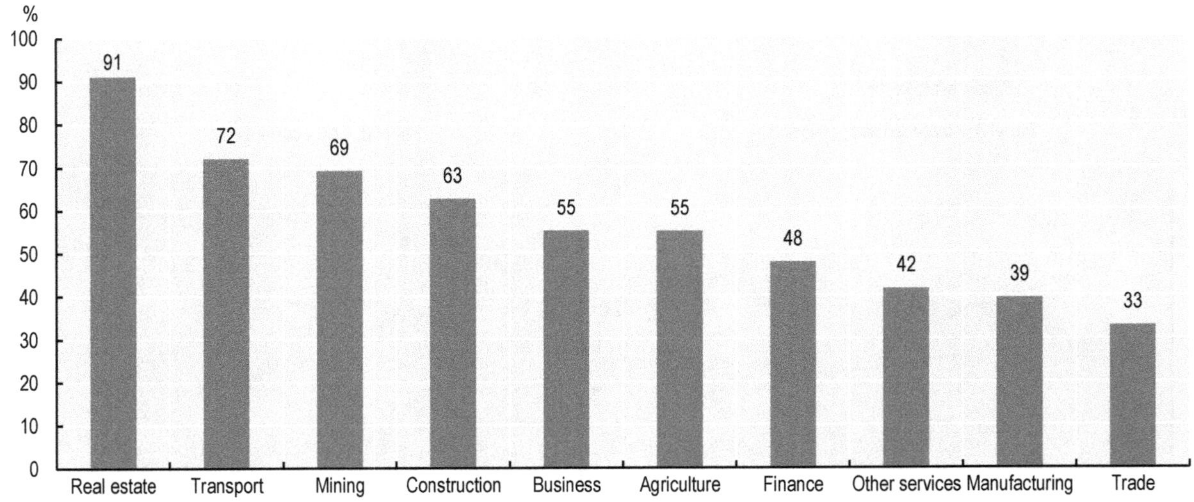

Note: Analysis based on the following nine LAC countries: Argentina, Bolivia, Brazil, Chile, Colombia, Costa Rica, Ecuador, Mexico and Peru. The most recent year with data available is 2017.
Source: Authors' calculations based on (Inklaar, Marapin and Gräler, 2023[5]).

StatLink https://stat.link/1o4d3r

The productivity challenges faced by LAC over several decades have impeded growth and development. Among the key factors contributing to this situation are the economic institutions that shape the business environment. These institutional factors encompass critical aspects such as safeguarding property rights, upholding the rule of law, enforcing contracts, and maintaining state capacity. Regulatory frameworks and public policies also play a significant role. These factors collectively influence how firms operate. They impact productivity through i) resource allocation across firms and industries; ii) firm-level innovation; and iii) the entry and exit of firms. A well-functioning financial system is essential to ensure the effectiveness of these mechanisms and to invest in strategic sectors (CAF, 2018[6]; OECD et al., 2023[7]).

A key factor for low productivity growth is underdeveloped financial systems, which are essential in financing of the development agenda (Chapter 3). Financial markets can have important effects on productivity through several channels. First, access to financing plays a key role in firms' decisions to innovate, expand and export. Second, lack of credit may also affect individuals' occupational choices and prevent talented entrepreneurs from pursuing projects with high potential. Third, a well-functioning financial system is key for firms to better absorb real shocks, allowing the most vulnerable and productive firms to survive. In an economy with little access to credit, the firms that survive adverse shocks are not necessarily those that are more productive but rather those with fewer liquidity problems. The increase in productivity that could be obtained by eliminating credit frictions is between 18% and 24% and could reach up to 36%. Similarly, if countries in the region were to adopt the best financial practices, they could achieve productivity gains of 18% and output per capita gains of up to 88% (CAF, 2018[6]).

Persistent challenges are more difficult to address when there is limited room for demand-side policies

As inflation eases, monetary authorities should remain cautious

As in the rest of the world, inflation in the region is converging towards pre-pandemic levels. After topping 10% on average (excluding Argentina and Venezuela) in the middle of 2022, inflation has dropped since the second half of 2023 in most LAC countries, independent of their monetary policy regime (Figure 1.6). Commodity prices were the main driver of recent increases in headline and core inflation rates (IDB, 2024[2]; OECD et al., 2023[7]). Since the beginning of 2023, declines in inflation have been particularly evident in economies where central banks are independent and follow inflation-targeting regimes. However, within inflation-targeting regimes, some economies – such as Colombia and, to a lesser extent, Mexico – have struggled to reduce headline inflation and anchor inflation expectations, while in other countries, such as Brazil, Chile and Peru, the normalisation of both inflation and interest rates was achieved more rapidly from the second half of 2023.

Figure 1.6. Monthly inflation in LAC economies under different inflation regimes

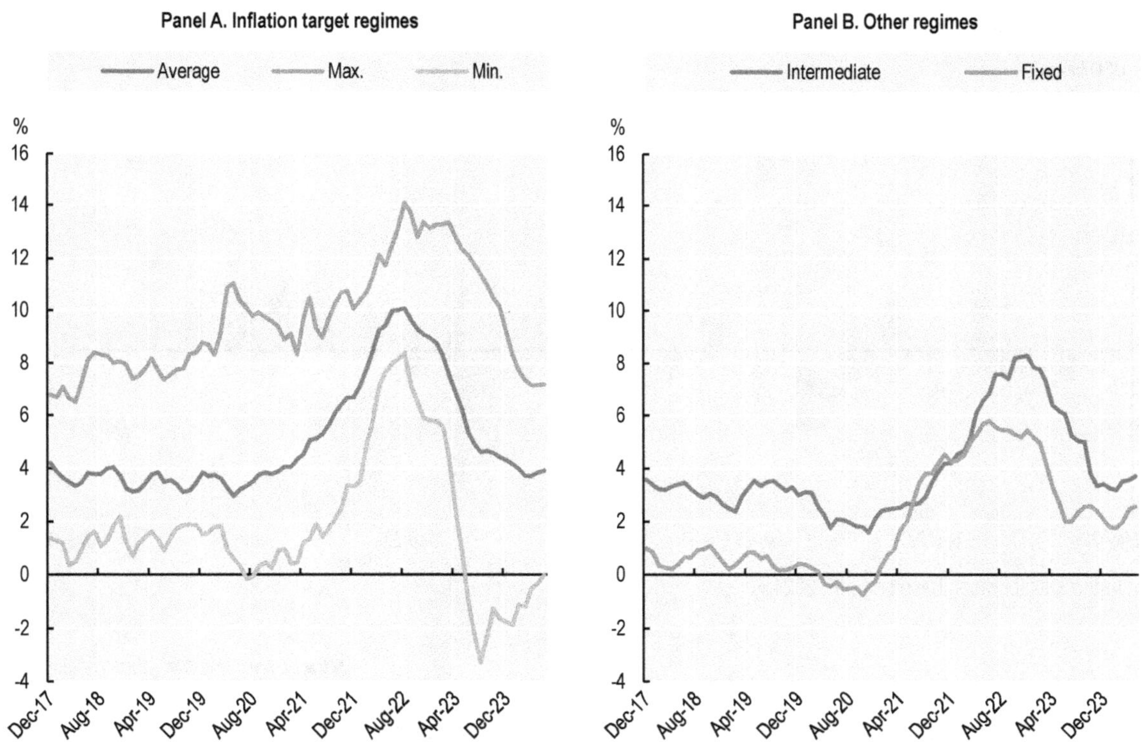

Note: The simple average for LAC countries with an inflation-targeting regime includes Brazil, Chile, Colombia, Costa Rica, the Dominican Republic, Guatemala, Jamaica, Mexico, Paraguay, Peru, and Uruguay. Max = maximum inflation among the countries per month. Min = minimum inflation among the countries per month. For intermediate regimes, the simple average includes Bolivia, Honduras, Nicaragua and Trinidad and Tobago. The simple average for fixed regimes includes Belize, Ecuador, El Salvador, Guyana, and Panama.
Source: Authors' calculations based on LSEG Data and Analytics.

StatLink https://stat.link/m0api6

Monetary policy has been fundamental in taming headline inflation and keeping inflation expectations in check. To control both headline inflation and inflation expectations, central banks in some LAC countries, such as Brazil, Colombia, Mexico and Peru, started tightening their monetary policies even before advanced economies. As inflation pressures diminished in these countries, central banks in the region also started to ease monetary conditions.

Monetary authorities should continue to be cautious. With local conditions putting pressure on inflation expectations in some countries (such as Brazil and Mexico), central banks in the region should be cautious and avoid easing monetary conditions too fast. This will prevent a significant reduction in interest rate gaps and therefore avoid capital flight and currency depreciation.

Capital flows to Latin America have been resilient

Short-term capital flows to LAC have continued to show resilience in the face of high interest rates in global financial markets. The region saw net short-term capital inflows of USD 42.9 billion in 2023 and USD 24.8 billion in the first semester of 2024, maintaining a positive flow in almost every month (Figure 1.7).

Figure 1.7. Total portfolio flows, May 2022-May 2024 (equity and debt)

USD billion (current values)

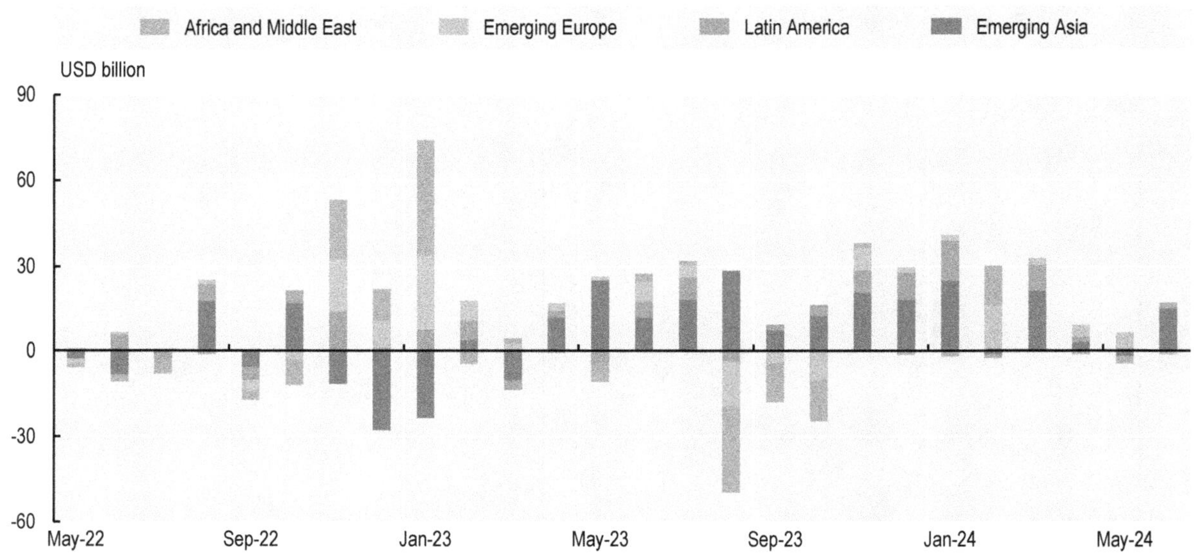

Source: Authors' elaboration based on (IIF, 2024[8]).

StatLink https://stat.link/kogsph

Positive portfolio inflows since 2023 can be partly explained by the region's interest rate hikes to address high inflation. This has created wide interest-rate gaps with the United States and other advanced economies. Interest rates in most LAC countries remain at higher levels than those of advanced economies, especially in Brazil and Mexico. These interest-rate gaps have made the region more attractive to investors, benefiting both equity and bond markets. In the case of equity markets, the price of financial assets in the region outperformed the group of 24 emerging economies measured by Morgan Stanley Capital International (MSCI), with a combined revaluation of close to 3.0%, compared to a 4.4% drop in the bloc of emerging economies, according to the MSCI Stock Price Index for the third quarter of 2023. In the case of the bond market, Latin America experienced a favourable year, adding net capital inflows of USD 44 billion in 2023.

In addition to these portfolio inflows, the region received historical inflows of foreign direct investment (FDI) in 2022, with a slight drop in 2023. Inflows reached record figures of USD 205.59 billion in 2022 but dropped 9.9% in 2023 down to USD 184.3 billion in 2023 (2.8% of GDP) on the back of a decline in global FDI inflows. The region remains one of the world's most attractive in terms of FDI (OECD et al., 2023[7]; ECLAC, 2024[9]). In 2022 and 2023, FDI inflows to the region accounted for more than 14% of total world FDI (Figure 1.8). Amid high FDI inflows, the focus should remain on quality. Quality FDI refers to investments that can contribute to increasing productivity, innovation, wages and skills development and to attaining decarbonisation goals (OECD et al., 2022[10]; OECD, 2019[11]; OECD et al., 2023[7]). To foster quality FDI, there is a need for stronger regulatory frameworks and well-defined investment strategies to ensure that FDI flows can be better oriented towards development goals (Chapter 4).

Figure 1.8. FDI inflows in LAC as a % total world FDI, 1990-2023

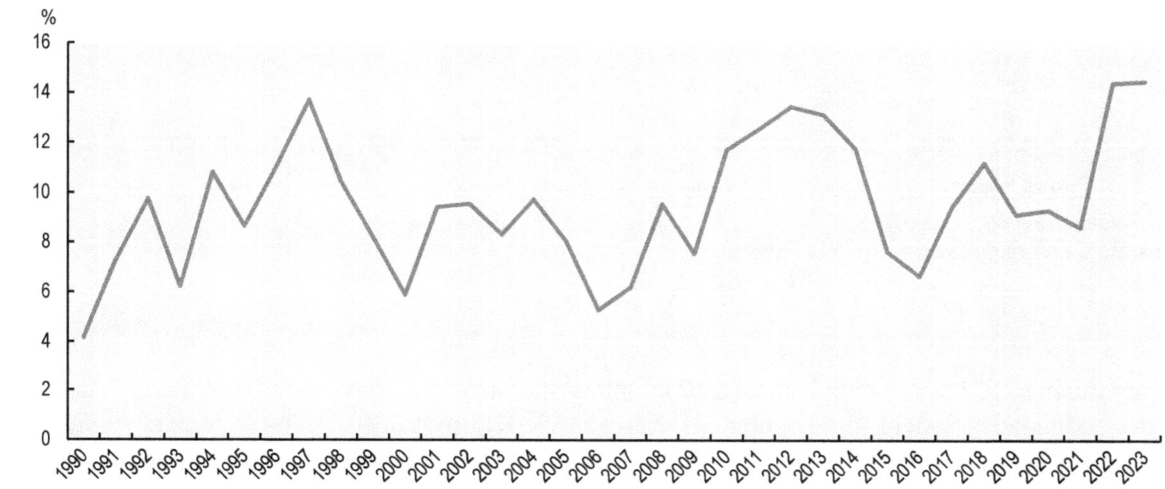

Source: Authors' calculations based on (UNCTAD, 2023[12]).

StatLink https://stat.link/590brt

Short-term and structural factors drove the increase in FDI towards LAC. As Russia's war of aggression against Ukraine, which began in February 2022, induced a forced reconfiguration of value chains on the European continent, the remoteness of the conflict made the Latin American region a reliable destination. A large part of the investment was directed towards the energy sector, with a growing weight on renewables (OECD, 2023[13]). FDI to the region also benefited from the withholding of profits by many transnational corporations in 2022. This was especially the case in Argentina, where the country's subsidiaries decided to reinvest the profits generated during the year rather than transfer them to the parent company. FDI to the region was also boosted by the development of nearshoring, which has expanded since 2020, especially in Mexico (OECD, 2024[14]).

Fiscal space remains limited while the region undergoes fiscal consolidation

After a significant fiscal stimulus in 2020-21, the region started a process of fiscal consolidation. The increase in fiscal revenues in 2022, coupled with a decrease in public spending after the fiscal stimuli adopted during the pandemic in 2020, resulted in narrowed fiscal deficits, which fell from -6.9% of GDP in 2020 to -2.2% in 2022 for the region. Similarly, the primary balance achieved a surplus of 0.3% of GDP in 2022, compared to -4.0% in 2020 (Figure 1.9) (ECLAC, 2024[15]).

Figure 1.9. Overall and primary fiscal balance in central governments in LAC as a % of GDP, 2010-23

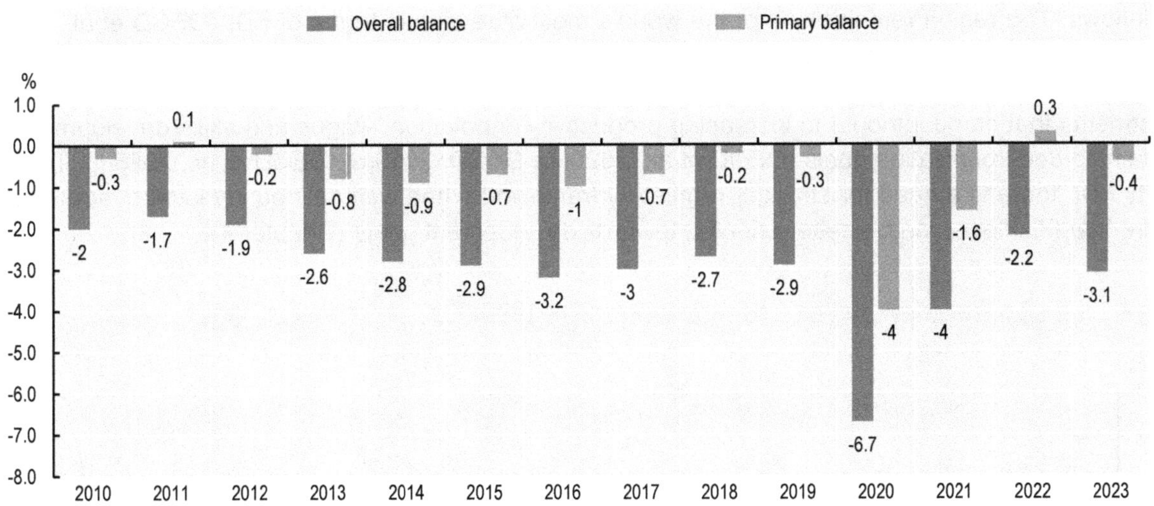

Note: Argentina, Brazil, Chile, Colombia, Costa Rica, the Dominican Republic, Ecuador, El Salvador, Guatemala, Honduras, Mexico, Nicaragua, Panama, Paraguay, Peru and Uruguay.
Source: Authors' elaboration based on (ECLAC, 2024[15]).

StatLink https://stat.link/er6n28

Fiscal revenues in 2022 increased in most LAC countries thanks to high commodity prices and better-than-expected economic growth in some countries. More specifically, tax-to-GDP ratios increased in more than three-quarters of LAC countries between 2021 and 2022, with the average tax-to-GDP ratio for the region rising by 0.3 percentage points to 21.5%, still slightly below its pre-pandemic level of 21.6% (Figure 1.10). The increase in the regional average was driven by corporate income tax amid higher profits by oil companies, although this was partially offset by a decline in revenue from excise taxes, due both to lower demand and to the adoption of a range of policy measures by countries to mitigate the impact of energy and food inflation on households and firms (OECD et al., 2024[16]) (Chapter 2).

Figure 1.10. Changes in tax-to-GDP ratio in LAC countries by main tax heading, 2022

Year-on-year change, percentage points

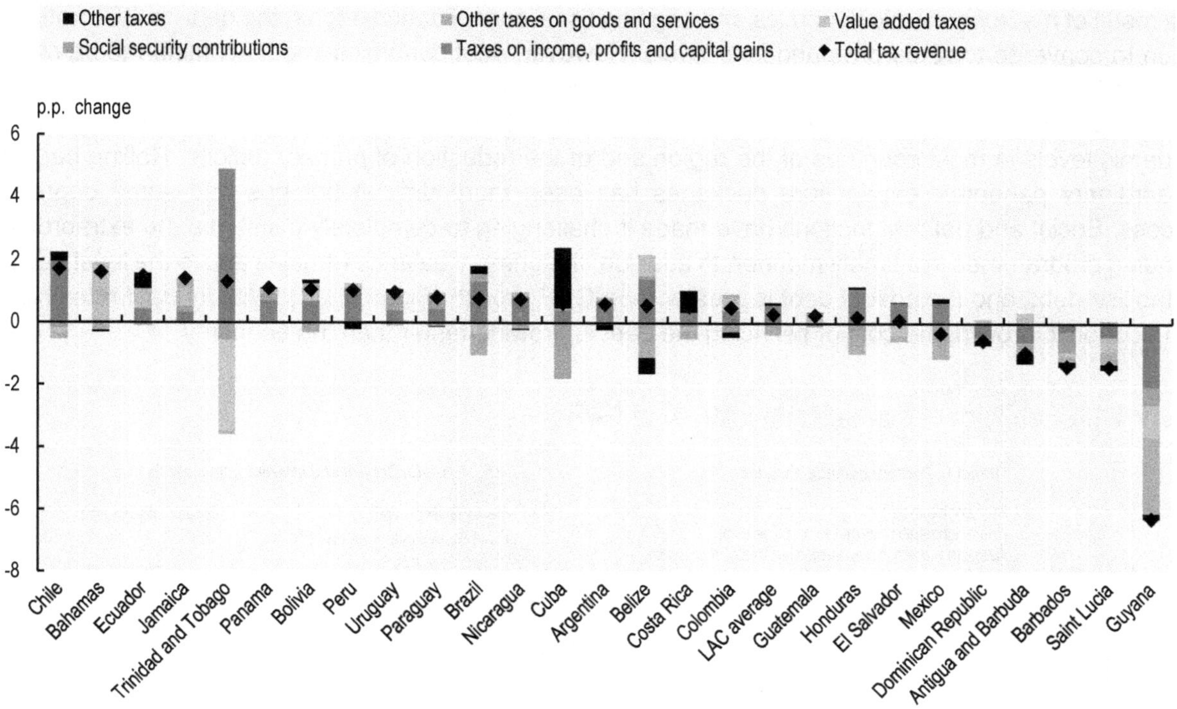

Note: The LAC average represents the unweighted average of 26 LAC countries included in (OECD et al., 2024[16]) and excludes Venezuela due to data availability issues.
Source: Authors' calculations based on (OECD et al., 2024[16]).

StatLink https://stat.link/jetnfv

Maintaining a restrictive fiscal stance is proving difficult for several reasons. First, growth is slowing in the region after the initial pandemic recovery, putting pressure on living standards and increasing social and political pressure on governments to spend more. Second, the financing of the fiscal stimulus packages adopted during the pandemic included the reallocation of resources from other expenditure lines towards subsidies and transfers. As the pandemic recedes, there is growing pressure to compensate for the spending losses in the areas neglected over 2020-21. Third, electoral events in several countries in the region are generating pressure to increase short-term spending. Fourth, inflationary pressures forced monetary authorities to increase interest rates, resulting in higher debt service. This is particularly the case in highly indebted countries, including some Caribbean countries, not only where debt is higher but where fiscal fragilities are associated with shorter-term debt profiles. These countries therefore have higher sensitivity to changes in short-term debt and are vulnerable to interactions between higher global interest rates and country risks. Finally, high volatility commodity prices are affecting fiscal revenues in major hydrocarbon and mining producers in LAC. Hydrocarbon-related revenues among major producers in the region increased to 4.4% of GDP on average in 2022, up from 2.6% in 2021, but are estimated to have dropped to 3.9% in 2023. Similarly, average revenues from mining increased from 0.7% of GDP in 2021 to 0.8% in 2022 but fell in 2023 to an estimated 0.5% of GDP as mineral prices trended down (OECD et al., 2024[16]).

Credible fiscal frameworks are essential for fiscal sustainability and to protect investments (Chapter 2). They can help to enhance fiscal discipline and reduce risk premiums on sovereign debt by establishing clear rules (e.g. fiscal rules) and guidelines for government spending, revenue collection and borrowing. Robust fiscal frameworks can improve investor confidence, thereby lowering the cost of borrowing for governments. They can also help to protect public investments during episodes of fiscal consolidation, as governments find it easier to cut spending on investment (Ardanaz and Izquierdo, 2022[17]). This not only has impacts on long-term growth but can also affect economic recovery (Arreaza et al., 2022[18]; OECD et al., 2023[7]).

As a result of macroeconomic dynamics and ongoing fiscal consolidation efforts, the debt-to-GDP ratio has begun to converge towards pre-pandemic levels. However, debt dynamics should continue to be closely monitored. In 2022, central government debt in the region accounted for 51.5% of GDP, down from 56.3% in 2020 (ECLAC, 2024[15]). This decrease is fundamentally a consequence of GDP returning to pre-pandemic levels in most countries of the region and of the reduction of primary deficits. Rolling back the extraordinary pandemic expenditure packages has been more difficult but has had some degree of success. Social and political frictions have made it challenging to completely dismantle the extraordinary spending programmes in a timely manner. In addition, the primary balance remains above the level needed to stabilise debt, and the cost of debt is greater than GDP growth (Figure 1.11). With interest rates higher than economic growth, the cost of servicing the debt is growing faster than the economy.

Figure 1.11. Public debt dynamics in LAC, % of GDP

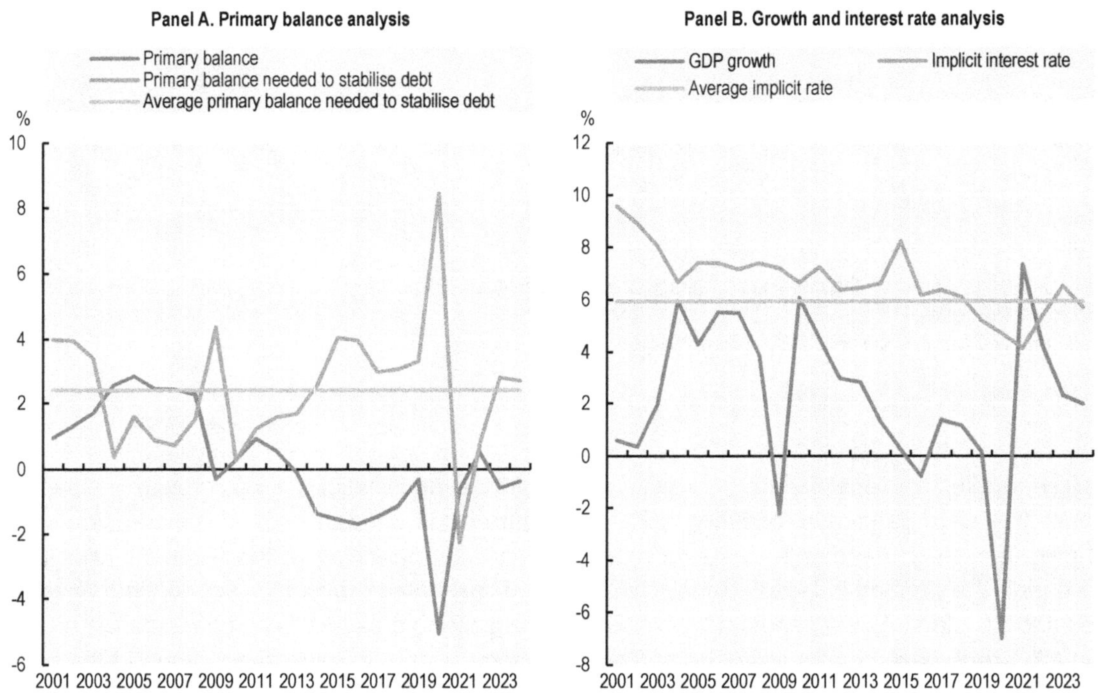

Note: Weighted average of the 33 LAC economies covered in the World Economic Outlook database. To calculate the primary balance needed to stabilise debt, an implicit rate is calculated as the ratio of debt service to total debt stock, reflecting the average borrowing cost, and we assume zero variation in the exchange rate or in other valuation effects. The primary balance needed to stabilise debt refers to how much the government needs to adjust its primary balance to keep the debt-to-GDP ratio constant, given the interest rate and growth dynamics $pb_t = d_{t-1}(i_t - g_t)/(1 + g_t)$ where pb_t is the balance needed to stabilise debt over GDP, d_{t-1} is the stock of public debt over GDP in the previous period, i_t is the implicit interest rate and g_t is the real rate of GDP growth.
Source: Authors' calculations based on (IMF, 2024[19]).

StatLink https://stat.link/mx9gkt

Public debt dynamics in the region display strong heterogeneity. In countries that had strong fiscal consolidation programmes even before the pandemic hit, like Barbados, Ecuador and Jamaica, debt-to-GDP ratios have resumed their downward trend after an initial increase. In other countries, such as Chile, Colombia, Paraguay, and Peru, despite their considerable heterogeneity in terms of public debt ratios and credit ratings, the debt-to-GDP ratio has stabilised. In still other economies, like Brazil, the debt-to-GDP ratio could stabilise at a higher level, which could lead to fiscal fragilities. In other countries (Argentina and, to a lesser extent, Mexico), there is no clear evidence yet that debt is on a stabilising trajectory (IMF, 2024[19]).

Social conditions and poverty: A multi-dimensional perspective

Poverty remains high in LAC countries although it has declined since the beginning of this century. In 2024, people living in poverty accounted for 26.8% of the region's total population (Figure 1.12). Two decades earlier, in 2001, the rate was 44.1%. Despite the overall reduction in poverty, the COVID-19 pandemic has had a lasting negative effect on people's welfare. Poverty and extreme poverty have remained above pre-pandemic levels in more than half of LAC countries. On average, the situation improved slightly in 2023 compared to 2020, when the poverty rate hit 32.8%. However, extreme poverty has remained persistently high since 2001. In 2024, one person out of ten (10.4%) lived in extreme poverty, compared to 12.2% in 2002 (ECLAC, 2024[20]).

Figure 1.12. Monetary poverty rates in selected Latin American countries, 2001-22

Percentage of people living under the poverty and extreme poverty lines

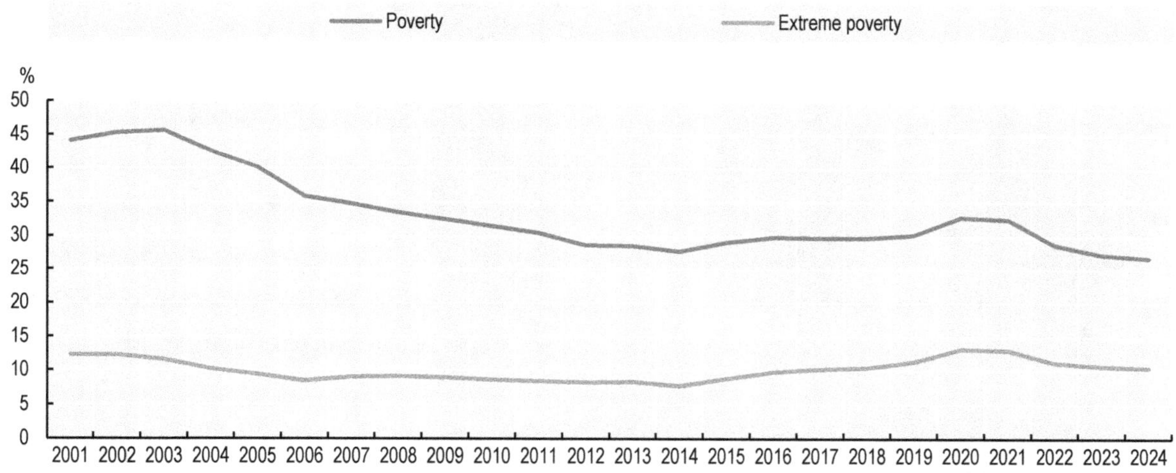

Note: Weighted average for the following countries: Argentina, Bolivia, Brazil, Chile, Colombia, Costa Rica, the Dominican Republic, Ecuador, El Salvador, Guatemala, Honduras, Mexico, Nicaragua, Panama, Paraguay, Peru, Uruguay and Venezuela. Data for 2023 are projections. Poverty and extreme poverty headcount rates refer to the number of people living under national estimated poverty lines. Extreme poverty lines are the product of multiplying the calorie requirement provided by international recommendations and the cost per kilocalorie, which is the indicator that summarises the information on the structure and prices of food consumption of the reference population, which is estimated through household income and expenditure surveys or living conditions surveys. In turn, the poverty line is obtained by multiplying the extreme poverty line by a factor that expresses expenditure on non-food goods and services (i.e. the Orshansky coefficient). For more details on the methodology, see (ECLAC, 2019[21]).
Source: Author's elaboration based on (ECLAC, 2024[20]).

StatLink https://stat.link/t0uqex

Inflation has had a negative impact on the living conditions of people living in LAC, especially the most vulnerable people. Indeed, the cumulative effect of inflation episodes impacts greatly on the most vulnerable households, particularly those with low income or headed by older people (Caisi et al., 2023[22]). In 2023, the general price level across the region was 13.1% higher than in 2021, while for people living in extreme poverty, the price of the basket of goods normally consumed was 20% higher (Figure 1.13, Panel A). The gap in inflation rates reached a peak of 4.4 percentage points in 2022, was still at 4.1 percentage points in the first half of 2023 (OECD et al., 2023[7]) and on average was 2.9 percentage points in 2023 (Figure 1.13, Panel B). It was still particularly high in Argentina (8.5 percentage points), Colombia (3.3), Guatemala (4.5) and Peru (4.2). The decrease in relative inflation since mid-2023 for people living under the national extreme poverty line is partly due to a decline in commodity prices, which began increasing when Russia's war of aggression against Ukraine pushed up prices of food and energy (OECD, 2023[23]; Rogoff, 2023[24]). This added further constraints to the pandemic-induced disruptions in global value chains (Arriola et al., 2020[25]; OECD et al., 2023[7]). Those pressures have recently eased (ECB, 2023[26]; Giordano and Michalczewsky, 2024[27]).

Figure 1.13. Impact of inflation on the most vulnerable people in LAC

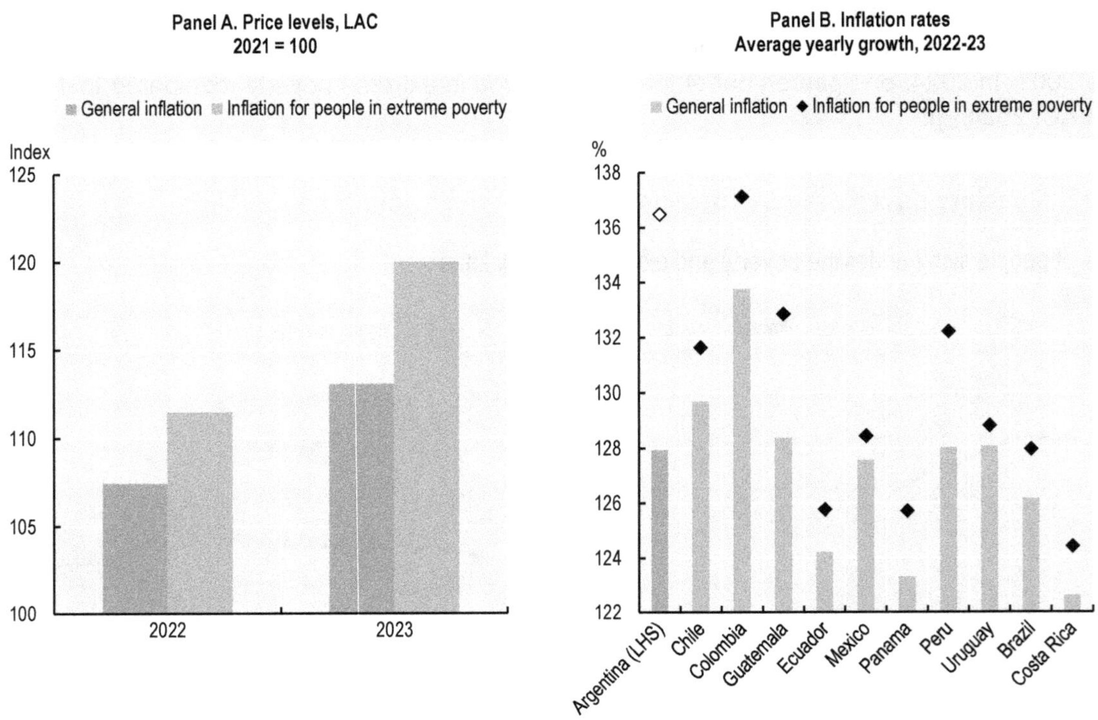

Note: Extreme poverty thresholds are based on the cost of a basic food basket that covers basic needs and provides the minimum caloric requirement of the members of a reference household. For Colombia and Peru, the food and non-alcoholic beverages item of their Consumer Price Index (CPI) was taken into consideration. In the case of Panama, the data include the districts of Panama and San Miguelito. For Uruguay, inflation in Montevideo is considered. To calculate inflation for people in extreme poverty in Brazil, the averages of the baskets of the 17 capitals were used. Panel A refers to the unweighted averages of price levels across LAC faced by general consumers (green) and by people in a situation of extreme poverty (orange). In Panel A, Argentina is excluded from the calculations of the average price levels. In Panel B, percentages for Argentina are shown on the left-hand axis.

Source: Authors' elaboration based on data from national statistical offices on CPI and poverty thresholds.

StatLink https://stat.link/seocf7

Despite progress, reducing poverty remains a major social concern in LAC and needs to be considered in all its dimensions. Lack of sufficient income correlates with other dimensions that are key for people's welfare, such as education, health, housing, and sanitation. Measurements of income and multi-dimensional poverty in the LAC region have advanced significantly in recent decades thanks to the availability of microdata from national household surveys carried over by government bodies and national statistical offices (Gasparini, Santos and Tornarolli, 2021[28]; OPHI and UNDP, 2023[29]). However, income poverty as measured through household surveys is not necessarily perfectly correlated with multi-dimensionally poverty (Alkire and Shen, 2017[30]; Tran, Klasen and Alkire, 2015[31]). United Nations (UN) initiatives to address the global challenge of ending poverty and material deprivation in all forms include the 2030 Agenda for Sustainable Development, adopted in 2015, and the UN Sustainable Development Goals (SDGs). Efforts to measure multi-dimensional poverty attempt to set out clear priorities for addressing these goals (Box 1.1).

Box 1.1. Measuring multi-dimensional poverty

Poverty measures are normally based on the assumption that a monetary poverty figure can capture the phenomenon of people's inability to live with adequate material means (Ravallion, 2016[32]). Although monetary poverty statistics are essential, poverty is associated with a shortage of particular material resources (Lister, 2004[33]). It should therefore be considered a multi-dimensional phenomenon (Sen, 1999[34]). Income poverty as measured through household surveys is not necessarily perfectly correlated with multi-dimensionally poverty. Recognition of poverty as a multi-dimensional phenomenon has increased rapidly over the last few decades. This is because, in the view of many economists, a monetary figure such as income cannot capture all aspects of the deprivation suffered by people living in poverty (Alkire and Shen, 2017[30]; Tran, Klasen and Alkire, 2015[31]). Recognition of poverty as a multi-dimensional phenomenon can be found in Sustainable Development Goal 1 on ending poverty in all its forms everywhere: SDG 1.1, on ending monetary poverty for people living on less than USD 1.90 per day, is complemented by SDG 1.2, which aims to reduce multi-dimensional poverty by at least half by 2030. The World Bank has also accepted the use of a multi-dimensional poverty indicator as a complement to the USD 1.90 per day measure (World Bank, 2017[35]).

Global estimates on multi-dimensional poverty across more than 100 developing countries are developed jointly by the United Nations Development Programme and the Oxford Poverty and Human Development Initiative (OPHI and UNDP, 2023[29]). The global Multi-dimensional Poverty Index (MPI) advances SDG 1.2 and measures interconnected deprivations across indicators related to SDGs 1, 2, 3, 4, 6, 7 and 11 (on poverty; hunger; health and well-being; education; clean water and sanitation; affordable and clean energy; and sustainable cities and communities). The index has the advantage of being methodologically consistent across countries.

The global MPI methodology begins by constructing a deprivation profile for each household and each person living in it. Deprivations are tracked using 10 indicators spanning health, education and standard of living. Examples of indicators are the child mortality rate, the school attendance rate, and the share of households that lack access to electricity or that do not have basic assets such as a phone, television, computer, refrigerator, bicycle or motorcycle. All indicators are equally weighted within each dimension. The deprivation score for each person is the sum of the weighted deprivations experienced. The global MPI considers people as multi-dimensionally poor if their deprivation score is one-third or higher.

Many countries have developed national adaptations based on the global MPI. Regional MPIs also exist, including for LAC (ECLAC, 2013[36]). Official multi-dimensional poverty measures have been released in Chile, Colombia, Costa Rica, Ecuador, El Salvador and Mexico, with specific national methodologies (CONEVAL, 2010[37]; Angulo, Diaz and Pardo Pinzon, 2013[38]; Ministerio de Desarrollo Social de Chile, 2015[39]; Castillo and Perez, 2015[40]; Gobierno de El Salvador, 2015[41]; INEC, 2015[42]). The data presented in this chapter refer to national estimates provided in (ECLAC, 2024[43]).

Source: Authors' elaboration based on (OPHI and UNDP, 2023[29]), (OPHI/University of Oxford/UNDP, 2019[44]) and (ECLAC, 2024[45]).

Multi-dimensional poverty as measured by the global MPI varies greatly across LAC countries. In 2022, multi-dimensional poverty was below 20% in six LAC countries, while it was particularly high in El Salvador (33.4%), Mexico (36.3%), Ecuador (38.1%) and Honduras (66.9%) (ECLAC, 2024[45]). According to estimates of the UN Development Programme, around 33 million people in LAC, or nearly 6% of the regional population, experienced acute multi-dimensional poverty in 2023 (OPHI and UNDP, 2023[29]).

Among the dimensions of poverty, living conditions, including housing and basic services, contribute the most to acute poverty in the region (38.9%), followed by health (33.5%) and education (27.6%) (ECLAC, 2024[45]). Meanwhile, the consequences of climate change have a greater impact on the most vulnerable groups. Globally, between 32 million and 132 million people risk falling into poverty due to climate change by 2030 under most scenarios (Jafino et al., 2020[46]).

Multi-dimensional poverty indices are an important tool for helping policy makers to better understand and tackle monetary poverty and other forms of deprivation. In Colombia, a simplified version of the national MPI was constructed using granular data from the census to identify critically deprived areas of the country. The information was used to prioritise certain regions and municipalities for better targeting of social benefits (DANE, 2020[47]). In Chile, the MPI has been used as a policy tool to complement existing poverty statistics and to design, monitor and evaluate public policy for attaining the SDGs (Gobierno del Chile, 2017[48]). In many cases, having people who are poor directly participate in validating the structure for the national MPI can provide the most straightforward focus on the dimensions and severity of multi-dimensional poverty. This process has been undertaken by some LAC countries, including El Salvador and Panama (OPHI/University of Oxford/UNDP, 2019[44]).

Some LAC countries have deepened the policy scope of MPIs. For instance, Costa Rica and Mexico have adopted and officially incorporated the MPI into their budget allocation processes, aligning resources with the results of the national MPI. Allocations may be adjusted to tackle deprivations more effectively, even using the same amount of aggregate budget resources. This kind of analysis allows governments to accelerate the reductions of multi-dimensional poverty by redistributing resources according to the needs of each region or of vulnerable groups (MPPN, 2017[49]; OPHI/University of Oxford/UNDP, 2019[44]). MPIs can also complement existing information with environmental indicators as a specific domain of multi-dimensional poverty. Much material deprivation is linked to natural disasters such as earthquakes, landslides, floods and storms (OECD et al., 2022[10]). Multitopic household surveys have the potential to identify which poor and vulnerable groups are the victims of specific deprivations related to the environment and natural resources. Chile, the Dominican Republic, El Salvador, and Panama have modified their household surveys to include a module on the risks of natural disasters and environmental pollution (OPHI/University of Oxford/UNDP, 2019[44]).

Informal work, widespread in the region, negatively impacts living conditions

Employment opportunities have stagnated in the LAC region in the last decade (ECLAC, 2024[43]). In 2022, the region's employment rate for people aged 15-64 stood at 65.1%, just slightly above the 2012 level of 64.4% and below the 2022 OECD average of 69.3% (which saw a substantial increase of 4.4 percentage points compared to ten years earlier).

Women and youth are extremely vulnerable in the region's labour market. In 2022, the gender gap in employment rates was 24.8 percentage points across LAC countries, varying from 38.3 percentage points in Honduras to 11.7 percentage points in Uruguay. Women's relative opportunities in the labour market have shown little progress over the last ten years: the gender gap has shrunk by just 3.5 percentage points since 2012. Young people aged 15-24 face a low likelihood of being employed. In 2022, the youth employment rate was 39.6%. These vulnerabilities are cumulative in LAC labour markets. Young women have an extremely low likelihood of being employed, with just three out of ten holding a job in 2022.

In addition, low-quality jobs and informality are widespread in the region's labour markets. In 2022, more than half of the workers in LAC were informal (55.7%) (ILO, 2024[50]).[2] This is only a slight improvement over 2010, when 59.4% of people employed were informal. The informality rate is particularly high in Bolivia (83.7%), Ecuador (68.5%), Guatemala (79.6%), Paraguay (67.9%) and Peru (74.4%). In contrast, effective fiscal policies have helped to cut informality rates almost in half in Chile and Uruguay (see Chapter 2 for more details). As of 2022, the rate stood at 27.4% in Chile and 22.1% in Uruguay.

Both men and women are exposed to informal work in the LAC region. In 2022, the share of informal workers within each gender group was 55.9% for men and 55.4% for women. However, in countries where informality is particularly high, women are much more likely than men to hold an informal job. The gender gap in the informality rate is substantial in Bolivia (5.0 percentage points), Ecuador (4.6 percentage points), Guatemala (4.8 percentage points), Paraguay (3 percentage points) and Peru (5.7 percentage points), countries where around seven workers out of ten are informal. Furthermore, the incidence of informal work is higher in sectors like agriculture (78.0%) and construction (75.8%), while it is lower in manufacturing (47.8%) and services (49.6%). Informality is higher in rural areas (71.4%) than in urban areas (50.5%).

Measuring informality at the household level is useful for understanding the labour market features of each country. The informal or formal status of working members within a household has important implications for dependent members. The formal employment status of at least one household member may increase the household's access to social insurance schemes, which often cover the contributor's spouse and/or children, as in the case of health insurance. For this reason, households with only informal workers face different vulnerabilities than mixed households. Adding the household dimension to the analysis of informality helps policy makers to identify the recipients of social assistance programmes and to design targeted public policies to address the vulnerabilities and negative consequences of informality on individuals and their households.

Across LAC in the years leading up to 2022, 64.9% of people lived in households where at least one of the principal earners held an informal job, 42.5% in households depending entirely on informal employment and 22.4% in mixed households with earners holding formal and informal jobs. People living in households where all earners were formal workers represented 25.1% of the population (Figure 1.14). However, heterogeneity is high across the region. The share of people living in completely informal households is substantial in countries like Honduras (73.9%), Bolivia (70.8%), Nicaragua (64.2%) and Peru (60.6%), while the share living in completely formal households is high in Uruguay (65.4%), the Bahamas (62.0%), Chile (59.2%) and Costa Rica (56.6%).

Figure 1.14. Distribution of the LAC population, by household informality status, latest available year

% of the population

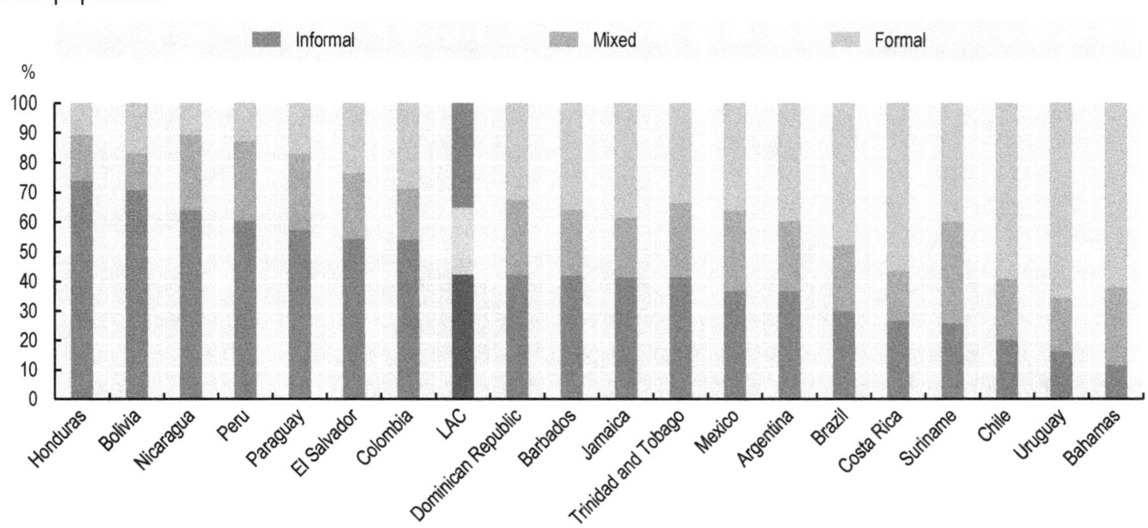

Note: Data from latest available year of each country's household survey. They refer to 2013 for the Bahamas; to 2016 for Barbados; to 2014 for Nicaragua and Trinidad and Tobago; to 2017 for Chile; to 2018 for Argentina, Bolivia, the Dominican Republic, Paraguay, and Uruguay; to 2019 for Brazil, Honduras, Jamaica and Peru; to 2020 for Costa Rica and Mexico; to 2021 for Colombia and El Salvador; to 2022 for Suriname.
Source: Authors' elaboration based on (OECD, 2024[51]).

StatLink https://stat.link/es7wtu

As a driver of low pay for individuals and of low income for households, informal work negatively impacts living conditions. In LAC during the 2020s, 65.5% of people in the lowest quintile of household income distribution lived in completely informal households, 13.9% in mixed households and 20.6% in formal ones. In the top income quintile, in contrast, those shares were respectively 22.2%, 24.1% and 53.7% (OECD, 2024[51]).

In other words, labour informality is associated with poverty in the LAC region (Figure 1.15). During the 2020s, 28.2% of informal workers were living under the national poverty line on average, while just 10.5% of formal workers were poor. The share of informal workers living beneath the poverty line was extremely high in Honduras (62.4), Argentina (58.5%) and Mexico (44.8%). Notably, across LAC countries, total poverty rates for workers are almost perfectly correlated with the gap in poverty between informal and formal workers.

Figure 1.15. Poverty rates of workers in LAC by informality status

% of workers who live under the national poverty line

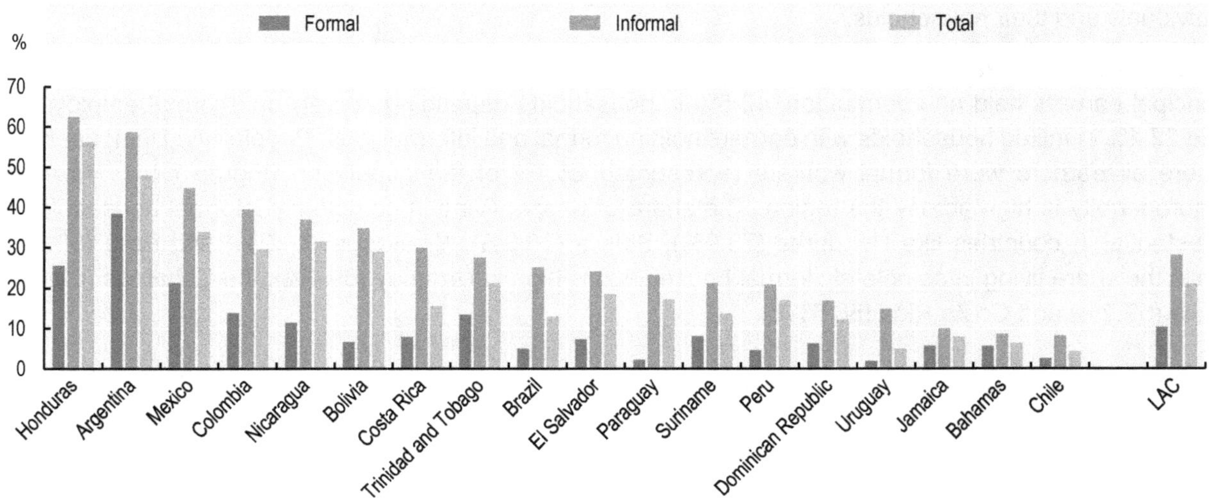

Note: Data from latest available year of each country's household survey. They refer to 2013 for the Bahamas; to 2014 for Nicaragua and Trinidad and Tobago; to 2017 for Chile; to 2018 for Argentina, Bolivia, the Dominican Republic, Paraguay and Uruguay; to 2019 for Brazil, Honduras, Jamaica and Peru; to 2020 for Costa Rica and Mexico; to 2021 for Colombia and El Salvador; to 2022 for Suriname.
Source: Authors' elaboration based on (OECD, 2024[51]).

StatLink https://stat.link/scy1xb

Beyond its direct impact on workers, informal work has deep negative consequences on household members. In LAC during the 2020s, 44.8% of children under the age of 5 depended entirely on the income of informal households. The same is true for older people: 48.7% of people over the age of 65 depended on completely informal households (OECD, 2024[51]). This means that almost half of the region's most vulnerable people may not have any effective social coverage, such as contributory pensions or health insurance. Targeting social assistance to this type of family must be a priority for LAC governments.

The use of information and communication technologies (ICTs) in formalisation policies can become a key tool for reducing informality in LAC (Chapter 3). Recent studies have highlighted how ICTs have helped in formalising small firms, through better traceability of informal activities, productivity enhancement due to digital applications, or better access to financial instruments for small firms or the self-employed due to financial technologies (fintech) (ILO, 2022[52]; Filipetto et al., 2022[53]). Fostering digital transformation in the region could therefore help in decreasing informality.

LAC economies are still profoundly unequal, although less so than in recent decades, due in part to high growth during the commodity price boom (Balakrishnan et al., 2021[54]). Measures of inequalities in household disposable income, such as the Gini index, show little variation since 2017, after significant declines since the start of the 2000s (Figure 1.16). In 2022, the Gini coefficient in LAC was 0.45. Countries with the highest Gini coefficients (indicating greater inequality) were Brazil and Colombia, above 0.50. The lowest Gini coefficients were registered in Argentina, the Dominican Republic and Uruguay, with indices between 0.38 and 0.40. At the global level, the region exhibited higher relative inequalities around 2015 than Africa (0.42), Asia (0.36) and Europe (0.31) (World Bank, 2024[55]).

Figure 1.16. Income inequalities in LAC countries, 2002-22

Gini coefficients

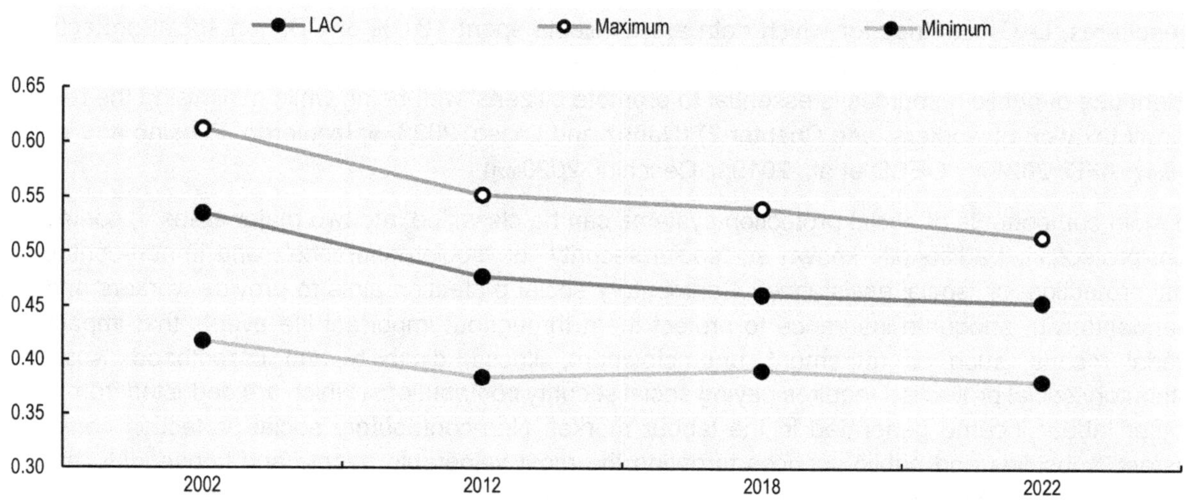

Note: The figure shows the unweighted average and the maximum and minimum levels of the Gini coefficients in the following LAC countries: Bolivia, Brazil, Chile, Colombia, Costa Rica, the Dominican Republic, Ecuador, El Salvador, Guatemala, Honduras, Mexico, Nicaragua, Panama, Paraguay, Peru, Uruguay and Venezuela.
Source: Authors' elaboration based on (ECLAC, 2024[43]).

StatLink https://stat.link/r3vpul

The structural decrease in inequality in the region over the last two decades was primarily driven by a significant decrease in unequal income outcomes in selected countries where inequality was particularly high. For instance, income inequality as expressed by the Gini coefficient was extremely high in the early 2000s in Bolivia (0.61), the Dominican Republic (0.50) and El Salvador (0.51). By 2022 the coefficient had shrunk respectively to 0.42, 0.38 and 0.40. This positive trend was partly linked to the commodity boom experienced in those countries (Balakrishnan et al., 2021[54]). However, inequality has been more persistent in some LAC countries, remaining above the LAC average in both 2002 and 2022. This was the case in Brazil (0.57 in 2002 and 0.51 in 2022), Panama (0.57 and 0.50) and Paraguay (0.58 and 0.47).

Informal work is a main driver of wage inequality. On average during the 2020s, formal employees in LAC earned an hourly wage two times larger than the wage earned by informal employees, contributing to the high dispersion of market labour income. The ratio is larger than the average in El Salvador (4.4 times), Honduras (2.5) and Peru (2.4). It is considerably smaller in Barbados (1.7), Chile (1.3), and Brazil and Colombia (1.6).

Better policy design of social protection systems can improve social inclusion

Enhancing social inclusion in LAC requires not just strengthened financing but also better policy design of social protection systems. In a context of limited resources, it is crucial to support the design of social protection policies that are both effective and efficient. This section focuses on the design of retirement pensions, health insurance, unemployment benefits and active labour market policies in LAC. It begins with a description of social spending levels in the region and an examination of the differences between contributory and non-contributory social protection systems.

In 2022, central government social spending relative to GDP in Latin America decreased for a second straight year, following substantial growth in 2020 with the emergency response to the COVID-19 pandemic (Chapter 2). In 2022, central government social spending stood at 11.5% of GDP, 2.2 percentage points lower than in 2020, yet slightly higher than the 2019 level (0.3 percentage points) (ECLAC, 2023[56]). Using the OECD Social Expenditure Database (SOCX), a classification of social expenditures, LAC countries for which data are available spent 12.6% of GDP on social protection on average in 2018, compared to 19.7% of GDP across the OECD (ECLAC, 2023[57]; OECD, 2023[58]). The efficient use of public resources is essential to promote citizens' well-being while minimising the recourse to direct taxation of workers (see Chapter 2) (Nuñez and Lasso, 2023[59]; Izquierdo, Pessino and Vuletin, 2018[60]; AFD, 2024[61]; OECD et al., 2019[1]; Cecchini, 2020[62]).

The main components of social protection systems can be classified into two major areas: i) contributory social protection, traditionally known as "social security" or "social insurance"; and ii) non-contributory social protection, or "social assistance". Contributory social protection aims to provide workers and their dependents with adequate insurance to protect them throughout important life events that impact their material means, such as retirement, unemployment, illness, disability and parenthood. Access to contributory social protection requires paying social security contributions, which are deducted from wages or other labour income generated in the labour market. Non-contributory social protection consists of transfers, subsidies and public services targeting the most vulnerable people and households, such as those living in poverty (either monetary or multi-dimensional). Those benefits are generally not funded by social security contributions but rather through the general budget, using resources from direct or indirect taxation (Cecchini, 2020[62]; ILO, 2021[63]; OECD, 2019[64]). Although basic social protection for both informal and formal workers would require additional fiscal revenues, it should be put in place. The incentives for formal job creation would be strengthened if such basic social protection was financed through general tax revenues instead of social security contributions, which tend to increase the cost of formalisation. Linking benefits and providing social protection rights may also make formal employment more attractive to workers (Arnold et al., 2024[65]).

An effective mix of well-targeted public finance programmes to increase the coverage of social protection schemes, along with well-designed and implemented policy interventions in LAC labour markets, can foster social inclusion and tackle current gaps in the protection of vulnerable groups that are closely linked with informal jobs. In this context, designing a single affiliation system for the different social security systems, including health and pensions, should contribute to enhancing social inclusion through job formalisation (OECD, 2024[66]).

While most pension systems like minimum contributory pensions fall under the contributory component of social protection systems, some programmes, such as social non-contributory pensions, are cash transfer programmes (Arenas De Mesa, 2019[67]; Arenas de Mesa, Robles and Vila, 2024[68]; OECD, 2024[66]; Arenas De Mesa and Robles, 2024[69]). The purpose of these non-contributory pensions is to even out consumption over the life cycle, to provide income following invalidity or the death of a breadwinner, and to alleviate poverty in old age.

Pension systems can be categorised according to the financial management of the resources, the rules on the granting of benefits and the distribution mechanism (Cecchini, 2020[62]; Uthoff, 2016[70]). The main differences concern financial management modalities. Pension systems can be categorised as i) pay-as-you-go (PAYG) systems, in which the economically active contribute to the system to pay for the pensions of those who have already retired; or ii) funded systems, where pension contributions are deposited in an investment savings account established for each affiliated worker for their personal use upon retirement.

Pension systems in LAC have undergone major structural reforms since the 1980s. This has generally consisted of transforming the institutional design of PAYG systems through the introduction of fully funded schemes. In general, structural reforms resulted in lengthy transition periods during which at least two pension systems, the old and the new, coexisted, like in the case of the Chilean reform of 1981. Since then, nine LAC countries (Argentina, Bolivia, Costa Rica, the Dominican Republic, El Salvador, Mexico, Panama, Peru and Uruguay) have added a fully funded regime to their systems, either to be as the main pillar or to complement the traditional PAYG system (ECLAC, 2018[71]; Cecchini, 2020[62]; OECD, 2023[72]). Colombia has recently passed new legislation, aiming at increasing coverage, by means of targeted subsidies to workers not reaching the minimum contributory time requirements, especially women (Ministerio del Trabajo, 2024[73]).

LAC countries have also undertaken parametric reforms aimed at changing the framework of PAYG systems, even if these reforms have also been applied to fully funded systems. Between 2008 and 2017, 11 Latin American countries – Brazil, Costa Rica, Cuba, Ecuador, Guatemala, Haiti, Honduras, Nicaragua, Paraguay, Uruguay, and Venezuela – adjusted their public PAYG systems, while 4 countries – Colombia, Chile, El Salvador and Peru – adjusted their fully funded systems (ECLAC, 2018[71]).

In this context, exclusively fully funded pension systems have started to attract criticism in the region. Economists argue that concentrating the efforts of the pension system exclusively on individual capacity to save seems not feasible, especially in the context of long-lasting labour informality (Arnold et al., 2024[65]; Uthoff, 2016[70]; Sojo, 2017[74]). Contributions to the region's pension systems dropped during the pandemic. Only 44.3% of the economically active population contributed in 2020, with a slight recovery in 2021 (45.7%), and coverage of the active population in 2021 was particularly low for those living in low-income families (7.1%) and in rural areas (21.8%) and for young people aged 15 to 19 (16%) (Robles and Holz, 2024[75]; Arenas de Mesa, Robles and Vila, 2024[68]; Arenas De Mesa and Robles, 2024[69]).

The high level of informality in the LAC labour market, the large proportion of unstable jobs in the formal sector with low contribution capacity and the rise of other non-standard jobs, like those linked to digital platforms, pose challenges in terms of boosting the low coverage rate of the region's pension systems, especially in fully funded systems (Robles and Holz, 2024[75]; ECLAC, 2018[71]). Current systems have already switched to a mix in which non-contributory social pensions complement the contributory system: the coverage of non-contributory pension systems for persons 65 years or over rose from 3.4% in 2000 to 26.7% in 2021 (ECLAC, 2018[71]; Robles and Holz, 2024[75]). Various studies have focused on the effects of non-contributory pensions on poverty reduction and inequality in LAC countries. Results are mixed, but some statistical evidence supports the hypothesis that poverty and extreme poverty are mitigated for people receiving social pensions without posing risks to financial sustainability (Arenas de Mesa, Robles and Vila, 2024[68]; Arenas De Mesa and Robles, 2024[69]).[3]

LAC also presents large gaps in terms of access to healthcare, with the region facing the challenge of moving towards more comprehensive care systems and policies (OECD, 2023[76]). Nonetheless, total spending on health has been increasing. From 2010 to 2017, the average annual growth rate in real per capita health expenditures was above 3% for most countries in the region (Rao et al., 2022[77]).

Public spending on health varies greatly across LAC. Government health expenditure stands at around 5% of GDP for countries like Argentina, Costa Rica, Nicaragua, Suriname, and Uruguay but is around 3% of GDP for others like Colombia, Grenada, Guatemala, Honduras, Mexico and Venezuela. This compares to health expenditure levels in OECD countries of 8-11% of GDP. Individuals and households still finance a large proportion of total health spending. Average out-of-pocket expenditure in the region reached 30.3% of total health spending around 2020, equivalent to 2.2% of regional GDP, with the figure exceeding 30%

in 14 of 33 LAC countries (Robles and Holz, 2024[75]). High out-of-pocket spending shows that access to universal healthcare is still unavailable for a significant portion of people in the region at a time when the risks of disease and natural disasters are impacting health expenditures, as shown by new epidemiological threats like the COVID-19 crisis (Marinho, Dahuabe and Arenas de Mesa, 2023[78]).

Nonetheless, health systems are highly integrated with other social protection programmes in the region, and overall social protection contributes significantly to improving the right to health thanks to programmes such as paid leave, cash transfer programmes, labour inclusion programmes, care systems and access to basic services. These support mechanisms contribute positively to people's health status and the reduction of health inequalities throughout the life cycle, while also lessening the financial burden for households and governments (Hone, 2018[79]). This approach, known as primary health care (PHC), is considered a priority area in LAC (ECLAC, 2022[80]; WHO and UNICEF, 2018[81]). PHC plays a strategic role in co-ordinating health systems with social protection and promoting the changes required by health systems to move towards universality. By strengthening PHC, it is possible to address the fragmentation of health services and the segmentation of the demand for care based on people's ability to pay.

Unemployment benefits are another fundamental aspect of social protection, as their primary goal is to secure the income conditions of persons who, though capable and willing to work, cannot find a job (Isgut and Weller, 2016[82]; ILO, 2021[83]; ILO, 2021[63]). Unemployment benefits are provided through contributory systems, with social security contributions paid by workers and/or employers (unemployment insurance), or through monetary transfers funded by the public budget (unemployment assistance) (ECLAC, 2023[56]).

Unemployment benefits are currently insufficient in LAC: only ten of the region's countries have unemployment insurance. This low coverage is explained by the structure of the region's labour markets, with high informality and few self-employed workers having the ability to pay voluntary contributions (Weller, 2023[84]). Countries had to adjust their social protection policies and programmes during the COVID-19 pandemic to provide adequate support for the unemployed (ECLAC, 2022[80]; Velásquez, 2021[85]; Velásquez Pinto, 2003[86]). The modifications involved lowering the minimum required contributions to access entitlements, extensions of coverage to other groups or for partial unemployment, extensions of the duration of the measures and an increase in amounts. Despite these efforts, unemployment benefits covered just 12.5% of the region's total unemployed population in 2021, with high heterogeneity across countries. Coverage did not exceed 10% of unemployed workers in Argentina, Ecuador and Venezuela, while countries with higher coverage than the rest of the region included Barbados (88.0%), Uruguay (31.4%), the Bahamas (26.9%) and Chile (24.3%) (Robles and Holz, 2024[75]). Adapting unemployment benefits to the characteristics of the labour market and linking them to active labour market programmes are key to promoting workers' reinsertion while protecting the most vulnerable groups without disincentivising job formalisation.

Finally, active labour market policies (ALMPs) are policy actions designed to foster employment opportunities, improve job quality in terms of formality and upgrade workers' skills and competencies (Espejo et al., 2023[87]; ECLAC, 2023[56]). As key elements in the implementation of social assistance programmes, well-designed ALMPs can help to narrow social disparities. The number of these programmes increased in 22 LAC countries from 70 in 2010 to 121 in 2019 (ECLAC, 2023[56]).

ALMPs in the region are targeted to different stages of people's lives, particularly to the unemployed and workers in informal employment. In 2022, 31 of the region's 120 programmes targeted the inclusion of young people in the labour market, but further efforts are needed given the significant gaps that youth face in labour market access. Other programmes meet the needs of vulnerable groups that face multiple barriers in LAC labour markets, like people with disabilities, women, and ethnic minorities such as indigenous peoples and Afro-descendants (ECLAC, 2023[56]). These programmes should be expanded, both in numbers and in scope, to break down barriers to entry and ensure the labour inclusion of vulnerable groups that experience multiple forms of inequality, discrimination, and exclusion (Espejo et al., 2023[87]).

Common types of initiatives in the LAC region include technical training and support for self-employment, which is particularly important in tackling informality given that own-account workers are overrepresented among informal workers. In 2022, 79 labour inclusion programmes provided technical and vocational training; 48 supported self-employment; 21 were indirect job creation schemes; 10 involved adult education and initiatives to encourage students to remain in school; and 9 were direct job creation initiatives. The focus of labour inclusion programmes varies depending on the targeted age group, as inclusion needs vary along the life cycle (Espejo et al., 2023[87]). Overall, the data suggest that technical and professional training are fundamental for youth and adults. Anticipating market demand for future skills is also key for designing effective labour market policies (ECLAC, 2023[56]; OECD et al., 2023[7]). ALMPs targeting the most vulnerable populations should promote both social inclusion and the efficient use of financial resources. One of the main challenges of the region is to systematically design impact evaluation studies. Existent empirical evidence suggests that training programmes generally have a positive impact on increasing the employment chances of beneficiaries and that they are effective in increasing the probability of having a formal job (Escudero et al., 2019[88]). The few available studies are less conclusive with respect to the countercyclical role of public works programmes, while wage subsidies generally boost employment probabilities, particularly when they are targeted directly at individuals (ILO, 2016[89]).

The role of public and private financing in closing development gaps

The rich diversity and abundant natural resources of LAC are juxtaposed against a backdrop of persistent inequalities, vulnerability to climate change and recent socio-economic upheavals. Structural social, economic and environmental challenges in the region call for strategic policy actions that put better and higher levels of investment at the centre (OECD et al., 2023[7]).

Well-sequenced and co-ordinated policy planning is essential in this landscape as development challenges are multi-dimensional and not easy to grasp. These challenges are deeply interconnected, requiring strategies that transcend sectoral boundaries and that leverage synergies between different development objectives (OECD, 2021[90]). Multi-dimensional measures of development offer a useful framework for designing policy strategies to address deeply interconnected problems. The multi-dimensional framework of the SDGs is perhaps the most important reference for quantifying progress towards multiple development goals and therefore useful for understanding the costs of this challenge (UNCTAD, 2023[91]). Ongoing discussions about a post-2030 agenda acknowledge the need for continued efforts to achieve sustainable development (UofT and UCL, 2024[92]; Partners for Impact, 2024[93]). The OECD's multi-dimensional well-being measurement framework also offers useful indicators for understanding progress in development and the challenges ahead (OECD, 2021[90]).

Evaluations show that the progress made to date on the SDGs in LAC is insufficient for achieving most targets by 2030. Although 73% of measurable indicators, representing 72% of the targets outlined in the 2030 Agenda, indicate progress in the intended direction, 41% of these indicators (equivalent to 47% of the targets) require intensified efforts to expedite progress. This acceleration is necessary to ensure that the benchmarks set for 2030 are met within the coming seven years (ECLAC, 2024[45]). According to available data, only 25% of the SDG targets look likely to be achieved by 2030 (Figure 1.17). There is slow progress on around 48% of the targets, while the remaining 27% are regressing (ECLAC, 2022[80]).

Figure 1.17. SDG targets by their likelihood of achievement in LAC by 2030

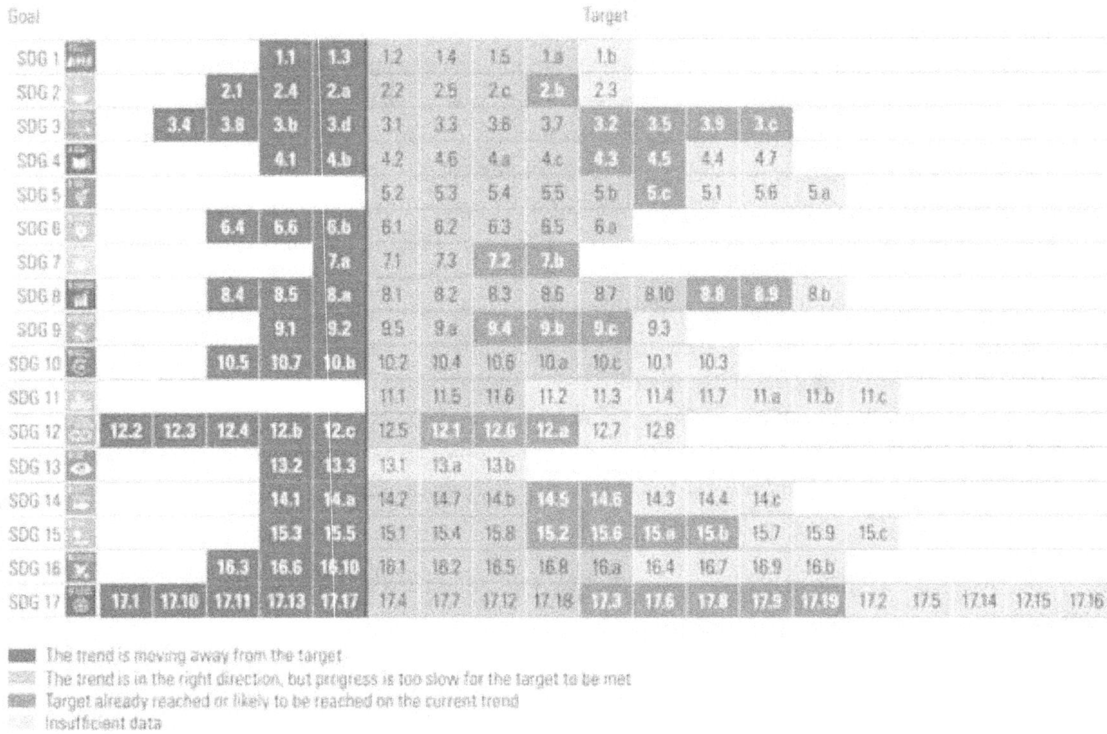

Source: From *The Challenge of Accelerating the 2030 Agenda in Latin America and the Caribbean: Transitions towards Sustainability*, by the Economic Commission for Latin America and the Caribbean (ECLAC), © 2024 United Nations. Reprinted with the permission of the United Nations (2024[45]).

The OECD's framework for measuring multi-dimensional well-being provides a complementary analytical tool for understanding the status and main challenges in advancing towards greater well-being for citizens (OECD, 2020[94]). Looking beyond averages reveals wide variations between and within countries. The two decades prior to the pandemic saw considerable gains in average well-being in the region, but the pace of progress has slowed since the mid-2010s, and structural problems such as informality and inequalities persisted through 2019 (OECD, 2021[90]). Furthermore, many of the resources that underpin the sustainability of well-being – natural, human, social and economic capital resources – are under threat or in decline. Adopting a policy approach focused on well-being[4] would help LAC countries to address their highly interconnected societal challenges more effectively.

The financing gap refers to the difference between the current levels of investment in sustainable development and the amount needed to achieve the SDGs by 2030. Measuring the financing gap for sustainable development in LAC is a key task that demands collective efforts across governments and multilateral institutions. Understanding the magnitude of the gap is essential for planning effective development initiatives. Despite the inherent challenges in quantifying such a complex gap, efforts have been made to estimate the resources required to meet global economic, social and environmental objectives (Box 1.2).

Box 1.2. Measuring the financing gap for sustainable development

The UN Conference on Trade and Development (UNCTAD), in partnership with the UN Department of Economic and Social Affairs (UNDESA) and the UN Development Programme (UNDP), has calculated the spending needed worldwide to accelerate progress towards achieving the 2030 Agenda for Sustainable Development.[5] Estimates of total spending needed along six "transition pathways" aligned with the SDGs range from USD 5.4 trillion to USD 6.4 trillion per pathway per year from 2023 to 2030, while the financing gap between current spending trajectories and the amount needed ranges from USD 275 billion to USD 469 billion per pathway per year. About 80% of the spending is anticipated to be needed in upper-middle-income and high-income developing countries, which face higher per-person costs and a wider financing gap than low-income and lower-middle-income developing economies.

For the LAC19[6] region, the cost of accelerating progress towards achieving the SDGs is estimated between USD 1.3 trillion and USD 1.6 trillion per development priority. This leaves an average annual gap of USD 99 billion between the required spending and the current trajectory. The global and regional gaps for the LAC19 group are outlined below.

Priority 1. Social protection and decent jobs

The SDG financing gap in this area is estimated at USD 294 billion per year between 2023 and 2030. Of this, USD 44 billion is needed for low- and lower-middle-income economies and USD 249 billion for upper-middle- and high-income developing economies (UNCTAD, 2023[91]). In 2017, the World Health Organization estimated that a substantial annual investment of USD 371 billion was needed to meet SDG 3 on health in low- and middle-income countries (WHO, 2017[95]). The International Labour Organization estimated a financing gap of USD 1.2 trillion for advancing the social protection and universal health care agenda in 134 developing countries (ILO, 2020[96]).

For LAC19, the total required annual spending in this area is approximately USD 1.3 trillion, with a yearly financing gap of USD 77 billion. In South America, this gap amounts to USD 55 billion – nearly three times larger than in Central America. In the Caribbean, while the gap is smaller at USD 1.5 billion, it represents 6.3% of the region's required spending.

Priority 2. Education transformation

The SDG spending gap in this area is estimated at USD 275 billion per year between 2023 and 2030. Of this, USD 128 billion is needed for low-income and lower middle-income economies and USD 147 billion for upper middle- and high-income developing economies. The UN Educational, Scientific and Cultural Organisation estimates that an annual average of USD 461 billion is needed from 2023 to 2030 to meet the financing gap for achieving SDG 4 on education for 79 low- and lower middle-income countries (UNESCO, 2015[97]; UNESCO, 2023[98]).

This development pathway requires an annual total expenditure of USD 1.4 trillion for the LAC19 countries. With current government spending levels, there remains a gap of USD 44 billion – the smallest financing gap among all pathways in the region.

Priority 3. Food systems

The SDG spending gap in this area is estimated at USD 328 billion per year between 2023 and 2030. Of this, USD 19 billion is needed for low-income and lower middle-income developing economies and USD 309 billion for upper middle- and high-income developing economies. In 2015, the UN Food and Agriculture Organization, the International Fund for Agricultural Development and the World Food Programme jointly estimated that USD 265 billion was needed annually from 2016 to 2030 to sustainably end hunger, with significant investments needed in both productive sectors and social protection programmes (FAO, IFAD and WFP, 2015[99]).

For the LAC19 countries, the financing gap amounts to USD 98 billion, requiring a 6.4% increase in annual spending to close it. South American countries face the largest annual gap of USD 73 billion, which represents approximately 6.2% of their required spending and the highest cost per capita in the region. Central American and Caribbean economies, while having smaller absolute gaps of USD 23 billion and USD 2 billion respectively, face relatively higher shortfalls, with each needing around 7% of their required spending on food systems.

Priority 4. Climate change, biodiversity loss and pollution

The SDG spending gap in this area is estimated at USD 337 billion per year between 2023 and 2030. Of this, USD 11 billion is needed for low-income and lower-middle-income developing economies and USD 327 billion for upper middle- and high-income developing economies.

In the LAC19 region, current government spending aimed at reducing emissions, protecting biodiversity and lowering domestic material consumption leaves an annual gap of USD 102 billion. To close this gap, a 7.3% increase in annual spending is needed. South American economies face the largest shortfall, with a gap of USD 76 billion – approximately 7.5% of their required funding. While Central American economies have a smaller gap of USD 2 billion and Caribbean economies USD 1 billion, these gaps still represent about 7% of their required spending.

Priority 5. Energy transition

The SDG spending gap in this area is estimated at USD 286 billion per year between 2023 and 2030. Of this, USD 5 billion is needed for low and lower middle-income developing economies and USD 281 billion for upper middle- and high-income developing economies. The International Energy Agency emphasises the need to increase clean energy investment to USD 4.5 trillion annually by 2030 to achieve universal access to clean energy and decarbonising the global energy sector (IEA, 2023[100]).

Excluding installed renewable energy infrastructure, current government spending in the LAC19 region leaves an annual gap of USD 92 billion, necessitating a 9.4% increase in spending. South American economies face the largest gap at USD 69 billion, equivalent to 6.4% of the required funding. Central America has a shortfall of USD 22 billion, while the Caribbean faces a gap of USD 1.4 billion, both representing roughly 6% of their needed spending.

Priority 6. Inclusive digitalisation

The SDG spending gap in this area is estimated at USD 469 billion per year between 2023 and 2030. Of this, USD 38 billion is needed for low-income and lower middle-income developing economies and USD 430 billion for upper middle- and high-income developing economies. The International Monetary Fund estimates the global digital infrastructure investment needed to achieve universal access to broadband and promote inclusive digitalisation at USD 418 billion annually, with emerging market economies requiring the most significant investment (IMF, 2023[101]; Oughton, Amaglobeli and Moszor, 2023[102]).

For the LAC19 countries, the annual financing gap in this area stands at USD 221 billion, the largest of all pathways in the region, requiring a 17% increase in annual funding. South American economies face the most significant shortfall, with a gap of USD 196 billion – 20% of their required spending. In contrast, Central American and Caribbean economies have smaller gaps, representing 7% of their total requirements, or approximately USD 23 billion and USD 1.6 billion respectively.

Source: (UNCTAD, 2023[91]).

The magnitude of the LAC region's challenges calls for substantially mobilising resources, far exceeding what public finance alone can provide, and for using those resources effectively. This underscores the urgent need for a collaborative effort that brings together government, the private sector, civil society and international partners to pool resources and expertise coherently and strategically. By fostering an environment that encourages private investment, and by developing innovative and efficient financing mechanisms and strengthening international co-operation, the region can mobilise the resources needed to achieve its development goals (Chapters 3 and 4). The path to a sustainable and resilient future for the LAC region lies in harnessing the power of collaborative financing, driving innovation, and ensuring that development efforts benefit all segments of society (OECD, 2022[103]).

The region can navigate its path towards sustainable growth and resilience by formulating a clear roadmap for development. Amid pressing development challenges and constrained fiscal capacities, the region requires a comprehensive development strategy with a delineated financing agenda at its core. Strategic policy actions to address the region's disparities and mobilise resources effectively require the identification of innovative financing mechanisms and the alignment of public and private investments with development goals (United Nations, 2024[104]).

National Development Plans (NDPs) are crucial in shaping coherent strategies – owned by the partner country governments – for the public and private sectors to mobilise resources towards achieving major development goals. This is particularly important for optimising resources in the region's tight fiscal landscape. For the public sector, NDPs serve as guiding frameworks, and even in some cases compulsory frameworks, that outline public investments and ensure efficient allocation of resources. For the private sector, NDPs provide direction on national strategies, enabling investors to channel resources into sectors vital for development (OECD et al., 2019[1]). By aligning public and private interests, NDPs foster synergy in resource mobilisation efforts, facilitating sustainable economic growth and social progress.

Sectoral plans should be aligned with NDPs to co-ordinate the implementation of multifaceted policy strategies, such as the "triple transition" encompassing the green, social and digital transitions. For instance, Colombia's National Strategy for Energy, Connectivity and Educational Communities provides a co-ordinated sectoral roadmap for parallel programmes that aim to provide green energy to schools and also digital infrastructure to guarantee Internet access in remote areas. Furthermore, productive development policies play a vital role, as they allow countries to focus on transforming sectors prioritised for sustainable growth (ECLAC, 2024[105]). These policies are essential for targeting efforts where they can have the greatest impact, fostering industrial diversification and enhancing competitiveness in selected sectors. By aligning financing with productive development goals, NDPs ensure that resources are channelled into sectors that offer high potential for economic and social returns, further driving the region's structural transformation.

Effective NDPs also establish the necessary conditions for collaboration between the public and private spheres, ultimately driving investment towards priority areas and fostering inclusive development. At only 20% of GDP, the LAC region exhibits one of the lowest levels of total investment across all regions globally (OECD et al., 2023[7]).

Public financing is crucial for tackling social challenges that are paramount to the region's sustainable development but that might not immediately attract private investment (Chapter 2). These include social programmes aimed at poverty reduction, educational equity, social protection, and universal access to health care – areas where the benefits are widely distributed across society and where the direct payback to private investors is more difficult to determine (Figure 1.18).

Figure 1.18. Public and private spending on social protection programmes in LAC, 2018

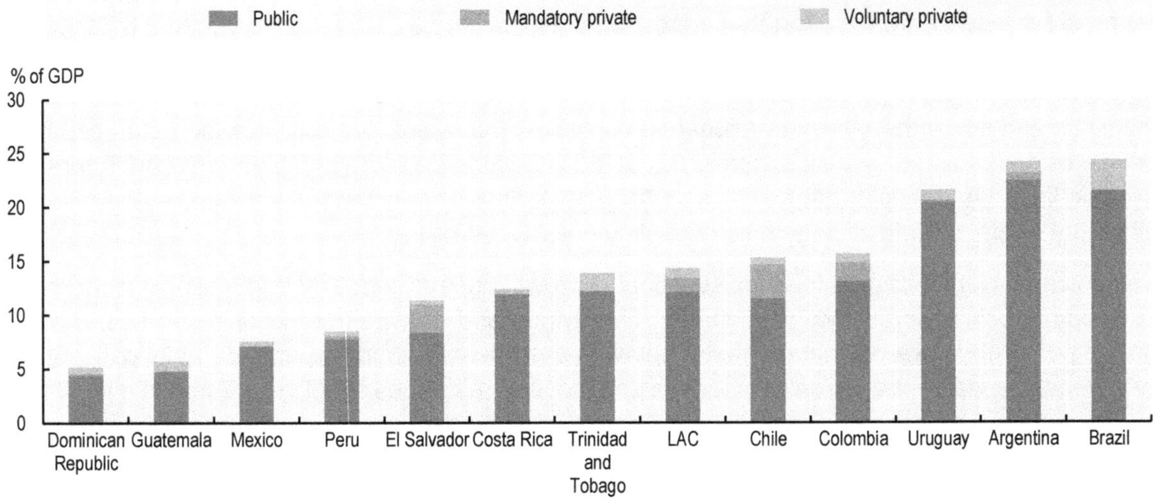

Note: In the OECD SOCX methodology, social spending is defined as: "The provision by public and private institutions of benefits and financial contributions directed to households and individuals in order to provide support in circumstances that negatively affect their well-being, provided that the provision of benefits and financial contributions does not constitute a direct payment for a particular good or service or an individual contract or transfer". Mandatory private social expenditures are legally required supports delivered by the private sector, while voluntary private social expenditures are benefits from privately operated, non-mandatory programmes, including non-governmental organisations and tax-advantaged plans. SOCX presents social spending grouped into nine policy areas: old age, survivorship, disability-related benefits, health, family, active labour market policies, unemployment, housing and other areas of social policy.
Source: Authors' elaboration based on (OECD/ECLAC, 2018[106]).

StatLink https://stat.link/157wzu

Likewise, certain environmental conservation areas require public investment due to their lack of profitability for the private sector. At a time when LAC is grappling with significant inequality and vulnerability to climate change, the region requires substantial investment in infrastructure resilient to environmental impacts and in social programmes that can bridge the inequality gap (Chapter 2). Public investment in renewable energy projects and the preservation of biodiversity hotspots, such as the Amazon rainforest, are critical for the region's sustainability goals and need to be supported by government-led financing and international aid (OECD et al., 2022[10]). Ensuring transparency and efficiency in public expenditure is vital for maximising the impact of these investments, as it builds public trust and ensures that resources are used effectively (IMF, 2019[107]).

Public funding is insufficient to finance all of the region's development needs (see above on fiscal policy and Chapter 2). Governments in LAC are grappling with fiscal constraints that have been exacerbated by the economic fallout of the COVID-19 pandemic, limiting their ability to invest in health, education, climate, environment and social protection at the levels required (Bierbaum and Schmitt, 2022[108]; OECD et al., 2021[109]). This fiscal reality accentuates the critical role of the private sector in filling the financing gap. While the private sector remains the main driver of investment in LAC, its 78% share in total investment in the region is below the OECD average of close to 84% (Figure 1.19) (OECD et al., 2023[7]).

Figure 1.19. Private vs. public investment as a share of total investment in LAC and OECD, 2019

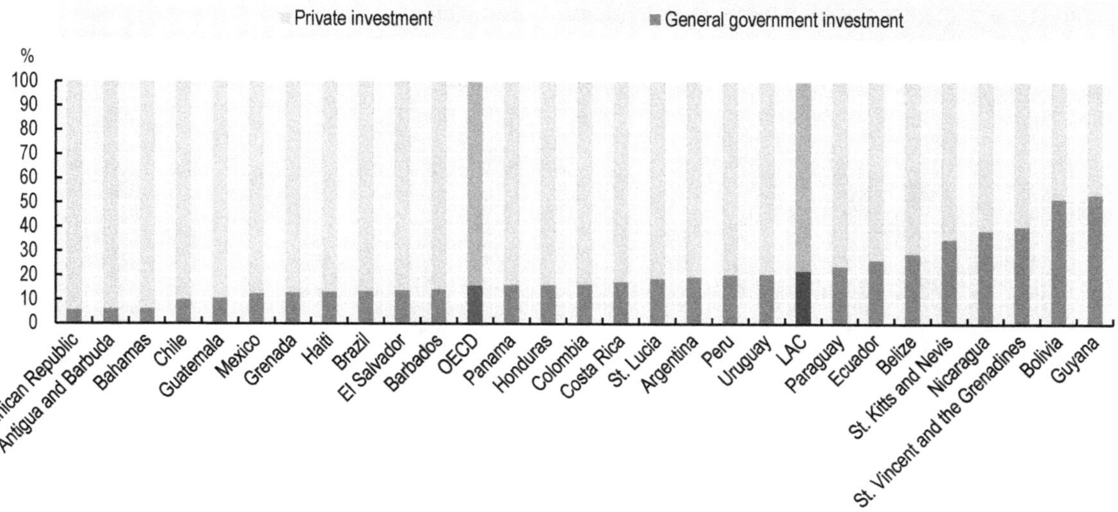

Note: The OECD average is a simple average of all member countries in 2019. The LAC average is a simple average of the countries for which data were available: Antigua and Barbuda, Argentina, the Bahamas, Barbados, Belize, Bolivia, Brazil, Chile, Colombia, Costa Rica, the Dominican Republic, Ecuador, El Salvador, Grenada, Guatemala, Guyana, Haiti, Honduras, Mexico, Nicaragua, Panama, Paraguay, Peru, St. Kitts and Nevis, St. Lucia, St. Vincent and the Grenadines, Uruguay, and Venezuela.
Source: Authors' elaboration based on OECD (2023[7]) and IMF (2022[110]).

StatLink https://stat.link/zf6xoe

Developing financing models involving the private sector, such as public-private partnerships (PPPs), can facilitate the infusion of private capital into crucial sectors, bringing efficiency, scalability, and innovation to development projects (IDB, 2021[111]). Some LAC countries have made strong improvements in the regulatory and institutional frameworks of PPPs, but significant regional disparities persist in project preparation and sustainability. Weak state institutions, unclear legislation and deficient contract design have allowed anomalies such as the frequent and costly renegotiation of road concessions (Bitran, Nieto-Parra and Robledo, 2013[112]). Specifically, substantial gaps exist in the management of PPPs, with improvements needed in risk management, project monitoring and assessment of the economic and social impacts of operational PPPs (OECD et al., 2023[7]; Economist Impact, 2022[113]).

Public financing in LAC often focuses on critical infrastructure investments, such as roads, highlighting the strategic emphasis placed by governments on essential physical networks (Figure 1.20). Private financing fuels economic growth through investments in sectors where commercial viability is clear and market-driven solutions can thrive, and it is thus pivotal in the region (Chapter 3). This includes industries such as technology, telecommunications, and transport connectivity, as well as certain infrastructure projects that can generate both direct economic returns and social benefits (OECD et al., 2020[114]; OECD et al., 2023[7]). As a dynamic growth sector, the telecommunications subsector in particular tends to attract private financing. Such digital investments are crucial for boosting connectivity and also enhance the green and social transitions.

Figure 1.20. Investment in infrastructure by subsector in selected LAC countries, 2021

By country, as a percentage of total public investment in infrastructure

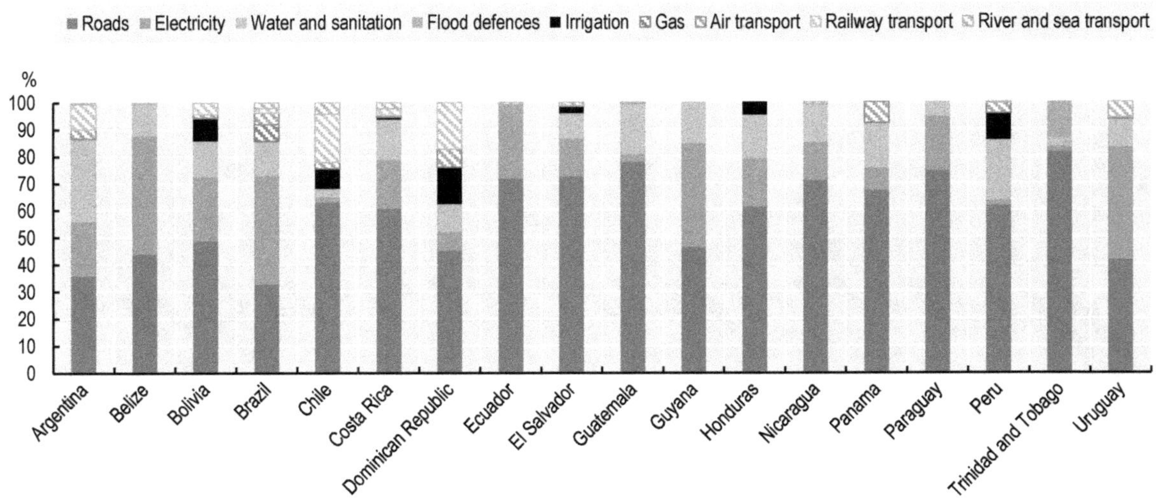

Note: Sectors under consideration focus primarily on infrastructure services and essential utilities. Infrastructure investment related to oil and gas production, oil refinement and petrochemistry is excluded. Social infrastructure is also excluded (e.g. schools, hospitals, dwellings and security infrastructure). The other sectors are subdivided into subsectors. Water includes water and sanitation (drinking water supply through the grid and provision of sanitation services), flood defences (urban and rural projects for mitigating the effects of flooding) and irrigation (facilities and systems of artificial irrigation). Transport includes roads and paths, urban mass transportation, railway transportation (infrastructure and rolling stock), air transport, and fluvial and maritime transportation. Energy includes generation, transmission and distribution of electricity, and transmission and distribution of natural gas.
Source: Authors' elaboration based on Infralatam (2024[115]).

StatLink https://stat.link/6a0ug9

Mobilising private sector resources entails more than just filling financing gaps: it represents an opportunity to support productive development policies by fostering economic transformation in priority sectors (Chapter 3). The private sector's involvement can introduce new technologies and business models that enhance productivity and competitiveness while addressing critical social and environmental issues. By encouraging investments aligned with productive development strategies, the private sector can drive sustainable growth while also supporting countries' development agendas (ECLAC, 2024[105]). Such targeted investments enable structural changes that boost competitiveness and promote high-impact industries, which are crucial for the region's resilience and long-term growth. For example, investments in renewable energy and sustainable agriculture can contribute to climate change mitigation and adaptation efforts, creating jobs and fostering economic resilience (OECD et al., 2022[10]). Furthermore, business opportunities that are aligned with environmental objectives and new regulations are growing, becoming increasingly attractive to the private sector. The region's growing tech startup ecosystem, for example, demonstrates how private capital can drive innovation in digital banking, e-commerce and fintech solutions, addressing both economic and access-related challenges (Chapter 3).

Investment in research and development (R&D) is a transformative sector that offers attractive opportunities and incentives for private investment. Unlike other sectors that rely heavily on public financing due to limited commercial appeal, R&D stands out as a dynamic area that can appeal to private capital, particularly when bolstered by incentives such as tax breaks and intellectual property rights (ECLAC, 2022[116]). Investment in R&D drives innovation and competitiveness, which are crucial for addressing regional challenges like economic stagnation and social inequality. By strategically enhancing R&D, private investment not only fosters technological advancements and high-skilled employment but also contributes significantly to sustainable economic growth (ECLAC, 2022[116]). Compared to other regions and countries, such as the European Union, OECD countries, China or the United States, LAC is still highly dependent on public financing for R&D, leaving room for growth in private sources of financing, including companies, higher education institutions, foreign funds and private non-profit organisations (Figure 1.21).

Figure 1.21. Share of R&D investment by funding source in LAC and other territories, 2011-20

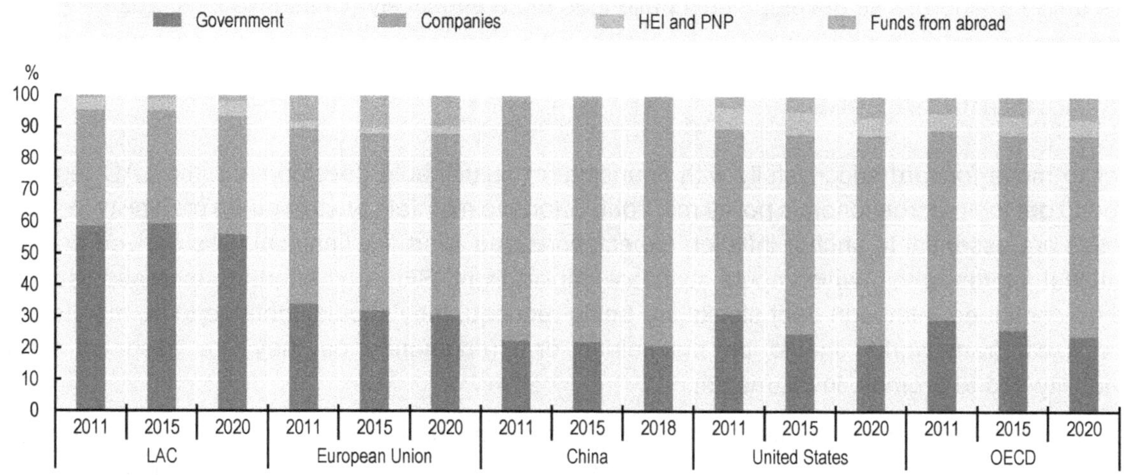

Note: HEI = higher education institutions. PNP = private non-profit organisations.
Source: Authors' elaboration based on OECD et al. (2023[7]) and RICYT (2020[117]) for LAC, and the Science, Technology and Innovation Scoreboard (OECD, 2024[118]) for the other territories.

StatLink https://stat.link/ycl3eb

Creating an enabling environment for private investment involves addressing structural challenges that can deter investors, such as political instability, regulatory uncertainty, and inadequate infrastructure. Unlocking private investment requires the creation of a conducive environment that mitigates risks and offers attractive returns while aligning with the SDGs (Chapter 3). The social contract plays a foundational role in this process by fostering inclusive, participatory governance that builds trust, strengthens fiscal systems, and aligns diverse stakeholders' interests with long-term, sustainable policy goals (OECD et al., 2021[109]). Strengthening legal and institutional frameworks and improving transparency and governance are crucial steps towards building investor confidence (OECD, 2015[119]). This implies a regulatory and policy framework that incentivises sustainable investments (e.g. taxonomies, disclosures), risk-sharing mechanisms and clear guidelines on sustainable practices (OECD et al., 2023[7]).

The LAC region faces significant challenges due to institutional and regulatory complexity, both internally and across different jurisdictions. This complexity includes issues such as unequal treatment of investors, inconsistent due diligence practices and regulatory requirements that vary between jurisdictions (OECD et al., 2023[7]). By fostering regulatory systems' interoperability and integrating sustainable development taxonomies, the LAC region could enhance investment quality, mitigate risks for private companies and create a coherent and supportive business environment, thus contributing to attracting domestic and international investors. Moreover, building trust and dialogue among the public sector, private investors and communities is vital not only for strengthening the social contract but also for ensuring that projects are aligned with local needs and development priorities. Financial innovations such as green, social, sustainability and sustainability-linked bonds, impact investing and blended finance instruments can offer viable pathways for channelling private funds into sustainable development projects (Chapter 4).

International co-operation and partnerships play a pivotal role in amplifying the impact of development financing. Multilateral development banks, international financial institutions and bilateral donors can provide not just financial resources but also valuable technical expertise, capacity building and policy support (OECD et al., 2019[1]). For instance, the GEMMES Colombia model offers scenarios for financing the trajectory of Nationally Determined Contributions (NDCs), aiding decision-makers in shaping political strategies to combat global warming (AFD, 2024[61]). This external support is crucial for leveraging additional resources, sharing risk and ensuring the sustainability of investments. Furthermore, international partnerships can facilitate access to global markets, technologies and best practices, enhancing the region's ability to address its development challenges more effectively (United Nations, 2024[104]).

Policy recommendations

In order to move forward successfully with financing for sustainable development, the LAC region must continue to get the macroeconomic policy mix right. Efforts to maintain or strengthen credibility in monetary authorities are essential to anchor inflation expectations and avert the financial risks derived from higher international interest rates, which could stimulate capital flight. Similarly, efforts to increase fiscal space should be continued. Although debt stocks are being reduced, they should continue to be monitored, and credible fiscal frameworks should be maintained or strengthened as they are essential for fiscal sustainability and to promote investments.

Moving forward, the region must address its long-term development challenges. Well-designed development strategies should be implemented by LAC countries through national development plans, in the form of multi-annual investment plans. Reshaping economic institutions – such as property rights protection, rule of law, contract enforcement, state capacity and regulatory frameworks – will help firms with the allocation of resources and innovation, which are key to increasing productivity and boosting sustainable growth. Building systems that facilitate financing is vital for firms to expand, export and survive adverse economic shocks. Removing the barriers that inhibit well-functioning financial systems is equally crucial. Easing access to credit will help individuals in their occupational choices, especially talented entrepreneurs pursuing high-potential projects.

Building more resilient societies will be key for a more inclusive development model. A good mix of structural policy reforms and well-designed social protection schemes will be essential to tackle persistent labour informality, poverty and socio-economic inequalities. In a context of limited financial resources, support for the design of effective and efficient policies is crucial. For example, policy interventions on social protection systems should aim for greater universality while recognising that the way in which contributory pension and health schemes are financed is fundamental to promoting job formalisation. In addition, well-targeted non-contributory social protection schemes, such as conditional cash transfers, could provide better protection to the most vulnerable groups.

Interconnected challenges must be addressed by well-sequenced, co-ordinated, and effective policy planning. The region should increase public investment in resolving social challenges, building resilient infrastructure and upgrading essential services, while at the same time enhancing transparency and efficiency in spending. Encouraging a stable regulatory environment will attract private investment, supported by sound institutional frameworks on public-private partnerships and other types of investments. This is fundamental given the relatively low participation of the LAC private sector, particularly in research and development.

Box 1.3. Key policy messages

Continue to strengthen fiscal and monetary institutions in LAC

- Continue to monitor public debt dynamics and the implementation of credible fiscal frameworks that are essential to ensure fiscal sustainability and enhance investments.
- Maintain or strengthen credibility in monetary authorities to control both headline inflation and inflation expectations and to reduce financial risks.

Address structural challenges that hold back productivity growth

- Continue developing human capital and increase investment in research and development.
- Foster economic institutions that enable a productive environment for firms: protection of property rights, rule of law, contract enforcement mechanisms, state capacity and the regulatory framework.

Move towards universal social protection systems and better protect the most vulnerable people

- Ensure that a basic set of social protection coverage is financially sustainable and fully funded through general tax revenues, rather than social security contributions.
- Assure that conditional cash transfer programmes are targeted to people living in the most vulnerable households. Conditionalities may be relaxed for programmes targeting people living in extreme poverty.

Define a policy planning strategy with a multi-dimensional approach

- Adopt well-sequenced and co-ordinated and effective policy planning to shape coherent strategies for the public and private sectors to mobilise resources towards achieving major development goals.

Enhance public sector financing for social challenges

- Focus public investment on tackling key social challenges that are paramount to the region's sustainable development but might not immediately attract private investment.
- Improve transparency in public spending to maximise impact.

Engage the private sector strategically

- Establish incentives for the private sector to drive sustainable economic growth by investing in strategic sectors. These investments should be market-driven, fostering solutions that not only thrive economically but also generate positive development externalities.
- Create a stable, transparent regulatory environment to attract private investment, with a focus on sustainable investment.

Notes

[1] This is the result of a development accounting exercise using the Penn World Table version 10.01 (Feenstra, Inklaar and Timmer, 2015[130]), a database with information on relative levels of income, output, input and productivity, covering 183 countries between 1950 and 2019. The results correspond to averages over the period 2010-19 and over 21 LAC countries (Argentina, Barbados, Belize, Brazil, Chile, Colombia, Costa Rica, the Dominican Republic, Ecuador, El Salvador, Guatemala, Haiti, Honduras, Jamaica, Mexico, Nicaragua, Panama, Paraguay, Peru, Trinidad and Tobago, and Uruguay).

[2] The definition of informal work followed the guidelines of the 17th International Conference of Labour Statisticians at the ILO (17th ICLS). Informal employment is conceptually defined as "all remunerative work (i.e. both self-employment and wage employment) that is not registered, regulated or protected by existing legal or regulatory frameworks, as well as non-remunerative work undertaken in an income-producing enterprise. Informal workers do not have secure employment contracts, workers' benefits or social protection. For more details see (ILO, 2003[131]).

[3] For more information, see (Bertranou and Grushka, 2002[122]; Escobar, Martínez and Mendizábal, 2013[124]; Mena and Hernani-Limarino, 2015[128]; Borrella-Mas, Bosch and Sartarelli, 2016[123]; Schwarzer and Querino, 2002[120]; Barrientos, 2003[121]; Joubert and Todd, 2011[126]; Bertranou, Solorio and van Ginneken, 2002[129]; Martínez, Pérez and Tejerina, 2015[127]; Galiani and Gertler, 2016[125]).

[4] A well-being approach in policy, as defined by the OECD, is designing and implementing policies that aim to improve the overall quality of life by considering a broad range of factors beyond traditional economic measures, focusing on multi-dimensional aspects of individual and community well-being (OECD, 2020[94]).

[5] UNCTAD's approach to measuring the financing gap for achieving the Sustainable Development Goals is structured around a series of questions and methodologies. It begins with collecting data on SDG indicators per economy and over time, alongside government expenditures across 11 sectors such as agriculture, health, education and social protection. Analysing the relationship between government spending and SDG progress involves fitting models considering factors beyond public expenditure alone, including moderator variables like GDP and corruption. UNCTAD's approach uses a formula incorporating log forms of SDG targets and spending per GDP on sectors and includes coefficients describing the elasticity of spending on each sector and sectoral synergies. Forecasting future spending patterns and their impact on SDG progress is crucial for understanding baseline scenarios and potential trajectories. Identification of economies that allocate spending optimally, considering diminishing returns and sectoral synergies, is essential. Comparing business-as-usual scenarios with optimal scenarios allows for the determination of additional spending required to reach more SDGs. Finally, in calculating the total cost of reaching SDG pathways, UNCTAD focuses on government spending but also considers other financing sources like foreign direct investment and official development assistance. The methodology emphasises the importance of government expenditure for achieving SDGs while acknowledging the role of private investment and external financing. It highlights the need for caution in interpreting results due to data limitations and assumptions, providing valuable insights into progress towards SDGs and identifying financing gaps for policy makers to address (UNCTAD, 2023[91]). Tools and resources to support all stakeholders in SDG costing were provided by numerous partners, namely UN Women, IFAD, IMF, IEA, ILO, ITU, ESCWA, UNEP, UNESCO, UN-Habitat and UNICEF.

[6] For LAC, the UNCTAD study focused on 19 countries (LAC19). The study covers 7 Central American countries – Belize, Costa Rica, El Salvador, Guatemala, Honduras, Mexico, and Panama; 3 Caribbean

countries –the Dominican Republic, Haiti, and Jamaica; and 9 South American countries – Argentina, Bolivia, Brazil, Chile, Colombia, Ecuador, Peru, Uruguay, and Venezuela.

References

AFD (2024), *GEMMES Colombia: Understanding Macroeconomic Vulnerabilities and Opportunities Related to Low Carbon Transition*, Agence Française de Développement (AFD), Paris, https://www.afd.fr/en/carte-des-projets/gemmes-colombia-understanding-macroeconomic-vulnerabilities-and-opportunities-related-low-carbon-transition. [61]

Alkire, S. and Y. Shen (2017), "Exploring multidimensional poverty in China: 2010 to 2014", *Research on Economic Inequality*, pp. 161-228, https://ophi.org.uk/publication/RP-47a. [30]

Angulo, R., B. Diaz and R. Pardo Pinzon (2013), "A Counting Multidimensional Poverty Index in Public Policy Context: The Case of Colombia", *OPHI Working Paper*, No. 62, University of Oxford. [38]

Ardanaz, M. and A. Izquierdo (2022), "Current expenditure upswings in good times and public investment downswings in bad times? New evidence from developing countries", *Journal of Comparative Economics*, Vol. 50/1, pp. 118-134, https://doi.org/10.1016/j.jce.2021.06.002. [17]

Arenas De Mesa, A. (2019), *Los sistemas de pensiones en la encrucijada: Desafíos para la sostenibilidad en América Latina*, United Nations Economic Commission for Latin America and the Caribbean, https://repositorio.cepal.org/server/api/core/bitstreams/ef2286b9-b700-45e9-ac66-e343faa75211/content. [67]

Arenas De Mesa, A. and C. Robles (eds.) (2024), *Non-contributory Pension Systems in Latin America and the Caribbean: Towards Solidarity with Sustainability*, United Nations Economic Commission for Latin America and the Caribbean, https://repositorio.cepal.org/server/api/core/bitstreams/4294d37f-3c2f-4ea3-be4e-e5fe8cc06d06/content. [69]

Arenas de Mesa, A., C. Robles and J. Vila (2024), "El desafío de avanzar hacia la sostenibilidad de los sistemas de pensiones en América Latina", *Social Policy Series*, United Nations Economic Commission for Latin American and the Caribbean. [68]

Arnold, J. et al. (2024), "Towards better social protection for more workers in Latin America: Challenges and policy considerations", *OECD Economics Department Working Papers*, No. 1804, OECD Publishing, Paris, https://doi.org/10.1787/76a04c6f-en. [65]

Arreaza, A. et al. (2022), *Reglas fiscales para la recuperación en América Latina: experiencias y principales lecciones*, Development Bank of Latin America and the Caribbean (CAF), Caracas, https://scioteca.caf.com/handle/123456789/1905. [18]

Arriola, C. et al. (2020), "Efficiency and risks in global value chains in the context of COVID-19", *OECD Economics Department Working Papers*, No. 1637, OECD Publishing, Paris, https://doi.org/10.1787/3e4b7ecf-en. [25]

Balakrishnan, R. et al. (2021), "Commodity Cycles, Inequality, and Poverty in Latin America", *IMF Departmental Papers*, International Monetary Fund, https://doi.org/10.5089/9781484326091.087. [54]

Barrientos, A. (2003), "What is the impact of non-contributory pensions on poverty? Estimates from Brazil and South Africa", *CPRC Working Paper*, No. 33, Chronic Poverty Research Centre (CPRC), https://www.files.ethz.ch/isn/128064/WP33_Barrientos.pdf. [121]

Bertranou, F. and C. Grushka (2002), "The non-contributory pension programme in Argentina: Assessing the impact on poverty reduction", *ESS Paper Series*, No. 5, International Labour Office, https://www.ilo.org/publications/non-contributory-pension-programme-argentina-assessing-impact-poverty. [122]

Bertranou, F., C. Solorio and W. van Ginneken (eds.) (2002), *Pensiones no contributivas y asistenciales: Argentina, Brasil, Chile, Costa Rica y Uruguay*, International Labour Office, https://webapps.ilo.org/public/libdoc/ilo/2002/102B09_259_span.pdf. [129]

Bierbaum, M. and V. Schmitt (2022), "Investing better in universal social protection: Applying international social security standards in social protection policy and financing", *ILO Working Paper*, No. 43, International Labour Organization, Geneva, https://www.ilo.org/wcmsp5/groups/public/---ed_protect/---soc_sec/documents/publication/wcms_834216.pdf. [108]

Bitran, E., S. Nieto-Parra and J. Robledo (2013), "Opening the Black Box of Contract Renegotiations: An Analysis of Road Concessions in Chile, Colombia and Peru", *OECD Development Centre Working Papers*, No. 317, OECD Publishing, Paris, https://doi.org/10.1787/5k46n3wwxxq3-en. [112]

Borrella-Mas, M., M. Bosch and M. Sartarelli (2016), "Non-contributory pensions number-gender effects on poverty and household decisions", *IVIE Working Paper*, No. 2016-02, Valencian Institute of Economic Research, https://www.ivie.es/downloads/docs/wpasad/wpasad-2016-02.pdf. [123]

CAF (2018), "RED 2018: Institutions for productivity: Towards a better business environment", https://scioteca.caf.com/handle/123456789/1410. [6]

Caisi, J. et al. (2023), "The uneven impact of high inflation", *OECD Papers on Well-being and Inequalities*, No. 18, OECD Publishing, https://doi.org/10.1787/59e2b8ae-en. [22]

Castillo, A. and F. Perez (2015), *Medicion de la Pobreza Multidimensional en Ecuador*, INEC (Instituto Nacional de Estadısticas y Censos), http://www.ecuadorencifras.gob.ec/documentos/web-inec/Sitios/Pobreza_Multidimensional/assets/ipm-metodologia-oficial.pdf. [40]

Cecchini, S. (ed.) (2020), *Universal Social Protection in Latin America and the Caribbean*, Select Pages of ECLAC, United Nations Economic Commission for Latin America and the Caribbean, https://repositorio.cepal.org/server/api/core/bitstreams/50cd7ff5-252f-4769-942d-19b447209709/content. [62]

CONEVAL (2010), *Informe de pobreza multidimensional en Mexico 2008*, Consejo Nacional de Evaluación de la Política de Desarrollo Social, https://www.coneval.org.mx/rw/resource/coneval/info_public/pdf_publicaciones/informe_pobreza_multi_web.pdf. [37]

DANE (2020), *Medida de Pobreza Multidimensional Municipal de Fuente Censal*, https://www.dane.gov.co/files/investigaciones/condiciones_vida/pobreza/2018/informacion-censal/bt-censal-pobreza-municipal-2018.pdf. [47]

ECB (2023), *Economic Bulletin Issue 6*, European Central Bank, https://www.ecb.europa.eu/press/economic-bulletin/html/eb202306.en.html. [26]

ECLAC (2024), *CEPALSTAT, Statistical Databases and Publications*, https://statistics.cepal.org/portal/cepalstat/dashboard.html?theme=1&lang=en. [43]

ECLAC (2024), *Fiscal Panorama of Latin America and the Caribbean, 2024: Fiscal Policy for Addressing the Challenges of Climate Change*, United Nations Economic Commission for Latin America and the Caribbean, https://www.cepal.org/en/publications/69217-fiscal-panorama-latin-america-and-caribbean-2024-fiscal-policy-addressing. [15]

ECLAC (2024), *Foreign Direct Investment in Latin America and the Caribbean 2024*, United Nations Economic Commission for Latin America and the Caribbean, https://repositorio.cepal.org/server/api/core/bitstreams/a450f098-bbcb-41d2-88fd-b8e426c92677/content. [9]

ECLAC (2024), *Panorama of Productive Development Policies in Latin America and the Caribbean*, Economic Commission for Latin America and the Caribbean, Santiago, https://repositorio.cepal.org/server/api/core/bitstreams/ef207540-b0d4-4cc9-8248-63b3ebac878d/content. [105]

ECLAC (2024), *Social Panorama of Latin America and the Caribbean, 2024*, United Nations Economic Commission for Latin America and the Caribbean, https://repositorio.cepal.org/items/e1403b62-ae38-461c-af18-00c8ed1610b3. [20]

ECLAC (2024), *The Challenge of Accelerating the 2030 Agenda in Latin America and the Caribbean, Transitions towards Sustainability*, United Nations Economic Commission for Latin America and the Caribbean, Santiago, https://repositorio.cepal.org/server/api/core/bitstreams/15388446-8b73-44c2-b6e1-44d5b687b32f/content. [45]

ECLAC (2023), *Public and private social expenditure (SOCX methodology), in percentages of GDP*, https://statistics.cepal.org/portal/cepalstat/dashboard.html?lang=en (accessed on 1 April 2024). [57]

ECLAC (2023), *Social Panorama of Latin America and the Caribbean, 2023*, United Nations Economic Commission for Latin America and the Caribbean, https://repositorio.cepal.org/server/api/core/bitstreams/7ddf434a-6073-4f1e-8b71-a6639e4586d5/content. [56]

ECLAC (2022), *Innovation for Development: The Key to a Transformative Recovery in Latin America and the Caribbean*, United Nations Economic Commission for Latin America and the Caribbean, Santiago. [116]

ECLAC (2022), *Social Panorama of Latin America 2021*, United Nations Economic Commission for Latin America and the Caribbean, https://repositorio.cepal.org/server/api/core/bitstreams/dcad3d5a-70c5-4ec6-8712-c68c8b220487/content. [80]

ECLAC (2019), "Income poverty measurement: Updated methodology and results", *ECLAC Methodologies*, No. 2, https://repositorio.cepal.org/server/api/core/bitstreams/b2dd4899-f5b4-4d6e-998c-64a916cb1eff/content. [21]

ECLAC (2018), *Social Panorama of Latin America, 2017*, United Nations Economic Commission for Latin America and the Caribbean, Santiago, https://repositorio.cepal.org/server/api/core/bitstreams/de7a8c8d-7c05-454d-b384-7fb8f73e0a31/content. [71]

ECLAC (2013), *Social Panorama of Latin America 2013*, United Nations Economic Commission for Latin America and the Caribbean, https://repositorio.cepal.org/bitstreams/98961ae6-d21f-4740-85a1-94769f542287/download. [36]

Economist Impact (2022), "Evaluating the environment for public-private partnerships in Latin America and the Caribbean: The 2021/22 Infrascope", *Economist Impact*, https://infrascope.wpengine. com/wp-content/uploads/2019/04/EIU_INFRASCOPE_2021_12.pdf. [113]

Escobar, F., S. Martínez and J. Mendizábal (2013), *El impacto de la Renta Dignidad: política de redistribución del ingreso, consumo y reducción de la pobreza en hogares con personas adultas mayores*, Economic and Social Policy Analysis Unit (UDAPE), Ministry of Development Planning (MDP), La Paz. [124]

Escudero, V. et al. (2019), "Active labour market programmes in Latin America and the Caribbean: Evidence from a meta analysis", *Journal of Development Studies*, Vol. 55/12, pp. 2644-2661, https://doi.org/10.1080/00220388.2018.1546843. [88]

Espejo, A. et al. (2023), "Desafíos y recomendaciones para la inclusión laboral de jóvenes en América Latina", in Huepe, M. (ed.), *Desigualdades, inclusión laboral y futuro del trabajo en América Latina*, United Nations Economic Commission for Latin America and the Caribbean, Santiago, https://repositorio.cepal.org/server/api/core/bitstreams/a25c634b-af42-4892-b8ba-21372a2b815a/content. [87]

FAO, IFAD and WFP (2015), *Achieving Zero Hunger: The Critical Role of Investments in Social Protection and Agriculture*, Policy Support and Governance, Food and Agriculture Organization of the United Nations, https://www.fao.org/policy-support/tools-and-publications/resources-details/en/c/422255. [99]

Feenstra, R., R. Inklaar and M. Timmer (2015), "The Next Generation of the Penn World Table", *American Economic Review*, pp. 05(10), 3150-3182, http://www.ggdc.net/pwt. [130]

Filipetto, S. et al. (2022), "Labour transitions that lead to platform work: Towards increased formality? Evidence from Argentina", *AFD Research Paper*, https://www.afd.fr/en/ressources/labour-transitions-lead-platform-work-towards-increased-formality-evidence-argentina. [53]

Galiani, S. and P. Gertler (2016), "Evaluación de Impacto del Programa Pensión 65: nueva evidencia causal de las pensiones no contributivas en Perú", *Documento de Trabajo*, No. IDB-WP-840, Inter-American Development Bank. [125]

Gasparini, L., M. Santos and L. Tornarolli (2021), "Poverty in Latin America", *Documentos de Trabajo*, No. 284, CEDLAS, https://www.cedlas.econo.unlp.edu.ar/wp/wp-content/uploads/doc_cedlas284.pdf. [28]

Giordano, P. and K. Michalczewsky (2024), *Trade Trends Estimates, Latin America and The Caribbean – 2024 Edition*, Inter-American Development Bank, https://doi.org/10.18235/0005513. [27]

Gobierno de El Salvador (2015), *Medicion multidimensional de la pobreza en El Salvador*, http://www.secretariatecnica.gob.sv/gobierno-oficializa-implementacion-de-medicion-de-la-pobreza-multidimensional. [41]

Gobierno del Chile (2017), *Informe Nacional Voluntario*, https://sustainabledevelopment.un.org/content/documents/15776Chile.pdf. [48]

Hone, T. (2018), "Revisiting Alma-Ata: What is the role of primary health care in achieving the Sustainable Development Goals?", *The Lancet*, Vol. 392, pp. 1461-1472. [79]

IDB (2024), *Ready for Take-Off? 2024 Latin American and Caribbean Macroeconomic Report*, Inter-American Development Bank, Washington, DC, https://doi.org/10.18235/0005667. [2]

IDB (2021), "Financing of public-private partnerships", *Discussion Paper*, No. IDB-DP-898, Inter-American Development Bank, Washington, DC, https://doi.org/10.18235/0003717. [111]

IEA (2023), *Scaling Up Private Finance for Clean Energy in Emerging and Developing Economies*, International Energy Agency, https://www.iea.org/reports/scaling-up-private-finance-for-clean-energy-in-emerging-and-developing-economies/executive-summary. [100]

IIF (2024), *Institute of International Finance website*, https://www.iif.com/. [8]

ILO (2024), *ILOSTAT*, https://ilostat.ilo.org/data/. [50]

ILO (2022), *E-formalización en América Latina: acelerando en una región llena de brechas*, International Labour Organization, https://www.ilo.org/es/media/371126/download. [52]

ILO (2021), *Informe Mundial sobre la Protección Social 2020-2022: La protección social en la encrucijada: en busca de un futuro mejor*, International Labour Organization, Geneva, https://www.ilo.org/global/publications/books/WCMS_817576/lang—es/index.htm. [83]

ILO (2021), *World Social Protection Report 2020-22: Regional Companion Report for Latin America and the Caribbean*, International Labour Organization, Geneva, https://www.ilo.org/wcmsp5/groups/public/@ed_protect/@soc_sec/documents/publication/wcms_842104.pdf. [63]

ILO (2020), "Financing gaps in social protection: Global estimates and strategies for developing countries in light of COVID-19 and beyond", *Working Paper*, International Labour Organization, Geneva, https://www.ilo.org/static/english/intserv/working-papers/wp014/index.html. [96]

ILO (2016), *What Works: Active Labour Market Policies in Latin America and the Caribbean*, International Labour Organization, Geneva, https://www.ilo.org/sites/default/files/wcmsp5/groups/public/@dgreports/@dcomm/@publ/documents/publication/wcms_492373.pdf. [89]

ILO (2003), *Guidelines Concerning a Statistical Definition of Informal Employment*, International Labour Organization, Geneva, https://www.ilo.org/resource/guidelines-concerning-statistical-definition-informal-employment-0. [131]

IMF (2024), *World Economic Outlook Database, April 2024*, International Monetary Fund, https://www.imf.org/en/Publications/WEO/weo-database/2024/April. [19]

IMF (2023), *Transforming Public Finance Through GovTech*, International Monetary Fund, Washington, DC, https://www.imf.org/en/Publications/Staff-Discussion-Notes/Issues/2023/09/06/Transforming-Public-Finance-Through-GovTech-535765. [101]

IMF (2023), *World Economic Outlook Database, October 2023*, International Monetary Fund, https://www.imf.org/en/Publications/WEO/weo-database/2023/October. [4]

IMF (2022), *Investment and Capital Stock Dataset*, International Monetary Fund, Washington, DC, https://data.imf.org/?sk=1CE8A55F-CFA7-4BC0-BCE2-256EE65AC0E4&sId=1390030341854. [110]

IMF (2019), *Public Investment Management Assessment (PIMA): Strengthening Infrastructure Governance*, International Monetary Fund, Washington, DC, https://www.imf.org/external/np/fad/publicinvestment/pdf/PIMA.pdf. [107]

INEC (2015), *Indice de Pobreza Multidimensional. Metodologıa, Costa Rica*, http://www.inec.go.cr/sites/default/files/documentos/pobreza_y_presupuesto_de_hogares/pobreza/metodologias/mepobrezaenaho2015-01.pdf. [42]

Infralatam (2024), *Data on Public Investment in Economic Infrastructure in Latin America and the Caribbean (database)*, http://infralatam.info/en/home. [115]

Inklaar, R., R. Marapin and K. Gräler (2023), *Tradability and Sectoral Productivity Differences across Countries*, GGDC Research Memorandum 195, https://www.rug.nl/ggdc/productivity/pld/releases/pld-2023?lang=en. [5]

Isgut, I. and J. Weller (eds.) (2016), *Protection and Training: Institutions for Improving Workforce Integration in Latin America and Asia*, United Nations Economic Commission for Latin America and the Caribbean, https://www.cepal.org/en/publications/40661-protection-and-training-institutions-improving-workforce-integration-latin. [82]

Izquierdo, A., C. Pessino and G. Vuletin (eds.) (2018), *Better Spending for Better Lives: How Latin America and the Caribbean Can Do More with Less*, Inter-American Development Bank, https://doi.org/10.18235/0001217-en. [60]

Jafino, B. et al. (2020), "Revised estimates of the impact of climate change on extreme poverty by 2030", *Policy Research Working Paper*, No. 9417, World Bank, https://openknowledge.worldbank.org/server/api/core/bitstreams/ad7eeab7-d3d8-567d-b804-59d620c3ab37/content. [46]

Joubert, C. and P. Todd (2011), *The Impact of Chile's 2008 Pension Reform on Labor Force Participation, Pension Savings, and Gender Equity*, Pension Council of Chile, https://previsionsocial.gob.cl/wp-content/uploads/2023/12/impacto-reforma-2008-fza-laboral-ahorro-genero-joubert-todd.pdf. [126]

Lister, R. (2004), *Poverty*, Polity Press, Cambridge. [33]

Marinho, M., A. Dahuabe and A. Arenas de Mesa (2023), "Salud y desigualdad en América Latina y el Caribe: la centralidad de la salud para el desarrollo social inclusivo y sostenible", *Social Policy Series*, No. 244, United Nations Economic Commission for Latin America and the Caribbean, https://repositorio.cepal.org/server/api/core/bitstreams/b816a7eb-10d7-4f37-8eba-e6cb8feb91cc/content. [78]

Martínez, S., M. Pérez and L. Tejerina (2015), "Atacando la vulnerabilidad en los adultos mayores: Evaluación de impacto de la Pensión Básica Universal, Programa Nuestros Mayores Derechos en El Salvador", *Nota Técnica*, No. IDB-TN-883, Inter-American Development Bank. [127]

Mena, G. and W. Hernani-Limarino (2015), "Intended and unintended effects of unconditional cash transfers: The case of Bolivia's Renta Dignidad", *IDB Working Paper Series*, No. IDB-WP-631, Inter-American Development Bank, https://doi.org/10.18235/0011709. [128]

Ministerio de Desarrollo Social de Chile (2015), *CASEN 2013: Situacion de la Pobreza en Chile. Presentacion de la Nueva Metodologia de Medicion de la Pobreza y Sintesis de los Principales Resultados*. [39]

Ministerio del Trabajo (2024), *Aprobada la reforma pensional en la Cámara de Representes*, https://www.mintrabajo.gov.co/comunicados/2024/junio/aprobada-la-reforma-pensional-en-la-camara-de-representes. [73]

MPPN (2017), *Using the MPI to Determine National Budgets in Costa Rica*, https://www.mppn.org/mpi-budgets-costa-rica/ (accessed on 1 March 2024). [49]

Nuñez, J. and D. Lasso (2023), "Incidencia de los impuestos y el gasto social: escenarios de política pública para Colombia", *AFD Research Papers*, No. 292, Agence Française de Développement, https://www.afd.fr/es/ressources/incidencia-de-los-impuestos-y-el-gasto-social-escenarios-de-politica-publica-para-colombia. [59]

OECD (2024), *Key Indicators of Informality Based on Individuals and Their Households (KIIbIH)*, https://shorturl.at/lZXl5. [51]

OECD (2024), *OECD Economic Outlook, Volume 2024 Issue 1: An unfolding recovery*, OECD Publishing, Paris, https://doi.org/10.1787/69a0c310-en. [14]

OECD (2024), *OECD Reviews of Labour Market and Social Policies: Colombia 2024*, OECD Reviews of Labour Market and Social Policies, OECD Publishing, Paris, https://doi.org/10.1787/6ed40726-en. [66]

OECD (2024), *Science, Technology and Innovation Scoreboard (database)*, OECD Publishing, Paris, https://www.oecd.org/en/data/datasets/science-technology-and-innovation-scoreboard.html. [118]

OECD (2023), *Harnessing the Potential of Foreign Direct Investment to Advance the Low-Carbon Transition in Latin America and the Caribbean*, OECD, https://www.oecd-events.org/investment-days-2023/content/keyresources. [13]

OECD (2023), *Health at a Glance 2023: OECD Indicators*, OECD Publishing, Paris, https://doi.org/10.1787/7a7afb35-en. [76]

OECD (2023), *OECD Economic Outlook, Volume 2023 Issue 2*, OECD Publishing, Paris, https://doi.org/10.1787/7a5f73ce-en. [23]

OECD (2023), *Pensions at a Glance 2023: OECD and G20 Indicators*, OECD Publishing, Paris, https://doi.org/10.1787/678055dd-en. [72]

OECD (2023), *Social Expenditure Database (SOCX)*, https://www.oecd.org/social/expenditure.htm. [58]

OECD (2022), *Global Outlook on Financing for Sustainable Development 2023: No Sustainability Without Equity*, OECD Publishing, Paris, https://doi.org/10.1787/fcbe6ce9-en. [103]

OECD (2021), *How's Life in Latin America?: Measuring Well-being for Policy Making*, OECD Publishing, Paris, https://doi.org/10.1787/2965f4fe-en. [90]

OECD (2020), *How's Life? 2020: Measuring Well-being*, OECD Publishing, Paris, https://doi.org/10.1787/9870c393-en. [94]

OECD (2019), *FDI Qualities Indicators: Measuring the Sustainable Development Impacts of Investment*, OECD Publishing, Paris, https://doi.org/10.1787/0894dfba-en. [11]

OECD (2019), *Society at a Glance 2019: OECD Social Indicators*, OECD Publishing, Paris, https://doi.org/10.1787/soc_glance-2019-en. [64]

OECD (2015), *Policy Framework for Investment, 2015 Edition*, OECD Publishing, Paris, https://doi.org/10.1787/9789264208667-en. [119]

OECD et al. (2019), *Latin American Economic Outlook 2019: Development in Transition*, OECD Publishing, Paris, https://doi.org/10.1787/g2g9ff18-en. [1]

OECD/ECLAC (2018), *Public and private social expenditure (SOCX methodology) database*, OECD Publishing, Paris, https://statistics.cepal.org/portal/databank/index.html?lang=en&indicator_id=4407 (accessed on 1 April 2024). [106]

OECD et al. (2023), *Latin American Economic Outlook 2023: Investing in Sustainable Development*, OECD Publishing, Paris, https://doi.org/10.1787/8c93ff6e-en. [7]

OECD et al. (2022), *Latin American Economic Outlook 2022: Towards a Green and Just Transition*, OECD Publishing, Paris, https://doi.org/10.1787/3d5554fc-en. [10]

OECD et al. (2021), *Latin American Economic Outlook 2021: Working Together for a Better Recovery*, OECD Publishing, Paris, https://doi.org/10.1787/5fedabe5-en. [109]

OECD et al. (2020), *Latin American Economic Outlook 2020: Digital Transformation for Building Back Better*, OECD Publishing, Paris, https://doi.org/10.1787/e6e864fb-en. [114]

OECD et al. (2024), *Revenue Statistics in Latin America and the Caribbean 2024*, OECD Publishing, Paris, https://doi.org/10.1787/33e226ae-en. [16]

OPHI and UNDP (2023), *Multidimensional Poverty Index 2023: Unstacking Global Poverty*, https://hdr.undp.org/system/files/documents/hdp-document/2023mpireporten.pdf. [29]

OPHI/University of Oxford/UNDP (2019), *How to Build a National Multidimensional Poverty Index (MPI): Using the MPI to Inform the SDGs*, https://ophi.org.uk/sites/default/files/2023-08/How_to_Build_Handbook_2019_PDF.pdf. [44]

Oughton, E., D. Amaglobeli and M. Moszor (2023), "Estimating digital infrastructure investment needs to achieve universal broadband", *IMF Working Papers*, No. WP/23/27, International Monetary Fund, Washington, DC, https://www.imf.org/en/Publications/WP/Issues/2023/02/10/Estimating-Digital-Infrastructure-Investment-Needs-to-Achieve-Universal-Broadband-529669. [102]

Partners for Impact (2024), *Partnerships – Preparing for a Post-2030 Era*, Partners for Impact, https://pfipartners.org/2024/02/21/partnerships-preparing-for-a-post-2030-era/. [93]

Rao, K. et al. (2022), "Future health spending in Latin America and the Caribbean: Health expenditure projections & scenario analysis", *IDB Technical Note*, No. IDB-TN-2457, Inter-American Development Bank, https://publications.iadb.org/en/future-health-spending-latin-america-and-caribbean-health-expenditure-projections-scenario-analysis. [77]

Ravallion, M. (2016), *The Economics of Poverty*, Oxford University Press, https://doi.org/10.1093/acprof:oso/9780190212766.001.0001. [32]

RICYT (2020), *Network for Science and Technology Indicators – Ibero-American and Inter-American (RICYT)*, http://www.ricyt.org/en/ (accessed on 18 September 2023). [117]

Robles, C. and R. Holz (eds.) (2024), *The Future of Social Protection in the Midst of a Protracted Social Crisis in Latin America: Advancing towards Universal, Comprehensive, Sustainable and Resilient Systems*, United Nations Economic Commission for Latin American and the Caribbean, https://repositorio.cepal.org/server/api/core/bitstreams/a78ff55b-7552-401f-bf14-d279e9c3c57a/content. [75]

Rogoff, K. (2023), "The long-lasting economic shock of war", *IMF Analytical Series*, International Monetary Fund, https://www.imf.org/en/Publications/fandd/issues/2022/03/the-long-lasting-economic-shock-of-war. [24]

Schwarzer, H. and A. Querino (2002), "Non-contributory pensions in Brazil: The impact on poverty reduction", *ESS Paper*, No. 11, International Labour Organization. [120]

Sen, A. (1999), *Development as Freedom*, Oxford University Press. [34]

Sojo, A. (2017), *Protección social en América Latina: la desigualdad en el banquillo*, United Nations Economic Commission for Latin America and the Caribbean, https://repositorio.cepal.org/entities/publication/e4050921-17d8-43de-8923-4dbc5f73c0bd. [74]

The Conference Board (2024), *Total Economy Database*, The Conference Board, https://www.conference-board.org/data/economydatabase. [3]

Tran, V., S. Klasen and S. Alkire (2015), "Static and dynamic disparities between monetary and multidimensional poverty measurement: Evidence", *Measurement of Poverty, Deprivation, and Economic Mobility*, Vol. 23, pp. 249–281, https://econpapers.repec.org/bookchap/emereinzz/s1049-258520150000023008.htm. [31]

UNCTAD (2023), *The Costs of Achieving the SDGs*, United Nations Conference on Trade and Development, Geneva, https://unctad.org/sdg-costing/about. [91]

UNCTAD (2023), *UNCTAD Statistics*, https://unctad.org/statistics. [12]

UNESCO (2023), "Can countries afford their national SDG 4 benchmarks?", *UNESCO Policy Paper*, No. 49, UNESCO, https://doi.org/10.54676/YHFN2611. [98]

UNESCO (2015), "Pricing the right to education: The cost of reaching new targets by 2030", *Global Education Monitoring Report*, https://www.unesco.org/gem-report/en/pricing-right-education. [97]

United Nations (2024), *Financing for Sustainable Development Report 2024: Financing for Development at a Crossroads*, United Nations, Inter-agency Task Force on Financing for Development. [104]

UofT and UCL (2024), *After2030 Project*, University of Toronto (UofT) and University College London (UCL), https://www.oise.utoronto.ca/after2030. [92]

Uthoff, A. (2016), "Aspectos institucionales de los sistemas de pensiones en América Latina", *Serie Políticas Sociales*, No. 221, United Nations Economic Commission for Latin America and the Caribbean, https://repositorio.cepal.org/server/api/core/bitstreams/facce907-83d4-4f98-a320-68dd40246fc0/content. [70]

Velásquez Pinto, M. (2003), "Seguros de desempleo, objetivos, características y situación en América Latina", *Serie Financiamiento para el Desarrollo*, No. 133, United Nations Economic Commission for Latin America and the Caribbean, https://repositorio.cepal.org/server/api/core/bitstreams/04c7fb8d-a5c1-462e-8567-3f2d31a74973/content. [86]

Velásquez, M. (2021), "La protección ante el desempleo: medidas aplicadas durante la crisis del COVID-19", *Documentos de proyectos*, No. (LC/TS.2021/214), United Nations Economic Commission for Latin America and the Caribbean, https://www.cepal.org/en/node/55421. [85]

Weller, J. (2023), "Principales tendencias globales y su impacto en la inclusión laboral", in Huepe, M. (ed.), *Desigualdades, inclusión y futuro del trabajo en América Latina*, United Nations Economic Commission for Latin America and the Caribbean, https://repositorio.cepal.org/server/api/core/bitstreams/75490d25-e918-4f30-9b5b-afabf8b70e6b/content. [84]

WHO (2017), "WHO estimates cost of reaching global health targets by 2030", World Health Organization (WHO), Geneva, https://www.who.int/news/item/17-07-2017-who-estimates-cost-of-reaching-global-health-targets-by-2030. [95]

WHO and UNICEF (2018), *A Vision for Primary Health Care in the 21st Century: Towards Universal Health Coverage and the Sustainable Development Goals*, https://apps.who.int/iris/handle/10665/328065. [81]

World Bank (2024), *Poverty and Inequality Platform*, https://pip.worldbank.org/home. [55]

World Bank (2017), *Monitoring Global Poverty: Report of the Commission on Global Poverty*, World Bank Group, Washington, DC, http://documents.worldbank.org/curated/en/353781479304286720/Monitoring-global-poverty-report-of-the-commission-on-global-poverty. [35]

2 Public finance for development

This chapter examines trends in the administration and mobilisation of public resources in Latin America and the Caribbean. It considers how best to manage them in order to maintain fiscal sustainability while achieving development agendas. The chapter highlights the importance of an efficient use of public funds. It explores strategies for achieving fairer, more efficient and simpler taxation systems and looks at various avenues for increasing tax revenues in the region. The chapter calls for a rethink on debt management practices and presents key considerations for strengthening fiscal frameworks. Finally, it analyses the drivers of tax morale and explores how policy makers in the region can boost voluntary compliance in order to strengthen long-term revenue mobilisation.

Infographic 2.1. LAC needs to improve tax collection, spending and debt management

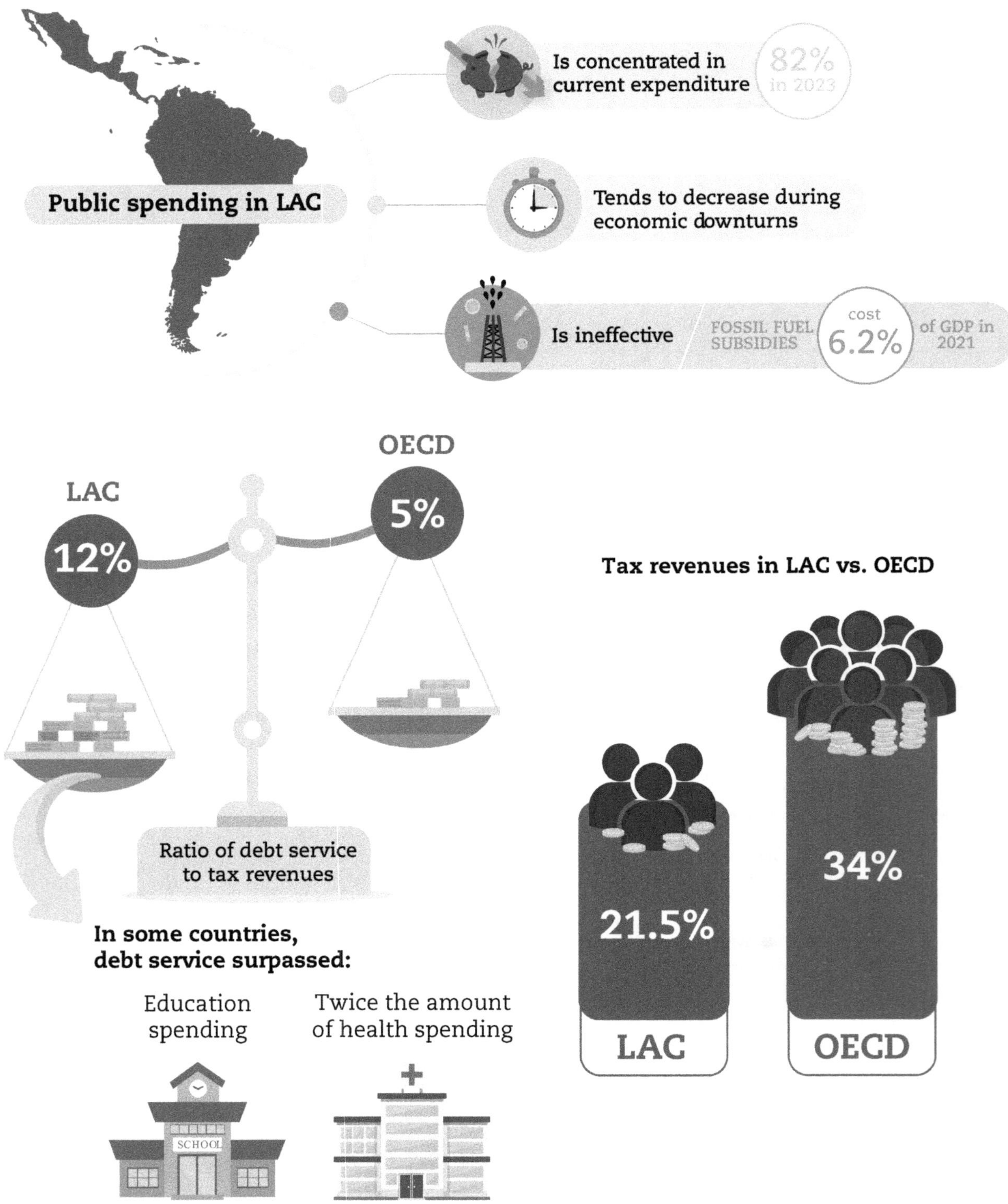

Introduction

Achieving development agendas while also maintaining fiscal sustainability requires that the countries of Latin America and the Caribbean (LAC) improve the way they spend their resources, collect taxes and manage public debt. Spending in LAC is currently insufficient, disproportionately focused on short-term expenditures and not optimally allocated. The public sector has a strategic role to play in financing crucial public services and goods for attaining the sustainable development of the region. However, low tax revenues in most LAC countries limit the state's capacity to strengthen institutions and to provide more and better public services. Given the region's heterogeneity, different combinations of policies tailored to each country will be required to improve tax collection and the progressivity of tax systems. But current debt levels in the region limit fiscal space for investment, and high debt service costs reduce spending capacity.

This chapter begins by examining the main trends of public spending in LAC and the need for more and better spending. It presents an analysis of current taxation systems in the region, highlighting the need to achieve fairer, more efficient and simpler designs. It explores possible actions to improve public debt management and promote the use of innovative and sustainable debt tools and examines the importance of developing a tax-paying culture in the region. It concludes with key policy messages.

Trends in public spending in LAC

Central government expenditure as a percentage of gross domestic product (GDP) has grown in LAC over the past 30 years, but it remains relatively low, is biased towards the short term and tends to be pro-cyclical. In 2023, central governments in LAC allocated a simple average of 25.5% of their GDP towards expenditure, compared to 19% in the 1990s (ECLAC, 2023[1]). Of this, a significant portion went to current spending, which accounted for 82% of total public expenditure across LAC in 2023. However, there is considerable heterogeneity. In Dominica, for example, government expenditure reached 56.9% of GDP in 2022, driven significantly by income from its Citizen by Investment (CBI) programme, which confers citizenship on foreigners who invest in the country. Other Caribbean nations, such as Antigua and Barbuda, Grenada, Saint Kitts and Nevis, and Saint Lucia, also received a substantial financial boost from CBI programmes. Public expenditure as a proportion of GDP was much lower in Paraguay, at 17.3%, and Guatemala, at 14%, in 2023. The composition of current versus capital expenditure also varies markedly in the region (Figure 2.1).

Figure 2.1. Central government total expenditure as % of GDP, by function and by country

2023 or latest available data

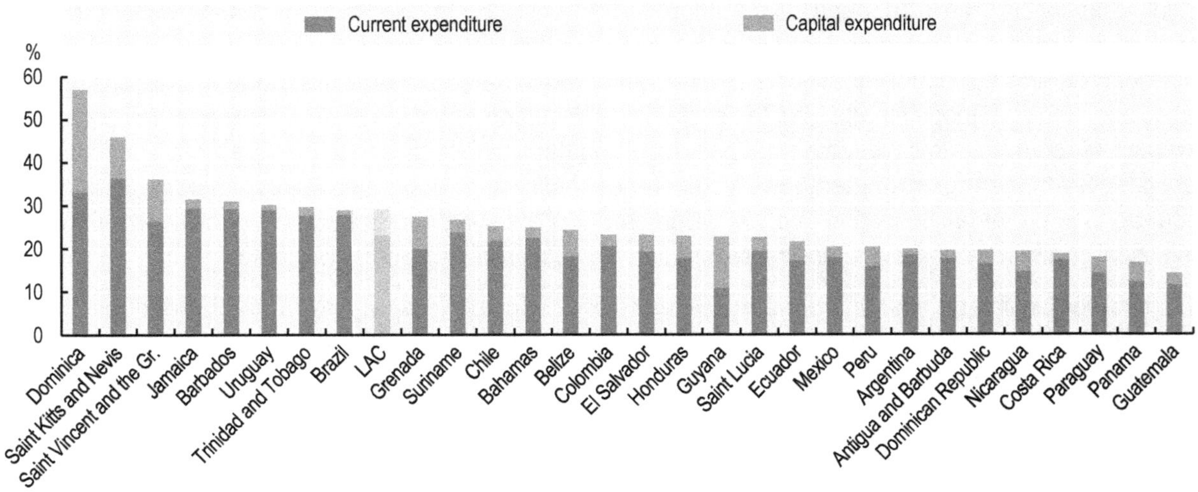

Note: Central government total expenditure refers to total expenditure and lending minus repayments. Data for Dominica correspond to 2022. Data for LAC correspond to a simple average.
Source: (ECLAC, 2023[1]).

StatLink https://stat.link/3n1wqj

Another aspect of public expenditure in LAC is its cyclical nature. As in other developing regions, countries in LAC tend to decrease public spending during economic downturns and artificially increase current expenditure during upswings (Ardanaz and Izquierdo, 2017[2]) and pre-electoral periods up to 1% of GDP, highlighting their financial restrictions, short political timelines and weak institutions (Nieto Parra and Santiso, 2009[3]). During the COVID-19 pandemic, most LAC economies responded with increases in health spending and economic support measures for households and businesses, but these varied widely in size and type (IMF, 2020[4]). The composition and timing of public expenditure are important in assessing the effect of fiscal stimulus on economic growth (Ilzetzki, Mendoza and Végh, 2013[5]). During downturns, cuts in public investment have a more harmful effect on growth than cuts in public consumption, potentially reducing output by USD 1.3 for every cut of USD 1 in public investment compared to USD 0.4 for public consumption (Ardanaz and Izquierdo, 2017[2]). In Peru, government current expenditure demonstrates multipliers ranging from 0.3 to 0.7, while capital expenditure exhibits multipliers ranging from 1.0 to 1.15 (Restrepo, 2020[6]; Raga, 2022[7]). These figures underscore the importance of strategic allocation in budget planning to maximise the impact of public spending.

Public expenditure in LAC can also promote the reduction of poverty and inequality (Lustig, 2018[8]). In 2024, 26.8% of LAC's total population lived in poverty, 10.6% in extreme poverty and the Gini coefficient reached 0.45 (Chapter 1). Despite the greater multiplier effect of capital compared to current expenditure, the latter remains high. Therefore, the efficiency in government spending on basic but transformative goods and services, such as education, is essential for citizens' well-being, and thus for the sustainable development of the region (AFD, 2024[9]; Lustig, 2018[8]).

Aligning government budgets with sustainable development

National budgets help align sustainable development priorities with available public expenditure. To ensure the best possible alignment, governments need to understand the importance of each strategic sector and the cost of developing them (Chapter 1). Many national budgets in LAC are not aligned with development agendas and have inconsistencies between sustainability objectives, the funds assigned and the efficiency of their implementation. For example, fossil-fuel subsidies have been rising in LAC since 2015, as will be discussed below (Figure 2.3) (UNCTAD, 2024[10]). A properly designed budget should not only fund the development agenda but also ensure that the amounts calculated for each objective are properly executed. Improved budget design and implementation and data availability can ensure that each priority is adequately funded and protected from unexpected cuts throughout the fiscal year. In 2021, on average, only 80% of the assigned budget was executed in LAC. Most of the countries executed between 60% and 80% of their budgets, with exceptions like Chile, which executed its entire budget (100%). Nicaragua exceeded its assigned budget with an execution rate of 110% (IDB, 2023[11]).

Co-ordination among public agencies and jurisdictions is key in aligning objectives designed nationally but financed locally. In recent years, subnational governments in LAC have taken a central role in the administration of public funds in some countries. Subnational governments have accounted for more than 30% of total general government expenditure in countries such as Argentina, Brazil, Colombia, Mexico and Peru, compared to 15% or less in nations like Chile, Costa Rica, Ecuador, Panama, Paraguay and Uruguay (OECD, 2022[12]). Multilevel governance and effective co-ordination among government levels are essential to ensure alignment between the objectives for sustainable development set at the national level and spending at the local level. Mechanisms and tools such as Programme Budgeting and Budget Trackers aim to prevent spending duplicity between national and local governments that does not achieve public policy objectives. There are many other variables that policy makers should consider when designing and implementing their budgets. The OECD has developed a set of recommendations on budgetary governance that might serve as a reference (Box 2.1).

Box 2.1. OECD recommendations on budgetary governance

The OECD's recommendations on budgetary governance cover ten priority areas, some of which are particularly pertinent to LAC. The OECD recommends that countries:

1. manage budgets within clear, credible and predictable limits for fiscal policy
2. closely align budgets with the medium-term strategic priorities of government
3. design the capital budgeting framework to meet national development needs in a cost-effective and coherent manner
4. ensure that budget documents and data are open, transparent and accessible
5. provide for an inclusive, participative and realistic debate on budgetary choices
6. present a comprehensive, accurate and reliable account of the public finances
7. actively plan, manage and monitor budget execution
8. ensure that performance, evaluation and value for money are integral to the budget process
9. identify, assess and manage prudently longer-term sustainability and other fiscal risks
10. promote the integrity and quality of budgetary forecasts, fiscal plans and budgetary implementation through rigorous quality assurance, including independent audit.

Of special interest for LAC is the recommendation inviting countries to closely align budgets with the medium-term strategic priorities of government. This will help policy makers to identify which priorities should be funded and with which amount of current and capital investment.

Other recommendations of interest to the region are those calling for participatory and transparent budget design, which can help to raise tax morale and thus generate more funds for national budgets.

Source: (OECD, 2015[13]).

Improving the effectiveness of public spending on education

In LAC, public expenditure in education illustrates that it is not only about how much is spent, but also how well it is spent (OECD/CAF/ECLAC, 2015[14]) (OECD et al., 2019[15]). LAC governments have consistently invested a higher proportion of their GDP in education (4.5%) than other developing regions, but there is strong heterogeneity across the region. Investment per student ranges from 22.2% of per capita GDP in Jamaica to 9.9% in the Dominican Republic (World Bank, 2023[16]). In 2022, LAC recorded a lower average PISA mathematics score for 15-year-old students (373) than the OECD average (472) (Figure 2.2). The comparison between educational outcomes of countries with comparable per capita GDP spending on students highlights how an efficient investment can promote better performance and results for the same amount of funds. Although the data suggest a positive correlation between government expenditure on education and academic performance, it is crucial to understand that it should not be taken as a causal effect, and other factors should be considered in the equation – such as education quality, curriculum effectiveness, different resource availability in rural and urban areas, teacher training, and the socio-economic conditions of both teaching staff and students. Understanding these drivers is necessary for targeted policy interventions that improve educational equity and quality across different countries and regions. By adopting the OECD's spending efficiency standards, countries could maintain current levels of education expenditure while simultaneously improving outcomes. For example, ceteris paribus, following the OECD's average performance, with current levels of investment Jamaica could achieve a PISA mathematics score of 501 if the funds were properly spent, while Costa Rica could reach a score of 475.

Figure 2.2. Government spending on education per student, 2000-18, vs. PISA maths scores, 2022

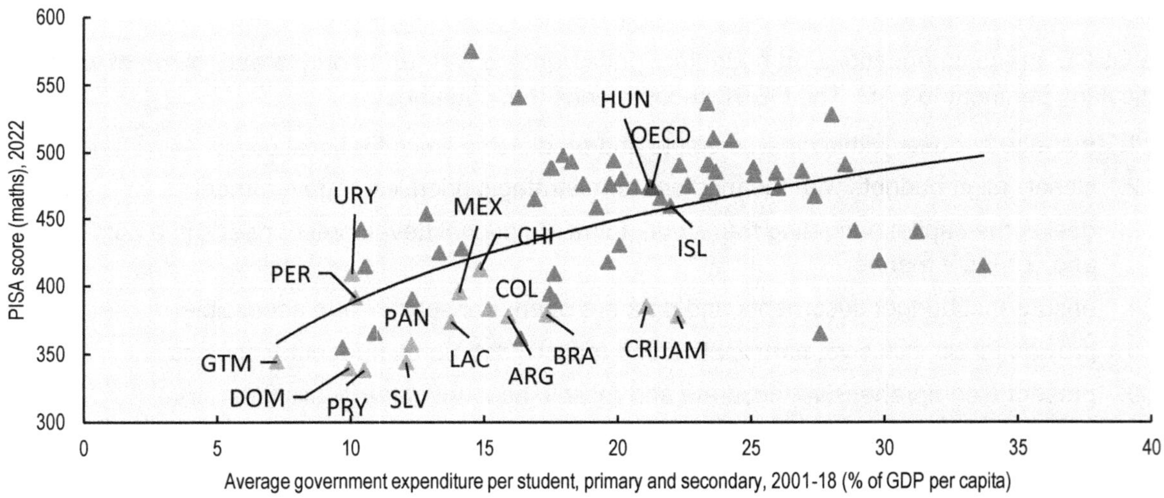

Note: The figure shows the correlation between the two dimensions and should not be taken as a causal effect. The PISA score corresponds to math performance for each region and country. The average government expenditure on education per student is a simple average of the available data for each country between 2000 and 2018 for primary and secondary levels of education. The total averages for OECD and LAC correspond to simple averages.

Source: (OECD, 2023[17]) and (World Bank, 2023[16]).

StatLink https://stat.link/pyl846

Phasing out inefficient fossil fuel subsidies to free up funds while promoting inclusivity

The rationalisation and sequential phase-out of fossil fuel subsidies could free up funds for other uses. However, to safeguard inclusivity in the transition to cleaner energy, it is crucial to pair subsidy phase-outs with policies that protect the most vulnerable against fuel price volatility (OECD et al., 2024[18]). Financing fossil fuel subsidies in LAC accounted for 7.4% of GDP in 2021 (Figure 2.3, Panel A). At the time, governments across the region were supporting customers and businesses in light of the global increase in energy prices, and many subsidies tended to be poorly targeted (OECD, 2023[19]). In 2023, Suriname allocated the highest proportion of GDP to fossil fuel subsidies, at 19.5%, followed by Bolivia (14.4%). The LAC countries with the lowest percentages of GDP dedicated to fossil fuel subsidies were Uruguay (1.5%), Barbados (1.4%) and Belize (0.4%) (Figure 2.3, Panel B). Oil remains the most subsidised fossil fuel in LAC (OECD et al., 2022[20]). In Colombia, all fossil fuel subsidies were allocated to the oil sector in 2022, and the same was true for most fossil fuel subsidies in Bolivia and Ecuador. Other LAC countries have diversified. For example, Argentina allocated 42% of its subsidies to oil, 21% to electricity and 37% to gas, while Mexico granted 46% to both oil and electricity, 5% to coal and 3% to gas.

Figure 2.3. Fossil fuel subsidies as a proportion of GDP (%)

Panel A. Fossil-fuel subsidies as a % of GDP, by region, 2015-21

Panel B. Fossil-fuel subsidies as a % of GDP, by country and region, 2023

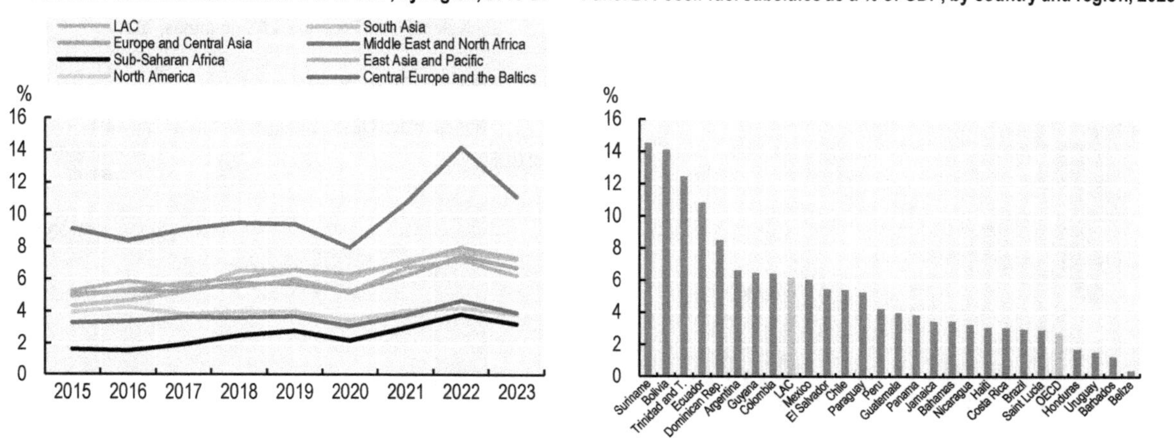

Note: Data for LAC and OECD refer to simple averages. In Panel B, the fuel subsidies included are oil (gasoline, diesel, kerosene, liquefied petroleum gas, and other oil derivates), coal and natural gas.
Source: (IMF, 2023[21]).

StatLink https://stat.link/4kiwte

In this context, well-designed budgets are crucial instruments for fostering sustainable and inclusive development models. Inclusiveness can be enhanced with targeted funding. For example, socially inclusive budgets can boost overall energy transition policies by reducing regressive subsidies, which sometimes benefit rich households and increase inequality, and by prioritising funding for compensatory policies for the most vulnerable groups, which can help to avoid setbacks and social unrest (OECD et al., 2022[20]).

Towards greater equity, efficiency and simplicity of taxation systems

For the majority of countries in LAC, funds raised through taxes serve as the primary and most stable revenue source for governments, enabling effective planning and budgeting, and facilitating the funding of vital public services, infrastructure projects and social welfare programmes. In most LAC economies, there is potential to increase tax revenues and improve the progressivity of the tax system. Given the region's heterogeneity, different policies are needed. Policies should focus on rebalancing the tax structure, rationalising tax expenditures, exploring additional revenue sources such as property, health and environmental taxes, and improving tax administration.

Tax revenues in LAC remain too low to finance increased public spending

Despite increased tax collection over the last three decades, tax revenues[1] in LAC remain insufficient to finance increased public spending. Tax revenues for the LAC region stood at 21.5% of GDP in 2022, well below the OECD average of 34.0%. Levels varied greatly, from 33.3% in Brazil to 10.6% in Guyana (Figure 2.4, Panel A). The tax-to-GDP ratio has steadily increased, from 14.6% in 1990 to 21.5% in 2022, but the gap with OECD economies persists. The increase in the tax-to-GDP ratio in LAC has been mainly driven by increases in revenue from taxes on income and profits, and by value-added tax (VAT) (OECD et al., 2024[22]) (Chapter 1).

Figure 2.4. Tax-to-GDP ratios and Equivalent Fiscal Pressure in the LAC region

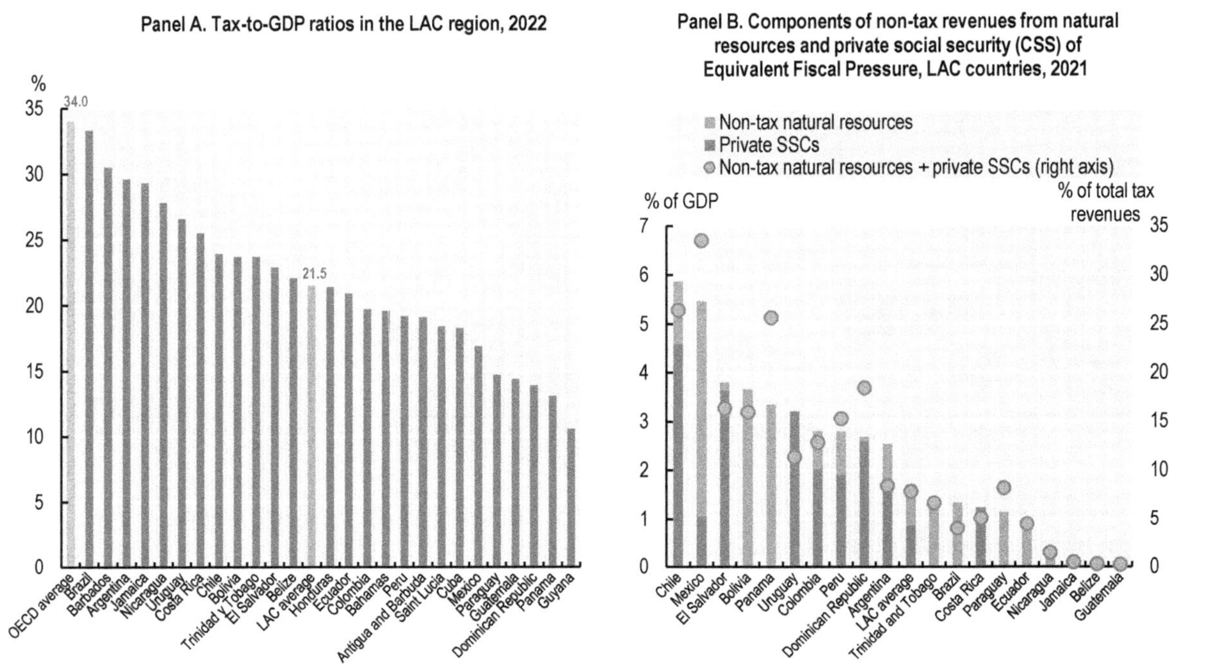

Note: In Panel A, the figures represent general government revenues, including those from subnational governments. The figures exclude local government revenues for Antigua and Barbuda, Argentina (but include provincial revenues), the Bahamas, Barbados, Cuba, the Dominican Republic, Saint Lucia, Trinidad and Tobago, and Venezuela, as the data are not available. The OECD average represents the unweighted average of the 38 OECD member countries (including Chile, Colombia, Costa Rica and Mexico). The LAC average represents the unweighted average of the 26 Latin American and Caribbean countries included in this publication, excluding Venezuela due to data availability issues.

Source: Panel A: (OECD et al., 2024[22]). Panel B: (Morán and Solera, 2023[23]).

StatLink https://stat.link/wudq7p

Equivalent Fiscal Pressure (EFP) can serve as a complementary measure to the tax-to-GDP ratio. EFP includes mandatory contributions to private social security and non-tax revenues from the exploitation of natural resources (Morán and Solera, 2023[23]; OECD et al., 2024[22]). As such, EFP can assist in evaluating the dependency of LAC countries on natural resources, their vulnerability to price fluctuation and the importance of private social security contributions (SSC) (i.e. non-tax compulsory payments) in the mobilisation of resources. EFP is particularly relevant for countries like Chile and Mexico, where private SSCs and non-tax revenues from natural resources play a significant role. In 2021, these revenues contributed an additional 5.9% of GDP to the traditional tax-to-GDP ratio in Chile, reaching a total of 28.1% of GDP (Figure 2.4, Panel B). In Mexico, they contributed an extra 5.5% of GDP. These contributions accounted for more than 3% of GDP in Bolivia, El Salvador, Panama and Uruguay, while in Argentina,

Colombia, the Dominican Republic and Peru they slightly exceeded 2% of GDP. In contrast, in Belize, Guatemala, Jamaica and Nicaragua, non-tax revenues from natural resources and private SSCs are practically non-existent (Morán and Solera, 2023[23]). With the exception of Guyana and Trinidad and Tobago, where non-tax revenue from oil production and exploitation are high, many other Caribbean countries rely significantly on non-tax revenue sources from Citizen by Investment (CBI) programmes and grants (ECLAC, 2024[24]).

Increasing the revenues from direct taxes can help to reduce inequality in LAC

The tax structure in the region is characterised by a low contribution of direct taxes and a high reliance on indirect taxes. In 2022, personal income tax (PIT) and SSC accounted for 26.7% of total tax revenue (5.7% of GDP) in LAC, compared to the OECD average of 48.4% of total tax revenue (16.9% of GDP) (Figure 2.5). In contrast, corporate income tax (CIT) contributed more to tax revenues in LAC than in OECD countries. CIT accounted for 16.3% of total tax revenues (3.4% of GDP) in LAC, compared to 12.0% of total tax revenues (3.9% of GDP) in OECD countries. Taxes on goods and services represented 48.4% of total tax revenues (10.4% of GDP) in LAC, compared to less than 32% of total tax revenues (10.6% of GDP) in OECD countries. In LAC, VAT accounted for most of the revenue from goods and services, contributing 28.3% of total tax revenues and 6.1% of GDP (OECD et al., 2024[22]).

Figure 2.5. Average tax structure in the LAC region and the OECD, 2022

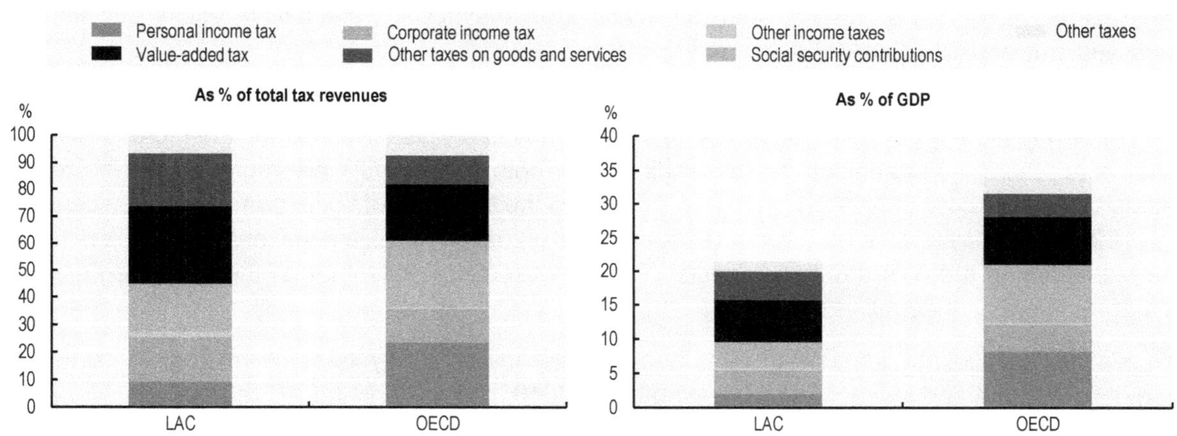

Note: The LAC average excludes Venezuela due to data issues. Ecuador is excluded from the LAC average for PIT and CIT revenues due to data quality issues. The OECD average represents the unweighted average of the 38 OECD member countries, which include Chile, Colombia, Costa Rica and Mexico.
Source: (OECD et al., 2024[22]).

StatLink https://stat.link/y7pme2

Reducing the regressivity of VAT entails revising exemptions and targeted spending

Indirect taxes, including VAT and import duties, tend to be regressive if measured against current income and proportional or slightly progressive when measured as a percentage of current expenditure. When poorly designed and targeted, these taxes can place a disproportionate burden on low-income populations. For instance, fiscal incidence analysis across ten countries in the LAC region showed that VAT is regressive, but that its impact on the current income of poorer households was mitigated by high levels of evasion and informality (Pessino et al., 2023[25]). In addition, substantial tax expenditures aimed at making VAT less regressive often primarily benefit the wealthy (the group with the highest levels of consumption) in absolute terms. In other words, a lack of household-level targeting of tax expenditures leads to higher-income households benefiting the most (Pessino et al., 2023[25]). To improve the progressivity of VAT, tax expenditures should be rationalised and designed in such a way as to minimise regressive effects and revenue losses, in some cases compensating poor households for their loss in purchasing power from paying VAT. It has been shown that social transfers (targeted benefit schemes or even universal transfer schemes) can deliver greater benefits to poorer households than reduced VAT rates or exemptions for the same fiscal cost in developing countries (Warwick et al., 2022[26]). Social programmes must be better targeted and designed to help lift households out of poverty (Chapter 1) (Núñez and Lasso, 2024[27]).

Redesigning direct taxes can enhance their progressivity

Low levels of personal income tax collection and inefficient tax expenditures weaken the ability of tax systems in LAC to promote equity and sustain long-term development. Factors contributing to low PIT collection include: i) high tax reliefs (such as personal deductions and income exemptions); ii) a narrow tax base that is comprised primarily of wages (since tax privileges are often granted to returns on capital); and iii) high levels of tax evasion (OECD et al., 2024[22]). Tax relief often includes provisions such as deferrals and allowances that limit potential tax revenue. In some cases, deductions and exemptions mainly favour taxpayers with higher incomes (Núñez and Lasso, 2024[27]). Enhancing and reassessing the design of PIT holds promise for increasing progressivity and revenue generation in the region. For instance, a reassessment could favour targeted tax relief measures for low-income individuals over more general tax benefits, such as broad-based deductions or credits that disproportionately benefit higher-income earners. Finally, it is imperative to overcome the political challenges associated with reforms that affect higher-income sectors. Achieving a balance between administrative simplicity, distributive equity and revenue sufficiency is crucial (ECLAC, 2023[28]).

The potentially positive impact on inequality and poverty of direct taxes suffers from the effect of SSCs, which is relatively high in LAC and tends to make taxation less progressive and thus to increase poverty (Pessino et al., 2023[25]). In addition, tax expenditures for both PIT and CIT are regressive in the region, averaging 0.8% and 0.4% of GDP respectively. Improving the targeting of tax expenditures is essential to improve the progressivity of direct taxes (Pessino et al., 2023[25]). Taking the analysis a step further requires considering the redistributive impacts of the net fiscal system – that is, the combined effect of taxes and transfers on inequality.

As tax evasion significantly impacts the equity and efficiency of tax systems in the region, combating evasion of both direct and indirect taxes is essential. In 2018, CIT evasion in LAC reached an average of 2.9% of GDP and PIT evasion 1.5% of GDP (Pessino et al., 2023[25]). High levels of evasion of SSCs also persist, although official estimates are scarce (OECD, 2019[29]). For indirect taxes such as VAT, estimates indicate an average evasion rate of 2.2% of GDP, representing about 30.0% of total tax evasion (Rasteletti and Saravia, 2023[30]). Evasion is examined in greater detail in the section on tax morale below.

High corporate tax rates in LAC could dampen incentives to invest in the region

Relatively high tax rates on corporate profits in the LAC region could deter competitiveness and investments. Average statutory CIT rates were 25.0% in LAC in 2021, above the OECD's 21.5%. However, revenue levels and statutory tax rates (STRs) do not show differences across jurisdictions regarding several important features, such as fiscal depreciation rules as well as other tax provisions. These provisions include allowances for fiscal depreciation, deductions for interest payments and equity financing. Because these provisions can significantly affect tax liabilities, their generosity is key for the correct measurement of effective taxation across tax systems.

LAC countries have relatively high forward-looking average and marginal effective tax rates (ETRs). They are a useful tool for best gauging the effective tax burdens on investment projects (Hanappi et al., 2023[31]; OECD, 2022[32]). This methodology is based on assumptions about the financial returns of hypothetical investment projects, to which existing tax provisions are applied to determine the amount of tax owed and do not require information from tax returns. In 2021, the effective average tax rate (EATR)[2] for a given investment project in the 21 LAC countries analysed[3] averaged 23.9%, compared to 21.9% in OECD countries and 17.1% in the remaining countries in the sample, which includes data from emerging Europe, Middle East and Central Asia, emerging Asia and Sub-Saharan Africa. In the case of effective marginal tax rates (EMTR), the average rate was 13.8% in the LAC region, almost double the average of 7.6% in OECD countries and 7.8% in the remaining countries (Figure 2.6). At the country level, Argentina, Brazil and Chile had the highest EATR of the 89 jurisdictions analysed. In the case of EMTR, Argentina, Bolivia, Chile, Jamaica and Peru were in the top ten (Hanappi et al., 2023[31]).

Figure 2.6. Corporate effective tax rates in LAC, 2021

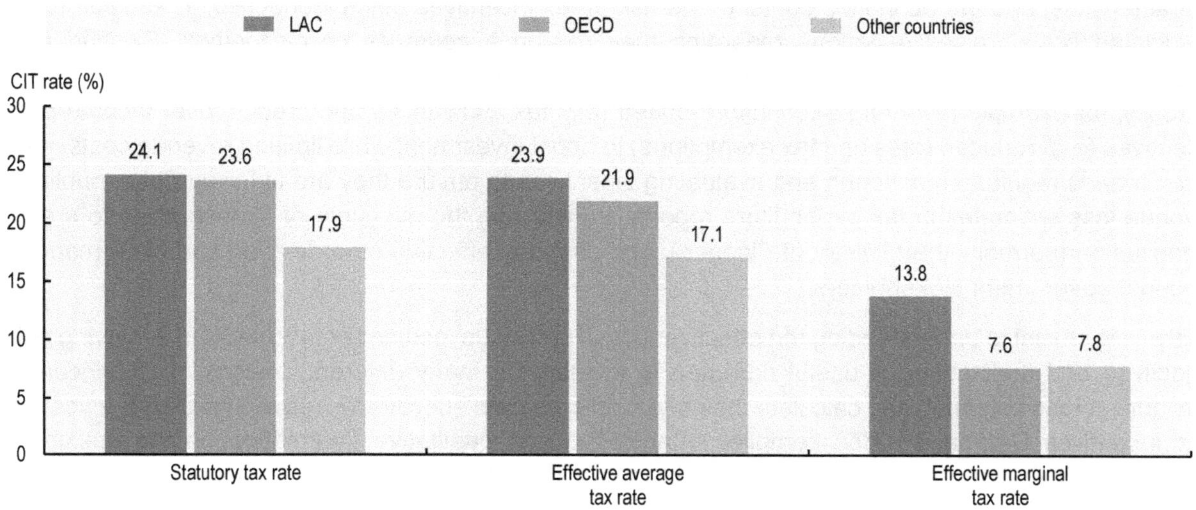

Note: "Other countries" includes data from emerging Europe, Middle East and Central Asia, emerging Asia, and Sub-Saharan Africa.
Source: (Hanappi et al., 2023[31]).

StatLink https://stat.link/0o47iq

The forward-looking high ETRs in LAC countries are mainly explained by the region's high statutory CIT rates, but also by ungenerous tax provisions that in some cases can even increase ETRs. The effect of tax provisions on ETRs can be observed by analysing the difference between STRs and EATRs. This difference is on average only 0.2 percentage point (p.p.) in LAC, while it reaches 1.7 p.p. in OECD countries and 0.8 p.p. in the remaining countries in the sample. However, the LAC figure is skewed by important outliers that present large decelerating tax treatment of capital expenditure. These countries are Argentina, Bolivia and Chile, where the tax treatment of acquired software drives high EATRs (Hanappi et al., 2023[31]).

Better designed CIT incentives can lower their costs in supporting investment and other policy goals

Incentives or preferential tax treatment in specific activities, sectors and locations affect CIT revenues and effective rates. Tax incentives provide a more favourable tax treatment compared to the standard treatment and are targeted to specific taxpayers. Incentives are often implemented to stimulate investment or support other policy objectives, like sustainable development goals. However, incentives may be of limited effectiveness when poorly designed and may provide windfall gains to projects already planned without incentives. They can also result in foregone government revenue, create economic distortions, erode the principle of equity and increase administrative costs (Celani, Dressler and Wermelinger, 2022[33]). The region needs more and better analysis of the costs and impact of incentives, which in some cases may need a redesign (OECD, 2022[34]). Such analysis is particularly important in view of new international agreements on the global minimum effective corporate tax rate (GMT). The GMT can have a significant impact on the effectiveness of certain tax incentives and may require a careful reconsideration of the design and implementation of tax incentives in the region (Box 2.2).

Tax incentives are a common feature of many CIT systems, including in LAC. In 2021, foregone revenue from CIT incentives averaged 3.7% of GDP in LAC countries, equivalent to 19% of central government tax revenues (OECD et al., 2023[35]).

Existing evidence and policy guidance emphasise that tax incentives can increase investment but that such effects are uncertain and heterogeneous and depend on incentive design, firm and asset characteristics, and the economic context. The risk of tax incentives being ineffective, in addition to their associated costs, raises questions regarding their role in a country's policy toolbox. Existing policy guidance cautions against their use and promotes few design and implementation principles (IMF et al., 2015[36]), for example favouring expenditure-based (e.g. tax allowances and credits) over income-based incentives (e.g. reduced rates and tax exemptions) to boost investment while limiting revenue costs. It also recommends regularly monitoring and evaluating incentives to ensure they are fit for purpose, publishing revenue loss estimates in tax expenditure reports, transferring the oversight of all incentives to a single organisation (normally the Ministry of Finance), and ensuring effective co-ordination and clear mandates amongst government stakeholders.

Analysis is crucial to understanding the effectiveness of corporate income tax incentives in achieving policy objectives and their costs. A useful first step is to map the many different designs of CIT incentives available across countries and calculate their effect on corporate effective tax rates. The OECD Investment Tax Incentives Database (ITID) compiles quantitative and qualitative information on the design and targeting of investment tax incentives available across economies, using a consistent data collection methodology. It focuses on incentives that are provided through the CIT system and that are only available to a specific group of corporate taxpayers, based on the taxpayers' sector, activity, location or other investor- or project-related characteristics (i.e. targeted provisions) (Celani, Dressler and Wermelinger, 2022[33]). The 2022 version of the ITID finds that, among 52 emerging and developing economies, almost 90% of economies use at least one tax exemption, while 69% and 65% of the economies use reduced rates and tax allowances respectively (OECD, 2022[37]).

More data and analysis on the use, design and impact of tax incentives are needed given their widespread use in the region. CIT incentive analysis can shed light on areas for improvement in the design of incentives and yield recommendations to make them simpler, more transparent and conducive to quality investment and reduce their costs. As part of a fiscal co-operation project with the Spanish Agency for International Development Co-operation (AECID), at least eight LAC economies[4] will be included in the ITID and relevant ETR measures evaluated by the end of 2024. The purpose is to help LAC policy makers make smarter use of tax incentives and rationalise and reform costly but inefficient ones.

As in many other countries, LAC countries tend to grant targeted tax incentives or preferential tax treatments that reduce ETRs in specific activities, sectors and locations. To illustrate how the tax incentive analysis can be used, ETRs were calculated for selected tax incentives in three economies in the region (the Dominican Republic, Ecuador and Paraguay) and three industries (textile, metals and tourism) (Figure 2.7). While the Dominican Republic and Ecuador have a 25% standard ETR, they offer sector-specific tax incentives that substantially lower effective taxation in two of the industries. For example, ETRs can be as low as 0% in textiles in the Dominican Republic and be 45% lower than standard taxation in the Ecuadorian metals industry (13.7% compared to 24.8%). While Paraguay does not use CIT incentives, it applies a relatively low standard CIT rate, resulting in the lowest ETR in the metals and tourism industries across the three countries.

Figure 2.7. EATRs under standard tax treatment and investment tax incentives in the corresponding sector

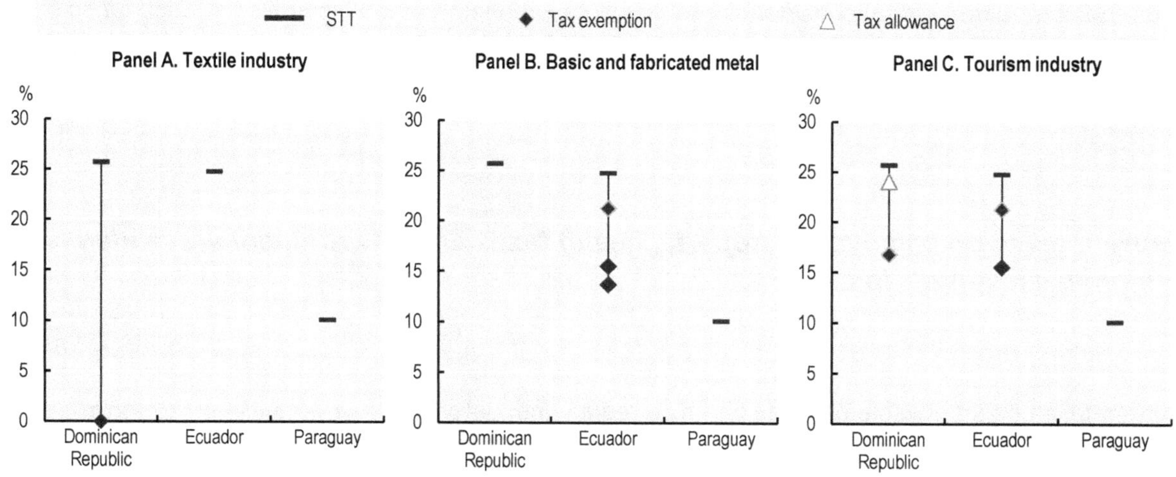

Note: This figure considers investment tax incentives and standard tax treatment (STT) on 1 January 2020. Effective average tax rates (EATRs) are calculated for a standardised investment in a single non-residential building asset. STT considers country-specific standard corporate income tax (CIT) rates, asset-specific capital allowance rates and cost recovery methods. Temporarily or permanently tax-exempt income does not give rise to standard capital allowances. Ecuador does not use CIT incentives and applies a relatively low standard CIT rate of 10%.
Source: (OECD et al., 2023[38]; Celani, Dressler and Wermelinger, 2022[33]).

StatLink https://stat.link/8dsoh7

Box 2.2. The new global minimum corporate tax rate can significantly impact LAC tax incentives

Pillar Two of the new international tax agreement establishes a global minimum effective corporate tax rate (GMT) of 15% for large multinational enterprises (MNEs) with consolidated revenues above EUR 750 million. This has important implications for the use of tax incentives globally. Wherever tax incentives drive an in-scope MNE's effective tax rate below 15% in a jurisdiction, the MNE could be subject to top-up taxes under the GMT, a core component of Pillar Two. Implementation of the rules can generate revenues for LAC countries, set multilaterally agreed limits on tax competition, and reduce profit-shifting. These rules may also have an impact on the effectiveness of certain tax incentives, particularly in cases where low-taxed profit is associated with little economic substance. Therefore, the design of tax incentives will require careful reconsideration in a post-Pillar Two environment.

The GMT will not affect all jurisdictions, MNEs and tax incentives in the same manner. The impact of the GMT on tax incentives will depend on the jurisdiction's tax system and on the characteristics of MNEs and the activities they perform in the jurisdiction. For example, tax incentives may continue to provide benefits for firms that are not in scope of the GMT, such as domestic firms or subsidiaries of MNE groups below the EUR 750 million revenue threshold. For firms within scope of the GMT, those with a greater amount of substance (tangible assets and payroll) in a given jurisdiction will be less affected than others, as they benefit from the Substance-Based Income Exclusion (SBIE) which restricts the application of the GMT to "excess profit".

The impact of the GMT will also depend on the design of tax incentives. For example, expenditure-based tax incentives that target payroll or tangible assets may be less affected than income-based incentives. Tax incentives that allow faster recovery of the cost of tangible assets, such as immediate expensing or accelerated depreciation for investment in tangible assets, will be unaffected by the GMT.

Cash grants and refundable tax credits are treated as income under the GMT, which means that these types of incentives have a smaller impact on effective tax rates for GMT purposes compared to incentives that reduce covered taxes. Understanding the degree to which tax incentives may be affected by the rules requires careful consideration of the detailed design of tax incentives in each jurisdiction. An OECD report prepared at the request of the G20 Indonesian Presidency explored the interactions of GMT with tax incentives (OECD, 2022[39]).

Source: (OECD, 2024[40]).

Recurrent taxes on immovable property, health taxes and environmentally related taxes can increase revenues in LAC

Simplifying the tax process for recurrent taxes on immovable property can increase funds

Recurrent taxes on immovable property can help reduce inequality, yet their potential in the region has not been fully realised. Recurrent taxes on immovable property accounted for 0.4% of the region's GDP on average in 2022, well below the OECD average of 1% (Figure 2.8). However, there is great heterogeneity in property tax collection across the region, ranging in 2022 from 1.8% of GDP in Barbados to 0.1% in the Dominican Republic. Recurrent taxes on immovable property remained largely unchanged between 2014 and 2022 in most LAC countries, with slight decreases in some cases. In Barbados, revenues from these taxes fell from 2.1% of GDP in 2014 to 1.8% in 2022, marking the largest decline in the region. Argentina, Guyana, Panama and Saint Lucia also saw a reduction of 0.1% of GDP. Fully leveraging property taxes on immovable property by updating current systems to simpler, more taxpayer-friendly valuation methods could potentially generate additional revenues of 1.5% to 2.0% of GDP (Ahmad, Brosio and Jiménez, 2019[41]).

Figure 2.8. Recurrent taxes on immovable property in LAC

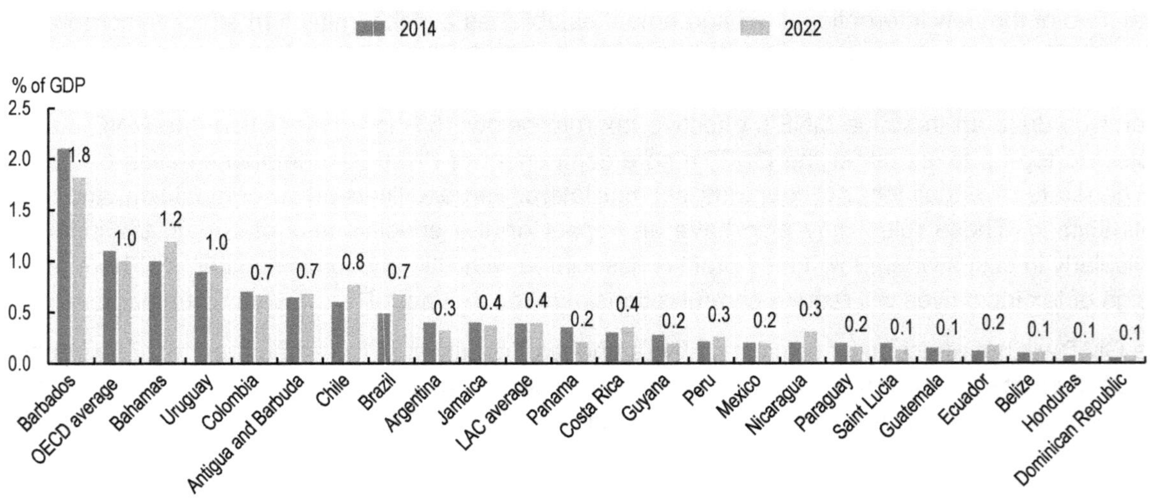

Note: The figure excludes local government revenues for Antigua and Barbuda, Argentina (but includes provincial revenues), the Bahamas, Barbados, Cuba (except for 2002-12), the Dominican Republic, Saint Lucia, Trinidad and Tobago, and Venezuela as the data are not available. Local government revenue data have been available since 1991 for Nicaragua, since 1994 for Bolivia, since 1995 for Guatemala, since 1998 for Jamaica, since 1999 for Panama, since 2000 for Peru, since 2002 for El Salvador and Guyana, since 2006 for Paraguay and since 1990 for all other countries. LAC average represents the unweighted average of 17 LAC countries and excludes Cuba and Venezuela due to data issues. Chile, Colombia, Costa Rica and Mexico are also part of the OECD (38) group. The OECD average represents the unweighted average for OECD member countries.
Source: (OECD et al., 2024[22]).

StatLink https://stat.link/s9ucmy

Most countries and municipalities in LAC use value-based approaches for property taxation, which are often difficult and costly to administer due to limited administrative capacity and the unpopularity of such taxes in certain regions (Ahmad, Brosio and Jiménez, 2019[41]). A value-based approach assesses taxes based on a property's market value, using either assessed or cadastral values, or a combination of both. They also require very precise information that can be hard to obtain in countries or municipalities with limited administrative capacity. To make the system more taxpayer-friendly and address issues of complexity and unpopularity, simpler alternatives include **self-assessment**, an area-based system and a banded system. In the case of the self-assessment system, property owners estimate their own property's value. Depending on the local context (e.g. the level of administrative capacity), area-based taxation can be implemented, where taxes are based on property size or characteristics, and taxpayers participate in determining the tax base. The area-based system, in particular, could generate significant revenue and reduce inequality, especially if the funds are directed toward social programmes (Ahmad, Brosio and Jiménez, 2019[41]). The banded system, which groups properties into categories to simplify tax calculations, could complement either approach (self-assessment or area-based) (Ahmad, Brosio and Jiménez, 2019[41]). Countries and municipalities in LAC should aim to progressively adopt valuation systems that simplify the tax process, improve transparency, and involve taxpayers in determining their tax liabilities.

While urban land constitutes the primary component of the tax base for recurring property taxes, it is crucial to also assess the potential revenue contribution from rural land. Special attention must be taken to avoid setting tax rates too high, as this could have negative economic effects, such as discouraging investment or burdening rural communities. On average, rural property makes up a notable 20.8% of the total property value recorded in the cadastre across the LAC region. Residential property constitutes the largest share at 64.2%, followed by vacant sites at 21.9%, and non-residential property at 4.6% (Lincoln Institute of Land Policy, 2014[42]).

Improving recurring property tax administration in the region is essential (Choga and Giwa, 2023[43]). For countries and municipalities with established value-based systems, it is essential to further enhance this capacity by investing in data collection and management systems (e.g. multipurpose cadastre), training personnel, and improving administrative infrastructure. For countries with numerous rural or hard-to-reach areas, exploring simpler methods such as self-assessment or area-based approaches may be more beneficial. Furthermore, to ensure the progressivity of recurring property taxes, it is essential to balance accurate property value assessments with managing administrative costs, while also ensuring that taxes are fair and contribute to the funding of essential services (Ahmad, Brosio and Jiménez, 2019[41]).

Health taxes can generate revenues while reducing long-term healthcare costs

Health taxes offer advantages for governments by simultaneously curbing the consumption of unhealthy products, generating additional tax revenue and potentially lowering long-term healthcare costs (Sassi et al., 2023[44]). By promoting healthier lifestyles, these taxes can also enhance long-term labour productivity (PAHO, 2023[45]). Across developing countries, health tax reforms remain relatively limited (OECD, 2023[46]). Most have focused on increasing excise duties on tobacco (and alternatives) and alcohol, while fewer have introduced taxes on sugar-sweetened beverages (SSBs) (OECD, 2023[46]).

Although health taxes on tobacco, SSBs, and alcohol have been implemented in LAC, there is still room to expand them. For example, revenues from tobacco taxes could be increased by raising the tax rates, and these tax increases could also reduce cigarette use (OECD/The World Bank, 2023[47]). Studies in 31 LAC countries indicate that a 50% excise tax increase on a pack of cigarettes can increase tobacco tax revenue by 32%, representing an additional USD 7.1 billion for the region (Goodchild, Sandoval and Belausteguigoitia, 2017[48]). At the same time, 21 countries in LAC have implemented some type of SSB tax. However, many countries' tax policies are misaligned with health goals as they continue to tax bottled water but not certain high-sugar beverages (PAHO, 2022[49]). In 2023, Colombia became one of the first countries in the world to tax ultra-processed products when it introduced a health tax on such products and

SBBs. The tax started at 10% and will rise to 20% by 2025 (OECD, 2023[46]). In Mexico, a study showed that an excise tax on SSBs that resulted in a 10% drop in consumption could save the country USD 983 million in health care costs, while a drop in consumption of 20% could save USD 1.9 billion in health care costs (Sánchez-Romero et al., 2016[50]). As for alcohol taxes, 28 LAC countries applied taxes to beer and spirits as of 2018, while 26 did so for wine (PAHO, 2022[49]).

A comprehensive fiscal policy approach to health taxes in LAC is crucial. These taxes should not be seen merely as tools to reduce the demand for unhealthy products, but also as instruments to promote and enable longer, healthier lives (Sassi et al., 2023[44]). They serve as important sources of information for both consumers and producers. For consumers, these taxes offer insights that help individuals understand their rationale and make more informed health choices, beyond just the financial impact. For example, for producers, particularly in the case of SSB taxes, the information helps them reformulate their products – a key intended outcome of such taxes (Sassi et al., 2023[44]). Health taxes frequently attract criticism for their potentially regressive financial effects, amplified by their high visibility and divisive nature (Sassi et al., 2023[44]). Policy makers need to establish a consistent policy framework and narrative to address and counter these critiques effectively (Sassi et al., 2023[44]). On the supply side, governments must regularly modify the design of health taxes to maintain their effectiveness in the face of evolving market structures and strategic reactions (Belloni and Sassi, 2023[51]). Therefore, it is important to consider industry responses, as these can impact tax revenue collection. For example, in the United Kingdom, a health tax on SSBs led to product reformulation and a shift in advertising towards non-taxed or lower-taxed products. While this outcome was successful in terms of product reformulation, the SSB tax generated only 0.03% of total tax revenue (Belloni and Sassi, 2023[51]).

Environmentally related taxes are still underdeveloped in the region

The adoption of environmentally related taxes in LAC countries has been slow, with a heavy reliance on fuel taxes. Environmentally related tax revenues (ERTR) can help to increase revenues in the short to medium term while pursuing environmental and social objectives. These measures should be implemented with the understanding that they may generate progressively less revenue over time if they successfully lead to changes in behaviour as the green transition advances. In 2022, ERTR in LAC averaged 0.8% of GDP, below the OECD average of 1.8% of GDP (Figure 2.9). In LAC, these values ranged from 0.1% of GDP in Belize to 2.0% in Costa Rica. Costa Rica's ERTR is the only one in LAC that surpassed the OECD average. In Costa Rica, fuel taxes are higher than in many other Latin American countries, while subsidies remain lower (OECD, 2023[52]). Several countries, such as Barbados, Honduras, Nicaragua, and Peru, source their ERTR almost exclusively from energy, with amounts ranging from 1.4% of GDP in Honduras to 0.4% of GDP in Peru. In contrast, Brazil and Trinidad and Tobago rely almost exclusively on transport for ERTR.

Countries such as Chile, Colombia and Mexico have undertaken significant green tax reforms, reflecting their commitment to environmental protection. The impact of these reforms is reflected in the wide variation of environmentally related tax revenues across the region (OECD et al., 2024[22]). For instance, in 2014, Mexico implemented a Special Tax on Carbon, replacing previously ineffective fuel subsidies with impactful fuel taxes. This green tax, aimed at mitigating emissions from fossil fuels, especially gasoline and diesel, led to a substantial increase in fiscal revenues, transitioning from a cost of MXN -300 billion (Mexican pesos) to a revenue of MXN +300 billion (AFD, 2022[53]).

Figure 2.9. Environmentally related tax revenues in LAC countries, by main tax base, 2022

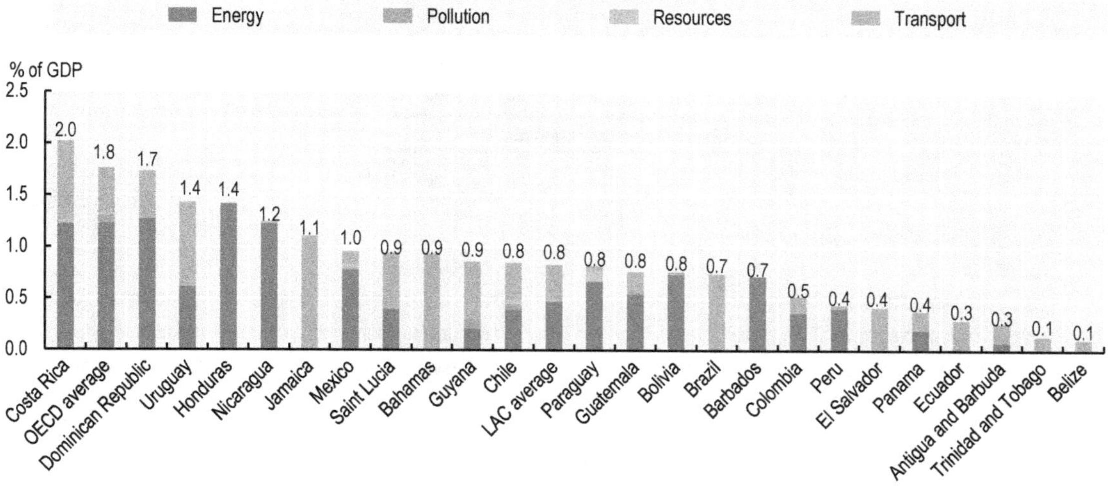

Note: The LAC average represents the unweighted average of 24 LAC countries and excludes Argentina, Cuba and Venezuela due to data issues. The figure does not include Jamaica's revenues from the special consumption tax on petroleum products (estimated to be more than 2.0% of GDP in 2018) as the data are not available. The OECD average represents the unweighted average of 37 OECD member countries.
Source: (OECD et al., 2024[22]).

StatLink https://stat.link/q3mwze

Further developing explicit carbon pricing mechanisms can help to increase revenues in LAC. On average, carbon pricing instruments have the potential to increase government revenues by up to 2.0% of GDP in the region (OECD et al., 2022[20]). In some LAC countries, these revenues could be as high as 4.2% of GDP, as observed in Ecuador, or as low as 0.3% of GDP for Costa Rica, when considering both carbon pricing and subsidy reforms. Governments can increase carbon prices through the introduction of new carbon taxes, increases in carbon tax rates, the phasing out of carbon tax reductions or exemptions, or increases in the stringency of minimum standards for carbon price benchmarks (OECD, 2023[54]).

Carbon taxes, emissions trading systems (ETS) and carbon credits are different carbon pricing methods that hold the potential to reduce emissions while generating additional revenues. Carbon taxes put a price on emissions. An ETS caps emissions and enables trading. Carbon credits involve trading emission reductions. In LAC, explicit carbon taxes are emerging, with countries like Argentina, Chile, Colombia, Mexico, and Uruguay adopting them (Table 2.1). For instance, in its latest tax reform (Law 2277 of 2022), Colombia expanded the base for the carbon tax. However, in most countries carbon taxes have only recently gained traction and are still being implemented at low rates with limited coverage (OECD, 2023[54]). ETS can generate significant revenues through allowance auctions of permits, which, if well designed, can support key sustainable development objectives. In the European Union, ETS auction revenues are used to spur investments in clean technologies (IEA, 2020[55]). As of March 2024 in LAC, only Mexico had implemented an ETS pilot policy, with legal and political hurdles still affecting the implementation of ETS in Brazil, Chile and Colombia (Table 2.1) (OECD et al., 2022[20]). The establishment of a carbon credit market can also open new avenues for revenue collection, such as taxes on transactions or administrative fees for the registration and transfer of credits. Since the LAC market is growing and maturing, these revenues can be significant (OECD, 2023[54]). LAC stands as the world's second-largest source of carbon credits, contributing approximately 20% of all global carbon credits generated in 2020 and 2021 (World Bank, 2023[56]). However, only Chile and Colombia have developed their own carbon credit mechanisms, which operate in conjunction with a carbon tax or an ETS policy (Table 2.1). To ensure the effectiveness of these credits in high-impact green projects, it is essential that environmental benefits are fully realised, fair distribution among local communities is guaranteed, and alignment with the national carbon finance strategy is achieved.

Table 2.1. Carbon taxes, ETS and carbon credit markets in LAC

	Compliance mechanisms			Credit markets
	Carbon tax	Subnational carbon tax	ETS	Government-administered carbon crediting mechanism
Argentina	Implemented in 2018	No	No	No
Brazil	No	No	Under consideration since 2022	No
Chile	Implemented in 2017	No	Under consideration since 2016	Implemented in 2022
Colombia	Implemented in 2017	No	Under development since 2016	Implemented since 2020
Mexico	Implemented in 2014	Yes (6 states)	Pilot implemented in 2020	Under development since 2020
Uruguay	Implemented in 2022	No	No	No

Note: Latest data available: 2023. ETS = emissions trading systems.
Source: Authors' elaboration based on (World Bank, 2023[56]).

Environmentally related taxes should be accompanied by protection schemes for vulnerable households. Developing and improving compensation and mitigation measures, such as cash transfers, in-kind support, active labour market policies and entrepreneurship programmes, are essential to cushion social costs and strengthen social protection systems. For instance, gasoline taxes have a direct impact on middle- and high-income households through private transportation costs. But, more importantly, gasoline taxes indirectly impact low-income households through public transportation and the transportation costs incorporated into the prices of goods and services they purchase, including food. Recent studies indicate that the increase in indirect tax pressure on poor households associated with gasoline taxes can even reverse the poverty-reducing effect of direct transfers (AFD, 2022[53]). This makes implementing gasoline taxes even more challenging during periods of high energy prices. Countries in the region can develop better support mechanisms to help households adapt to higher energy costs through technological changes and public transport development. More precisely targeted mechanisms using carbon tax revenues for income support policies are necessary to address distributional consequences. Compensation policies should be complemented by programmes facilitating relocation, retraining and the promotion of decent work (OECD et al., 2022[20]).

Presumptive tax regimes can improve compliance and encourage formalisation

Well-designed presumptive tax regimes, hold the potential to bolster tax compliance and promote business formalisation. Presumptive tax regimes offer a practical solution, for example by applying taxes on an assumed income base, making them more straightforward and efficient than standard methods. This approach not only facilitates the formal registration of businesses but it could also aid in broadening the social safety net by subsidising social security contributions for micro firm workers (Azuara Herrera et al., 2019[57]; Mas-Montserrat et al., 2023[58]). By reducing compliance costs and imposing lower tax rates compared to standard tax systems, they primarily target micro and small businesses in both the formal and informal sectors. Though not primarily aimed at immediate revenue generation, these regimes can significantly enhance long-term tax compliance, yielding positive revenue effects over time (Azuara Herrera et al., 2019[57]).

For presumptive tax systems to be effective, their design should include identifying specific target groups, establishing clear and verifiable eligibility criteria, reducing compliance costs for taxpayers and enforcement costs for the tax administration, providing an incentive to formalise, and ensuring that the system is affordable for the target group. It should also facilitate, rather than deter, migration into the standard tax system (Mas-Montserrat, Colin and Brys, 2024[59]; Mas-Montserrat et al., 2023[58]). Poorly designed regimes may yield adverse effects on revenue and equity and increase tax evasion. A presumptive tax regime focused solely on short-term revenue gains could deter taxpayers from joining the formal economy. Thus, gradual implementation is advisable to improve compliance. These regimes may also inadvertently foster tax evasion by creating discontinuities in the tax schedule, such as sudden changes or gaps in tax rates or thresholds. These discontinuities can provide opportunities for individuals or businesses to exploit loopholes or ambiguities in the tax system, thereby reducing their tax obligations or avoiding taxes altogether. Such distortions could ultimately hamper overall productivity and GDP growth (Azuara Herrera et al., 2019[57]). To combat tax evasion, it is crucial to further digitalise services, enabling tax authorities to verify compliance through digital means such as mobile phone or Internet-based tax returns and payments (Mas-Montserrat et al., 2023[58]). Digital solutions can simplify tax regimes and increase trust in governments through digital governance initiatives (see below on tax morale). A simpler, digitally enabled tax system encourages compliance and facilitates the tracking of payments, which in turn raises awareness and reduces evasion (Arsovska, 2021[60]).

Presumptive tax systems have the potential to expand social protection coverage and gradually increase revenue generation, especially when they incorporate social security contributions (OECD, 2024[61]). Under such a regime, small businesses could be allowed to pay a single tax that replaces as many taxes as possible, including social security contributions. By offering social protection access, these systems may encourage individuals to formalise their businesses. Specific cases in LAC demonstrate that simplified tax regimes can effectively reduce informality (Mas-Montserrat, Colin and Brys, 2024[59]). Uruguay now boasts the lowest level of informal employment in the region following implementation of the Monotributo regime (Mas-Montserrat, Colin and Brys, 2024[59]; Mas-Montserrat et al., 2023[58]). Introduced in 2001 and expanded in 2006, Monotributo offers a simplified framework by consolidating social security contributions and income tax into a single payment. It allows self-employed individuals to register as personal enterprises with one employee, as partnerships with two partners or as family businesses with a maximum of three partners and no employees (Azuara Herrera et al., 2019[57]).

Tax systems in LAC can also serve to promote gender equality

Tax policy can contribute to gender equality and to governments' efforts to reduce inequalities (OECD, 2022[62]). The payment of taxes can directly or indirectly exacerbate gender inequality, depending on how and on whom the tax burden is imposed, as well as its size (ECLAC, 2021[63]). While men and women are generally subject to the same tax regulations, gender inequalities within the tax system can inadvertently be perpetuated by social and economic differences, such as income disparities or varying levels of labour participation (OECD et al., 2023[38]). Identifying biases that perpetuate these inequalities is crucial for phasing them out and promoting gender non-discrimination in taxation. In LAC, countries must develop more gender-responsive tax systems. While some countries have made progress in reforming tax policies to enhance gender equity, further measures are necessary.

Identifying and addressing both explicit and implicit biases are essential for moving towards more gender-equal tax systems. Explicit biases are written into laws or seen in informal practices, while implicit biases lead to unequal impacts despite similar treatment. In direct taxation, biases arise from joint taxation, differential treatment by income source, tax allowances and the different relative share of women and men in different occupational categories. In the Dominican Republic, for instance, joint filing is standard unless a woman proves that she has independent income (ECLAC, 2021[63]). In indirect taxation, there may be implicit biases that can contribute to regressivity, as these biases may disproportionately affect lower-income women who spend a larger share of their income on taxed goods and services. Here, strengthening the progressivity of tax policies is key. While a progressive tax system does not equate to a gender-responsive one, it generally exhibits greater sensitivity to gender-specific impacts (ECLAC, 2021[63]).

Moreover, tax policy may contribute to gender-related inequalities in labour market outcomes, especially with respect to labour market participation. Studies indicate that tax burdens on households' secondary earners (who are mostly women) can discourage their participation in the labour market (ECLAC, 2021[63]). Studies show that in some countries second earners face higher effective tax rates than single workers when they enter the workforce (OECD, 2024[64]). Additionally, tax-induced disincentives for second earners are more significant in countries that employ household-level taxation or in jurisdictions with individual-level taxation where tax benefits are calculated on a household basis (OECD, 2024[64]).

Formalising the care sector would significantly benefit women and potentially increase tax revenues. Through well-designed care policy packages that improve earnings and expand employment, countries in the region can unlock significant tax revenue potential (OECD, 2024[65]). Formalisation of this sector can help to expand tax bases and promote greater labour market attachment. In LAC, unpaid care work is equivalent to 21% of GDP (significantly above the OECD average of 15%), with women contributing three-fourths of this share (UNDP, 2024[66]). Globally, closing the care sector formalisation gap requires a 4.2% of GDP investment by 2035. However, this investment could be partially offset by increased tax revenue from a wider tax base due to formalisation. Estimates suggest that this could reduce the net funding requirement to 3.2% of GDP by 2035. Women would benefit significantly, holding 78% of the new jobs created, with 84% of these being formal positions (ILO, 2022[67]).

Gender-sensitive tax policies should also foster the development of women's entrepreneurship. Women face challenges in raising capital, and cultural norms and stereotypes often hinder their access to emerging technology and entrepreneurial industries. Although the financing gap for women-owned micro-enterprises in LAC remains significant, it is currently the smallest among developing regions due to concerted multi-stakeholder efforts. This demonstrates that co-ordinated efforts among international co-operation agencies, governments, civil society and the private sector can have a long-term positive impact, consolidating more gender-sensitive policies (Berg, Rubio and Laske, 2024[68]).

Rethinking debt management and strengthening fiscal frameworks

Public debt enables governments to finance human and physical capital investments, facilitating long-term economic growth. It helps to smooth macroeconomic fluctuations by providing fiscal stimuli during recessions to support economic activity. However, the benefits of public debt depend on the productivity and efficiency of its utilisation, the stage of the economic cycle and the level of financial market development (Ayhan, Ohnsorge and Sugawara, 2020[69]).

High debt levels may pose several risks for countries. First, high debt levels increase vulnerability to financial crises. Rising debt ratios may lead to an erosion of investor confidence and demand for higher risk premiums, potentially leading to a debt crisis when debt levels are considered unsustainable (Ayhan, Ohnsorge and Sugawara, 2020[69]). They may also constrain government responses during economic downturns, since resources to implement fiscal policy are constrained (Romer and Romer, 2018[70]). Furthermore, rising debt ratios have a negative impact on economic growth since they displace productive public expenditures, increase domestic interest rates and diminish private-sector investment (Powell and Valencia, 2023[71]). In LAC, debt levels have decreased since the COVID-19 pandemic, but the current global context has given rise to public debt sustainability concerns (Chapter 1).

Public debt levels relative to the size of the economy exhibit heterogeneity across countries in the region. For instance, Barbados' public debt as percentage of its GDP stood at 140% in 2021, while figures for Colombia and Chile were 57% and 21% respectively. Heterogeneity persists across multiple dimensions of debt composition, including the currency of issuance (whether domestic or foreign), the legislative framework of issuance and the maturity profile. The composition of creditors can also vary, encompassing different levels of participation from the private sector and bilateral and multilateral banks. These diverse characteristics shape distinct debt profiles for countries.

The composition of public debt can exacerbate or minimise vulnerabilities

There is heterogeneity in the composition of public debt across LAC economies (Figure 2.10). While domestic debt is predominant, with 74% of public debt in the region issued under internal legislation, external debt continues to serve as an important source of financing for some countries. For instance, in Brazil, Mexico and Costa Rica, domestic public debt accounts for 98%, 78% and 75% of total debt, respectively, while in Nicaragua, Paraguay and Panama, external debt makes up 90%, 90% and 81% of total debt, respectively. Issuing bonds under domestic legislation presents several advantages, including the use of national custody and settlement systems, lower required volumes per issue than in international markets and the resolution of any litigation in national courts with lower costs and less uncertainty (Powell and Valencia, 2023[71]). However, there are risks. For instance, domestic debt may be subject to higher interest rates than debt issued under external legislation. Moreover, sustaining domestic issuances relies on the level of financial market development, which tends to be low in the region. Countries face challenges related to liquidity and the creation of a broad and diversified investor base (Jonasson and Papaioannou, 2018[72]).

Although 69% of public debt in LAC is held in domestic currency, foreign currency issuances are significant in several countries, exposing them to exchange rate fluctuations. Allocation varies across countries. Debt in domestic currency represents 66% to 95% of the total debt of Brazil, Mexico and Chile (Figure 2.10). High local currency debt issuance reduces debt sustainability risks in the face of large exchange rate depreciations (OECD et al., 2020[73]). Although foreign currency debt is typically associated with external debt, certain countries in the region also issue domestic debt in foreign currency. Ecuador, El Salvador, Nicaragua and Panama hold domestic debt exclusively denominated in foreign currency. Countries such as Argentina, the Dominican Republic, Paraguay and Suriname hold sizeable issuances in non-domestic currency, amounting to 70% to 90% of their total debt. For these countries, debt service has the potential to increase significantly in national currency terms, creating pressure to mobilise additional resources or cut public spending to meet obligations (ECLAC, 2023[74]).

Figure 2.10. Public debt by legislation and currency as % of GDP, 2021

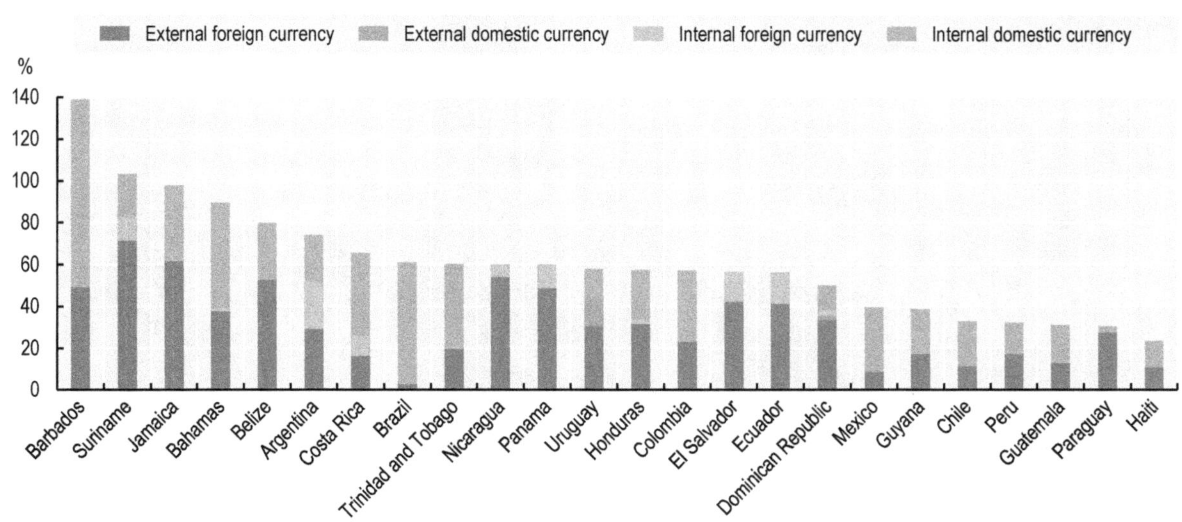

Note: Internal debt refers to debt issued within a country's borders and regulated by its domestic laws. External debt refers to debt issued in foreign countries and subject to the jurisdiction of foreign courts.
Source: Authors' elaboration based on (IDB, 2021[75]).

StatLink https://stat.link/8vxdbr

Historical trends in debt issued under domestic currency also exhibit heterogeneity. Between 2015 and 2021, a consistent share of total debt denominated in domestic currency was maintained by Brazil (95%) and Mexico (78%). In contrast, countries such as Belize, Guatemala, Guyana, Haiti, Honduras and Uruguay experienced notable increases in their domestic currency debt over this period. The share increased from 26% to 55% in Guyana, for instance, and from 18% to 34% in Belize. At the same time, significant declines were registered in Suriname (from 49% to 20%) and Paraguay (from 25% to 10%), indicating a shift towards debt denominated in foreign currency (IDB, 2021[75]).

An increase in the share of local currency debt has long been a policy objective in LAC. An excessive level of foreign currency debt has been associated with recurrent currency crises and debt defaults. Foreign currency debt increases financial vulnerability because the exchange rate would need to depreciate sharply after a negative shock, and this causes an automatic jump in the public debt-to-GDP ratio. Gains in the share of local currency government debt have resulted from a stronger macroeconomic policy framework in many economies in the region, and from a growing domestic institutional investor base (Powell and Valencia, 2023[71]).

A long-term structuring of external debt reduces exposure to financial market volatility. However, some countries face medium- and short-term obligations, rendering them vulnerable during periods of rising interest rates. The bulk of the region's public debt is long-term (more than 5 years), followed by medium term (1-5 years), with a slight proportion of short-term debt (less than a year) (Figure 2.11). The average remaining maturity stands at 13 years. Longer amortisation profiles are associated with less exposure to financial market fluctuations (mainly interest rate shifts). Countries such as Argentina, Brazil and Suriname face obligations over the next five years, representing about 40% of their GDP.

Figure 2.11. Public debt by remaining maturity as % of GDP, 2021

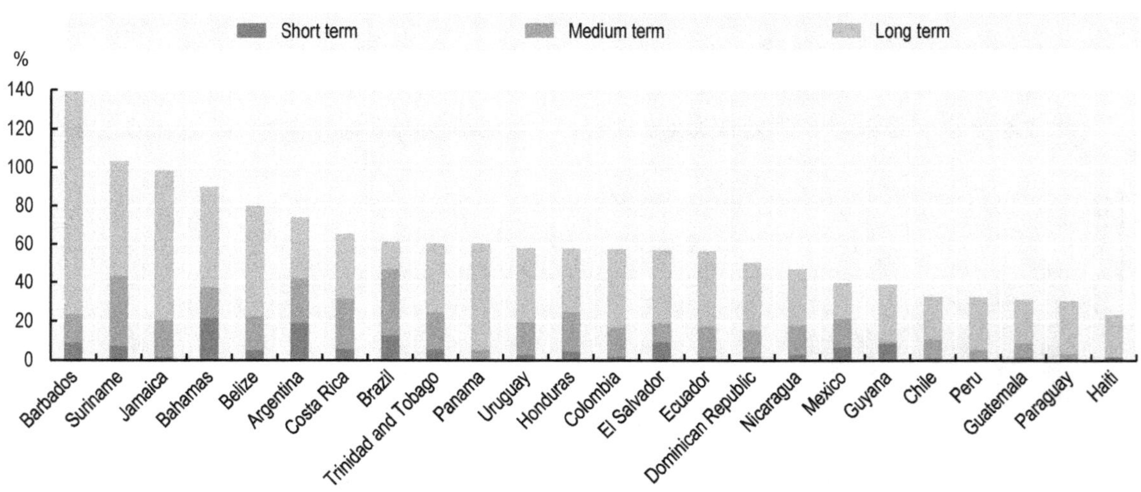

Note: Short term refers to a remaining maturity of less than one year, medium term is from one to five years, and long term exceeds five years.
Source: Authors' elaboration based on (IDB, 2021[75]).

StatLink https://stat.link/53z7oq

External debt in Latin America is mainly held with private creditors. However, multilateral and bilateral lenders remain the main financing source for countries with constrained access to financial markets. External resources raised vary across the region. On average, the creditor structure of the region is composed of bonds (51%), multilateral banks (19%), bilateral creditors (13%) and commercial banks (11%) (Figure 2.12). Caribbean economies like Dominica, Haiti, and Saint Vincent and the Grenadines, and Latin

America countries such as Bolivia, Guatemala, Honduras and Nicaragua, mainly rely on debt issued through multilateral and bilateral creditors. Countries that have traditionally had access to capital markets such as Argentina, Brazil, Colombia, the Dominican Republic, Mexico and Peru, mainly raise funds through bond issuances.

Figure 2.12. External public debt stock by creditor (public and private), 2022

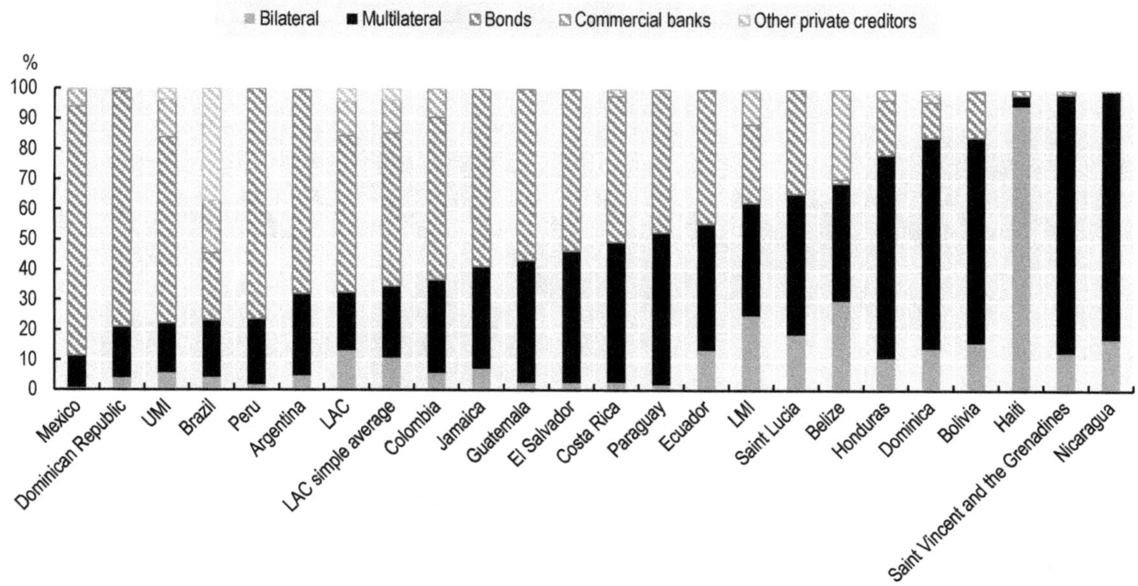

Note: LAC simple average gives equal weight to all countries on their distribution of credit holders; LAC takes into consideration the amount issued by each LAC country. LMI and UMI are all lower middle-income and upper middle-income countries in the world as classified by the World Bank in *International Debt Statistics*.
Source: Authors' calculation based on (World Bank, 2022[76]).

StatLink https://stat.link/1xpjey

Credit quality improved in LAC in 2023 after deteriorating in previous years, with 14 more positive than negative actions by credit rating agencies (Figure 2.13). The credit outlook was revised upward for 11 countries in the region, and eight countries were upgraded: Argentina, Barbados, Brazil, Costa Rica, El Salvador, Guatemala, Jamaica and Uruguay. The outlook was revised downward for four countries, and five were downgraded: Argentina, Bolivia, Ecuador, El Salvador and Panama. Reasons for positive actions included completed distressed exchanges or debt restructurings, better economic conditions and resilient fiscal performance. Reasons for negative actions included heightened risks and vulnerability, political uncertainty and depletion of external liquidity buffers (ECLAC, 2023[77]). Moreover, in 2024, Paraguay's credit rating was upgraded, achieving investment grade for the first time. This was driven by sustained economic growth, enhanced fiscal stability, greater resilience to external shocks, and reforms that strengthened public institutions.

Figure 2.13. Number of positive and negative sovereign credit rating actions by country, 2023

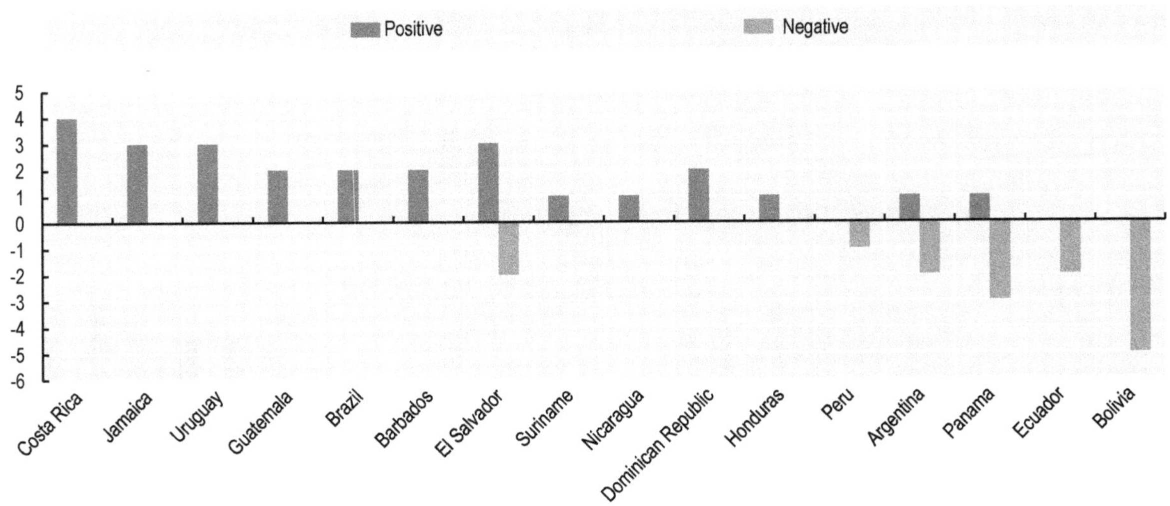

Source: (ECLAC, 2023[77]).

StatLink https://stat.link/ckg05f

High debt service payments constrain social expenditure

Debt service as a proportion of tax revenues has increased due to higher debt levels and interest rates, constraining fiscal space for development-oriented government spending and investment. Developing countries face higher borrowing costs in financial markets, even after considering default risk and market volatility. This results in many governments dedicating a high share of revenue to debt service payments that could be crowding out public spending (Gray Molina and Jensen, 2023[78]). Across the region, the ratio of debt service to tax revenue reached 12.2% in 2022, up from 9.8% in 2012 (Figure 2.14). Most countries in LAC have experienced increases, with the highest levels in 2022 seen in Mexico (30%), the Bahamas (23%), the Dominican Republic (20%) and El Salvador (20%). In contrast, countries such as Barbados, Chile and Jamaica have achieved significant reductions. Jamaica stands out as a notable case of debt reduction due to the adoption of well-designed fiscal rules and a partnership agreement that ensured the equitable distribution of adjustment burdens (Arslanalp, Eichengreen and Blair, 2024[79]) (Chapter 1).

Figure 2.14. Debt service-to-tax revenues ratio in LAC, 2012 and 2022

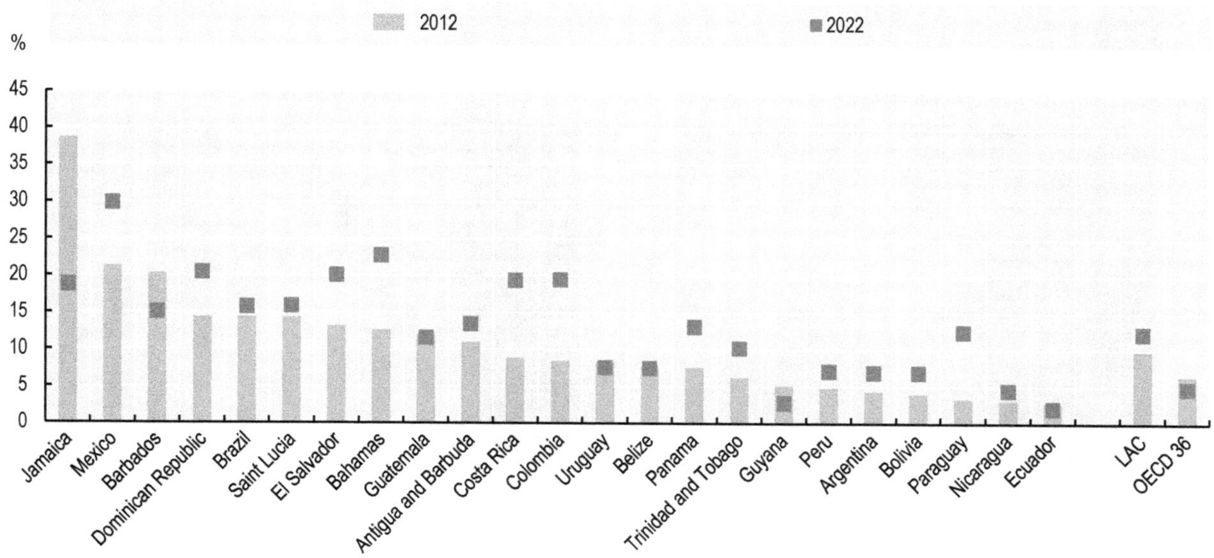

Source: Authors' calculation based on (OECD et al., 2024[22]) and (IMF, 2023[80]).

StatLink https://stat.link/50tebv

Over the past decade, interest payments on debt have surpassed core government expenditures in several countries. For instance, in some cases, debt service has exceeded the spending on education and reached two times that on healthcare and capital investment. However, the differences in research and development are even more pronounced (Figure 2.15). At the same time, the weight of debt service relative to expenditure in other priority areas varies across the region. While countries such as Chile and Paraguay face lower debt service burdens, others like Brazil and Jamaica experience higher ratios. Debt service constitutes more than 25% of all government spending in some LAC countries (Martin and Waddock, 2022[81]).

Figure 2.15. Ratio of LAC central government interest payments to expenditure in key fields, 2010-23 average

Percentages

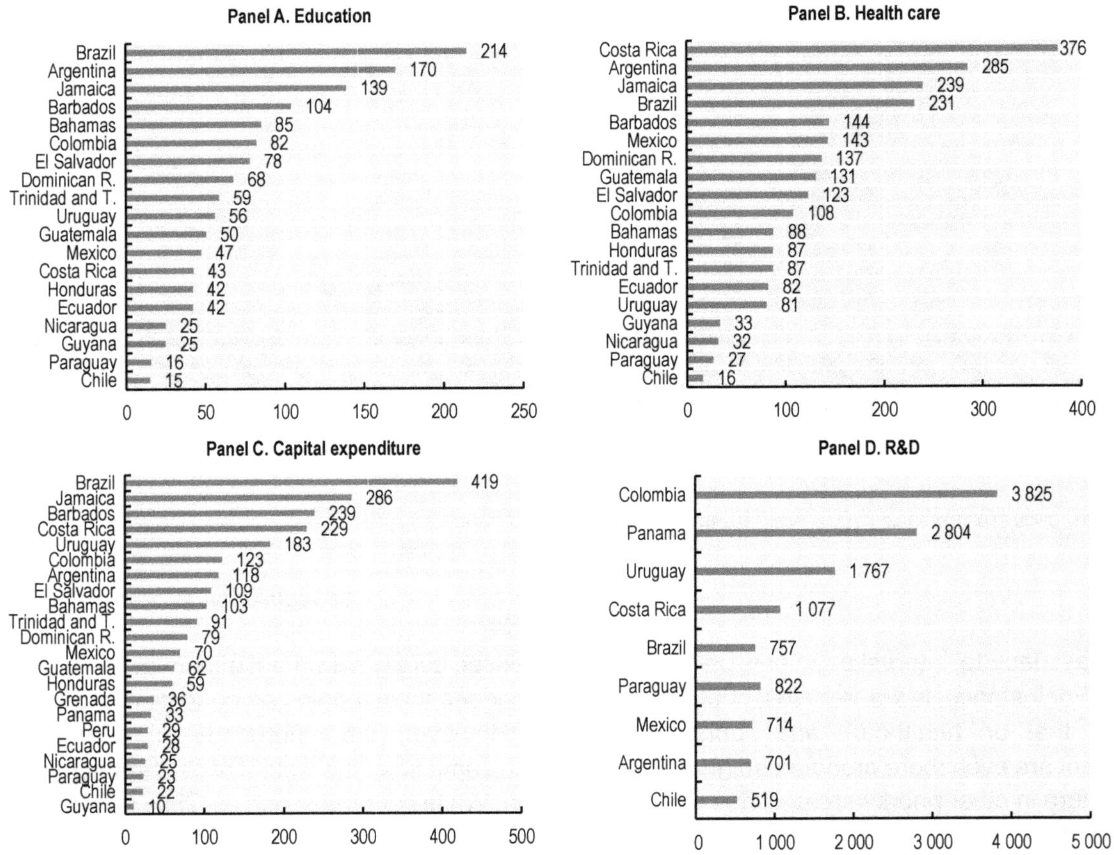

Note: Panels A and B show the average for 2010-20, Panel C for 2013-23 and Panel D for 2013-22 due to data availability.
Source: Authors' calculation based on (ECLAC, 2023[1]) and (RICYT, 2023[82]).

StatLink https://stat.link/h0bafi

Fiscal frameworks are essential for protecting investment and guaranteeing fiscal sustainability

Fiscal frameworks are an essential tool to preserve medium- and long-term stability. They establish rules that can help fiscal policy to be countercyclical, reduce discretionality of public spending and guarantee debt sustainability (Chapter 1). Within them, Medium-Term Fiscal Frameworks (MTFFs) focus on a 3- to 5-year perspective of fiscal aggregates, promoting fiscal discipline, guiding annual budgets and enabling governments to better manage risks and policy trade-offs (Curristine et al., 2024[83]). Fiscal frameworks can also help to protect public investments that are essential for the production transformation. Without fiscal frameworks, governments may find it easier to reduce public investment rather than cut current expenditures during episodes of fiscal consolidation due to political considerations (Ardanaz and Izquierdo, 2017[2]). This can affect economic recovery and impact long-term growth. In contrast, protecting investment during a fiscal consolidation period can mitigate economic contraction and, in some cases, lead to an expansion (Arreaza et al., 2022[84]; OECD et al., 2023[38]).

Fiscal rules are a central component of the fiscal framework. They are designed to solve the temporal inconsistency of public finances and mitigate the accumulation of debt by establishing debt limits (Andrian et al., 2023[85]). By decoupling spending from the business cycle, fiscal rules prevent spending from rising during economic upturns and protect public investment during downturns (Ardanaz and Izquierdo, 2017[2]). Moreover, fiscal rules help to stabilise debt-to-GDP ratios, ensuring long-term fiscal stability. Additionally, they have the potential to alleviate the perception of sovereign risk (Gomez-Gonzalez, Valencia and Sánchez, 2024[86]). Sustainability depends not only on the existence of fiscal rules but also on their quality and on compliance. Quality rules are supported by institutions. They have robust legal frameworks, flexibility against economic shocks and monitoring and enforcement mechanisms. High quality fiscal rules stabilise debt growth and reduce its volatility (Galindo and Izquierdo, 2024[87]). Compliance is crucial, since periods of adherence correlate with fewer events of debt acceleration, lower bond spreads and higher credit ratings (Ardanaz, Ulloa-Suarez and Valencia, 2023[88]).

Fiscal rules are widely used in LAC. Most are concentrated in expenditure or budget balance rules, with some economies using a combination of these. For instance, Argentina, the Bahamas, Brazil, Colombia and Costa Rica are currently implementing expenditure rules that aim to set a limit on total, primary or current government expenditures. Similarly, the Bahamas, Brazil, Chile, Colombia, Costa Rica and Peru are using budget balance rules, while the Bahamas and Peru are using the debt rule. Some economies base their budget balance rules on fiscal balances that consider the (structural) cycle. Some also have clauses that aim to protect investment. For instance, Costa Rica included a golden rule in its framework according to which borrowing can be used only to finance investment spending (Hamid et al., 2022[89]; OECD et al., 2023[38]).

Fiscal rules must be flexible enough to accommodate exogenous shocks. The importance of flexible fiscal rules is evidenced by the fact that economies with no fiscal rules or with rigid ones can reduce their public investment by 10% in a fiscal consolidation amounting to 2% of GDP, while in countries with flexible fiscal rules, fiscal consolidation does not affect investment. This flexibility can take the form of cyclically adjusted fiscal targets, well-defined escape clauses or differential treatment of investment expenditures (Ardanaz et al., 2021[90]).

A strengthened fiscal pact to sustain long-term revenue mobilisation

New fiscal pacts are key pillars to implementing social contracts in the region and they would allow to sustain long-term revenue mobilisation policies and reforms. Citizens are more inclined to pay taxes when they see the government using collected funds efficiently for quality public goods and services (Carrillo, Castro and Scartascini, 2021[91]). However, low tax revenues in LAC limit the state's capacity to strengthen institutions and provide better quality public services. To create a virtuous cycle, countries in the region must reconnect with citizens and design taxation systems that both raise the needed revenues and spend them in a more progressive and transparent manner. This requires better tax administration and a broad consensus built through national dialogue and clear communication. It also requires the development of a tax-paying culture.

A tax-paying culture is a fundamental pillar of the fiscal pact. Strengthening tax compliance is not only a question of improving tax enforcement and "enforced compliance" but also of pursuing "quasi-voluntary compliance" by building trust, providing quality public services, and facilitating tax payments. This requires addressing persistent challenges in tax systems, such as unequal tax burdens, questionable interactions with tax officials and poor translation of revenue into service delivery. There is an urgent need in LAC for innovative technical strategies to boost revenue collection while fostering taxpayer trust, building political support for reform, and reinforcing social contracts (Dom et al., 2022[92]). It is therefore important to understand the drivers of voluntary compliance.

The importance of understanding tax morale

Tax morale is generally defined as the intrinsic motivation to pay taxes (Torgler, 2005[93]; OECD, 2019[29]). It is often measured using perception surveys and is frequently proxied by a question referring to the percentage of the population that declares that cheating on taxes is never justified. In LAC, tax morale has fluctuated over the last decade but seems to be deteriorating. After a period of increasing tax morale between 2008 and 2011, the trend reversed: the proportion of those saying that not paying taxes was justifiable rose from 45.5% in 2011 to 57.9% in 2023 (Figure 2.16, Panel A) (WVS, 2022[94]; OECD, 2019[29]).

Three determinants can help policy makers understand the low levels of tax morale in LAC: i) socio-economic factors that condition citizens' perceptions of taxes and their capacity to pay them; ii) how institutions influence and promote tax payment; and iii) the quality of public services and goods, which can incentivise citizens to contribute via taxes (OECD, 2019[29]). These determinants are important because understanding the sources of a country's tax morale is a first step to developing a tax-paying culture.

Socio-economic factors that can affect willingness to pay taxes include level of education, age, gender and religion. People with more education are generally more predisposed to pay taxes, as are older people, women and those who are more religious. As such, educational policies have the potential to raise tax morale. Policy makers can use targeted policies, like taxpayer education per socio-economic group. For instance, enforcement may be more effective if targeted at high-income groups, where evasion is higher, while facilitating compliance could be emphasised for lower-income groups (OECD, Forthcoming[95]). Similarly, women tend to have higher compliance at lower levels of tax liability, and the use of deterrence messages has been proven to be more effective with them (Lopez-Luzuriaga and Scartascini, 2023[96])

The quality of public services may directly affect willingness to pay taxes because it demonstrates how public funds are used (OECD, 2019[29]). Citizen satisfaction with healthcare and education declined in several LAC countries between 2011 and 2022 (Figure 2.16, Panel B). Declining satisfaction with public services has been accompanied by an erosion of tax morale in the region, as LAC citizens who believe that the government uses tax revenues efficiently to provide quality public goods are more likely to consider paying taxes as a civic duty (Castañeda, 2024[97]).

Figure 2.16. Motivation to pay taxes vs. satisfaction with public services in LAC

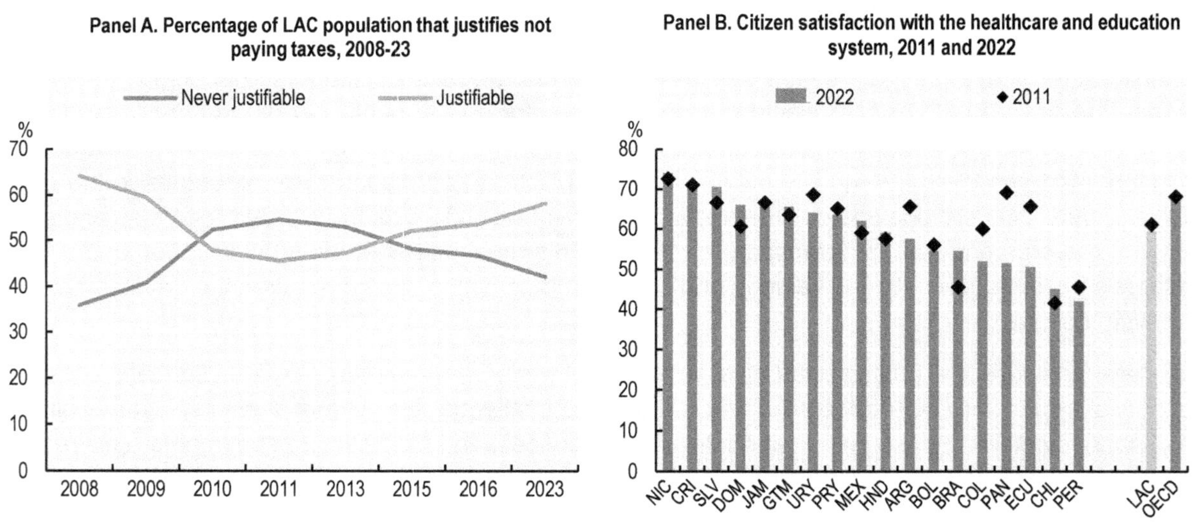

Note: The data in Panel A is based on the question: "How justifiable do you think it is to evade taxes?". The polling was conducted by Latinobarometro. The data in Panel B refer to averages of satisfaction with the education and healthcare systems, based on the questions: "In the city or area where you live, are you satisfied or dissatisfied with the educational system and the schools?" and "In the city or area where you live, are you satisfied or dissatisfied with the availability of quality health care?". The polling was conducted by Gallup. Due to missing data, the OECD average for 2011 was calculated using 2012 data for Norway and Iceland.
Source: Authors' calculations based on (Gallup, 2023[98]) and (Latinobarometro, 2023[99]).

StatLink https://stat.link/31eyf4

Taxpayers' trust in government plays a fundamental role in tax morale. The interaction between citizens and institutions is marked by the institutional trap in LAC. As living conditions improved in LAC and the middle class consolidated, citizens' expectations grew only to face the slow response of inequitable institutions and poor governance (OECD et al., 2019[15]). Trust in government could be strengthened by investing the higher tax revenues stemming from improved compliance in redistributive policies. This would strengthen the social contract, which fosters trust and collaboration between stakeholders by creating an inclusive framework for mobilising public and private resources towards financing development objectives, while also delivering on the sustainable development agenda (Chapter 1) (OECD et al., 2021[100]). Countries that spend more on social programmes tend to be more successful in reducing inequality, while inequality tends to increase in those that spend less (Lustig, Martinez Pabon and Pessino, 2023[101]). Efforts to strengthen tax morale should include businesses and various private-sector representatives. Multinational enterprises represent a considerable source of public revenue. Through responsible business conduct actions, they can play a transformative role in advancing the sustainable agenda and can help to spread a culture of compliance through their supply chains (OECD, 2022[102]). Moreover, communication strategies can significantly influence public perceptions of taxation. Providing information about fiscal reforms and their impact on inequality can enhance social acceptance of taxation, increase trust in the authorities and raise overall tax morale, while at the same time working to counter tax evasion and corruption (Ormeño Pérez, 2017[103]; Goenaga Ruiz de Zuazu, 2020[104]; Durán-Fernández and de las Mercedes Torres-Negrete, 2024[105]; Salgado and Ugarte, 2024[106]).

Transparency policies can strengthen citizens' trust by helping governments better evidence how common funds are used and better account for their redistributive impact. Cases have shown that the positive impact of digital solutions can also have a positive impact on tax morale and trust. Digital programmes can enhance transparency, reduce both actual corruption and public perceptions of it, simplify the tax payment structure and provide citizens with more accessible, efficient and higher-quality public services at lower costs. For example, LAC countries such as Brazil, Chile and Colombia have integrated artificial intelligence (AI) systems into their tax administrations to enhance efficiency and compliance. Brazil's Risk Analysis and Applied Artificial Intelligence System of the Tax Administration project utilises AI for advanced risk analysis in detecting tax fraud, while Chile's Integrated Taxpayer Assistance System employs clustering algorithms to manage VAT taxpayer categorisation. Similarly, Colombia uses AI to enhance the identification of eligible recipients for its social programmes (Valencia and Camilo Díaz, 2024[107]). Similarly, participatory processes can help policy makers design policies that truly cover citizens' perspectives and priorities (Box 2.4).

Box 2.3. OECD recommendations on citizen participation

The OECD Guidelines for Citizen Participation Processes recommend a ten-step path for involving citizens in the planning, implementation and evaluation of public decision making:

1. identifying the problem to solve and the moment for participation
2. defining the expected objectives and results
3. identifying the relevant group of people to involve and recruiting participants
4. choosing the participation method
5. choosing the right digital tools
6. communicating about the process
7. implementing a participatory process
8. using citizen input and providing feedback
9. evaluating the participation process
10. fostering a culture of participation

Identifying the relevant group of people to involve is of special interest for LAC as it could help to close social gaps that characterise the region. Policy design could be strengthened by targeting particular groups for participation, such as rural populations, lower-income women or informal workers.

Choosing the right digital tools for citizen participation is also an issue in LAC, which still experiences low levels of digitalisation. 5G deployment has been slow in the region, with a penetration rate of just 12% projected for 2025 (OECD et al., 2023[38]). Policy makers in the region will thus need to broaden the tools available to communicate and implement participative activities.

Source: (OECD, 2022[108]).

Policy recommendations

Public expenditure in the LAC region has expanded over the past three decades, accounting for an average of 25.5% of GDP in 2023. However, it remains predominantly short-term and pro-cyclical, with current spending constituting 82% of total expenditure. Given that 26.8% of the population is living in poverty in 2024, optimising public spending efficiency, especially in critical areas like education, and ensuring strategic budget allocation are crucial for fostering sustainable and inclusive development models.

Most LAC economies have the potential to increase tax revenues and improve the progressivity of the tax system. In the majority of economies, policies need to focus on improving the design of indirect taxes, raising more revenues from direct taxes, rationalising tax expenditures, formalising the economy, strengthening tax compliance, tapping into the revenue potential of international tax co-operation and exploring new revenue sources such as recurrent taxes on immovable property, health taxes and environmentally related taxes. Addressing gender biases in tax policies as much as possible is essential for promoting gender equality. As countries in the region face different challenges, tax reform or tax policy recommendations require country-specific analysis, design and implementation, as a one-size-fits-all approach does not exist.

Elevated levels of debt in LAC countries and its vulnerable composition constrain fiscal space for development-oriented spending and investment. High debt levels heighten susceptibility to financial crises and limit fiscal responses during recessions. Effective debt management is imperative to finance both human and physical capital, promote long-term economic growth and provide stability throughout the economic cycle.

Maintaining medium- and long-term fiscal stability hinges on robust fiscal frameworks that support countercyclical fiscal policies, curtail discretionary spending and uphold debt sustainability. Such frameworks safeguard essential public investments during fiscal consolidations, thereby bolstering economic recovery and paving the green and digital transitions. Fostering flexible fiscal rules, implementing effective compliance mechanisms and cultivating a robust tax-paying culture are vital for sustaining long-term revenue mobilisation for sustainable development, enhancing tax morale and bolstering public trust in governmental institutions.

The key policy messages for LAC on public finance for development are presented in Box 2.4.

Box 2.4. Key policy messages

Improve the effectiveness of public spending

- Identify and address the key elements determining public spending efficiency to liberate further resources.
- Promote counter-cyclical spending and increase capital expenditure relative to current expenditure.
- Strategically allocate the available budget to maximise the impact of public spending. Budget design should be human-centred, prioritising the strategic sectors for sustainable development and reducing inequality.
- Ensure multilevel governance and effective co-ordination among government to efficiently allocate resources.
- Redesign or phase out inefficient energy subsidies, while ensuring that social programmes compensate the most vulnerable.

Enhance collection and progressivity of tax systems

- Increase tax collection while considering the redistributive impact of tax revenues and fostering investment and entrepreneurship.
- Improve the design of the VAT and foster progressivity by minimising regressive tax exemptions, refining targeted tax relief measures for low-income households, and enhancing the design and focus of social programmes.
- Improve PIT collection and progressivity by eliminating regressive tax expenditures, broadening the tax base and implementing measures to combat tax evasion.
- Further explore recurrent taxes on immovable property, progressively adopt valuation systems to simplify the tax process, improve transparency, and involve taxpayers in determining their tax liabilities.
- Improve the design and effectiveness of taxes on tobacco and alcohol and introduce additional health taxes such as taxes on sugar-sweetened beverages.
- Increase revenues from environmentally related taxes by implementing carbon taxes. Consider expanding emissions trading systems and carbon credits.
- Develop compensation mechanisms for vulnerable households affected negatively by climate reform policies, including complementary transition support policies.
- Reassess inefficient tax incentives in the corporate income tax, including exemptions and deductions.
- Implement and improve the design of simplified tax regimes to boost compliance and encourage formalisation.
- Strengthen tax systems to advance gender equality, including measures to formalise the care sector.
- Eliminate gender explicit biases by reassessing measures such as joint filing, differential treatment by income source and tax allowances. Reassess implicit gender bias caused by differentiated tax burdens resulting from men's and women's consumption patterns.
- Implement measures to formalise the care sector through well-designed care policy packages that benefit women.

Foster resilient public debt management and solid fiscal frameworks

- Promote financial market development to expand financing sources, diversify creditors, and explore innovative financial instruments.
- Advance in the establishment of tailored fiscal rules to promote debt sustainability within countries. These mechanisms include expenditure rules, budget balance rules and debt rules, and should be flexible enough to accommodate the economic cycle.
- Strengthen institutions and improve monitoring, evaluation and compliance mechanisms for fiscal rules, ensuring its proper implementation and efficiency.

Understand and promote tax morale

- Understand the drivers of voluntary compliance and develop a fiscal pact among all stakeholders to increase the levels of tax collection and its progressiveness.
- Direct tax revenues to strengthen institutions and provide better-quality public services. This could increase citizens' willingness to pay taxes as they perceive that the government effectively utilises the funds it collects.
- Design targeted policies to improve tax morale, including targeted taxpayer education programmes (e.g. per socio-economic group) that can help increase tax revenues. In addition, focus enforcement actions on those with lower tax morale and facilitate compliance for those with higher tax morale.

Notes

[1] Tax revenues comprise not only taxes under the authority of central, national or federal governments, but also taxes under the competence of subnational governments and social security contributions.

[2] EATRs evaluate investment decisions at the extensive margin. They summarise the effect of taxation on the decision to invest in comparable but mutually exclusive projects, assuming that investment projects earn economic rents over their lifetime. The EMTR measures the tax burden on a project that is just breaking even before tax to evaluate investment decisions at the intensive margin, that is, on how much to invest once the location or activity has been defined.

[3] The 21 LAC countries analysed include: Argentina, Bahamas, Belize, Bolivia, Brazil, Chile, Colombia, Costa Rica, Curaçao, Dominican Republic, Ecuador, El Salvador, Guatemala, Honduras, Jamaica, Mexico, Nicaragua, Panama, Paraguay, Peru, and Uruguay.

[4] The eight LAC economies include: Brazil, Colombia, Dominican Republic, Ecuador, El Salvador, Peru, Paraguay, and Uruguay.

References

AFD (2024), "Fiscal Incidence and Public Spending. Public Policy Scenarios for Colombia", *Research Papers*, No. 307, Agence Française de Développement, https://www.afd.fr/en/ressources/fiscal-incidence-and-public-spending-public-policy-scenarios-colombia. [9]

AFD (2022), *"El Impacto distributiv de los impuestos verdes en México"*, Agence Française de Développement, https://www.afd.fr/es/carte-des-projets/el-impacto-distributivo-de-los-impuestos-verdes-en-mexico. [53]

Ahmad, E., G. Brosio and J. Jiménez (2019), "Options for retooling property taxation in Latin America"*, Macroeconomics of Development Series*, No. 202, Economic Commission for Latin America and the Caribbean, Santiago, https://repositorio.cepal.org/server/api/core/bitstreams/9282c2cf-003c-4239-ba4e-1e3c77adf51c/content. [41]

Andrian, L. et al. (2023), "Fiscal Rules and Economic Cycles: Quality (Always) Matters"*, IDB Working Paper Series*, No. IDB-WP-01374, Inter-American Development Bank, Washington, DC, https://doi.org/10.18235/0004570. [85]

Ardanaz, M. et al. (2021), "Growth-friendly fiscal rules? Safeguarding public investment from budget cuts through fiscal rule design", *Journal of International Money and Finance*, Vol. 111, https://doi.org/10.1016/j.jimonfin.2020.102319. [90]

Ardanaz, M. and A. Izquierdo (2017), "Current expenditure upswings in good times and capital expenditure downswings in bad times? New evidence from developing countries"*, IDB Working Paper Series*, No. 838, Inter-American Development Bank, Washington, DC, https://www.econstor.eu/bitstream/10419/173892/1/IDB-WP-838.pdf. [2]

Ardanaz, M., C. Ulloa-Suarez and O. Valencia (2023), "Why Don't We Follow the Rules? Drivers of Compliance with Fiscal Policy Rules in Emerging Markets"*, IBD Working Paper Series*, No. 1497, Inter-American Development Bank, Washington, DC, https://doi.org/10.18235/0005165. [88]

Arreaza, A. et al. (2022), *Reglas fiscales para la recuperación en América Latina: Experiencias y principales lecciones*, Development Bank of Latin America and the Caribbean (CAF), Caracas, https://scioteca.caf.com/handle/123456789/1905. [84]

Arslanalp, S., B. Eichengreen and P. Blair (2024), "Sustained Debt Reduction: The Jamaica exception"*, Brookings Papers on Economic Activity*, Brookings Institution, Washington, DC, https://www.brookings.edu/articles/sustained-debt-reduction-the-jamaica-exception/. [79]

Arsovska, M. (2021), "The future of government: Serbia's growing bet on digital transformation pays off"*, World Bank Blogs*, https://blogs.worldbank.org/en/governance/future-government-serbias-growing-bet-digital-transformation-pays. [60]

Ayhan, M., F. Ohnsorge and N. Sugawara (2020), "Benefits and Costs of Debt: The dose makes the poison"*, Policy Research Working Paper*, No. 9166, World Bank, Washington DC, https://documents1.worldbank.org/curated/en/648141582830563001/pdf/Benefits-and-Costs-of-Debt-The-Dose-Makes-the-Poison.pdf. [69]

Azuara Herrera, O. et al. (2019), "Special Tax Regimes in Latin America and the Caribbean: Compliance, social protection and resource misallocation", *IDB Working Paper Series*, No. 970, Inter-American Development Bank, Washington, DC, https://doi.org/10.18235/0001586. [57]

Belloni, A. and F. Sassi (2023), "Supply-Side Responses to Health Taxes", in Lauer, J. et al. (eds.), *Health Taxes: Policy and Practice*, World Scientific, https://doi.org/10.1142/9781800612396_0004. [51]

Berg, R., J. Rubio and N. Laske (2024), *Catalysts of change: How Entrepreneurs are Transforming Latin America*, Centre for Strategic and International Studies, https://csis-website-prod.s3.amazonaws.com/s3fs-public/2024-03/240308_Berg_Catalysts_Change.pdf?VersionId=WmAhPHJBDXCr7ah9amXNSVSJaG_4a8.f. [68]

Carrillo, P., E. Castro and C. Scartascini (2021), "Public good provision and property tax compliance: Evidence from a natural experiment", *Journal of Public Economics*, Vol. 198, https://www.sciencedirect.com/science/article/pii/S004727272100058X. [91]

Castañeda, N. (2024), "Fairness and Tax Morale in Developing Countries", *Studies in Comparative International Development*, Vol. 59, pp. 113-137, https://doi.org/10.1007/s12116-023-09394-z. [97]

Celani, A., L. Dressler and M. Wermelinger (2022), "Building an Investment Tax Incentives database: Methodology and initial findings for 36 developing countries", *OECD Working Papers on International Investment*, No. 2022/01, OECD Publishing, Paris, https://doi.org/10.1787/62e075a9-en. [33]

Choga, I. and F. Giwa (2023), "The Effect of Property Tax on Income Redistribution in Selected African Countries", *Sustainability 2023, 15(7), 5891*, https://doi.org/10.3390/su15075891. [43]

Curristine, T. et al. (2024), "How to Develop and Implement a Medium-term Fiscal Framework", *IMF How to Note*, No. 2024/005, International Monetary Fund, Washington, DC, https://www.imf.org/-/media/Files/Publications/HowToNotes/2024/English/HTNEA2024005.ashx. [83]

Dom, R. et al. (2022), *Innovations in Tax Compliance: Building Trust, Navigating Politics, and Tailoring Reform*, World Bank, Washington, DC, https://www.worldbank.org/en/events/2022/02/17/innovations-in-tax-compliance-building-trust-navigating-politics-and-tailoring-reform. [92]

Durán-Fernández, A. and A. de las Mercedes Torres-Negrete (2024), "Impacto de las reformas tributarias: Comportamiento de los contribuyentes y su cumplimiento en Latinoamérica", *Revista Metropolitana de Ciencias Aplicadas*, Vol. 7, pp. 71-84, https://remca.umet.edu.ec/index.php/REMCA/article/view/701/694. [105]

ECLAC (2024), *Fiscal Panorama of Latin America and the Caribbean, 2024: Fiscal Policy For Addressing The Challenges Of Climate Change*, United Nations Economic Commission for Latin America and the Caribbean, https://repositorio.cepal.org/server/api/core/bitstreams/7b6e3da2-68e3-431e-a9ed-29a931883693/content. [24]

ECLAC (2023), *"Statistics and Indicators", CEPALSTAT Statistical Databases and Publications (database)*, United Nations Economic Commission for Latin America and the Caribbean, https://statistics.cepal.org/portal/cepalstat/dashboard.html?indicator_id=1246&area_id=482&lang=en. [1]

ECLAC (2023), *Capital Flows to Latin America and the Caribbean: 2023 Year-In-Review And Early 2024 developments*, United Nations Economic Commission for Latin America and the Caribbean, http://www.issuu.com/publicacionescepal/stacks. [77]

ECLAC (2023), *Fiscal Panorama of Latin America and the Caribbean: Fiscal Policy for Growth, Redistribution and Productive Transformation*, United Nations Economic Commission for Latin America and the Caribbean, Santiago, https://www.cepal.org/en/publications/48900-fiscal-panorama-latin-america-and-caribbean-2023-fiscal-policy-growth. [28]

ECLAC (2023), *Public debt And Development Distress in Latin America*, United Nations Economic Commission for Latin America and the Caribbean, Santiago, https://www.cepal.org/en/publications/48910-public-debt-and-development-distress-latin-america-and-caribbean. [74]

ECLAC (2021), *Fiscal Panorama of Latin America and the Caribbean: Fiscal Policy Challenges For Transformative Recovery Post-COVID-19*, United Nations Economic Commission for Latin America and the Caribbean, Santiago, https://repositorio.cepal.org/server/api/core/bitstreams/8869b40e-8aca-4c73-b722-fb592377b14f/content. [63]

Galindo, A. and A. Izquierdo (2024), *Ready for Take-Off? Building on Macroeconomic Stability for Growth*, 2024 Latin American and Caribbean Macroeconomic Report, Inter-American Development Bank, Washington, DC, https://doi.org/10.18235/0005667. [87]

Gallup (2023), *Gallup World Poll 2023 (database)*, https://www.gallup.com/analytics/318875/global-research.aspx. [98]

Goenaga Ruiz de Zuazu, M. (2020), "Los relatos tributarios en la prensa española", *Revista Internacional De Sociología*, Vol. 78, https://doi.org/10.3989/ris.2020.78.1.18.191. [104]

Gomez-Gonzalez, J., O. Valencia and G. Sánchez (2024), "Debt affordability in developed and emerging market economies: The role of fiscal rules", *Journal of Economic Finance*, Vol. 48, pp. 377-393, https://doi.org/10.1007/s12197-024-09660-3. [86]

Goodchild, M., R. Sandoval and I. Belausteguigoitia (2017), "Generating revenue by raising tobacco taxes in Latin America and the Caribbean", *Revista Panamericana de Salud Pública*, Vol. 41, https://doi.org/10.26633/RPSP.2017.151. [48]

Gray Molina, G. and L. Jensen (2023), "Building blocks out of the crisis: The UN's SDG Stimulus Plan", *Global Policy Network Brief*, United Nations Development Programme, https://www.undp.org/sites/g/files/zskgke326/files/2023-02/Development%20Series%20-%20Building%20blocks%20out%20of%20crisis%20-%20The%20UN%27s%20SDG%20Stimulus%20Plan.pdf. [78]

Hamid, P. et al. (2022), *Fiscal Rules Dataset: 1985-2021*, IMF Fiscal Affairs Department, International Monetary Fund, Washington, DC, https://www.imf.org/external/datamapper/fiscalrules/map/map.htm. [89]

Hanappi, T. et al. (2023), *Corporate Effective Tax Rates in Latin America and the Caribbean*, Inter-American Development Bank, Washington, DC, https://doi.org/10.18235/0005168. [31]

IDB (2023), *Towards development: Public investment in Latin America (FISLAC)*, Inter-American Development Bank, Washington, DC, https://fislac.com/report-public/public-investment/. [11]

IDB (2021), *Standardized Public Debt Database*, Inter-American Development Bank, Washington, DC, https://mydata.iadb.org/Finance/Standardized-Public-Debt-Database/3bvi-edbq/about_data. [75]

IEA (2020), *Implementing Effective Emissions Trading Systems: Lessons from International Experiences*, International Energy Agency, Paris, https://iea.blob.core.windows.net/assets/2551e81a-a401-43a4-bebd-a52e5a8fc853/Implementing_Effective_Emissions_Trading_Systems.pdf. [55]

ILO (2022), *Care at work: Investing in care leave and services for a more gender equal world of work*, International Labour Organization, Geneva, https://www.ilo.org/sites/default/files/wcmsp5/groups/public/@dgreports/@dcomm/documents/publication/wcms_838653.pdf. [67]

Ilzetzki, E., E. Mendoza and C. Végh (2013), "How big (small?) are fiscal multipliers?", *NBER Working Papers*, No. 16479, National Bureau of Economic Research, https://www.nber.org/system/files/working_papers/w16479/w16479.pdf. [5]

IMF (2023), *IMF Fossil Fuel Subsidies Data: 2023 Update (database)*, International Monetary Fund, Washington, DC, https://www.imf.org/en/Publications/WP/Issues/2023/08/22/IMF-Fossil-Fuel-Subsidies-Data-2023-Update-537281. [21]

IMF (2023), *World Economic Outlook Database: October 2023 Edition*, International Monetary Fund, Washington, DC, https://www.imf.org/en/Publications/WEO/weo-database/2023/October. [80]

IMF (2020), *Regional Economic Outlook for Western Hemisphere*, International Monetary Fund, Washington, DC, https://www.imf.org/en/Publications/REO/WH/Issues/2020/10/13/regional-economic-outlook-western-hemisphere. [4]

IMF et al. (2015), *Options for Low Income Countries' Effective and Efficient Use of Tax Incentives for Investment*, https://www.imf.org/external/np/g20/pdf/101515.pdf. [36]

Jonasson, T. and M. Papaioannou (2018), "A primer on managing sovereign debt-portfolio risks", *IMF Working Papers*, No. 2018/074, International Monetary Fund, Washington, DC, https://www.imf.org/en/Publications/WP/Issues/2018/04/06/A-Primer-on-Managing-Sovereign-Debt-Portfolio-Risks-45746. [72]

Latinobarometro (2023), *Latinobarometro (database)*, https://www.latinobarometro.org/latContents.jsp. [99]

Lincoln Institute of Land Policy (2014), *Property Tax in Latin America*, https://www.lincolninst.edu/research-data/data/property-tax-latin-america. [42]

Lopez-Luzuriaga, A. and C. Scartascini (2023), "Willing but unable to pay? The role of gender in tax compliance", *IDB Working Papers*, No. 1330, Inter-American Development Bank, Washington, DC, https://publications.iadb.org/publications/english/document/Willing-but-Unable-to-Pay-The-Role-of-Gender-in-Tax-Compliance.pdf. [96]

Lustig, N. (2018), *Commitment to Equity Handbook: Estimating the Impact of Fiscal Policy on Inequality and Poverty*, Brookings Institution Press and CEQ Institute, Tulane University, https://www.brookings.edu/books/commitment-to-equity-handbook/#:~:text=Edited%20by%20Nora%20Lustig%2C%20the,taxation%20and%20public%20spending%20on. [8]

Lustig, N., V. Martinez Pabon and C. Pessino (2023), "Fiscal policy, income redistribution, and poverty reduction in Latin America", *IDB Working Papers*, No. 01530, Inter-American Development Bank, Washington, DC, https://doi.org/10.18235/0005237. [101]

Martin, M. and D. Waddock (2022), *A Nordic Initiative to Resolve the New Debt Crisis*, Debt Relief International, https://www.kirkensnodhjelp.no/contentassets/c1403acd5da84d39a120090004899173/a-nordic-solution-to-the-new-debt-crisis-sep22.pdf. [81]

Mas-Montserrat, M., C. Colin and B. Brys (2024), "The design of presumptive tax regimes in selected countries", *OECD Taxation Working Papers*, No. 69, OECD Publishing, Paris, https://doi.org/10.1787/58b6103c-en. [59]

Mas-Montserrat, M. et al. (2023), "The design of presumptive tax regimes", *OECD Taxation Working Papers*, No. 59, OECD Publishing, Paris, https://doi.org/10.1787/141239bb-en. [58]

Morán, D. and M. Solera (2023), *La presión fiscal equivalente en América Latina y el Caribe (1990-2021): Actualización y estado de situación en la salida de la pandemia de COVID-19*, Inter-American Development Bank, Washington, DC, https://doi.org/10.18235/0005326. [23]

Nieto Parra, S. and J. Santiso (2009), "Revisiting Political Budget Cycles in Latin America", *OECD Development Centre Working Papers*, No. 281, OECD Publishing, Paris, https://doi.org/10.1787/221383354183. [3]

Núñez, J. and D. Lasso (2024), "Fiscal Incidence and Public Spending: Public Policy Scenarios for Colombia", *Research Papers*, No. 307, Agence Française de Développement (AFD), https://www.afd.fr/en/ressources/fiscal-incidence-and-public-spending-public-policy-scenarios-colombia. [27]

OECD (2024), *Breaking the Vicious Circles of Informal Employment and Low-Paying Work*, OECD Publishing, Paris, https://doi.org/10.1787/f95c5a74-en. [61]

OECD (2024), *SIGI 2024 Regional Report for Southeast Asia: Time to Care, Social Institutions and Gender Index*, OECD Publishing, Paris, https://doi.org/10.1787/7fc15e1c-en. [65]

OECD (2024), *Tax Challenges Arising from the Digitalisation of the Economy –Global Anti-Base Erosion Model Rules (Pillar Two) Examples*, OECD, Paris, https://www.oecd.org/tax/beps/tax-challenges-arising-from-the-digitalisation-of-the-economy-global-anti-base-erosion-model-rules-pillar-two-examples.pdf. [40]

OECD (2024), *Taxing Wages 2024: Tax and Gender Through the Lens of the Second Earner*, OECD Publishing, Paris, https://doi.org/10.1787/dbcbac85-en. [64]

OECD (2023), *Environment at a Glance in Latin America and the Caribbean: Spotlight on Climate Change*, OECD Publishing, Paris, https://doi.org/10.1787/2431bd6c-en. [54]

OECD (2023), *OECD Environmental Performance Reviews: Costa Rica 2023*, OECD Environmental Performance Reviews, OECD Publishing, Paris, https://doi.org/10.1787/ec94fd4e-en. [52]

OECD (2023), *OECD Inventory of Support Measures for Fossil Fuels 2023*, OECD Publishing, Paris, https://doi.org/10.1787/87dc4a55-en. [19]

OECD (2023), *Programme for International Student Assessment (PISA)*, https://www.oecd.org/pisa/. [17]

OECD (2023), *Tax Policy Reforms 2023: OECD and Selected Partner Economies*, OECD Publishing, Paris, https://doi.org/10.1787/d8bc45d9-en. [46]

OECD (2022), *Corporate Tax Statistics: Fourth Edition*, OECD Publishing, Paris, https://doi.org/10.1787/5c8d8887-en. [32]

OECD (2022), *Multi-dimensional Review of the Dominican Republic: Towards Greater Well-being for All*, OECD Development Pathways, OECD Publishing, Paris, https://doi.org/10.1787/560c12bf-en. [34]

OECD (2022), *OECD Guidelines for Citizen Participation Processes*, OECD Public Governance Reviews, OECD Publishing, Paris, https://doi.org/10.1787/f765caf6-en. [108]

OECD (2022), *OECD Investment Tax Incentives Database – 2022 Update: Tax incentives for sustainable development (brochure)*, OECD Publishing, Paris, https://www.oecd.org/investment/investment-policy/oecd-investment-tax-incentives-database-2022-update-brochure.pdf. [37]

OECD (2022), *Tax Incentives and the Global Minimum Corporate Tax: Reconsidering Tax Incentives after the GloBE Rules*, OECD Publishing, Paris, https://doi.org/10.1787/25d30b96-en. [39]

OECD (2022), *Tax Morale II: Building Trust between Tax Administrations and Large Businesses*, OECD Publishing, Paris, https://doi.org/10.1787/7587f25c-en. [102]

OECD (2022), *Tax Policy and Gender Equality: A Stocktake of Country Approaches*, OECD Publishing, Paris, https://doi.org/10.1787/b8177aea-en. [62]

OECD (2022), *World Observatory on Subnational Government Finance and Investment (SNG-WOFI) (database)*, https://www.sng-wofi.org/. [12]

OECD (2019), *Tax Morale: What Drives People and Businesses to Pay Tax?*, OECD Publishing, Paris, https://doi.org/10.1787/f3d8ea10-en. [29]

OECD (2015), *Recommendation of the Council on Budgetary Governance*, OECD Publishing, Paris, https://legalinstruments.oecd.org/en/instruments/OECD-LEGAL-0410. [13]

OECD (Forthcoming), *Tax Morale Policy Brief.* [95]

OECD et al. (2024), *Revenue Statistics in Latin America and the Caribbean 2024*, OECD Publishing, Paris, https://doi.org/10.1787/33e226ae-en. [22]

OECD et al. (2024), *The Role of the G20 in Promoting Green And Just Transitions*, OECD Publishing, Paris, https://doi.org/10.1787/548e71cd-en. [18]

OECD et al. (2023), *Latin American Economic Outlook 2023: Investing in Sustainable Development*, OECD Publishing, Paris, https://doi.org/10.1787/8c93ff6e-en. [38]

OECD et al. (2023), *Revenue Statistics in Latin America and the Caribbean 2023*, OECD Publishing, Paris, https://doi.org/10.1787/a7640683-en. [35]

OECD et al. (2022), *Latin American Economic Outlook 2022: Towards a Green and Just Transition*, OECD Publishing, Paris, https://doi.org/10.1787/3d5554fc-en. [20]

OECD et al. (2021), *Latin American Economic Outlook 2021: Working Together for a Better Recovery*, OECD Publishing, Paris, https://doi.org/10.1787/5fedabe5-en. [100]

OECD et al. (2020), *Latin American Economic Outlook 2020: Digital Transformation for Building Back Better*, OECD Publishing, Paris, https://doi.org/10.1787/e6e864fb-en. [73]

OECD et al. (2019), *Latin American Economic Outlook 2019: Development in Transition*, OECD Publishing, Paris, https://doi.org/10.1787/g2g9ff18-en. [15]

OECD/CAF/ECLAC (2015), *Latin American Economic Outlook 2015: Education, Skills and Innovation for Development*, OECD Publishing, Paris, https://doi.org/10.1787/leo-2015-en. [14]

OECD/The World Bank (2023), *Health at a Glance: Latin America and the Caribbean 2023*, OECD Publishing, Paris, https://doi.org/10.1787/532b0e2d-en. [47]

Ormeño Pérez, R. (2017), "Comprendiendo el cumplimiento tributario de los individuos: Una revisión bibliográfica", *Revista de Estudios Tributarios*, Vol. 17, pp. 199-226, https://revistas.uchile.cl/index.php/RET/article/view/46987. [103]

PAHO (2023), "Health taxes", Pan American Health Organization, https://www.paho.org/en/topics/health-taxes. [45]

PAHO (2022), "Seminar: Health Taxes Policies in Latin America and the Caribbean: Are we making progress?", Pan American Health Organization, https://www.paho.org/en/events/seminar-health-taxes-policies-latin-america-and-caribbean-are-we-making-progress. [49]

Pessino, C. et al. (2023), "Distributional Effects of Taxation in Latin America", *IDB Working Papers*, No. 01534, Inter-American Development Bank, Washington, DC, https://doi.org/10.18235/0005230. [25]

Powell, A. and O. Valencia (2023), *Dealing with Debt: Less Risk for More Growth in Latin America and the Caribbean*, Inter-American Development Bank, Washington, DC, https://doi.org/10.18235/0004707. [71]

Raga, S. (2022), *Fiscal multipliers: A review of fiscal stimulus options and impact on developing countries*, Supporting Economic Transformation, https://set.odi.org/wp-content/uploads/2022/01/Fiscal-multipliers-review.pdf. [7]

Rasteletti, A. and E. Saravia (2023), *Tax expenditure and evasion in the value added tax in Latin America*, Hacienda Pública Española/Review of Public Economics, https://hpe-rpe.org/ief/109/forthcoming-articles/5418/tax-expenditure-and-evasion-in-the-value-added-tax-in-latin-america.pdf. [30]

Restrepo, J. (2020), “How big are fiscal multipliers in Latin America?”, *IMF Working Papers*, No. 20/17, International Monetary Fund, Washington, DC, https://doi.org/10.5089/9781513526836.001. [6]

RICYT (2023), *Network for Science and Technology Indicators – Ibero-American and Inter-American*, https://www.ricyt.org/en/. [82]

Romer, C. and D. Romer (2018), “Phillips Lecture – Why Some Times are Different: Macroeconomic Policy and the Aftermath of Financial Crises”, *Economica*, Vol. 85/337, pp. 1-40. [70]

Salgado, M. and G. Ugarte (2024), *Moral tributaria y sus determinantes en el mundo y en Chile*, Centro de Estudios Públicos, https://static.cepchile.cl/uploads/cepchile/2024/02/pder686_Salgado-y-Ugarte.pdf. [106]

Sánchez-Romero, L. et al. (2016), “Projected Impact of Mexico’s Sugar-Sweetened Beverage Tax Policy on Diabetes and Cardiovascular Disease: A Modeling Study”, *PLoS Medicine*, https://doi.org/10.1371/journal.pmed.1002158. [50]

Sassi, F. et al. (2023), “Introduction”, in Lauer, J. et al. (eds.), *Health Taxes: Policy and Practice*, World Scientific, https://doi.org/10.1142/9781800612396_0001. [44]

Torgler, B. (2005), “Tax morale and direct democracy”, *European Journal of Political Economy*, Vol. 21/2, pp. 525-531, https://doi.org/10.1016/j.ejpoleco.2004.08.002. [93]

UNCTAD (2024), *Financing for Sustainable Development Report 2024*, UN Trade and Development, https://unctad.org/publication/financing-sustainable-development-report-2024?trk=public_post_comment-text. [10]

UNDP (2024), *The Missing Piece: Valuing women’s unrecognized contribution to the economy*, https://www.undp.org/latin-america/blog/missing-piece-valuing-womens-unrecognized-contribution-economy. [66]

Valencia, O. and J. Camilo Díaz (2024), “Leveraging AI to Transform Macroeconomic and Fiscal Policymaking in Latin America and the Caribbean”, *IADB blog*, Inter-American Development Bank, Washington, DC, https://blogs.iadb.org/gestion-fiscal/en/ai-to-transform-macroeconomic-and-fiscal-policymaking/. [107]

Warwick, R. et al. (2022), “The redistributive power of cash transfers vs VAT exemptions: A multi-country study”, *World Development*, Vol. 151, https://doi.org/10.1016/j.worlddev.2021.105742. [26]

World Bank (2023), *States and Trends of Carbon Pricing Dashboard*, World Bank Group, Washington, DC, https://carbonpricingdashboard.worldbank.org/compliance/instrument-detail. [56]

World Bank (2023), *World Bank Indicators (database)*, https://data.worldbank.org/indicator. [16]

World Bank (2022), *International Debt Statistics*, World Bank, Washington, DC, https://www.worldbank.org/en/programs/debt-statistics/ids. [76]

WVS (2022), *WVS Database - 7th wave (2017-2022) (database)*, http://worldvaluessurvey.org. [94]

3 Rallying financial market resources for development

This chapter provides a comprehensive analysis of financial markets in Latin America and the Caribbean, highlighting their potential role towards achieving sustainable development. It examines the region's financial landscape, assessing the banking sector's depth, accessibility, efficiency, risks, and solvency. The chapter then identifies gaps in financial inclusion among households and firms, and opportunities for expanding access, such as digital innovations and financial literacy education. It considers the role of public development finance institutions in mobilising resources towards development goals. The chapter next explores the region's capital markets, focusing on how their development can foster liquidity and inclusivity, broaden access to markets, improve solvency and manage risks. It underscores the crucial importance of regulatory frameworks in nurturing these markets. The chapter concludes by examining LAC's position in international debt markets and regional financial integration.

Infographic 3.1. Financial markets can mobilise additional resources from the private sector in LAC

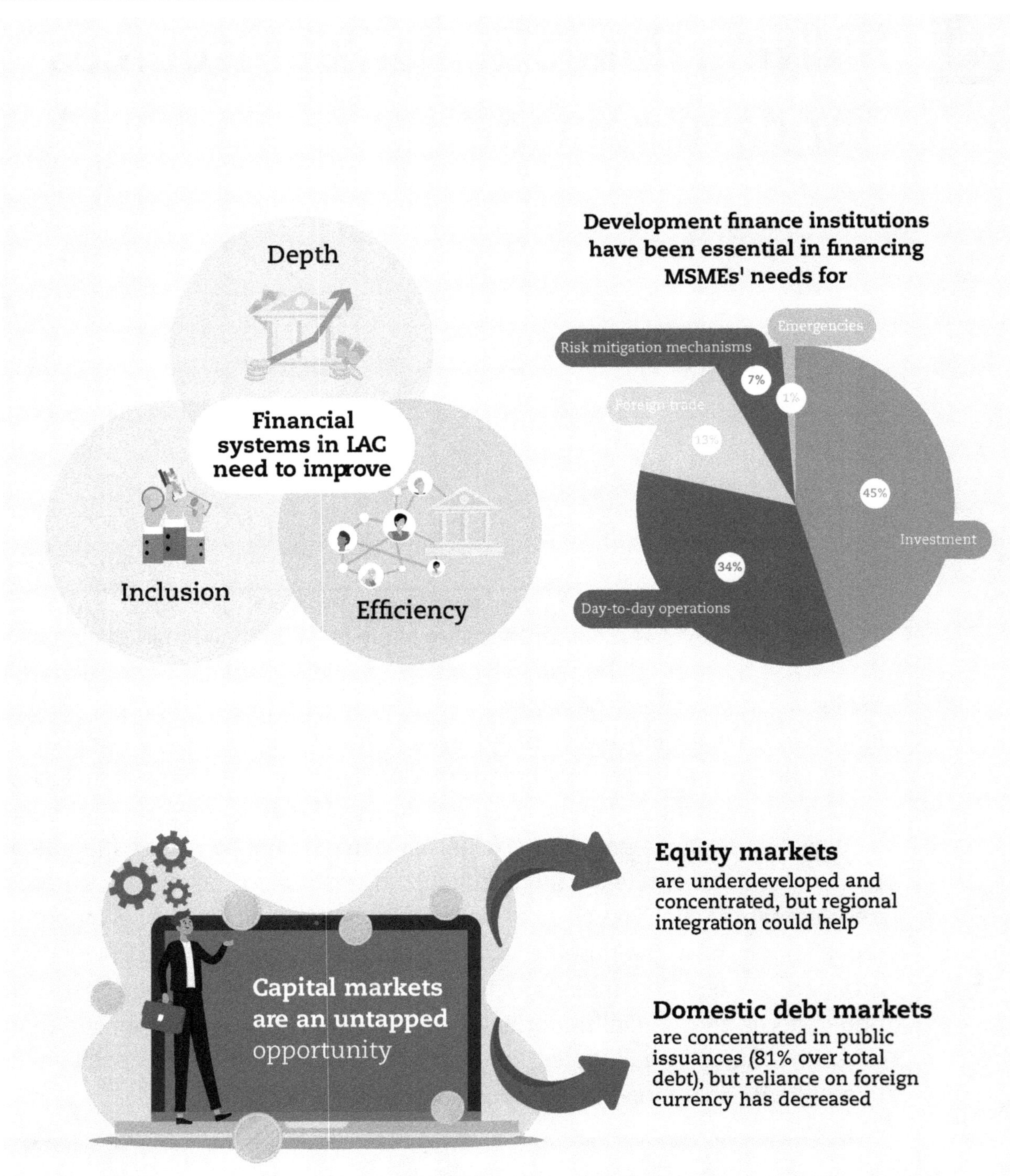

Introduction

A well-functioning financial system has the potential to mobilise and channel private resources towards development objectives. A developed financial system provides access to essential financial services such as loans, saving products and insurance for individuals and businesses, allowing them to improve or smooth consumption and increase investment in physical and human capital. Furthermore, the financial system plays a pivotal role in promoting entrepreneurship and fostering job creation, thereby improving economic welfare, reducing inequality and fostering economic growth (Levine, 2018[1]; World Bank, 2008[2]; OECD, 2020[3]). A fundamental condition for achieving these objectives is to ensure well-regulated and supervised financial markets, as this should foster soundness and stability, and mitigate vulnerabilities to prevent systemic risks (Boikos, Panagiotidis and Voucharas, 2022[4]; Strobbe, Nie and Rab, 2023[5]).

Financial markets have experienced significant growth over the last three decades in Latin America and the Caribbean (LAC) in terms of volume, participants, instruments, and products. Households have greatly increased their participation in financial markets through access to savings accounts and borrowing, although a large proportion of informal households still do not have a credit account. The expansion of the financial sector has benefited the growth and development of large companies, including the largest companies. However, micro, small and medium-sized enterprises (MSMEs) in the LAC region still face challenges in accessing financial markets, where they face the second-largest financing gap of any region in the developing world (OECD et al., 2023[6]). Regarding the development of capital markets, while a large majority of LAC countries face limited financial access to private companies through domestic equity and fixed-income markets, the region has increased its presence in international markets through debt issuance and the use of depositary receipts, and it continues to work towards regional financial integration.

This chapter explores the current status of financial markets in LAC and their role in achieving the region's development objectives. It discusses the region's banking system in terms of depth, access and efficiency, alongside the issues of risk and solvency. This overview of the region's financial development landscape is followed by an examination of gaps in financial inclusion, the impact of digital innovation in removing barriers to access and the crucial role of financial education. The chapter then analyses the region's capital markets, emphasising that their development can enhance liquidity and inclusion and increase access for medium-sized companies, especially in conditions of high solvency and balanced risk. It highlights the importance of regulation and concludes by exploring LAC's role in international debt markets and efforts to transcend national borders in financial market development via regional financial integration.

The functioning of the banking system in LAC

Within the financial system, banks are the main intermediaries for households and business. In regions with underdeveloped capital markets, such as Latin America, banking credit is particularly important since it serves as the primary source of financing for firms (Christiano Silva, Miranda Tabak and Tetzner Laiz, 2021[7]). Enhancing financial inclusion for small and medium-sized enterprises (SMEs) and households within the banking system, and developing more diversified and efficient financial markets, are critical imperatives for driving inclusive development in LAC (Arellano et al., 2018[8]).

To assess the functioning of the banking system, three aspects are commonly considered: depth, access, and efficiency (Čihák et al., 2012[9]). Depth measures the size of financial markets; access examines the extent to which individuals can use them; and efficiency evaluates the system's effectiveness in delivering services. This approach can capture the key features of financial systems and the evolution of the financial structure in the region (De la Torre et al., 2011[10]).

A review of financial development in LAC: Depth, access and efficiency

Depth

Despite improvements over the last decade, financial depth in LAC remains low. Domestic credit to the private sector has doubled over the last 20 years, reaching 50% of gross domestic product (GDP) in 2022. Despite this growth, LAC lags behind regions such as the European Union (85%) and East Asia (170%), with depth similar to the levels of South Asia and sub-Saharan Africa (Figure 3.1). Domestic credit is mainly provided by banks. However, bank deposits as a percentage of GDP stood at 55.1% for LAC In 2021, compared to 99.3% for OECD countries (Figure 3.1). These figures highlight the importance of addressing barriers to financial inclusion for individuals and businesses. Although financial depth correlates positively with economic growth and stability, research suggests that there is a threshold beyond which its benefits diminish, notably when private sector credit reaches 80-100% of GDP (Almarzoqi, Naceur and Kotak, 2015[11]; Arcand, Berkes and Panizza, 2012[12]; Easterly, Islam and Stiglitz, 2000[13]). Similarly, rapid expansion of the financial sector enhances risk-taking abilities but in the absence of a strong regulatory and institutional framework based on international standards and practices, it can also amplify systemic risks, heightening vulnerability to severe market downturns (Rajan, 2006[14]).

Figure 3.1. Domestic credit to the private sector as percentage of GDP, and financial depth in LAC, 2022

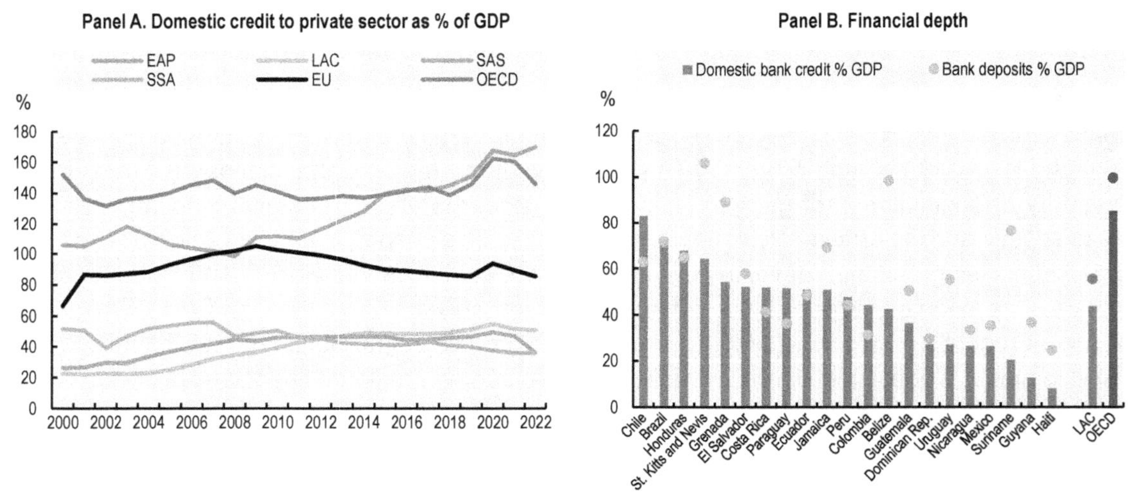

Note: Figures for bank deposits as percentage of GDP correspond to 2021 due to data availability. EAP = East Asia and the Pacific; SSA = Sub-Saharan Africa and SAS = South Asia.
Source: Authors' elaboration based on (World Bank, 2022[15]).

StatLink https://stat.link/eapqt0

Financial depth exhibits heterogeneity across countries in the region. Countries such as Chile and Brazil exhibit greater levels of depth, with domestic private credit to GDP – an indicator of financial systems' contribution to the real economy – standing at 83% and 71% respectively. In contrast, the ratio stands at 12% in Guyana and 8% in Haiti. In terms of bank deposits relative to GDP – an indicator of households and businesses' savings levels –, the highest values are recorded in St. Kitts and Nevis (105%) and Belize (98%), while the lowest are seen in the Dominican Republic (29%) and Haiti (24%).

Savings in LAC have historically remained low, constraining credit provision and capital accumulation. Over the last two decades, gross saving levels in LAC have consistently been modest, reaching a peak of 22% of GDP in 2006 and stabilising in 2022 at 18%. In comparison, the level of gross savings as a percentage of GDP in 2022 stood at 38% in East Asia and the Pacific, at 25% in the European Union and at 23% in the OECD countries (World Bank, 2024[16]). Savings play a crucial role in providing funds for credit and facilitating investments. A rise in savings typically leads to increased investment opportunities (David, Goncalves and Werner, 2020[17]). Persistent low national saving rates are a significant constraint for capital accumulation in LAC (Cavallo and Pedemonte, 2015[18]).

Access

The LAC region has seen an improvement in access to financial services for both households and MSMEs. Nonetheless, challenges persist, such as high costs, financial illiteracy, informality, and regulatory hurdles. Overcoming these barriers is crucial to ensuring broader access to financial services and for promoting inclusive economic growth across LAC.

Households

Account ownership has doubled in LAC over a decade, but disparities in access to formal financial services and reliance on informal borrowing persist. Access to saving and borrowing instruments enables households to manage their finances, reducing their economic vulnerability by smoothing consumption over time and facilitating wealth accumulation. The share of LAC individuals aged 15+ reporting ownership of an account at a formal financial institution increased from an average of 29.6% in 2011 to 57.2% in 2021 (World Bank, 2021[19]; 2008[2]). However, significant disparities persist across the region. As of 2021, Chile led in access to formal saving mechanisms, at 87% of its adult population, while Nicaragua lagged with just 26%. This contrasts with OECD countries, where on average 93.7% of the age 15+ population report having an account at a formal financial institution (Figure 3.2, Panel A). As for borrowing, Latin Americans still frequently turn to informal lending sources. On average, 42% of the region's population take out loans, yet only 20.1% do so from formal financial institutions (Figure 3.2, Panel B).

Figure 3.2. Access to formal saving and borrowing mechanisms in LAC, 2021

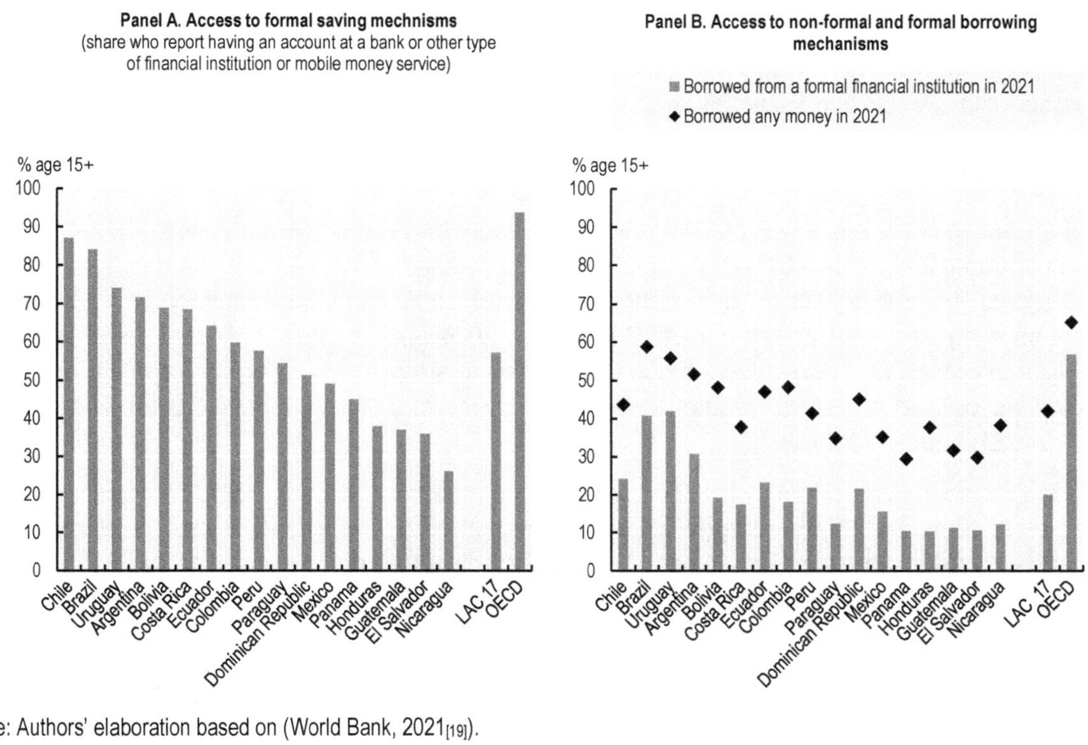

Source: Authors' elaboration based on (World Bank, 2021[19]).

StatLink https://stat.link/7iuvw5

Advancing financial access requires addressing several barriers. These include high transaction costs, lack of access to banking infrastructure, lack of quality products, limited scope of credit scores, regulatory hurdles and the need for financial literacy and digital skills (World Bank, 2021[19]). In 2021, among adults in LAC without an account, 59% on average said it was because they did not have sufficient resources and 55% declared that financial services were too expensive (Figure 3.3).

Figure 3.3. Reasons declared by adults in LAC for not having a bank account, 2021

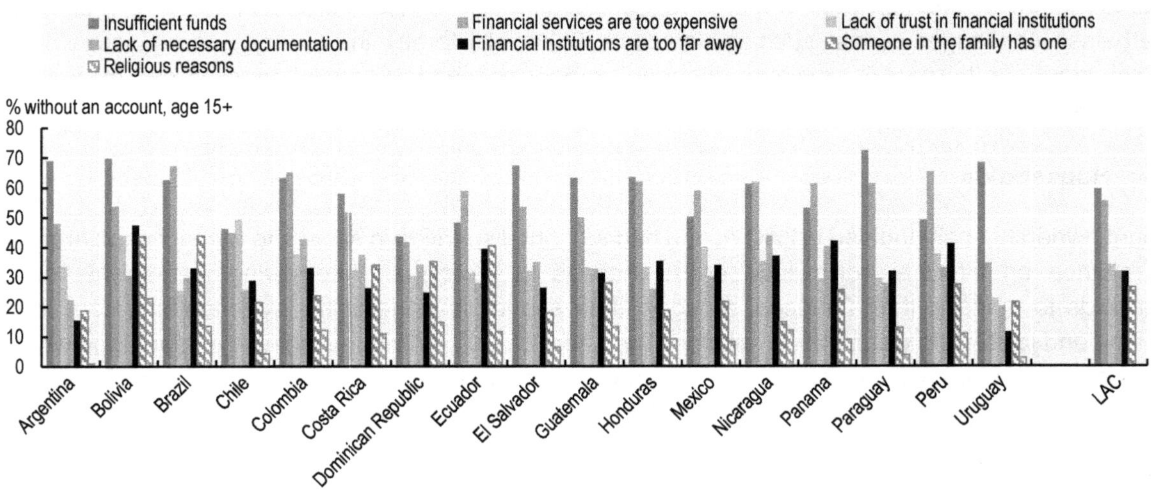

Source: Authors' elaboration based on (World Bank, 2021[19]).

StatLink https://stat.link/u02zct

Despite improvements in access to financial accounts across socio-economic groups in LAC, gender disparity has amplified. While access gaps based on income, labour market participation, education and age have all shown reductions, gender disparity in financial account ownership widened by three percentage points between 2011 and 2021. Women are seven percentage points less likely than men to have an account in LAC (World Bank, 2021[19]).

Enterprises

Improving access to finance is key for MSMEs, which account for 60% of the employed population in LAC and contribute about 25% to its GDP (Herrera, 2020[20]). Providing businesses with the necessary financial resources allows them to invest in new technologies, hire staff, increase inventory and expand their operational capacity and productivity (OECD/CAF/SELA, 2024[21]) (Chapter 1). Access to other financial products, like insurance and derivatives, helps businesses to survive and safeguard against unforeseen events such as natural disasters, market volatility or operational disruptions (Morgan and Pontines, 2014[22]; Bruhn and Love, 2013[23]).

Firms use the financial system mostly for deposits and as a means of payment. 89% of small firms, 94.3% of medium-sized firms and 96.6% of large firms in the region have a checking or savings account in the formal financial system. However, less than 15% of total credit in the region goes to MSMEs, compared to OECD countries where it exceeds 25% (World Bank, 2024[24]).

The use of the financial system in LAC is proportional to the size of the company. For instance, on average, the share of small, medium-sized and large companies in the region with a bank loan or line of credit is 40.9%, 56.7% and 69.0%, respectively. In contrast, the value of collateral needed for a loan, expressed as a percentage of the loan, declines with the size of the firm (200.9% for small firms, 172.1% for medium-sized firms and 155.1% for large firms) (Figure 3.4).

Figure 3.4. Financial inclusion in LAC by firm size, 2009-20

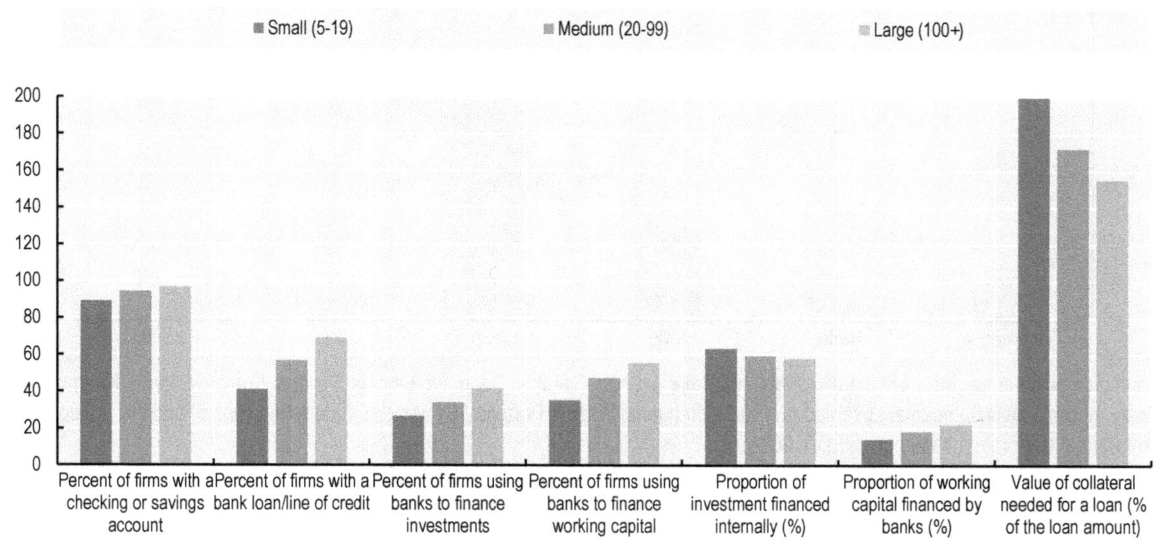

Note: Available surveys, such as the World Bank Surveys, sample between 1 200 and 1 800 firms for larger economies, 360 for medium-sized economies and 150 for smaller economies. The firm size is defined in terms of employment.
Source: Authors' elaboration based on (World Bank, 2024[24]).

StatLink https://stat.link/eiorpu

Formal MSMEs face difficulties in accessing credit due to the high cost of financing. They typically pay higher interest rates than large firms due to their riskier profile. Around 30% of MSMEs in the region face credit constraints (IFC, 2017[25]). In 2022, the spread of interest rates between loans to SMEs and large firms was notably high in LAC countries (Figure 3.5). Apart from Mexico, where the spread has decreased since 2020, the rest of the region's countries have experienced increases. Current spread levels in LAC exceed those of high-income countries (0.84%) (OECD, 2024[26]). Informality also increases the cost of financing. Borrowers often lack documents like financial statements and tax declarations, which limits the information they can provide to lenders. This can result in higher interest rates being imposed to mitigate the risks associated with adverse selection (Herrera, 2020[20]).

Figure 3.5. Interest rate spreads between loans to SMEs and to large firms, 2020-22

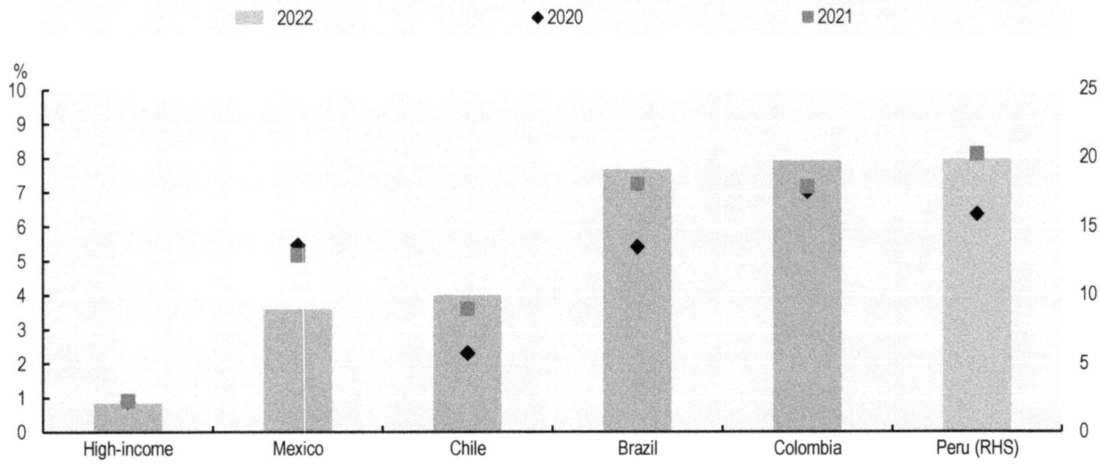

Note: High Income countries include Australia, Belgium, Canada, Chile, Czechia, Denmark, Estonia, Finland, France, Greece, Hungary, Ireland, Israel, Italy, Korea, Latvia, Lithuania, Luxembourg, the Netherlands, Poland, Portugal, Slovenia, Sweden, Switzerland and the United Kingdom.
Source: Authors' elaboration based on (OECD, 2024[26]).

StatLink https://stat.link/f1jn47

Lack of collateral is a main barrier for the region's MSMEs in terms of accessing credit. For instance, collateral is needed by 9 out of 10 SMEs in Colombia to access bank credit. There is also a mismatch between the types of collateral demanded by lenders and the assets typically held by SMEs. Approximately 80% of lenders primarily request real property as collateral, while the asset base of around 75% of the region's SMEs consists of movables such as inventory and equipment (OECD, 2024[26]).

Efficiency

In 2021 the average return on assets (ROA) in the region stood at 1.6%, higher than the OECD average of 0.9% (Figure 3.6). The ROA measures a bank's net income relative to its total assets, assessing the ability of the bank's management to generate profits from its asset base. While the ROA may be used as a measure of efficiency, high profitability can signal inefficiencies within the financial system and more generally in the economy (e.g. lack of reliable information on households and firms). While there is a high heterogeneity across LAC countries, the region's net interest margin (NIM), at 5%, was superior to the OECD average of 1.7%. The NIM measures the difference between interest income from assets like loans and securities, and interest paid to depositors for savings. A high credit spread may limit access to credit, making it costly for both individuals and businesses, and discourages savings. Due mainly to their high net interest margins, banks in emerging economies may be more profitable than those in high income countries, rendering them more attractive to investors but also limiting access to credit (Arellano et al., 2018[8]). Profitability in the region is not driven by high interest rates, which had a limited direct impact in Brazil, Chile, Colombia, Mexico and Peru (IMF, 2023[27]). Previous studies show that it is rather associated with limited revenue diversification, high concentration, higher macroeconomic risks and weak legal and regulatory systems (Saona, 2016[28]; Bejar et al., 2022[29]).

High banking costs are prevalent in the region. In 2021, banks in LAC faced an overhead cost to total assets ratio of 3.7%, higher than the OECD average of 1.4%. This indicator evaluates the operational efficiency of a bank by quantifying the magnitude of its operating expenses relative to its total assets. Levels observed may be attributed to several factors and they differ across LAC countries. These include premiums associated with greater underlying macroeconomic risks, high levels of informality, tighter and inefficient regulatory requirements and the absence of strong competitive pressures within the banking sector (Maudos and Solís,

2009[30]; Gelos, 2006[31]). High overhead costs in banks can lower their profitability, causing them to charge higher fees or to offer less favourable terms to businesses and households. They may also limit banks' ability to invest in new technologies and services that could benefit users.

Figure 3.6. Banking system profitability in selected LAC countries, 2021

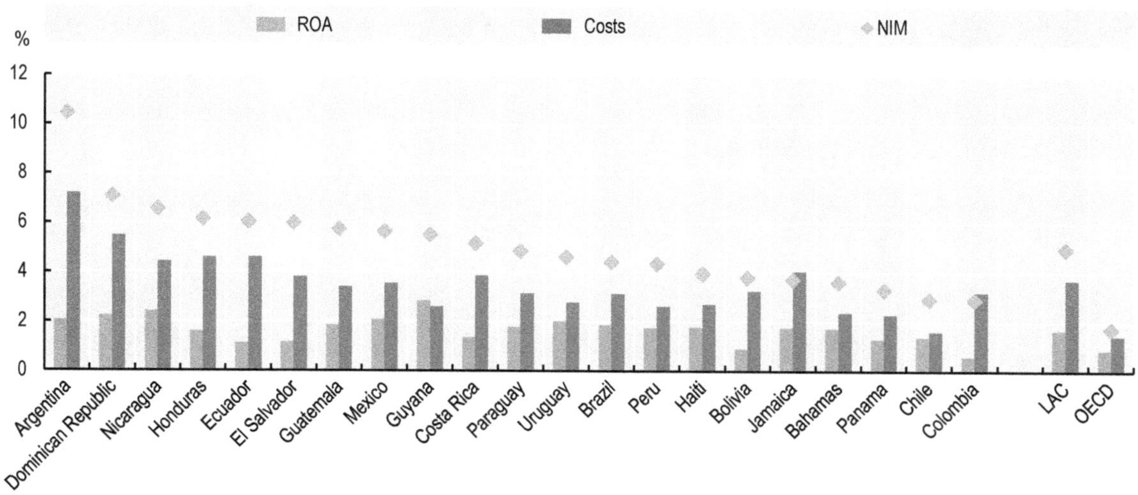

Note: ROA = return on assets, Costs = overhead costs to total assets and NIM = net interest margin.
Source: Authors' elaboration based on (World Bank, 2022[15]).

StatLink https://stat.link/b2j9cz

Banking competition policies contribute to lower financial services costs and are associated with fintech emergence. Markets with high levels of competition and low entry barriers not only can reduce the cost of financial services, but they also tend to offer more credit (Carlson, Correia and Luck, 2022[32]). They are associated with lower lending spreads and fees, and with a broader offer of financial products (Joaquim, Van Doornik and Haas, 2023[33]). Banking competition also promotes digital transformation and increases investment in research and development (R&D), improving efficiency and customer service. In Brazil and Mexico, for instance, banking innovation, lower NIMs and lower fees in the payments segment are associated with less concentrated markets in the context of fintech emergence (Bejar et al., 2022[29]). Furthermore, in countries where transparency within the banking sector is encouraged, the banking industry tends to be characterised by higher levels of competitiveness and decreasing interest margins (Abuselidze, 2021[34]).

Risks and solvency of the banking system

A sound financial regulatory framework and a well-supervised financial system are critical for minimising the risk of financial crises and financial system fragility, while also promoting orderly financial sector development and enhancing its contribution to the real economy. Such regulation is particularly essential in emerging economies and developing countries to support sustainable growth and avoid past experiences of banking crises and economic downturns.

The banking system in LAC maintains strong capitalisation, enhancing stability and an adequate environment to ensure access to finance. In 2022, the capital adequacy ratio of banks in the region stood at 16.9%, slightly below the 19.9% observed in OECD countries and above the regulatory minimum of 8% stipulated by the Basel framework (BIS, 2020[35]). National authorities in countries such as Brazil, Colombia, Peru, and Argentina require banks to maintain higher requirement levels than the Basel minimum requirement (OECD, 2010[36]). This indicates a robust capital position that provides a buffer against financial shocks. Regarding the impact of higher capital requirements on lending, it has been associated in Peru with lower credit growth only in the short term, with insignificant effect approximately after half a year. This effect is stronger during periods of lower GDP growth and for less profitable and less capitalised banks (Fang et al., 2022[37]).

High liquidity levels in LAC compared to advanced economies have supported the resilience of the banking system. The ratio of liquid assets to deposits and short-term funding remained robust in 2022 at 57.2%, surpassing the OECD average of 50.5% (Figure 3.7). High liquidity levels reflect the ability of banks to meet short-term obligations and cover unexpected liquidity shocks.

Figure 3.7. Banking system soundness indicators in LAC, 2022

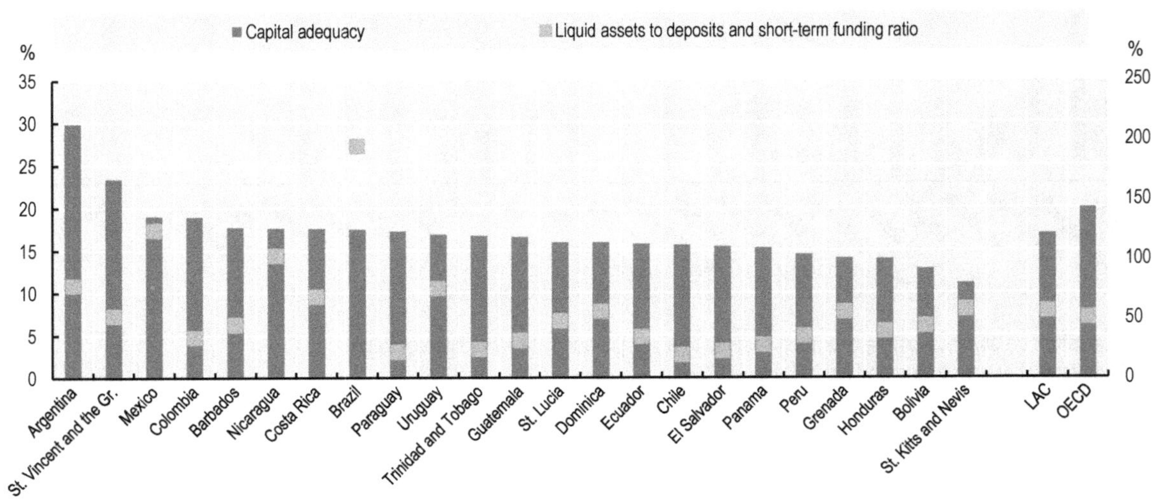

Note: Capital adequacy is displayed on the left axis. Liquid assets to deposits and short-term funding ratio is displayed on the right axis.
Source: Authors' elaboration based on (IMF, 2022[38]).

StatLink https://stat.link/al2wq1

Adapting Basel III standards to the specific conditions of LAC countries is essential for fostering financial system stability without impeding development in the region. Although the adoption of Basel regulations is optional for the large majority of emerging economies, and Basel III recommendations were calibrated primarily for advanced economies, several developing countries are in the process of adapting them to their local regulatory frameworks. Over half of the countries in LAC have incorporated some form of Basel III into their banking regulation framework (Galindo and Izquierdo, 2024[39]). However, developing and emerging markets countries exhibit specific characteristics that should be acknowledged, such as restricted access to international capital markets, underdeveloped domestic financial markets, high macroeconomic volatility and challenges related to transparency, regulatory effectiveness and institutional capacity (Beck and Rojas-Suarez, 2019[40]). For instance, Basel III implementation may impact lending for infrastructure projects, as the tightening of the large exposure rule restricts lending from small and domestic banks, and as tighter capital requirements for these projects increase lending costs. Additionally, liquidity requirements compel banks to align long-term lending with long-term funding and to hold more liquid assets for project financing, which is challenging due to limited access to capital markets in the region (Beck, 2018[41]). Finally, most assets and firms in LAC, especially SMEs, do not necessarily have the ratings or market information needed to adopt internal models to quantify their risk-weighted assets, and therefore the required capital could be higher than that required using the standardised approach.

Credit quality

The banking system in the region continues to manage credit risk effectively, demonstrating preparedness for economic downturns and potential for increased lending capacity. In 2022, the ratio of non-performing loans (NPL) to gross loans in the region stood at 4.8%, above the OECD average of 2.2% (Figure 3.8). However, this figure is largely influenced by elevated levels in five Caribbean countries; when they are excluded, the NPL ratio aligns with OECD trends, at 2.5%. In addition, NPL provisions in LAC remain adequate at 122%, compared to 70.6% for the OECD, while levels in some Caribbean countries are particularly low. NPL provisions indicate the level of preparedness for potential loan defaults, as they represent banks' available resources to absorb potential losses from non-performing loans.

Figure 3.8. Credit quality in LAC, 2022

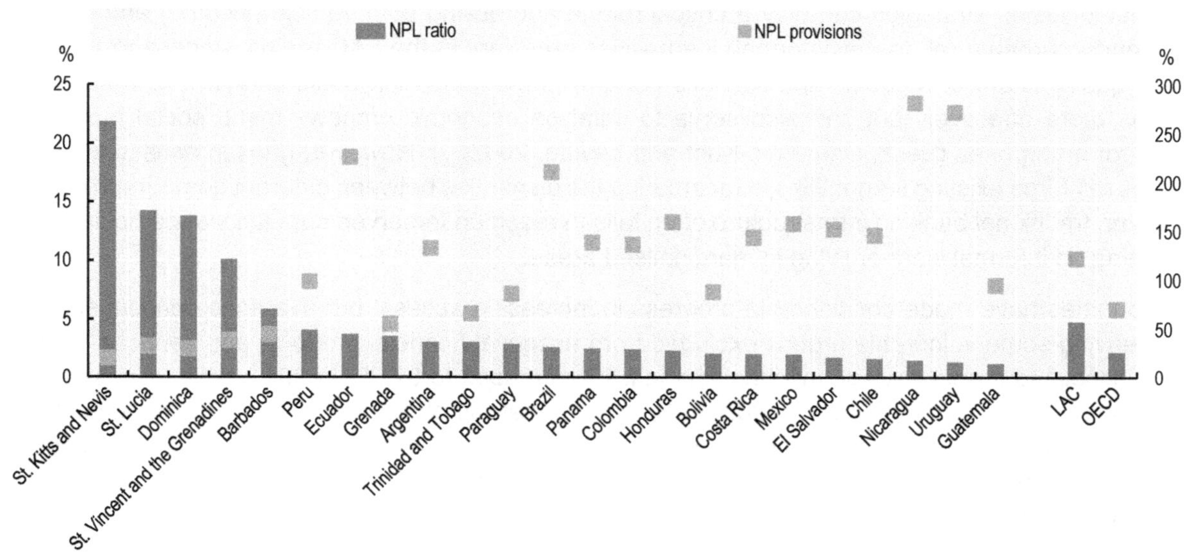

Note: NPL ratio is displayed on the left axis and NPL provisions on the right axis.
Source: Authors' elaboration based on (IMF, 2022[38]).

StatLink https://stat.link/fgw37b

Challenges and opportunities for greater financial inclusion

Financial inclusion is a multidimensional concept encompassing at least three key dimensions: access, usage and quality of financial services and products. The access dimension refers to making financial services and products available to all, especially underserved and lower-income populations. Over the last decade, all countries in the LAC region have made significant progress in terms of financial access. However, persistent vertical and horizontal inequalities leave some sectors marginalised and unable to access key financial products (Chapter 1). The usage dimension assesses how people engage with these services, measuring factors such as the regularity and frequency of transactions. This dimension is experiencing accelerated growth in LAC due to the proliferation of innovative digital solutions, which have exponentially increased digital payments in the region. The quality dimension of financial inclusion covers the ability of financial services and products to meet the needs of consumers, as well as clients' awareness and understanding of financial products. This involves promoting financial literacy, implementing strong consumer protection frameworks, and offering responsible financial products tailored to individual needs (OECD, 2022[42]). In this dimension, LAC countries still face significant challenges in terms of financial education, which is crucial for people to better understand, responsibly use and benefit from financial products and services.

Increased financial inclusion, when paired with quality financial products and services, can bring significant benefits for households and firms in LAC, driving economic growth and people's well-being (OECD, 2022[42]). Enhanced access to high-quality financial products and services, within the context of a strong financial consumer protection framework and with adequate levels of financial literacy, can allow households to increase their savings, smooth consumption and invest in housing, education and health, leading to improved living standards and reduced poverty (Banerjee and Duflo, 2011[43]). For firms, especially SMEs, quality financial inclusion facilitates access to credit, enabling investment in technology and expansion, which boosts productivity and job creation. At the societal level, broader financial inclusion with quality can contribute to reducing income inequality, promoting resource allocation efficiency, and fostering overall economic stability and resilience (Pal and Bandyopadhyayv, 2022[44]).

Gaps in access leave financial services out of reach for the most vulnerable

Financial inclusion strategies can play a critical role in addressing both vertical (income) and horizontal (e.g. gender, urban/rural, formal/informal) inequalities prevalent in the LAC region. Access to and usage of high-quality financial products and services not only can enable individuals and firms to manage their finances more effectively but can also serve to catalyse economic empowerment, social mobility and growth for enterprises (Beck, Demirgüç-Kunt and Levine, 2007[45]). However, gaps in access to financial services reinforce existing inequalities, exacerbating the disparities between different demographic groups. Moreover, traditional banking infrastructure often fails to reach underserved populations, particularly those depending on informal work or living in marginalised areas.

LAC countries have made considerable progress in increasing access, but averages conceal significant gaps, leaving some vulnerable groups excluded from essential financial products and services. As noted above, access to formal savings mechanisms in LAC increased to 57.2% in 2021, while access to loans in formal financial institutions grew to 20.1%. However, analysis of factors such as income level and the informal or formal nature of employment still reveals significant gaps in access. Access can be improved by identifying these gaps and removing barriers that prevent people from using financial services, alongside efforts to increase financial literacy.

Low income and poverty

Low income remains a significant barrier to accessing high-quality financial products and services in LAC. Financial products and services are both more accessible and more diverse for households in the richest quintile, facilitating investment in real estate, education and business ventures. This ease of access is largely due to higher incomes and the availability of collateral, which together reduce perceived lending risks for financial institutions. Conversely, households in the poorest quintile often find their financial options severely limited by their lack of collateral and lower incomes. This not only restricts their immediate financial mobility but also hampers their long-term economic growth, as they are unable to invest in opportunities that could improve their economic standing (Beck and de La Torre, 2007[46]). The disparity in access to credit starkly illustrates the economic divide: in LAC countries, a reduced number of individuals from the poorest quintile had access to homeownership loans compared to the wealthiest households (Figure 3.9, Panel A). In OECD countries, 24.7% of people live in households owned with a mortgage (OECD, 2024[47]).

Poverty drastically reduces access to financial products and services in LAC. This exclusion is primarily due to strict financial criteria, such as income thresholds, robust credit histories and collateral requirements, which are often unattainable for poor individuals, many of whom depend on informal work (Beck and de La Torre, 2007[46]). Without access to credit, the poor are more likely to remain trapped in a cycle of financial instability, unable to invest in assets that could offer long-term benefits, financial security, and economic mobility (Banerjee and Duflo, 2011[43]).

Figure 3.9. Access to homeownership loans in selected LAC countries, poorest and richest quintiles

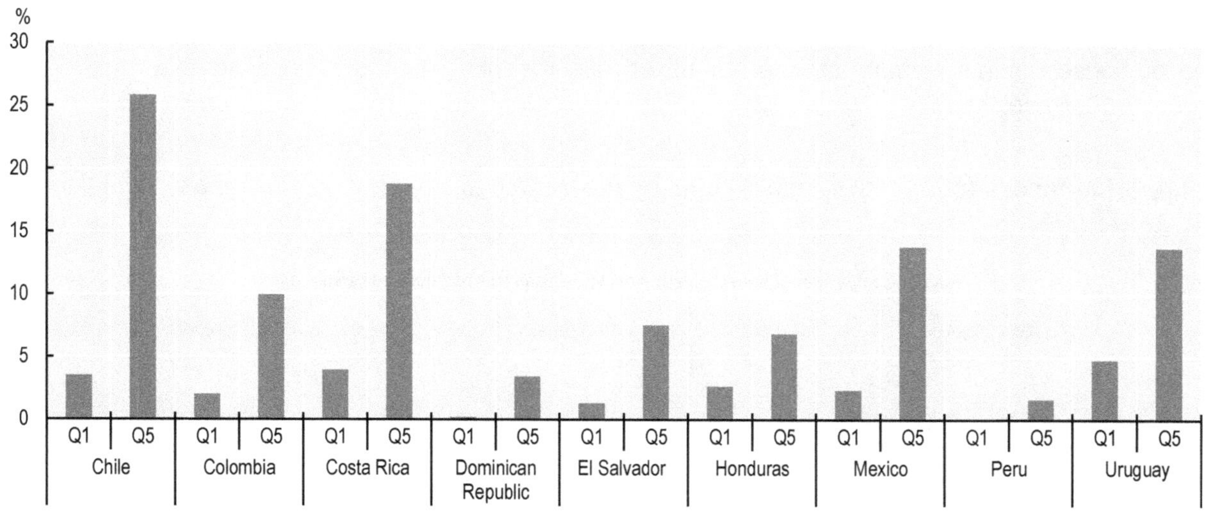

Note: This figure is based on data from household surveys conducted in the selected countries. The surveys included a question about the respondent's current housing status, with answers typically classified into three categories: homeowner, homeowner with a mortgage, or tenant. The figure represents the percentage of individuals who indicated they are homeowners currently paying a mortgage, whether financed through a public or private financial institution. The data for Chile is from 2017, Colombia 2021, Costa Rica 2021, the Dominican Republic 2018, El Salvador 2021, Mexico 2020, and Uruguay 2018.
Source: Authors' calculation based on Key Indicators of Informality based on Individuals and their Household (KIIbIH) database (OECD, 2021[48]) using national household surveys.

StatLink https://stat.link/dr1s72

The widening gap in access to financial services between the rich and the poor underscores the need for targeted financial inclusion policies. Empirical evidence has shown that financial development benefits the poor by accelerating their income growth faster than the average per capita GDP, thereby reducing income inequality (Beck, Demirgüç-Kunt and Levine, 2007[45]). Alternative credit scoring and open finance offer significant opportunities for financial inclusion. By leveraging alternative data, fintech companies can extend credit access to underserved populations. Open finance regulations in countries like Brazil, Mexico, Chile and Colombia are fostering increased competition and innovation in financial services, ultimately enhancing financial inclusion and economic participation. These regulations mandate data sharing among financial institutions, which can lead to more tailored and accessible financial products for consumers. For example, positive information from payments can complement traditional data used in credit scoring, improving the prediction of credit behaviour for typically excluded populations and SMEs (Herrera et al., 2023[49]).

Informal employment

Informal workers also face access barriers to financial products. This is primarily due to their lack of formal employment records, which are crucial for financial institutions when assessing creditworthiness, and to a scarcity of assets that can be used as collateral (Beck and de La Torre, 2007[46]). Additionally, the lower and irregular incomes often associated with informal work exacerbate these challenges, creating compounding effects that further limit access to financial products. Households with formally employed individuals typically possess a greater array of assets suitable for collateral, thereby enjoying broader access to financial products. This facilitates investments in physical capital, such as real estate, and human capital through educational advancements (Banerjee and Duflo, 2011[43]).

While in some countries, including Chile, Costa Rica and Uruguay, a relatively notable share of the population resides in households with homeownership loans, the share is considerably lower in countries like the Dominican Republic and El Salvador. Furthermore, formal households represent the highest proportion of households with homeownership loans in selected LAC countries, compared to informal households and mixed households (i.e. households with both formal and informal workers). In contrast, depending on the degree of informality across LAC countries, there is no single pattern regarding which type of household (i.e. formal, informal, or mixed) is most likely not to have a homeownership loan (Figure 3.10, Panel A).

Figure 3.10. Access to homeownership loans by the degree of households' informality in selected LAC countries

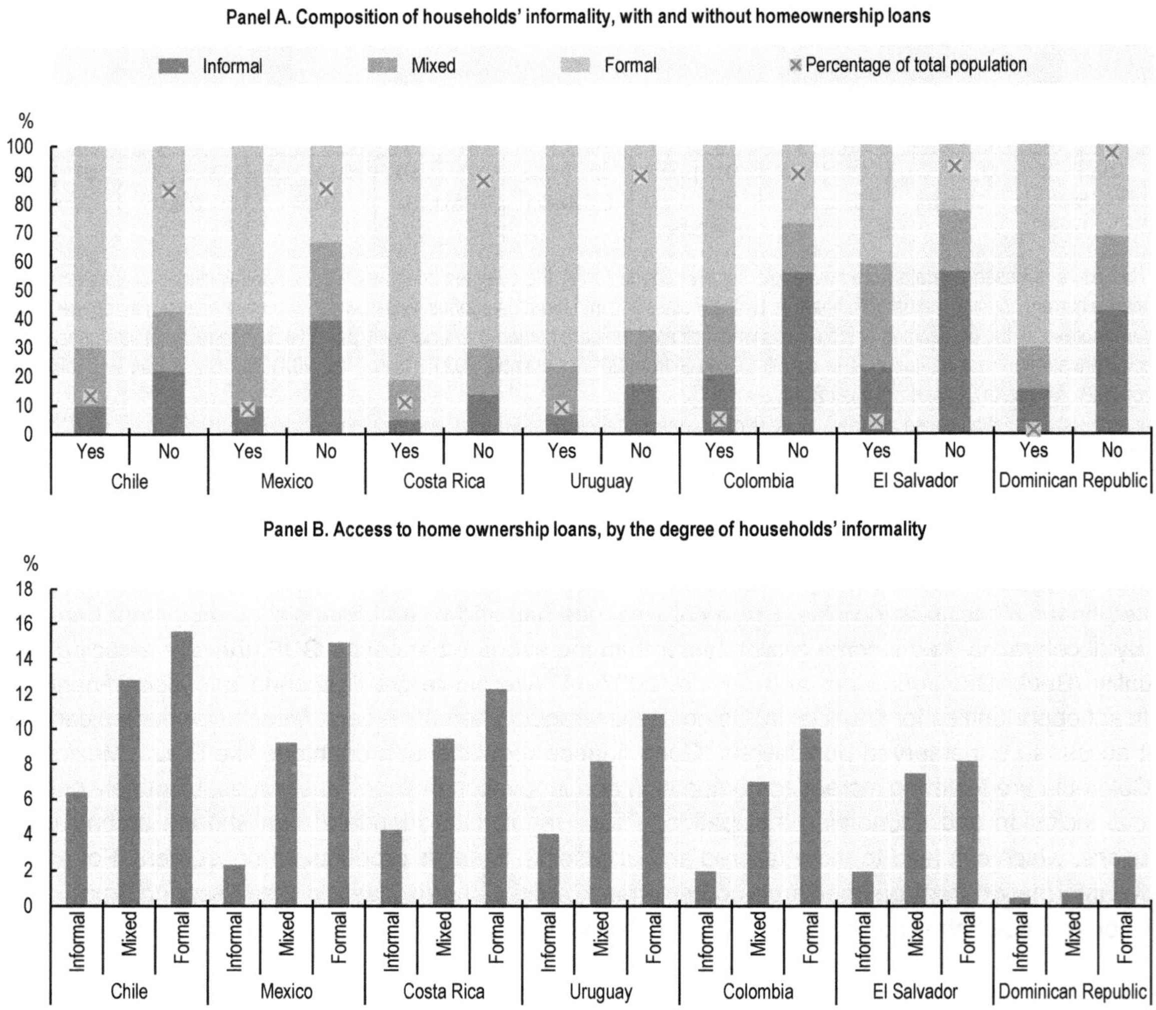

Note: The figure is based on household survey data from the selected countries. These surveys included a question about the respondent's current housing status, with responses generally categorised into three groups: homeowners, homeowners with a mortgage, and tenants. Households were classified into three types of household informality: formal households (where all workers have formal jobs), informal households (where all workers have informal jobs), and mixed households (with both formal and informal workers). The bars in the figure /represent the percentage of individuals within each household type who reported being homeowners with an active mortgage, whether financed by a public or private financial institution. The survey years are as follows: Chile (2017), Colombia (2021), Costa Rica (2021), the Dominican Republic (2018), El Salvador (2021), Mexico (2020) and Uruguay (2018).

Source: Authors' calculation based on the Key Indicators of Informality based on Individuals and their Household (KIIbIH) database (OECD, 2021[48]) and national household surveys.

StatLink https://stat.link/yu4div

Important differences exist in access to credit between formal and informal households. For instance, in Mexico, close to 15% of formal households had access to housing loans in 2020, compared to a mere 2.3% of informal households. Costa Rica also reflected this trend, with more than 12% of formal households accessing housing loans in 2021, compared to only 4.2% of informal households (Figure 3.10, Panel B).

Higher levels of financial inclusion are associated with lower informality, after controlling for GDP per capita (Figure 3.11). Formal employment promotes financial inclusion by integrating individuals into the financial system, as it typically requires employees to have bank accounts for salary deposits. With proper documentation and a banking history, these individuals are more likely to access credit and other financial products (Aurazo and Gasmi, 2024[50]). Additionally, broader access to financial services allows enterprises to secure capital, stabilize cash flow, and enhance productivity and profitability. These benefits can encourage informal businesses to transition into the formal economy, creating more formal employment opportunities (Lahura and Vargas, 2021[51]).

Figure 3.11. Informality and financial inclusion, 2021: Partial correlations

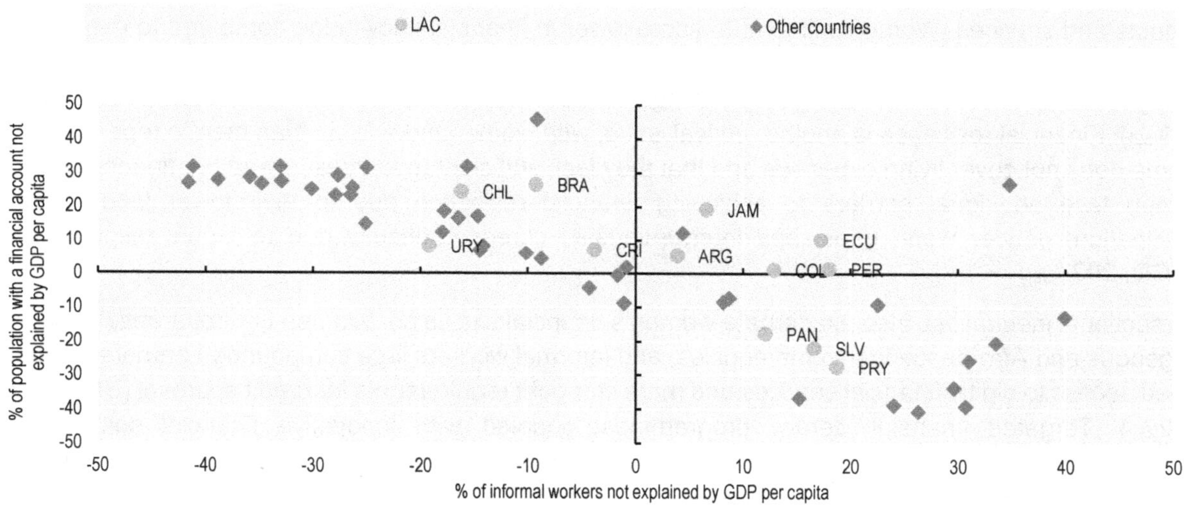

Note: Financial inclusion is measured by the percentage of the population with an account in a financial institution. Informality is measured by the percentage of informal workers in each country. GDP per capita (constant 2015 USD) was used as a control variable.
Source: Authors' calculation based on (ILOSTAT, 2024[52]) and (World Bank, 2021[19]).

StatLink https://stat.link/7bkeu6

Gender

Recent advances in women's access to financial products and services have contributed significantly to narrowing the gender gap in financial access in LAC. Access to financial products empowers women to invest in education, housing, health, and businesses, enhancing their economic standing. Between 2011 and 2021, the percentage of women with a bank account increased from 34.9% to 69.3%, compared to 77% of men. The percentage of women who borrowed from a formal financial institution increased from 7.4% to 24.3% during this period (World Bank, 2021[19]), illustrating positive strides toward gender equality in financial access.

However, despite these improvements, women in LAC still face systemic barriers that hinder their ability to fully benefit from financial inclusion (Demirgüç-Kunt, Klapper and Sin, 2013[53]). Cultural norms, gendered expectations, and legal frameworks in many LAC countries continue to limit women's autonomy and decision-making power over financial resources (Banca de las Oportunidades and CAF, 2024[54]; CMF,

2022[55]). For instance, women's access to credit remains significantly lower than men's, with only 25% of women borrowing from financial institutions – 11 percentage points behind their male counterparts. Furthermore, less than 5% of women who borrow funds use them for business purposes, highlighting a gap in women's entrepreneurial opportunities (World Bank, 2021[19]). This imbalance is further reflected in the ownership of firms, where only 18.7% of businesses in LAC are majority female-owned (World Bank, 2024[24]). Moreover, women in developing countries are largely concentrated in small firms and hence are likely to face greater financial constraints (Maquera Sardon, 2022[56]).

Achieving gender equality in the region is not only a social imperative but also carries substantial economic costs. Recent estimates suggest that achieving gender equality, as measured by eight sex-disaggregated Sustainable Development Goals indicators, will require an annual investment of USD 1.6 trillion from 2023 to 2030 for the 19 LAC economies studied (see Chapter 1 (UNCTAD, 2024[57])).This is equivalent to 28.4% of their collective GDP needed to close gender gaps in crucial areas such as poverty eradication, hunger alleviation, and women's equal participation in decision-making and the economy. This highlights the scale of investment required to promote gender equality, particularly through financial inclusion, as a key driver of broader development outcomes (Andrade et al., 2023[58]).

Gender differences in financial knowledge and resilience further complicate women's access to financial products and services. Women still tend to score lower in financial knowledge compared to men in most LAC countries (Figure 3.14). This knowledge gap has significant implications, affecting women's ability to manage their finances, build emergency savings, or access credit for entrepreneurial purposes (OECD, 2023[59]). Financial resilience is another critical issue, with women more likely than men to report that their income does not cover living expenses and that they lack sufficient resources to weather financial shocks. Women face additional barriers to achieving financial resilience due to their lower labour market participation, gender wage gaps, and interruptions in career continuity due to family responsibilities (OECD, 2023[59]).

Intersectional inequalities also exacerbate women's financial exclusion. Women in rural areas, those from Indigenous and Afro-descendant communities, and informal workers face compounded barriers, including limited access to digital financial services and more stringent requirements for credit approval (UN Women, 2022[60]). Targeted financial literacy programmes, coupled with innovative financial solutions like microcredit and alternative credit scoring, could bridge this gap. For instance, leveraging non-traditional data sources for credit scoring – such as utility payments or mobile phone usage – can expand credit access to women in informal employment, a sector where they are disproportionately represented (Herrera et al., 2023[49]).

Addressing biases, both on the supply and demand sides, is also essential. Studies show that women often lack the self-confidence needed to engage with financial products or present credit characteristics clearly, leading to lower loan approval rates (Banca de las Oportunidades and CAF, 2024[54]). Financial institutions should consider implementing further gender-sensitive lending practices, such as offering tailored financial products for women or reducing collateral requirements, which disproportionately affect women who often lack property rights or formal employment records.

Digital innovation is reshaping the financial landscape in LAC

Digital innovation has emerged as a powerful driver of financial inclusion. By leveraging new digital technologies, financial services in LAC can become significantly more inclusive (Sahay et al., 2020[61]). Emerging fintech platforms offer innovative, accessible and affordable financial services, bypassing the access barriers and limitations of traditional banking systems and reaching previously underserved segments of society (Bakker et al., 2023[62]). They encompass a wide range of innovative technologies and digital solutions, including online and mobile banking, lending, investment, and payments. This swift change can be seen through the proliferation of digital payment systems, the emergence of digital banks or neobanks, and the growth of alternative finance[1] and insurance (Sahay et al., 2020[61]; Mastercard and

AMI, 2023[63]). Digital payments also encompass payments made at physical or online merchants, sending or receiving remittances, paying utility bills, as well as receiving wages, government transfers or public pensions (Demirgüç-Kunt et al., 2022[64]). The integration of these technological advancements is not only streamlining and securing financial transactions but also fostering competition, reducing costs, and encouraging a culture of financial literacy and innovation (Chapter 1).

Although digital innovations are already supporting financial inclusion in LAC, gaps remain. Between 2014 and 2021, the percentage of age 15+ people who made or received a digital payment grew from 35.9% to 49.0% on average in LAC (Figure 3.12, Panel A). In some countries, such as Brazil or Chile, around 80% have made or received a digital payment, approaching the levels of OECD countries (95.6%). Similarly, the growth of mobile money accounts has surged in LAC, with countries like Argentina seeing an increase from 0.8% in 2014 to 27.0% in 2021. By delivering financial services via mobile devices, these platforms serve as crucial gateways into the financial system for individuals who have been excluded from traditional banking. This inclusivity not only expands the market but also plays a pivotal role in promoting financial literacy and stability among the population. Despite this expansion, significant gaps persist in most countries. For example, in 2021, 20.2% of men over 15 in Peru reported having a mobile money account, compared to only 8.9% of women (Figure 3.12, Panel B).

Figure 3.12. Growth of digital payments and neobanking in LAC

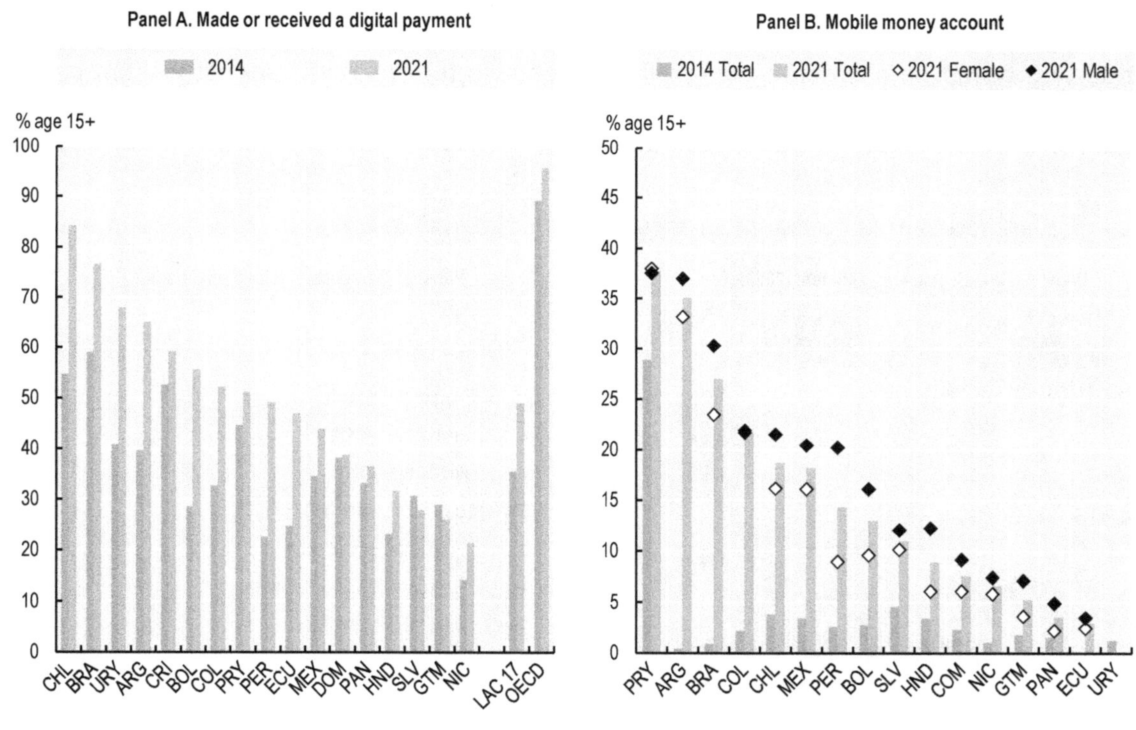

Note: Panel A: The percentage of respondents who, in 2021, reported using mobile money, a debit or credit card, or a mobile phone to make a payment from an account or reported using the Internet to pay bills or to buy something online or in a store in the previous year. This includes respondents who reported paying bills, sending, or receiving remittances, receiving payments for agricultural products, receiving government transfers, receiving wages, or receiving a public-sector pension directly from or into a financial institution account or through a mobile money account in the previous year. Panel B: The percentage of respondents who, in 2021, reported personally using a mobile money service in the previous year.
Source: Authors' elaboration based on (World Bank, 2021[19]).

StatLink https://stat.link/xd0hsa

Fintech has simplified how financial services are accessed and used across the region. The fastest growing fintech verticals in LAC include digital payments, digital banks, alternative finance by fintech, insurtech (technological innovations transforming the insurance sector) and big tech, among others. While at a nascent stage, the alternative finance and insurtech sectors are expanding swiftly. Fintech transformation in LAC is characterised by the rapid growth of digital payment systems, which had 262.8 million users by 2023, and digital banks, with more than 58.7 million users by 2023, primarily in Brazil and Mexico. Other segments such as digital investments and digital assets, also led by Brazil, reached 43.2 million and 62.5 million users respectively in 2023 (Figure 3.13, Panel A). Digital payments in LAC grew from USD 89 billion in 2017 to USD 215 billion in 2021 (Bakker et al., 2023[62]). The transaction volume of fully online digital banks in the LAC-6 – Argentina, Brazil, Chile, Colombia, Costa Rica and Mexico – grew from USD 17 billion in 2017 to USD 123 billion in 2021 (Statista, 2024[65]).

Fintech innovations have made financial transactions instantaneous and facilitated online access to traditional banking services, enhancing competition and reducing lending spreads. Moreover, fintech has played a critical role in financial inclusion, bringing banking to the previously unbanked and underbanked, as well as fostering SME growth through alternative finance. This inclusive growth has contributed to reducing income inequality (Bakker et al., 2023[62]). In fact, about three-quarters of digital banks' customers in LAC are previously unbanked and underbanked consumers and SMEs (Figure 3.13, Panel B). By extending financial services to previously unbanked and underbanked populations, as well as underserved SMEs, fintech innovations are dismantling longstanding barriers to financial access and promoting economic participation.

Credit scoring based on alternative data in their algorithms (e.g. positive information from payments) seems a promising path for complementing traditional data used in credit scores by improving the prediction of credit behaviour for typically excluded populations and SMEs (Herrera et al., 2023[49]).

Figure 3.13. Fintech users and markets served by digital banks in LAC

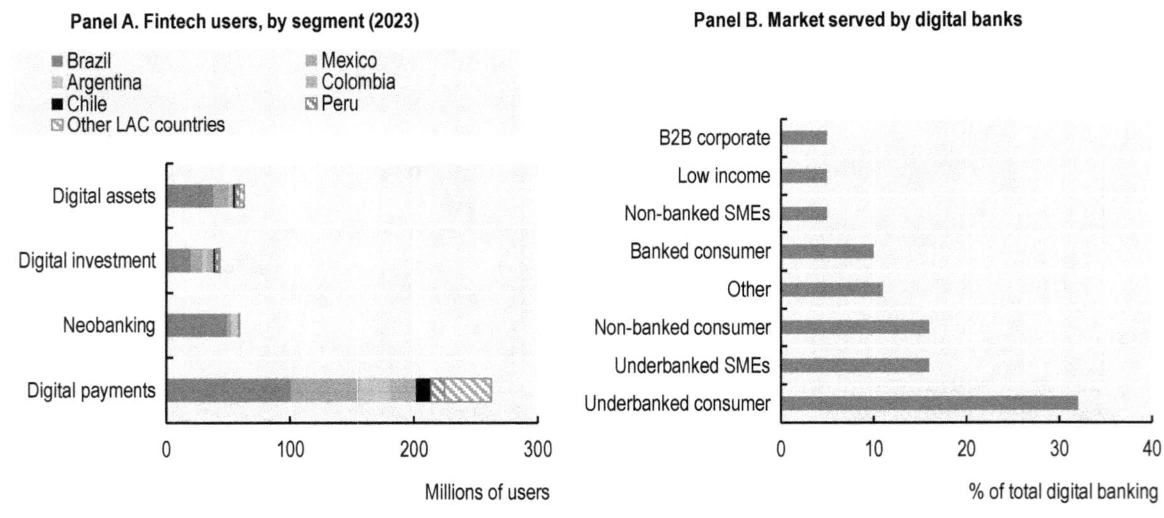

Note: Panel A: Other LAC countries include Bolivia, Costa Rica, Cuba, the Dominican Republic, Ecuador, El Salvador, Guatemala, Honduras, Nicaragua, Panama, Paraguay, Uruguay and Venezuela. Panel B: Unbanked refers to individuals or firms that do not have access to traditional banking services, such as a savings or checking account at a formal financial institution. Underbanked describes those that have a bank account but still rely on alternative financial services, like payday loans or check-cashing services, due to limited access to mainstream credit or banking products.

Source: Authors' elaboration based on (Statista, 2024[65]).

StatLink https://stat.link/rwlpxj

The adoption by businesses of digital payment systems, online banking and mobile money solutions can streamline business operations, reduce transaction costs, and save time, as well as increase financial inclusion. These technological advances not only enhance the operational efficiency of businesses but also open up new avenues for reaching customers and markets. Fintech is particularly resilient in times of stress. During the COVID-19 pandemic, for instance, as fintech supported the continuity of economic activities, it attracted increased investment, further fuelling the sector's expansion and highlighting its vital role in both economic stability and growth. During the COVID-19 pandemic in Brazil, nearly 50% of MSMEs with up to 9 employees increased their use of digital financial products. This figure rose to over 60% for MSMEs with 10-49 employees. In contrast, in Mexico, the increase was more modest, with around 30% of MSMEs with up to 9 employees and approximately 45% of MSMEs with 10-49 employees increasing their use of digital financial products (OECD, 2021[66]). As of 2023, 92% of small businesses in LAC accepted any digital payment, and 82% accepted bank transfers, while fewer than 33% accepted other digital payment methods (Mastercard and AMI, 2023[63]).

However, the rapid expansion of digital financial services, accelerated by the COVID-19 pandemic, highlights the importance of equipping individuals with the knowledge and skills to use these services safely. Current levels of digital financial literacy may be inadequate to navigate the opportunities and risks associated with these services (OECD, 2023[67]). Enhancing digital financial literacy is essential for ensuring the safe use of digital financial products.

Bolstering financial education and regulatory frameworks can enhance well-being

The quality of financial products and services is crucial to ensuring that increased access and usage in LAC contribute to greater well-being. High-quality financial services must be responsibly designed and delivered, incorporating strong consumer protection frameworks and promoting financial literacy (OECD, 2022[42]; OECD, 2023[67]). Financial literacy is defined by the OECD as a combination of "financial awareness, knowledge, skills, attitudes and behaviours necessary to make sound financial decisions and ultimately achieve financial well-being" (OECD, 2020[68]). It empowers consumers to make informed decisions, helping them to choose appropriate products and avoid pitfalls like over-indebtedness. Regulatory frameworks safeguard against predatory practices and ensure transparency, building trust in the financial system. Without these elements, increased financial inclusion can have unintended consequences, such as encouraging unhealthy financial behaviours and exacerbating financial stress, ultimately deteriorating people's well-being.

Despite recognition of financial literacy as a core 21st-century skill, financial literacy remains limited in LAC, with a significant portion of the population unfamiliar with basic financial concepts. Many adults lack the understanding and application of basic financial concepts necessary for making sound decisions in today's economically pressured environment. Key economic concepts, such as inflation and interest rates, remain unknown to many LAC citizens, with women being disproportionately affected. On average in nine selected LAC countries, more men understand the concept of interest rates (27%) than women (18%). In Colombia, only 13% of men understand interest rates, compared to just 6% of women (Figure 3.14, Panel A). Although Latin Americans and Caribbeans have a slightly better understanding of the concept of inflation and its effect on money, the gender gap remains, with an average of 50% of men understanding this concept compared to 44% of women in the nine countries. In Uruguay, for example, 65% of men and 53% of women understand the concept of inflation (Figure 3.14, Panel B). Moreover, in Brazil, Mexico, and Peru, male MSME owners have higher financial literacy than their female counterparts (OECD, 2021[66]).

Figure 3.14. Understanding of interest rates and inflation in LAC, 2023

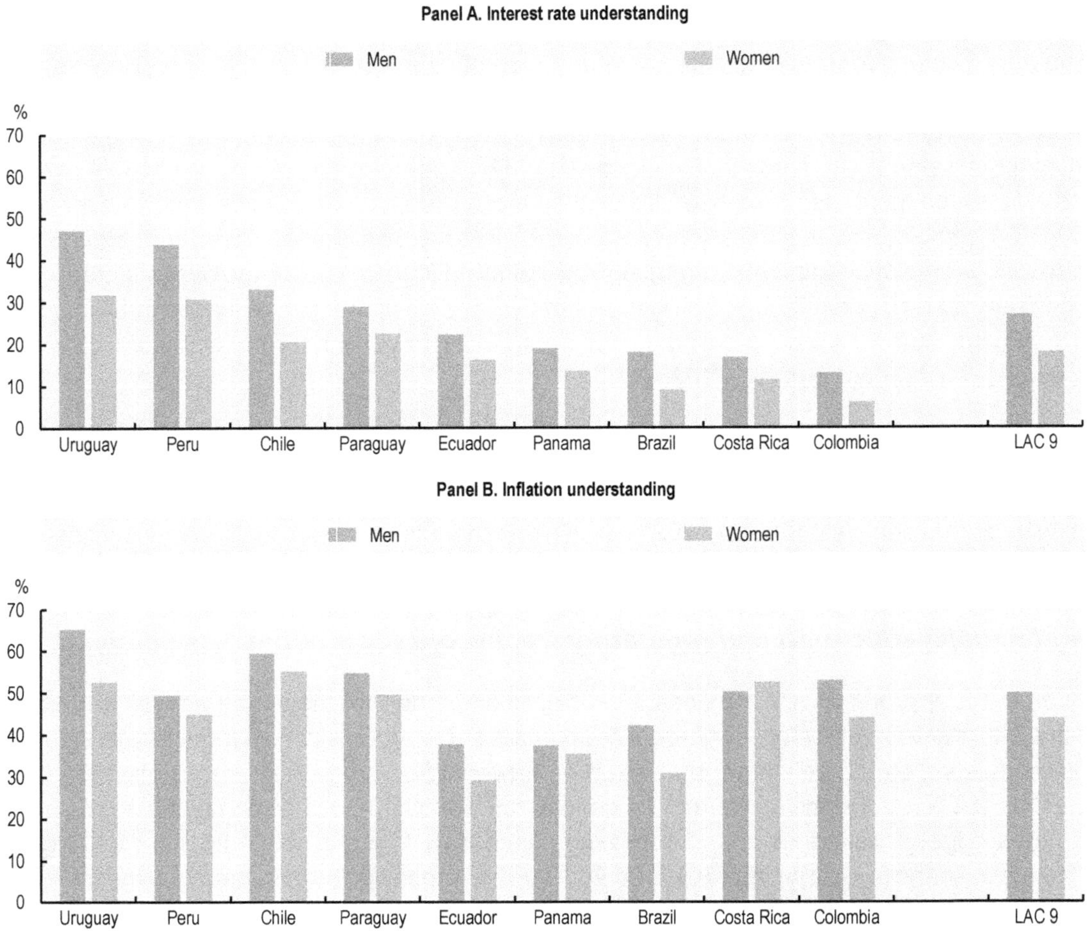

Note: Panel A: The series displays the percentage of respondents who answered the following question correctly: "Suppose you put $100 into a savings account with an interest rate of 2% per year. You make no additional deposits into this account and do not withdraw any money. No fees are charged to the account. How much would be in the account at the end of the first year, after the interest payment has been made?". Panel B: The series displays the percentage of respondents who answered the following question correctly: "Imagine that some siblings who have just received an inheritance must wait a year to access their share, and inflation remains at 3% annually. After a year, will they be able to buy more, less or the same compared to the present?"

Source: Authors' elaboration based on (CAF, 2023[69]), and (OECD, 2023[67]).

StatLink https://stat.link/x9j1kv

Improving financial literacy not only facilitates sound financial decisions but also significantly enhances individuals' financial well-being and resilience. According to the 2022 Programme for International Student Assessment (PISA), financial literacy performance in Brazil, Costa Rica and Peru lagged behind the OECD average. In these countries, 45%, 43% and 42% of students respectively did not achieve the baseline proficiency level (Level 2), compared to 18% of students in the OECD on average. At Level 2, students can identify common financial products and terms, distinguish between needs and wants, and make basic decisions on everyday spending based on personal experiences. The highest proficiency level in financial literacy, Level 5, was reached by only 2% of students in Brazil and 1% in Costa Rica and Peru, compared to 11% on average in the OECD. Level 5 students demonstrate advanced abilities in analysing complex financial products, solving unconventional financial challenges and understanding the broader financial landscape (OECD, 2024[70]).

The implementation of a National Financial Inclusion Strategy with a strong financial literacy component can significantly contribute to higher levels of financial literacy, lower market concentration[2] (OECD,

2022[42]) and the adoption of new digital financial technologies. Evidence from nine LAC countries suggests that the implementation of a National Financial Inclusion Strategy has led to increased adoption of deposit products (López Marmolejo and Ruiz Arranz, 2024[71]). However, there has been no notable impact on other financial services, such as loans, highlighting the need for more effective design and implementation to achieve broader outcomes. Furthermore, improving financial literacy can help individuals and businesses better understand and evaluate their financing options, reducing involuntary exclusion by enabling more informed decisions about seeking credit (Zuleta, 2017[72]).

The linkage between higher financial literacy and greater individual financial well-being, as outlined in the OECD Recommendation on Financial Literacy (Box 3.1), serves as a foundation for policy recommendations aimed at enhancing financial resilience and well-being among populations. Policy suggestions include enhancing basic financial knowledge, fostering positive financial behaviours and attitudes, improving digital financial literacy, and targeting support to those with the lowest financial literacy levels, all aimed at bolstering individual financial well-being and resilience against economic shocks (OECD, 2023[67]).

Box 3.1. OECD Recommendation on Financial Literacy

The OECD Recommendation on Financial Literacy presents a framework for improving financial literacy, recognising it as a cornerstone for individual empowerment and societal financial stability. This is particularly relevant for addressing the unique challenges in LAC, which has an urgent need for comprehensive financial education and inclusion strategies. The recommendation advocates national strategies that promote financial literacy through a sustained, co-ordinated approach that is coherent with other strategies on financial inclusion and consumer protection. This approach is vital for LAC, where disparities in financial access and education persist, with the digital divide accentuating these challenges. By tailoring financial literacy strategies to the region's diverse socio-economic landscape and leveraging collaboration among stakeholders, such strategies can significantly contribute to overcoming barriers to financial services and supporting economic and social prosperity (Grifoni et al., 2020[73]). All LAC countries that are members of the OECD, along with Brazil as a non-member, adhered to these recommendations of the Council when they were adopted.

The recommendation highlights the importance of using data to understand the financial behaviour and needs of a population, including those most vulnerable to financial exclusion. Its call for national surveys and international studies to collect data on financial literacy levels is particularly pertinent for LAC, where varying levels of financial literacy and access necessitate targeted interventions. Many countries in the LAC region already collect financial literacy data using an OECD methodology, with some of them also participating in the PISA financial literacy assessment. By addressing the specific needs of underserved communities, including rural populations and indigenous groups, and by recognising the critical role of digital financial literacy in bridging the digital divide, the recommendation provides a roadmap for LAC to enhance financial inclusion and literacy effectively.

Equipping individuals with the knowledge to make informed financial decisions is critical in LAC countries, where economic volatility, inflation and informal economies pose significant challenges. Promoting an understanding of saving, investment, retirement planning, and risk management tailored to the LAC context can empower individuals to navigate financial challenges and opportunities. The effective delivery of financial literacy programmes adapted to the cultural and economic contexts of LAC countries can facilitate greater financial resilience and well-being. This tailored approach to financial literacy, emphasising the inclusion of all segments of society, is crucial for fostering sustainable economic development and reducing inequalities in LAC.

Source: (OECD, 2020[68]).

Most LAC countries still need to build robust regulatory frameworks to protect consumers from fraud, misconduct, error and abuse, and to sanction such activities when they occur. These frameworks, alongside strong supervisory mechanisms, build trust in the financial system by enforcing transparency in financial product offerings, which helps consumers to make informed decisions and avoid financial pitfalls (OECD, 2022[42]). Effective supervision plays a crucial role by ensuring that regulations are followed and that unethical practices are identified and penalised in a timely manner. This combination of regulation and supervision helps prevent predatory lending practices – unethical or exploitative actions by financial institutions that take advantage of vulnerable consumers by offering unfair loan terms, excessive fees or misleading information – by allowing regulatory bodies to monitor and penalise unethical behaviour (OECD, 2022[42]). Strong regulations also promote the development of financial products tailored to the needs of marginalised communities and support fintech innovations for more accessible services. By fostering a competitive and transparent financial market, these regulations enhance the quality of financial products and services, ultimately creating a safe and supportive financial ecosystem that drives economic growth and resilience (OECD, 2024[74]).

Furthermore, as financial institutions increasingly adopt emerging technologies, they must take proactive measures to protect themselves against escalating cyber risks (Atkins et al., 2024[75]). Cybersecurity has become a critical pillar of consumer trust and a key enabler of equitable financial inclusion to prevent fraud and predatory practices.

Boosting financing through public development finance institutions

National and subnational development finance institutions (DFIs) play a crucial role in mobilising resources towards development goals. Public DFIs[3] include mostly public development banks (PDBs). They also include specialised financial institutions and funds at the national and local levels. These institutions are mandated to promote economic development, employment and investment aligned with the country's development objectives (Chapter 4). DFIs remain crucial in promoting economic growth and development by providing credit and capacity-building services where private banks and capital markets fall short (De Luna-Martínez, 2017[76]). Besides, they address market failures such as information asymmetries and pro-cyclical lending from the private sector (Xu, Ren and Wu, 2019[77]).Moreover, they can help to address financial market depth issues, redistribute risks and foster inclusive markets. The LAC region currently has approximately 107 DFIs that operate at the national level. Of these, 73% function as first-tier banks and 20% as second-tier banks. The total assets of DFIs vary greatly across LAC countries, from almost 8% of GDP in Brazil to 0.2% in Argentina (AFD/Peking University, 2023[78]). These institutions vary significantly in size, financial profile and regional coverage, as observed in balance sheet indicators such as capital, equity, assets, liabilities and loan portfolios. DFIs, including national and subnational development banks, have extensive knowledge of local markets and strong relationships with both private and public sector actors. By leveraging their advantageous position, they can assess risks, develop project pipelines and facilitate domestic and international capital flows (OECD et al., 2023[6]). International initiatives, including Finance in Common, are fundamental for sharing experiences and information across DFIs, and therefore achieving greater impacts on sustainable development in emerging and developing economies (Box 3.2).

Box 3.2. Finance in Common

Finance in Common is a global network that seeks to align PDBs with the 2030 Agenda and Paris Agreement. Building on the recent Rio de Janeiro Finance in Common Summit Joint Event with the G20, held in May 2024, development banks have identified several recommendations for improving co-ordination and co-operation to achieve development goals and mobilise the private sector. The recommendations concern the global financial architecture, country platforms and financial solutions for biodiversity and climate, as well as an increase in blended finance and private capital mobilisation. Namely, development banks identified the importance of capital markets for financial mobilisation. They recommend creating an open and singular accreditation process to ease access by development banks to other multilateral funds, like the Green Climate Fund; streamlining co-ordination and implementation of sustainable finance taxonomies; and contributing further to the Fourth International Conference on Financing for Development, to be held in Spain in 2025. These recommendations aim to tackle the fragmentation issues facing the development finance sphere and seek to create more common sustainable investment criteria.

To catalyse the role of PDBs in achieving sustainable development, more information is needed about these institutions. In this regard, the Institute of New Structural Economics of Beijing University and the French Development Agency have created the first comprehensive database on PDBs and DFIs. The database collects information on the role, functioning and effectiveness of PDBs and DFIs around the world with the objective of filling the gap in data on the global financial architecture. This initiative aims to promote research on PDBs and DFIs in order to enhance understanding of such institutions, realise their potential and verify that development goals are incorporated into their corporate strategies.

Source: (Finance in Common, 2024[79]) and (Finance in Common, 2024[80]).

DFIs play a clear role in the funding of MSMEs in LAC

The classification of DFIs by mandate shows a clear productive specialisation in MSMEs. Out of a sample of 76 development banks and finance institutions in LAC, 34% have an institutional mandate focused on financial support of MSMEs (Xu et al., 2021[81]). Throughout the region, there is great heterogeneity in institutional mandates, with South America having the most DFIs focused on SMEs, while many in Central America focus on financial support for the agriculture sector (Figure 3.15, Panel A). DFIs offer the region's MSMEs a variety of tailored financial instruments that cater to financial needs at every stage of development. These instruments can be grouped into five types of financing: i) financing day-to-day operations (working capital, payroll, inventory, rent); ii) financing investment; iii) financing foreign trade; iv) emergency financing; and v) risk mitigation and security instruments. A sample of 473 financial instruments from 38 DFIs across 13 LAC countries showed that the main types of financing offered are for investment (45%) and day-to-day operations (34%) (Figure 3.15, Panel B). This shows the commitment of DFIs to guaranteeing the working capital, liquidity and long-term investment needs of MSMEs. Other types of financing are less common and are primarily intended to enhance the financial inclusion and competitiveness of MSMEs (OECD et al., 2023[6]).

Figure 3.15. Institutional mandate of DFIs and financing types offered to MSMEs in LAC, 2023

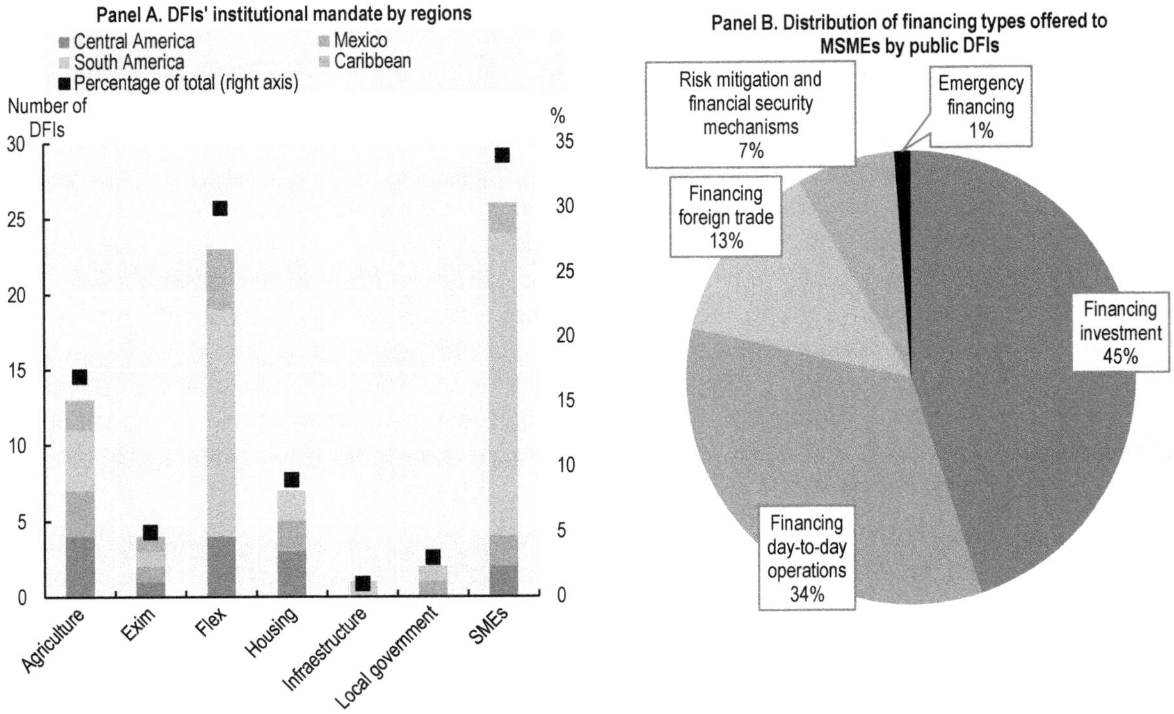

Note: Panel A: Exim = international trade; Flex = flexible. Panel B: This database covers 38 national and subnational public DFIs in 13 LAC countries: Argentina, Brazil, Chile, Colombia, Costa Rica, Dominican Republic, El Salvador, Guatemala, Mexico, Paraguay, Panama, Peru and Uruguay.

Source: Authors' elaboration based on ECLAC based on (AFD/Peking University, 2023[78]) and public data from 38 public DFIs in 13 LAC countries.

StatLink https://stat.link/iqn6hu

In the aftermath of the pandemic, DFIs significantly expanded their lending activities and introduced innovations in their financial services to address the growing demand for financing among MSMEs. These efforts included new loan programmes tailored to payroll and working capital needs, expanded credit availability and the postponement of loan repayments. DFIs also provided guarantees for SME bond issuances, covering up to 98% of the loan amount (80-98% in the case of Argentina, and varying depending on the enterprise size in Peru). Innovative measures were introduced to benefit MSME financing, such as web platforms for enterprise-market connections and financial intermediary funding (for instance utilising fintech companies). In Mexico, Nafin and Bancomext allocated approximately USD 2.5 billion through financial intermediaries, extending creditor loan and grace periods, providing new working capital loans and offering stock market guarantees to improve liquidity (ALIDE, 2023[82]).

DFIs play a crucial role in promoting financial inclusion for MSMEs through key instruments such as guarantee schemes, loans and lines of credit, among others. Guarantee schemes prioritise MSMEs due to their structural vulnerability and significance in employment generation. They offer several advantages, including expanding credit supply, granting access to the formal financial system for companies lacking collateral or for startups, and improving credit conditions. Credit mobilised by guarantee funds in LAC increased from USD 3.6 million in 2004 to a historical high of USD 88.6 million in 2020 before declining to USD 66.9 million in 2021 (Figure 3.16, Panel A). Similarly, the number of SMEs covered by guarantee schemes increased from 688 000 in 2000 to nearly 6 million in 2021. The coverage by guarantees across the region is highly heterogeneous. Larger economies in terms of GDP levels, like Colombia, Mexico and Brazil, lead in SME coverage, accounting for 34%, 27%, and 18%, respectively, of the total SMEs covered, while smaller countries like Bolivia, Costa Rica, Ecuador, El Salvador, Honduras and Uruguay account for less than 1% (Figure 3.16, Panel B) (Red Iberoamericana de Garantías, 2023[83]).

Figure 3.16. Evolution of guarantee funds and coverage of SMEs by guarantee schemes in LAC

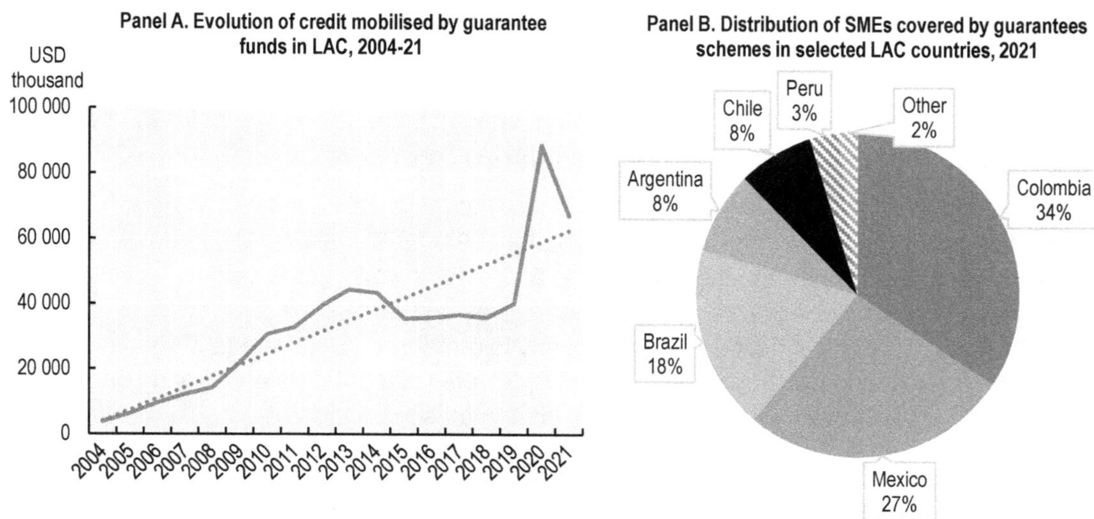

Note: Panel B: "Other" includes Bolivia, Costa Rica, Ecuador, El Salvador, Honduras and Uruguay.
Source: Authors' elaboration based on (Red Iberoamericana de Garantías, 2023[83]).

StatLink https://stat.link/5d4wpo

Expanding the impact of DFIs on the green transition and the digital transformation

DFIs have evolved across emerging and developing economies to confront more effectively new global challenges like the green transition and digital transformation (Rogozinski, 2017[84]). For instance, DFIs have expanded their role to confront the emerging challenge of double vulnerability, in which a nation faces both climate and financial insecurity. DFIs have adapted their financial instruments to address these intersecting vulnerabilities while ensuring that governments can still finance socio-economic policies (AFD, 2023[85]). DFIs are increasingly balancing commercial activities with their social mission, actively creating and developing markets in key sectors such as agriculture, infrastructure, energy, education and health.

While public DFIs in LAC have expanded their participation in the financial system, their activities in the green, gender, and digital agendas remain limited. During the COVID-19 pandemic in 2020, the loan portfolios of DFIs grew in most countries in LAC, with 71.2% of DFIs increasing their portfolios by 21%, primarily to support the production sector (ALIDE, 2023[82]). However, further commitment of DFIs to the SDGs could support the development of financial instruments for MSMEs that incorporate sustainable, gender-sensitive, and digital objectives. This can help channel private investments towards achieving key development goals. Of the 473 financial instruments for MSMEs offered by public DFIs in the LAC region in 2023, only 19% address at least one of the three cross-cutting challenges – 9.7% target the green transition, 5.5% target gender equality, and 3.8% target digital transformation or innovation (OECD et al., 2023[6]). Looking ahead, to further support climate financing, it is crucial for DFIs to build technical capacity both for their clients and themselves. (Box 3.3)

Box 3.3. How are PDBs in LAC supporting the climate transition?

A forthcoming joint publication between the European Investment Bank (EIB) and the Latin American Association of Development Financing Institutions (ALIDE) analyses how PDBs in LAC are supporting the green transition and what is holding them back from scaling up financing. This study will include a sample of 29 PDBs in 15 different countries covering close to 50% of the total assets of all PDBs in the region. Because PDBs are such relevant players in the region, it is important to understand their climate strategy, climate risk management, monitoring and impact measurement practices, their current products on offer and, ultimately, obstacles to increasing lending for climate.

As of 2023, extreme weather events have damaged the physical assets of 40% of PDBs and deteriorated the asset quality of the portfolio of another 59%. Still, despite 93% seeing the climate transition as an opportunity as opposed to a risk, and 77% following the targets set in the Paris agreement, just under 50% of the banks see themselves as leaders or promoters of the climate transition, 46% are followers of industry practices mostly to remain competitive and 7% are still sceptical to the needs of a green transition (Figure 3.17, Panel A). Overall, either PDBs are already offering green finance products (75%) or, even if they do not, they plan to do so soon (21%).

When asked about the main constraints to green lending, PDBs first identify demand-related factors. Namely, 55% of PDBs rank among the top three barriers to lending the clients' lack of technical capacities and the fact that climate strategy still has a low priority, together with the fact that often clients are unaware of available green finance of opportunities (mentioned by 45% of PDBs) (Figure 3.17, Panel B). Only after these factors do PDBs mention their own shortcomings, related to the supply-slide, including their own risk management and monitoring and impact measurement practices.

Figure 3.17. PDBs' climate strategy and main obstacles to climate financing

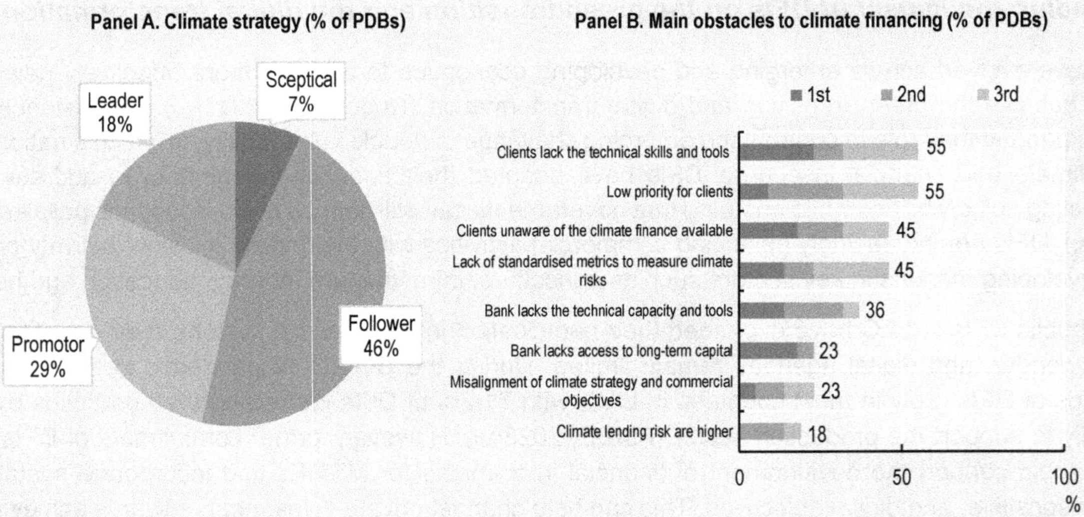

Note: Panel A: Sceptical: We do not acknowledge climate change as a significant risk for our bank and have not yet implemented any specific policies beyond any minimum regulatory requirements; Follower: We have implemented some climate-related policies (e.g. limiting carbon footprint, climate stress, pricing in climate on loans) following what other banks did in order to remain competitive; Promoter: We have a comprehensive strategy in place to address our impact on climate change and mitigate active risks on our portfolio; Leader: Climate change is a central consideration in all our policies and operations and is embedded in all our internal processes.
Source: Authors' elaboration based on (EIB, 2021[86]).

StatLink https://stat.link/s5wj1v

The survey's main message is that to support climate financing further, it is crucial for PDBs to build technical capacity both for clients and for themselves, for example through Technical Assistance (TA) programmes. A good example of such programmes is the EIB's Greening of the Financial Sector TA that so far, covers 15 countries in Europe and Africa.

Source: (EIB, 2021[86]) and (EIB, 2023[87]).

DFIs can play a pivotal role in facilitating the adoption of digital tools and emerging technologies across key sectors. In 2023, DFIs offered financial and non-financial services to multiple sectors with the aim of enhancing enterprises' digital capabilities and fostering investment. The most targeted sectors were information and communications technology (ICT) and the transport, storage and communications sector, each accounting for 20%, followed by the electricity, gas and water supply sector, and the agriculture, hunting and forestry sector, both at 15%. These services, tailored for digital transformation, can also lay the groundwork for developing sustainable digital financing ecosystems aligned with the Sustainable Development Goals (SDGs). For instance, these ecosystems can encompass infrastructure promotion including connectivity, digital identification and accessible data markets. In the agricultural sector, such services can stimulate projects for technological innovation in agricultural enterprises, addressing rural investments and associated costs. This may involve implementing activities with high technological content, ultimately leading to the generation of greater added value in regional economies.

DFIs will need to embrace digitalisation swiftly to maintain the competitiveness of financial products and boost financing. They will have to adapt their operations to the rapid consumer adoption of digital products and services. With the closure of physical branch offices during pandemic lockdowns, online and mobile banking emerged as the primary channels for bank interaction, resulting in a notable increase in usage worldwide (ALIDE, 2023[82]).

To adapt to digital transformation, DFIs require innovative strategies, especially in the competitive landscape of LAC. This involves forming strategic alliances with tech firms, startups and venture capital funds to invest in fintech. Such collaborations not only validate fintech ventures and attract investment but also provide valuable expertise. In return, DFIs can offer access to a wide clientele, stability and know-how about regulatory compliance. Advancing virtual assistants based on artificial intelligence (AI) and chatbots for enhanced customer service is also essential to adapt to the new digital economy. With the rise of challenger banks and neobanks, DFIs need internal reforms to fully embrace the digital economy, including developing "banking as a service" to enhance customer retention. It is also imperative for DFIs to adapt to the growing trend of decentralised finance, aimed at eliminating intermediaries in financial transactions (ALIDE, 2023[82]).

Deepening capital markets in LAC

Developing capital markets can increase liquidity and enhance inclusion

Capital markets provide opportunities for firms and governments to long-term funding for productive development. These markets consist of equity markets and debt markets. Both equity and bonds can be acquired through the primary market where new securities are issued, such as new bonds and initial public offerings (IPOs), or directly from private companies that are not listed on a public stock exchange (private capital markets). They can also be acquired through the secondary market, which involves trading existing securities. These mechanisms enable efficient allocation of capital, supporting economic growth and development (OECD, 2023[88]). For example, capital markets instruments have proven useful to promote development priorities, such as the circular economy transition (UNEP, 2023[89]) (Chapter 4).

Equity markets

Equity markets play a key role in economic development by enabling long-term capital raising, providing markets with liquidity and expanding investment opportunities. Equity markets facilitate access to long-term financing that helps companies to invest and develop productive and innovative activities. They also provide an opportunity for households to participate in corporate value creation, giving them additional options for managing savings (OECD, 2023[88]).

Equity markets in LAC remain small and lack liquidity, with strong heterogeneity between countries. In 2022, market capitalisation in LAC stood at 35.9% of GDP on average, compared to 64.7% for OECD countries (Figure 3.18, Panel A). However, the depth of equity markets is heterogeneous, ranging from 94.4% of GDP in Chile to just 3.2% in Costa Rica. Moreover, the stock turnover ratio, which measures the frequency at which stocks are bought and sold within a given period, shows low levels of market liquidity and activity. In 2022, the LAC turnover ratio was 24.0%, compared to 53.8% for the OECD (Figure 3.18, Panel B). This ratio also varies widely among LAC countries. Brazil showcases robust trading activity and market liquidity, with a turnover ratio of 162.7%, while Mexico, the second most active country, has a ratio of 23.3% and Jamaica stands last with 1.4%.

Figure 3.18. Market capitalisation and stock turnover ratio in LAC, 2022 or latest year available

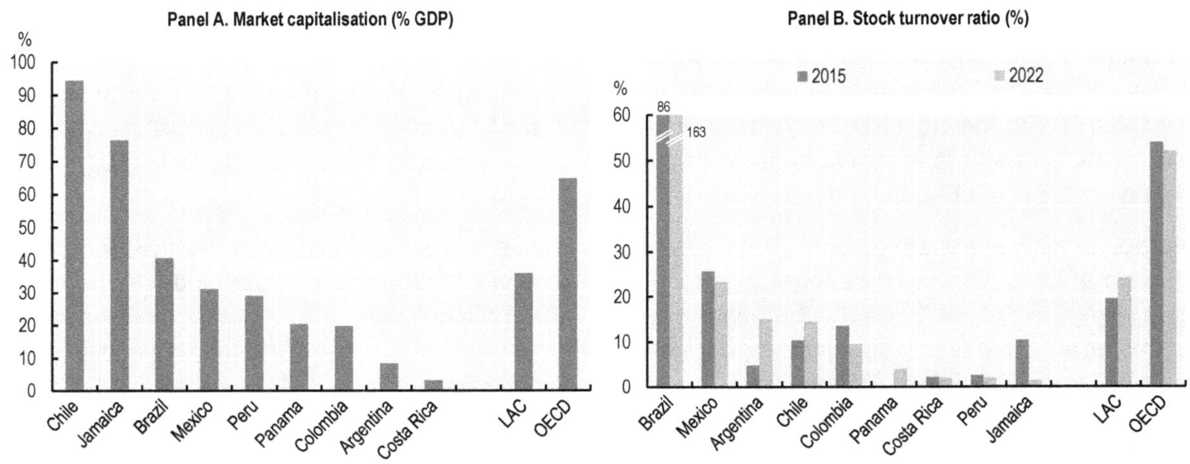

Note: Argentina corresponds to 2021 data. The LAC simple average includes 9 countries: Argentina, Brazil, Chile, Colombia, Costa Rica, Jamaica, Mexico, Panama and Peru. The OECD simple average includes 29 countries: Australia, Austria, Belgium, Canada, Chile, Colombia, Costa Rica, Czechia, France, Germany, Greece, Hungary, Ireland, Israel, Japan, Korea, Luxembourg, Mexico, Netherlands, New Zealand, Norway, Poland, Portugal, Slovenia, Spain, Switzerland, Türkiye, the United Kingdom and the United States. Norway corresponds to 2019 data; Belgium, France, Ireland and Portugal correspond to 2018 data, and Netherlands corresponds to 2017 data.
Source: Authors' elaboration based on (World Bank, 2024[16]).

StatLink https://stat.link/ho3zpk

For LAC economies, market concentration in equity markets is heterogeneous. The Herfindahl-Hirschman Index (HHI) is a measure of market concentration. The closer the index is to 0, the less concentrated the market, while a higher value indicates greater market concentration (FTC, 2023[90]). The HHI shows that there is high heterogeneity in market concentration across countries (Figure 3.19, Panel A). With the exception of Brazil and Chile, most LAC countries exhibit higher levels of concentration than Korea, which achieved high-income status in 1995 (Melguizo et al., 2017[91]). Moreover, concentration in the region is higher in all economies than in the New York Stock Exchange (NYSE). These results are consistent when measuring concentration based on the market capitalisation attributed to the top five companies in each country (Figure 3.19, Panel B). Similarly, large companies in LAC represent 80% of market capitalisation on average (OECD, 2023[88]).[4]

Figure 3.19. Concentration of equity markets in LAC, 2019 and 2024

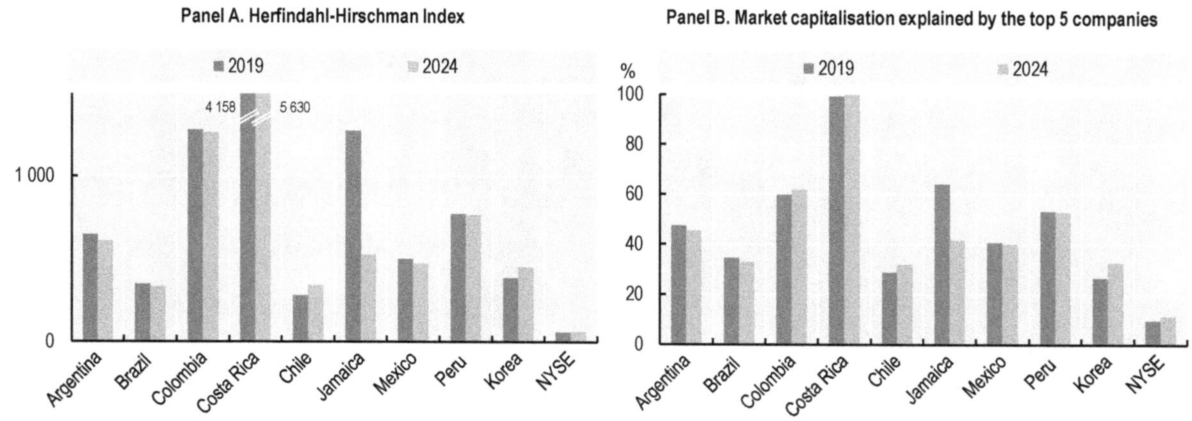

Note: A market is considered highly concentrated if the HHI exceeds 1 800 points and moderately concentrated if it is between 1 000 and 1 800 points. The exchanges analysed were: Bolsa de Comercio de Buenos Aires in Argentina, BM&F Bovespa SA and Bolsa de Valores Mercadorias e Futuros in Brazil, Bolsa de Santiago in Chile, Bolsa de Valores de Colombia, Costa Rica Stock Exchange, Jamaica Stock Exchange, Bolsa Mexicana de Valores, Bolsa de Valores de Lima S.A. in Peru, Korea Exchange, and New York Stock Exchange. Data were extracted on 12 June 2024.

Source: Authors' calculation based on (London Stock Exchange Group, 2024[92]).

StatLink https://stat.link/z64dei

Secondary Public Offerings (SPOs) account for most equity market activity in LAC, as there has been a trend of negative net listings over the last two decades. In 2021, net listings in the region reached 30 after 13 years of continuous negative net listings. Nevertheless, the improvement was only temporary, and in 2022 and 2023, the negative trend continued (Figure 3.20). This delisting phenomenon is present in many markets, as large companies migrate to the US market while medium-sized enterprises have difficulties listing in domestic markets (Vest, 2023[93]; OECD, 2019[94]). SPOs therefore represented 75% of the total amount raised in public offerings in the region between 2012 and 2023. Over that period, Brazil, which was responsible for most activity in the region, represented 71% of the total amount raised in IPOs and 68% of the total amount raised in SPOs in LAC. The second-best performers in the region are Mexico in IPOs (18% of the total amount raised) and Chile in SPOs (14% of the total amount raised) (OECD, 2024[95]).

Figure 3.20. Newly listed and delisted companies in LAC, 2000-23

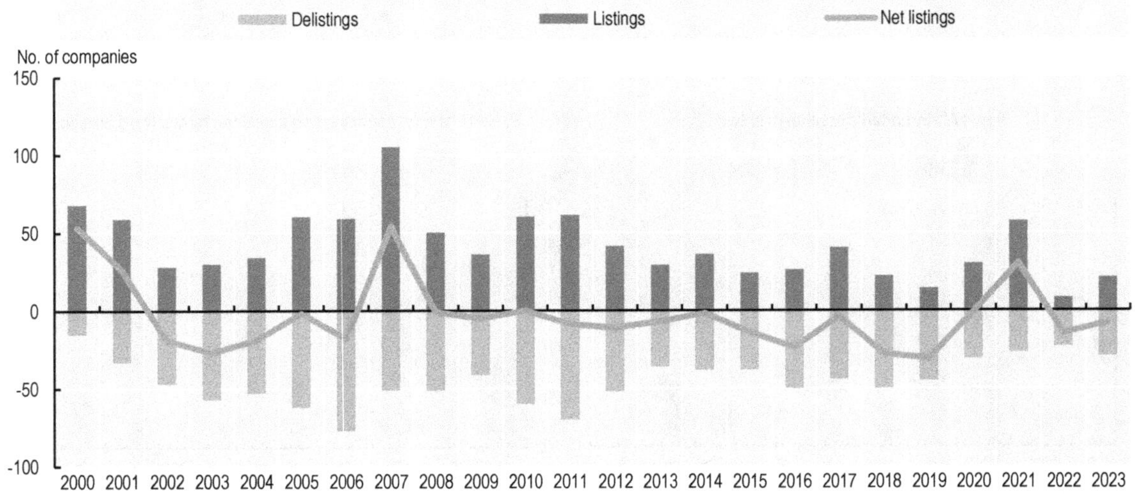

Source: Authors' elaboration based on (OECD, 2024[95]).

StatLink https://stat.link/jqucmt

The equity markets in the LAC region have the highest ownership concentration in the world, predominantly driven by corporate investors. The region's top 1% of shareholders hold an average of 46% of a company's total holdings, while the global average is 31% (Figure 3.21, Panel A). Furthermore, corporations hold almost one-third of listed equity in LAC, while institutional investors dominate globally, with 45% of equity. Corporations hold up to 72.8% of listed equity in Peru, while institutional investors in the region hold between 6.3% (Peru) and 27.1% (Brazil), a minor share in terms of the global landscape. This is evidence of the strong presence of company group structures in the region. In Colombia, Argentina and Brazil, the public sector is an important investor, at 37.8%, 20.5% and 14.8%, respectively (Figure 3.21, Panel B).

Figure 3.21. Ownership concentration and public equity holdings by type of investor, 2023

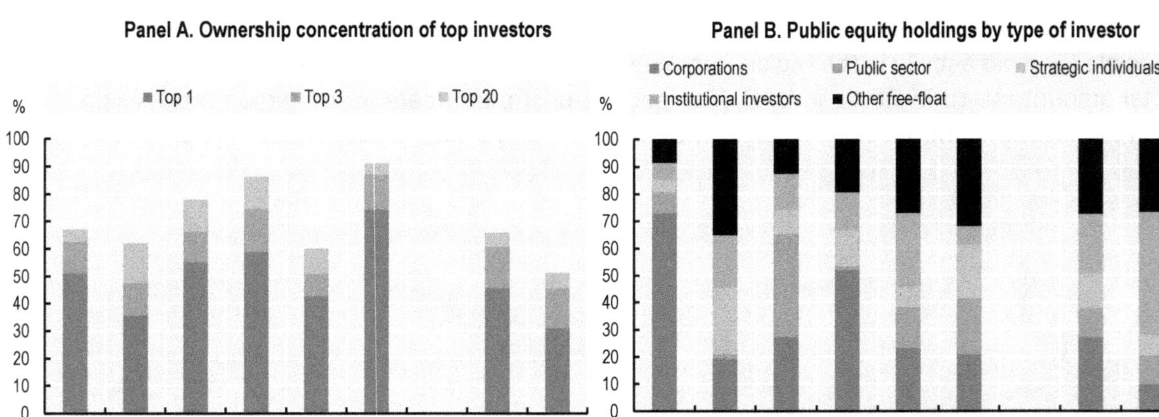

Note: Corporations include listed and unlisted private companies, their subsidiaries, joint ventures and operating divisions. Public sector refers to direct ownership by central governments, local governments, public pension funds, state-owned enterprises and sovereign wealth funds. Strategic individuals refer to physical persons that are controlling owners, members of a controlling family or block-holders and family offices. Institutional investors include pension funds, insurance companies, mutual funds and hedge funds. Other free-float refers to holdings by shareholders that do not reach the threshold for mandatory disclosure of their ownership records or retail investors that are not required to disclose (De La Cruz, Medina and Tang, 2019[96]).

Source: Authors' elaboration based on (OECD, 2024[95]).

StatLink https://stat.link/1uto4n

Access to private markets

Capital markets are further divided into public and private markets. Companies can finance themselves in the private or public debt market by issuing securities; in the public equity market by being listed in a stock exchange; or in the private equity market by privately selling stock. Medium-sized enterprises face difficulties in entering the public equity market and tend to resort to private markets (OECD, 2019[94]).

In private capital markets, venture capital (VC) accounts for the majority of operations. Investment in these markets can take the form of private equity, private credit or venture capital, or it can go specifically to infrastructure and natural resource projects. Venture capital is a type of equity financing for innovative young companies that have difficulties attracting standard financing. While it can provide high returns, it also brings high risk to investors (Rudolph, Miguel and Gonzalez-Uribe, 2023[97]). In the third quarter of 2023, venture capital accounted for 82% of the deal count (the total number of deals) and 47% of the total capital invested in LAC (Figure 3.22). Combined, other assets represented a larger share of capital invested, indicating larger deals. Private equity represented 27% of the capital invested in LAC, private credit 19% of the capital invested, and infrastructure and natural resources 7% of the total capital invested.

Figure 3.22. Investment by type of asset in LAC, Q3 2023

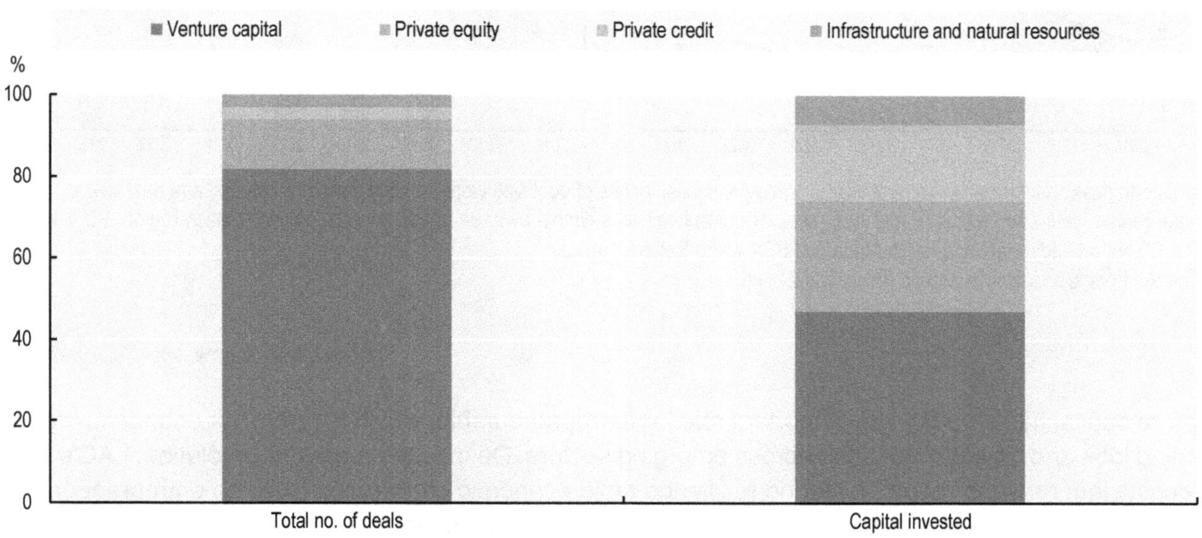

Note: Venture capital is a type of equity financing for new or growing businesses with perceived long-term growth potential. Private equity refers to a type of alternative investment in which investors buy shares in a privately held firm, generally in mature companies. Private credit refers to loans given by investors to businesses or individuals, which generates returns in the form of interest payments. Infrastructure and natural resources refer to capital invested specifically in projects related to natural resources and infrastructure development (Preqin, 2024[98]).
Source: Authors' elaboration based on (LAVCA, 2023[99]).

StatLink https://stat.link/9vbp05

LAC has historically maintained low venture capital investments compared to other global regions. North America dominates as the primary investor in this field, while Europe and Asia also surpass LAC in terms of VC funding per capita (Rudolph, Miguel and Gonzalez-Uribe, 2023[97]). North America and Asia are also the regions with the largest deals on average, while LAC trails behind. After surging in 2021, it became the region with the lowest average deal size in 2023. Meanwhile, the Middle East and North Africa (MENA) region has strengthened its position since 2016 and now surpasses Europe (Figure 3.23, Panel A).

Venture capital dynamics have slowed recently in LAC after a boom in 2021. VC funding in the region increased from USD 1.1 billion (249 deals) in 2016 to USD 25.1 billion (859 deals) in 2021 (Figure 3.23,

Panel B). This growth was driven by factors including post-COVID-19 incentives to reactivate the market; increased demand for digital services since the pandemic; participation of a few deep-pocketed, non-domestic investors; a surge of profitable exit opportunities; and the development of a supportive local ecosystem for startups (Rudolph, Miguel and Gonzalez-Uribe, 2023[97]). However, similar to other regions, investment in the region fell below pre-pandemic levels after 2021, declining to USD 5.4 billion in 2023.

Figure 3.23. Average venture capital deal size by region and annual venture capital investment in LAC, 2016-23

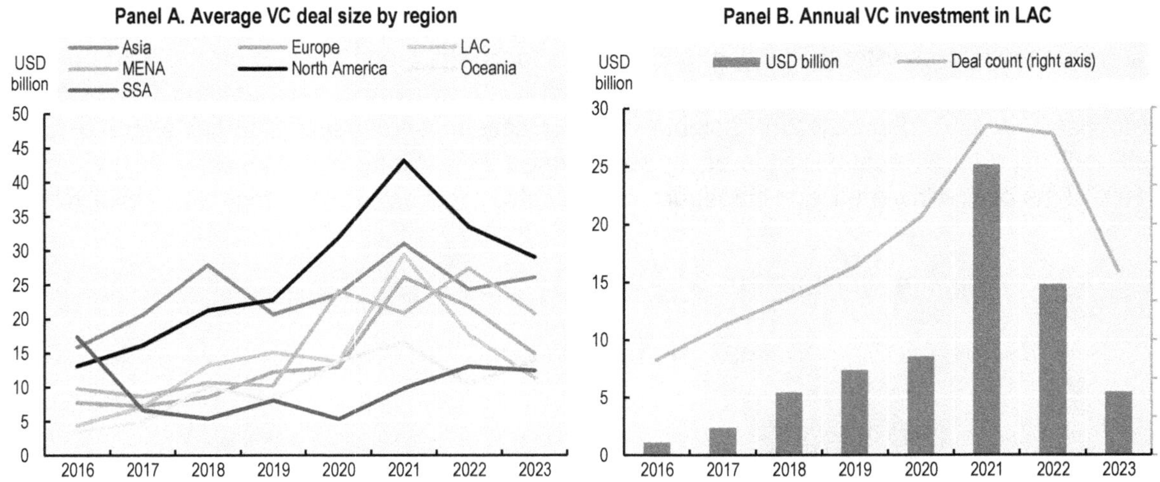

Note: Due to missing information on deal size in some instances, values of deal size were imputed based on the average deal size by groups of target region, year and vertical. Panel A: Figures are calculated as a simple average of countries belonging to each region. VC = venture capital, MENA = Middle East and North Africa and SSA = sub-Saharan Africa.
Source: Authors' calculation based on (Preqin, 2024[100]).

StatLink https://stat.link/fsdh7q

Venture capital has a particularly important role for entrepreneurship, which is pivotal for economic growth, creating jobs and driving innovation across emerging sectors. Despite the recent VC evolution, LAC's start-up ecosystem remains robust, fostering resilience amid economic challenges. Start-up entrepreneurs are vital in leveraging digital technologies to address socio-economic issues. By disrupting traditional industries, VC-backed ventures are poised to enhance accessibility to technology and financial services, shaping a promising future for the region (Berg, Rubio and Lask, 2024[101]).

Compared to other global regions, LAC allocates significant VC funding towards the mobile apps and fintech verticals while trailing behind in manufacturing, Artificial Intelligence and clean technology. Mobile apps, which accounted for almost 28% of the capital invested in 2023, are the industry's vertical[5] that receive the most investment in the region (Figure 3.24). Other outstanding verticals include blockchain technology, health tech and e-commerce. Regarding industries, the financial services industry accounts for roughly 19% of all VC funding in LAC, after information technology (41%) and the business-to-consumer (B2C) industry (29%). Globally, VC funding in LAC ranks first in terms of its concentration in the financial services industry and second in terms of the relevance of the fintech vertical (Rudolph, Miguel and Gonzalez-Uribe, 2023[97]).

Figure 3.24. VC investment by industry vertical in LAC (2016-23) and by region (2023)

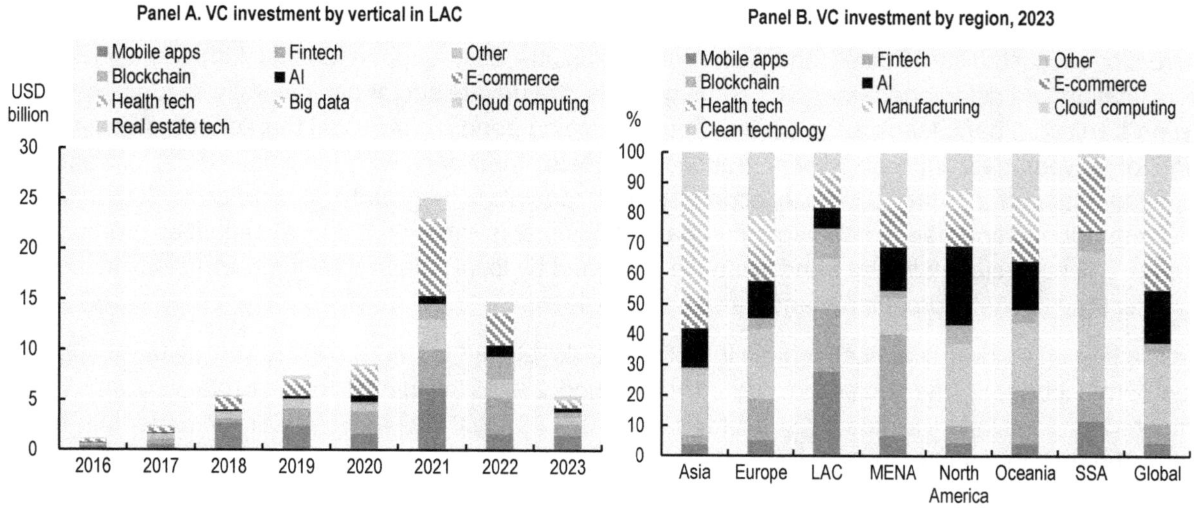

Note: AI = artificial intelligence, MENA = Middle East and North America and SSA = sub-Saharan Africa. Due to missing information on deal size in some instances, values of deal size were imputed based on the average deal size by groups of target region, year and vertical.
Source: Authors' calculation based on (Preqin, 2024[100]).

StatLink https://stat.link/jkzwys

VC investment in the region has been mainly supported by foreign firms. Non-domestic investors participated in about 74% of the value of the deals conducted during 2016-23 on average (Figure 3.25). This type of investor has also been important in terms of the number of deals: over the same period, about 68% of the deals had at least one non-domestic investor. However, not all foreign investors hold the same level of significance in the region, as 70% of the surge in non-domestic VC investment since 2019 can be attributed to four key investors: SoftBank, Tiger Global, DST Global and Ribbit Capital (Rudolph, Miguel and Gonzalez-Uribe, 2023[97]).

Figure 3.25. Domestic vs. non-domestic venture capital investors in LAC, 2016-23

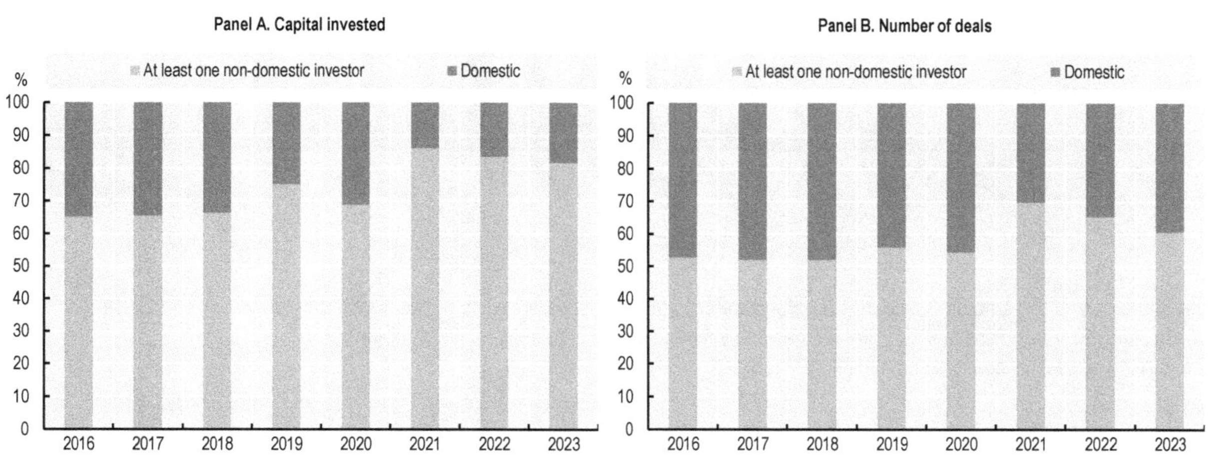

Note: Due to missing information on deal size in some instances, values of deal size were imputed based on the average deal size by groups of target region, year and vertical. This figure is based on a reduced sample of observations with information for both investor and target country.
Source: Authors' calculation based on (Preqin, 2024[100]).

StatLink https://stat.link/fs02re

Domestic corporate bond markets

Corporate domestic bond markets play a crucial role in spurring economic growth and supporting macroeconomic stability (Powell and Valencia, 2023[102]). They support capital formation, investment diversification and risk management. By issuing bonds, the private sector can diversify its funding sources beyond traditional bank loans and equity financing. Issuing bonds in the local market offers companies a range of advantages, including lower transaction costs, familiarity with local investors, currency risk mitigation, support for the domestic economy and regulatory familiarity. A corporate bond issue is considered domestic when it meets four criteria: i) the issuer is listed on the local securities market; ii) the issuer is a fiscal resident; iii) the bond issued is governed by local law; and iv) the place of issuance is the domestic market (Aldasoro, Hardy and Tarashev, 2021[103]).[6]

Corporate bond market issuances remain largely underdeveloped in LAC. In 2023, the outstanding amount of corporate bonds in the region accounted for around 2% of the global total, a relatively small share compared to the United States (US), Europe and Asia (OECD, 2024[104]). Local fundamentals help to explain the development of local currency bond markets, while they have played a minimal role in foreign currency bond markets (Ayala Pena, Nedeljkovic and Saborowski, 2015[105]).

In most LAC economies, the public sector is the main issuer in domestic bond markets. Between 2015 and 2023, public national or subnational entities (including the Central Bank) accounted for 81% of the total amount of local bond issuances in LAC on average, while corporate bonds accounted for the remaining 19% (Figure 3.26). However, there is large heterogeneity in the region, with corporate issuances reaching the highest levels in Caribbean economies such as Bahamas, Barbados and Trinidad and Tobago.

Figure 3.26. Domestic corporate and public bond issuance in LAC, 2015-23

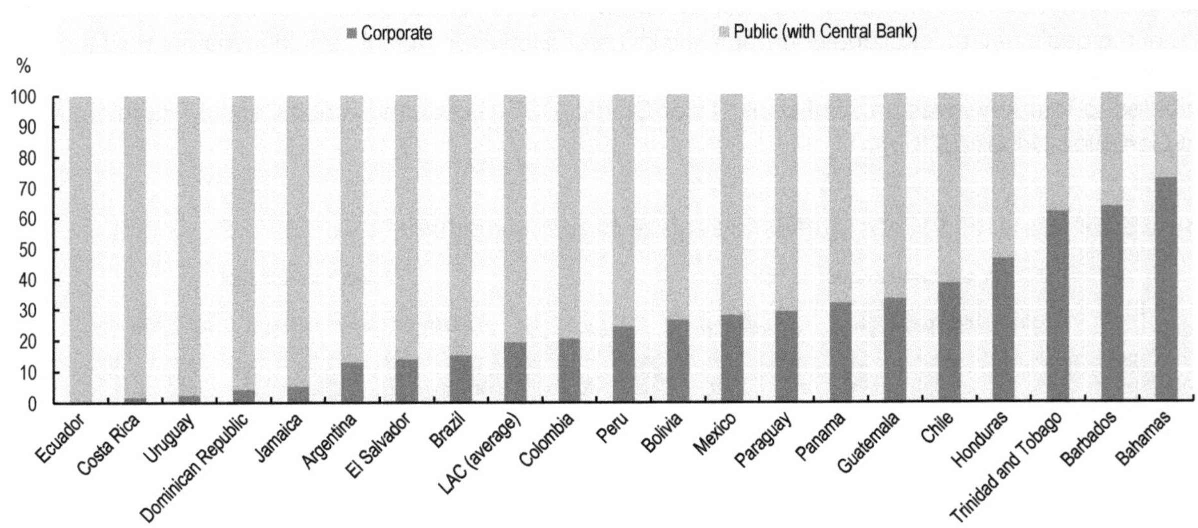

Note: Shares are of the amount issued in USD. Bonds refer to those issued during the period from 1 January 2015 to 31 December 2023. It includes bonds with an original maturity greater than one year and issues greater than USD 1 million.
Source: Authors' calculation based on (OECD, 2024[95]).

StatLink https://stat.link/kva1sl

The local corporate bond market in LAC is highly concentrated in a few economies. Between 2015 and 2023, 73% of the total amount of corporate bonds issued in domestic markets came from Brazil (37.7%) and Mexico (35.7%), followed by Chile (9.2%), Argentina (5.3%) and Colombia (4.3%). Other LAC economies have an active but much smaller private bond market; 13 countries in the region have participations smaller than 1%, making evident the need to develop local bond markets.

The demand for corporate bond market securities in the region is mainly driven by large pension funds, which mostly invest in investment-grade papers, keeping the lower-rated firms out of the market and subjecting them to funding through banks. The insurance sector and mutual funds are also relevant players in the "buy" side of private bonds (Vtyurina, Robles and Sutton, 2017[106]).The strong preference for top-rated issuers is a hurdle for new issuers, especially SMEs, which are usually considered riskier than investment-grade companies and face lower demand from institutional investors.

Non-financial firms are the most important issuers in corporate bond markets in the region.[7] They account for around 67% of the total corporate amount issued and 63% of the total number of issuances from the corporate sector (Figure 3.27, Panel A). This implies that the average amount issued by a non-financial firm is 1.2 times higher than that of the average financial company (Figure 3.27, Panel B). This can be partly attributed to the types of bonds included in the analysis. Banks and other financial institutions tend to issue more instruments of smaller amounts compared to non-financial entities, particularly certificates of deposit and short-term bills, to address their short-term financing needs.

Figure 3.27. Domestic corporate bond issuers in LAC and average amount issued, 2015-23

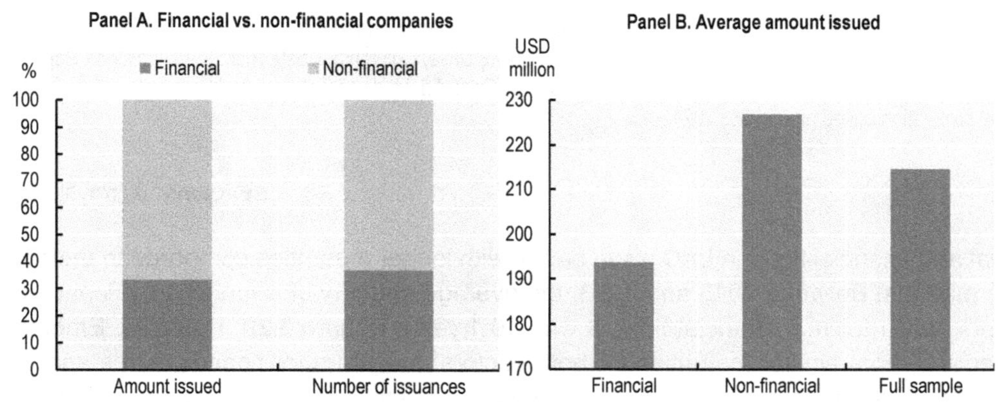

Note: Bonds issued during the period from 1 January 2015 to 31 December 2023. It includes bonds with an original maturity greater than one year and issues greater than USD 1 million. Countries included in the sample are: Argentina, the Bahamas, Barbados, Bolivia, Brazil, Chile, Colombia, Costa Rica, the Dominican Republic, Ecuador, El Salvador, Guatemala, Honduras, Jamaica, Mexico, Panama, Paraguay, Peru, Trinidad and Tobago, and Uruguay.
Source: Authors' calculation based on (OECD, 2024[95]).

StatLink https://stat.link/dsnul4

There is space to improve the currency composition of non-financial corporate bond issuances in domestic markets. Between 2015 and 2023, an average of 42% of the amount issued in LAC was denominated in local currency, while 58% was in foreign currencies. In contrast, globally, local currency accounted for 83% of the total issued amount and 86% in emerging markets (Figure 3.28, Panel A). This highlights the region's reliance on foreign currency borrowing and the currency mismatch in the firms' balance sheets, which exposes them to exchange rate risk (Eichengreen, Hausmann and Panizza, 2005[107]). Nevertheless, the share of the amount issued in domestic currency has increased in the region in the last few years. Between 2022 and 2023, this share reached 71%, changing the landscape of currency composition (Figure 3.28, Panel B). This was due to two factors. On the one hand, there was an increase in domestic currency issuance, even above pre-pandemic levels. From 2019 to 2023, the amount of USD issued in domestic currency in LAC increased by 53%. On the other hand, over the same period the region decreased the amount issued in foreign currency significantly, showing lower net debt and no actual correction of the currency mismatches (Haussmann and Panizza, 2011[108]). Strengthening local currency bond markets is essential to mitigate these risks.

Figure 3.28. Currency composition of non-financial corporate bonds issued by country group 2015-23

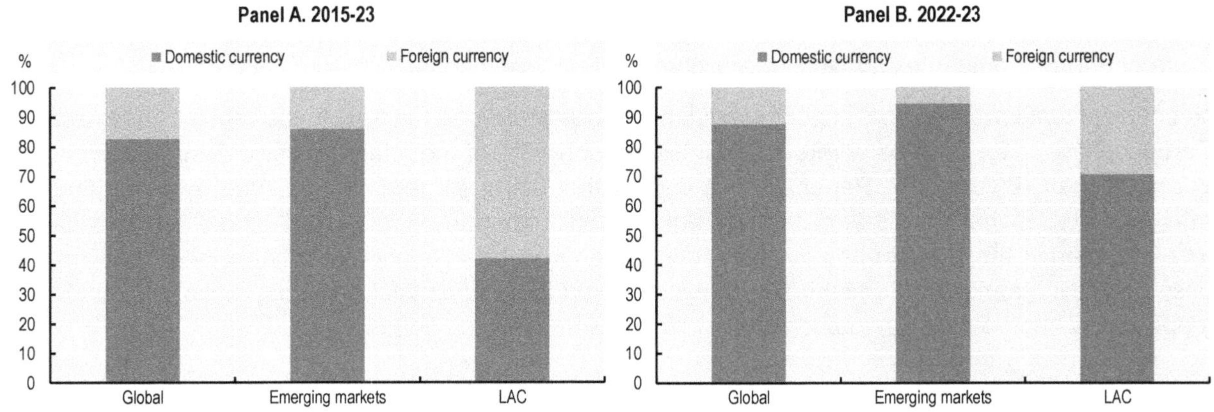

Note: Shares computed correspond to the amount issued in USD. Bonds refer to those issued during the period from 1 January 2015 to 31 December 2023. It includes bonds with an original maturity greater than one year and issues greater than USD 1 million. Countries included in the LAC group are: Argentina, the Bahamas, Barbados, Bolivia, Brazil, Chile, Colombia, Costa Rica, the Dominican Republic, Ecuador, El Salvador, Guatemala, Honduras, Jamaica, Mexico, Panama, Paraguay, Peru, Trinidad and Tobago, and Uruguay.
Source: Authors' calculation based on (OECD, 2024[95]).

StatLink https://stat.link/7zkuf0

Non-financial and financial firms in LAC issue bonds with longer maturities compared to their counterparts in emerging markets. Between 2015 and 2023, the average maturity of issuances by financial companies was 7.7 years, while for non-financial firms it was 10.1 years (Figure 3.29, Panel A). Emerging markets show shorter and more similar maturities for both sectors: 5.3 years for financial firms and 5.1 years for non-financial firms. Average maturity has decreased in the last two years, particularly for non-financial firms. Between 2022 and 2023, average maturity in LAC for financial firms reached 6.7 years and for non-financial firms 7.5 years (Figure 3.29, Panel B). This decrease brings LAC closer to emerging markets, although the difference is still over 2.5 years for the average maturity. This change in maturity might be due to the decrease in foreign issuance mentioned before. The results for financial firms should be interpreted with caution, as many financial firms in LAC often use debt securities with maturities of less than one year, which are not included in the sample.

Local corporate bond markets continue to develop in LAC, but there is still potential for growth. These markets could develop further by increasing the amounts issued and thereby the market size; expanding and/or diversifying the number of issuers; lengthening maturity in non-financial bonds; and decreasing market access costs. Expanding maturities in local-currency issuances by non-financial firms is also important to avoid currency mismatches and to mobilise internal savings to finance long-term projects in the region. Similarly, the development of a robust sovereign local-currency bond market yield curve in markets could give the private sector a benchmark for medium- and long-term financing costs. Moreover, the role of Environmental, Social, and Governance (ESG) bonds in the market has increased in the last few years and they represent an opportunity for market development (Chapter 4).

Figure 3.29. Average maturity of corporate bonds issued by country group and sector, 2015-23

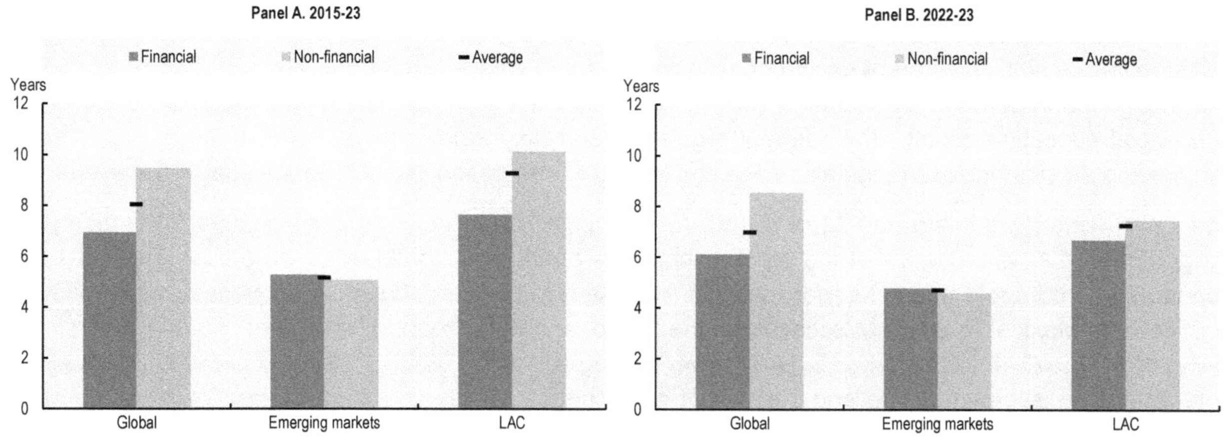

Note: Average maturity by year is weighted by the issued amount. Average maturity over a period of years is computed as the simple average of the yearly average maturity. Bonds refer to those issued during the period from 1 January 2015 to 31 December 2023. It includes bonds with an original maturity greater than one year and issues greater than USD 1 million. Countries included in the LAC group are: Argentina, the Bahamas, Barbados, Bolivia, Brazil, Chile, Colombia, Costa Rica, the Dominican Republic, Ecuador, El Salvador, Guatemala, Honduras, Jamaica, Mexico, Panama, Paraguay, Peru, Trinidad and Tobago, and Uruguay.
Source: Authors' calculation based on (OECD, 2024[95]).

StatLink https://stat.link/rwzku6

Multiple policies could help to achieve the development of corporate bond markets. For instance, a partial private-public subsidy for the price of credit ratings wherever they are a requirement for first-time issuers could help lower the issuance cost. A similar initiative was implemented in Africa in 2004 with successful results (Grandes and Pinaud, 2005[109]). Correctly used tax exemptions could also help to lower issuance costs. In Brazil, for example, the government introduced a new framework in 2011 under which private companies could issue infrastructure bonds to promote the development of long-term private capital markets and strengthen financing for infrastructure projects. If funds are used to finance infrastructure projects, the securities' interest and capital gains enjoy a tax exemption (Cavallo, 2023[110]).

Policy makers should consider the trade-offs between promoting the development of small local bond markets or encouraging regional domestic bond-market integration. Under the regional approach, smaller LAC countries could integrate into relatively more developed markets to decrease issuance costs and benefit from a more diversified, deeper and more liquid pool of investors. This could lead to the emergence of regional "financial bond market hubs" in the medium term, yielding benefits in terms of economies of scale and lower borrowing costs, as these hubs will provide deeper and broader pools of capital, in particular for medium-sized enterprises. However, less developed LAC economies would have to issue bonds in currencies other than their own, most likely in USD, and would need to be able to afford the technological, regulatory and cultural costs of integrating into those hubs.

Regional financial integration

Regional financial integration has the potential to expand access to capital markets, as it can increase efficiency, reduce transaction costs for investors, improve liquidity conditions and reduce risks. Integration can create incentives for foreign investors to acquire assets from different countries and therefore to diversify their portfolios in a single market. Moreover – considering that access to capital markets in LAC is mostly restricted to governments, large companies and state-owned enterprises – regional integration could increase the issuer base and bring investment into new sectors (Bown et al., 2017[111]). Finally, an increase in demand for assets quoted in a single market should contribute to reducing financing costs for issuers.

The region presents barriers to integration. These obstacles include the macroeconomic environment, low market supply and demand, regulatory frameworks, and market infrastructure. Regarding the macroeconomic aspect, the region presents high heterogeneity across countries in both the environment and stability, as well as different exchange rate regimes and volatile exchange rates. Furthermore, there is low supply of and demand for securities given both the small number of issuers and investors and the lack of financial education. Finally, the different regulatory and tax frameworks, as well as the use of different platforms in every stock exchange also pose challenges to integration in LAC (Bonita et al., 2020[112]).

The Latin American Integrated Market (MILA), launched in 2011, was the region's first attempt at integration. MILA, an initiative of the stock exchanges of Chile, Colombia and Peru, was created as an opportunity to compete against larger markets. However, MILA's trading volumes remained below those of Brazil and Mexico. In 2014, Mexico joined the group, and MILA reached a market capitalisation similar to that of the Brazil stock exchange but with lower trading volumes (OECD, 2019[94]).On paper, MILA aimed to facilitate the issuance, trade and settlement of securities across countries while allowing each stock exchange to maintain its independence (IDB/Wilson Center, 2016[113]). In practice, MILA did not achieve the expected performance and was largely led by Chile and Mexico, which reached more than 90% of the total traded volumes in 2018, leading the platform to stop operations (Figure 3.30).

Figure 3.30. Share by country in MILA total traded volume, 2012-18

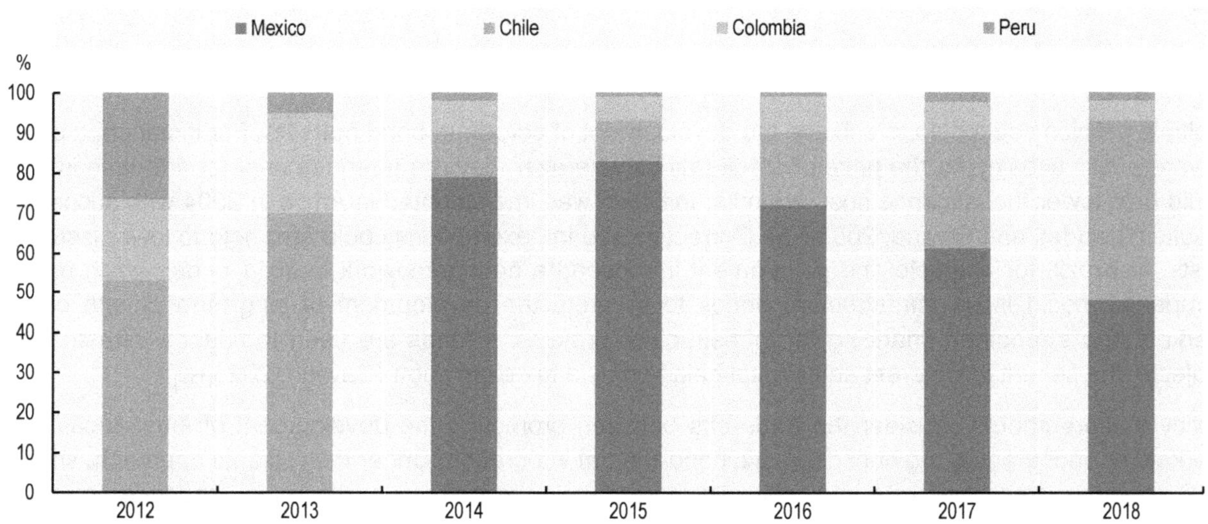

Note: MILA = Latin American Integrated Market.
Source: Authors' elaboration based on (Botero-Guzmán et al., 2023[114]).

StatLink https://stat.link/uoz3ty

Since 2020, nuam exchange has emerged as a new possibility for regional integration. Nuam exchange is a joint private initiative to build a regional market infrastructure, starting by integrating the stock exchanges of Santiago, Lima, and Colombia into one stock exchange. This initiative aims to integrate property and business models, by using one single platform and by advocating for harmonising regulations across countries (nuam exchange, 2024[115]).The three stock exchanges are now in the process of their integration. They are already legally integrated under nuam exchange and are working on the integration of operations and their trading platform, which is expected to be launched in 2025 (Rodríguez Martínez, 2024[116]). Nuam exchange is following the steps of Euronext, the leading pan-european market infrastructure born in 2000 with the merger of the Amsterdam, Brussels, and Paris exchanges.

This market integration has the potential to further develop local capital markets and attract international investors. In August 2024, nuam exchange reported a market capitalisation of almost USD 450 billion, 43% of this value coming from Bolsa de Valores de Lima, 39% from Bolsa de Comercio de Santiago and 18% from Bolsa de Valores de Colombia. In terms of the number of issuers, the integrated market reached 445 equity issuers and 345 fixed rent issuers (Figure 3.31). Under these conditions, nuam exchange is similar in size to the Malaysia exchange (in market capitalisation), the Istanbul exchange (in number of equity issuers), and the London Exchange (in number of brokers) (nuam exchange, 2024[117]). Moreover, between January and August of 2024, over USD 721 billion was traded on nuam exchange in over 12 million operations, including equity market, especial trades, fixed income, derivatives and monetary operations (nuam exchange, 2024[118]). To achieve the next steps of integration it is necessary for the authorities of Chile, Colombia, and Peru to approve mutual recognition of broker dealers and interoperability between central counterparty clearing houses (CCP).[8] These translate into brokers from any of the three countries being able to enter any of the three markets and the CCPs of all three countries being able to communicate and work between them. Features that are common practice in the European markets.

Figure 3.31. Market capitalisation and number of issuers of nuam exchange by country, August 2024

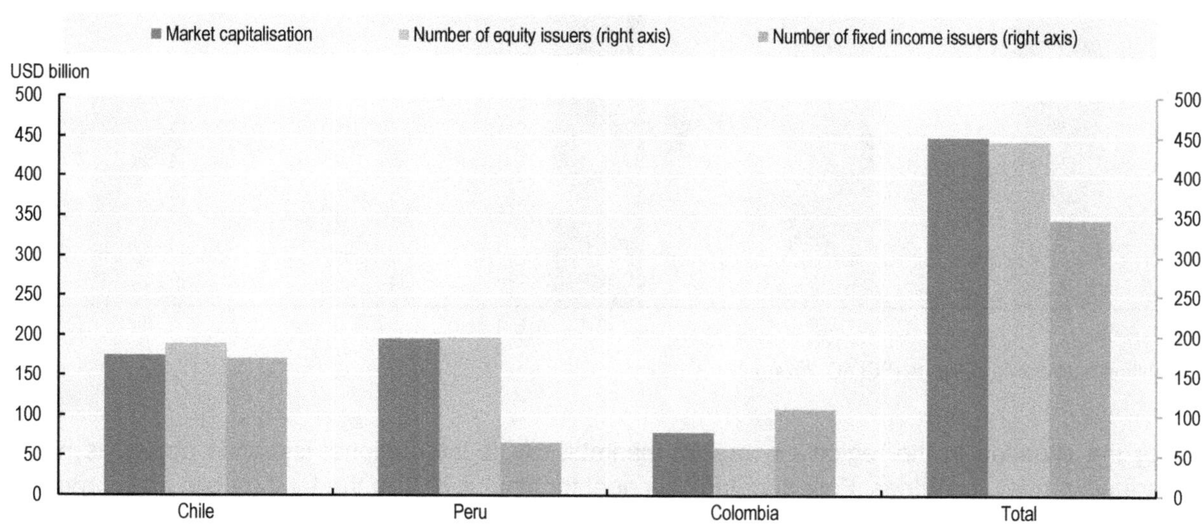

Note: the number of equity issuers does not include listed funds and ETF.
Source: Authors' elaboration based on (nuam exchange, 2024[118]) and (nuam exchange, 2024[117]).

StatLink https://stat.link/ix29de

Historically, regional integration of stock markets has been pursued via two paths: the creation of trading platforms, such as the no longer operational MILA, and the full integration of stock exchanges, as with the nuam exchange. The first type of integration has mostly been used by emerging markets. Examples are the South Eastern Europe Link, the Association of Southeast Asian Nations Trading Link and the Shanghai-Hong Kong Stock/Bond Connect (Pirgaip, Ertuğrul and Ulussever, 2021[119]). Full integration has been mostly used in Europe, with the Euronext merger, OMX integration, the merger between the London Stock Exchange and the Borsa Italiana, and the Central and Eastern Europe Stock Exchange Group (Dorodnykh, 2014[120]). Yet, it has been shown that integration with full harmonisation has a bigger impact on trading volume (Pirgaip, Ertuğrul and Ulussever, 2021[119]).

International capital markets

LAC in the international debt markets

The issuance of LAC bonds by the public and corporate sectors in international markets increased in 2023, following a slowdown in 2022. This increase was supported by currency appreciation, decelerating inflation and the end of interest rate hikes. The region's bond issuance (public and corporate) in international markets reached USD 89.15 billion in 2023, an increase of 39.7% over the year before (Figure 3.32). The region's participation in the international bond market is very balanced between sovereign and corporate issuers. In 2023, sovereign bonds accounted for 51.8% of the total issuance (USD 46.17 billion) and corporate bonds for 48.2% (USD 42.98 billion) (ECLAC, 2024[121]).

Figure 3.32. LAC public and corporate international bond issuance, 2019-23

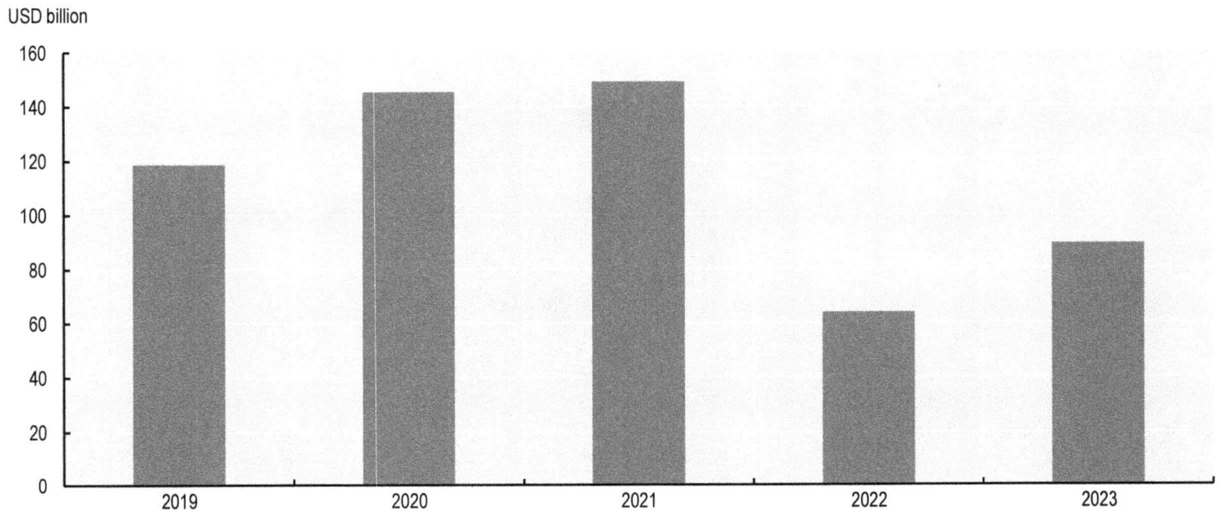

Source: Authors' elaboration based on (ECLAC, 2024[121]).

Mirroring the situation in the region's domestic markets, LAC's international issuance activity is highly concentrated in a few countries. Four countries account for almost 70% of the total (public and corporate) international issuance: Brazil (21.1%), Chile (19.3%), Mexico (17%) and Colombia (10.1%) (Figure 3.33). Moreover, supranational[9] bonds account for 8.6% of the total issuance, outperforming Costa Rica, the Dominican Republic, Panama and Peru, among others.

Figure 3.33. LAC public and corporate international bond issuance by country, 2023

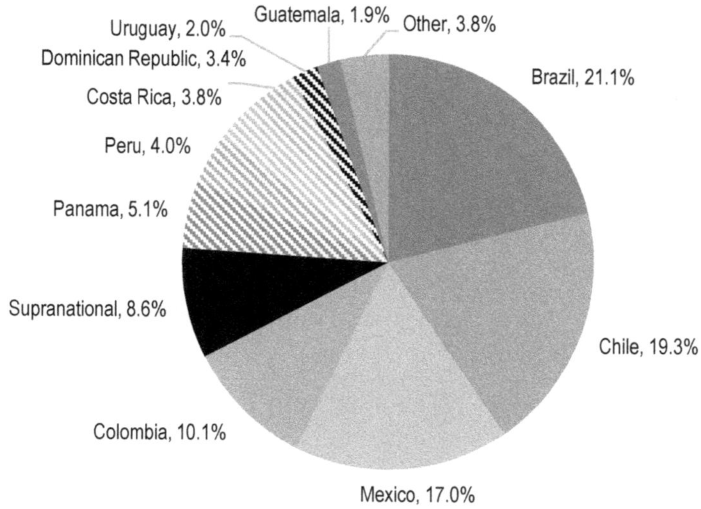

Source: Authors' elaboration based on (ECLAC, 2024[121]).

StatLink https://stat.link/mq1sok

Risks and solvency of the international capital markets

High solvency and balanced risk are crucial factors for maintaining well-developed and strong capital markets. Solvency is the ability to meet long-term obligations, like debt. It represents whether investors, creditors and other stakeholders can be confident enough that companies will repay their debts or produce returns, allowing the good functioning of the market (Factris, 2023[122]). As investors look for high returns, they will also look for higher risks. Therefore, it is in the best interest of investors and institutions to manage the risks the market is exposed to, in order to help maintain the stability of the market even when it faces shocks (Karacadag, Sundararajan and Elliott, 2003[123]).

Risk in the region decreased in 2023 after a difficult first quarter. Compared to other regions, LAC stood in the middle of the corporate bond spread ranking. The JP Morgan Corporate Emerging Markets Bond Index (CEMBI) measures the extra interest (in basis points) that a corporate international bond pays over a government international bond in emerging markets. This is a measure of how much risk emerging market corporations are perceived to have. The CEMBI for the region stood at 321 basis points at the end of December 2023 after losing 36 basis points during the year. This was 62 basis points lower than the region's sovereign counterpart, the EMBIG. After an increase in corporate spreads in the region in the first quarter of 2023 due to the default of Brazilian Lojas Americanas in January, the region was able to readjust in the following quarters and outperformed the Middle East and Asia (Figure 3.34) (ECLAC, 2024[121]).

Figure 3.34. CEMBI spread (basis points) year change by region, 2023

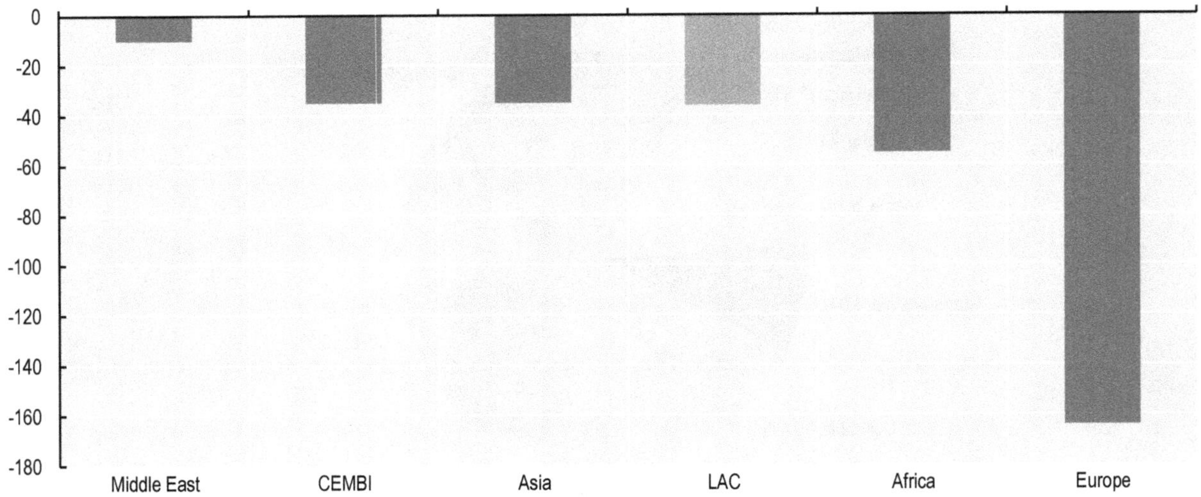

Note: CEMBI = JP Morgan Corporate Emerging Markets Bond Index.
Source: Authors' elaboration based on (ECLAC, 2024[121]).

StatLink https://stat.link/hmzv3j

Regulation of capital markets in LAC has undergone various transformations in recent years in the aim of keeping risk low and increasing efficiency. In Chile, reforms were implemented to improve the international integration of the bond market, facilitating the participation of foreign investors. In Brazil, efforts have been initiated to modernise regulation with the purpose of reducing compliance costs for companies accessing capital markets and enhancing regulatory efficiency via new regulatory technologies (Miranda, 2018[124]). While Colombia has continued improving its implementation of the IOSCO principles of securities regulation (Superintendencia Financiera de Colombia, 2024[125]).

Significant regulatory challenges remain to be addressed in the region, especially in terms of facilitating processes and incentivising new issuers. Actions by regulators must underscore the importance of dynamic and adaptive regulation that can respond effectively to changing market conditions and technological advances, ensuring sustained growth and stability of capital markets in the region. Elements to have in mind are adapting regulations to encourage greater diversification in investments, reducing operational and fiscal barriers for foreign investors, improving the protection of minority investors' rights and promoting greater financial education among the population (Miranda, 2018[124]).

The role of American Depositary Receipts

Large companies in LAC continue to use American Depositary Receipts (ADRs) to reach the equity market in the US. An ADR is a security representing shares of non-US companies held by a US depositary bank. For LAC companies, these instruments facilitate raising capital abroad, since they do not have to fulfil the listing requirements of the US market (SEC, 2012[126]). Brazil is the country in LAC with the most issuers of ADRs (72), followed by Mexico (38) (Figure 3.35). However, this is not necessarily the best option to gain access to markets, as it prevents the development of local capital markets and perpetuates the exit of companies from them. It is therefore necessary to explore other possibilities to facilitate the entry to local markets in LAC for them to expand.

Figure 3.35. Number of issuers of American Depositary Receipts in LAC by country, March 2024

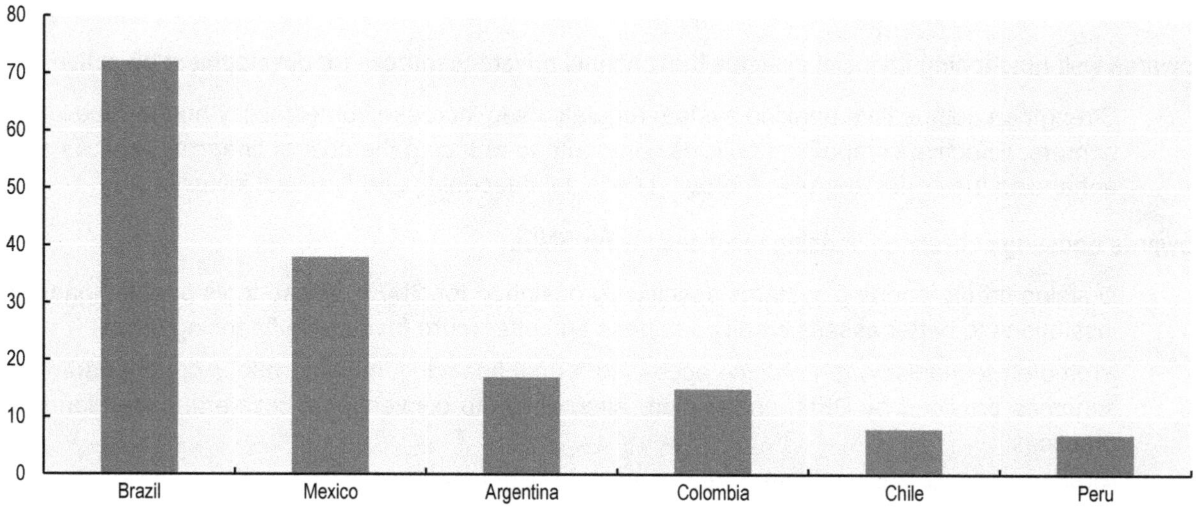

Source: Authors' calculation based on (Investing.com, 2024[127]).

StatLink https://stat.link/a6qpiy

Policy recommendations

Exploiting the potential of financial markets for advancing sustainable and inclusive growth in LAC requires channelling public and private resources effectively, boosting financing opportunities for SMEs, promoting financial inclusion and deepening capital markets. To achieve these goals, it is imperative that LAC governments formulate a co-ordinated, long-term strategy, using institutional mechanisms like national and sectoral development planning. This approach will be effective in mobilising both public and private sectors towards national strategic objectives, transcending political cycles to establish enduring policies centred on improving people's well-being (OECD et al., 2019[128]; OECD, 2021[129]).

Such a strategy has three important aspects. First, enhancing competitive banking system regulations and reducing entry barriers can foster a more dynamic financial sector, lowering costs and broadening access to financial services. Targeted measures aimed at improving access to finance for SMEs include developing specialised credit reporting systems and promoting alternative financing mechanisms beyond traditional collateral-based lending. Second, to promote inclusive economic growth, it is essential to ensure that high-quality financial products are accessible to underserved populations, to leverage digital innovations and to promote financial literacy. Finally, deepening capital markets through regulatory modernisation, encouraging institutional investor participation and promoting regional financial integration are crucial steps towards enhancing market efficiency and resilience across the region (Box 3.4).

Box 3.4. Key policy messages

Towards well-functioning financial systems that channel private resources for development objectives

- Strengthen competitive banking system regulations to increase contestability and reduce entry barriers. Effective competition policies contribute to reducing the cost of financial services and enhancing their offer, thereby improving financial deepening and financial inclusion.

Towards boosting access to financing mechanisms for SMEs

- Develop credit reporting systems specifically designed for SMEs. These tools enable financial institutions to better assess creditworthiness and offer more favourable financing terms.
- Promote mechanisms to enhance access to formal financing, such as public credit guarantee schemes provided by DFIs, and explore alternatives to conventional collateral-based lending practices.
- Strengthen data collection and statistical information related to SME financing in order to develop effective and evidence-based policies.
- Adopt the OECD recommendations on SME financing to: i) enhance access to a variety of financing instruments and channels tailored to their specific needs; ii) design regulation that supports a range of financing instruments for SMEs; and iii) foster innovation by providing appropriate incentives and market conditions.
- To support climate financing, national and subnational DFIs should build further technical capacity, both for clients and for themselves.

Towards financial inclusion

Ensure that high-quality financial products and services are accessible to all.

- Develop a comprehensive, evidenced-based and multiagency National Financial Inclusion Strategy defining regulatory frameworks and detailed work plans, including clear monitoring and evaluation strategies for tracking progress and making adjustments.
- Facilitate access to credit and other financial services for SMEs and informal workers to enhance their economic opportunities and growth potential. Promote the formalisation of informal workers to improve their access to financial products and services.
- Implement targeted interventions to close the gender gap in financial access, ensuring that women have equal opportunities to benefit from financial services. Support women-owned businesses through tailored financial products and services to promote their economic participation and growth.
- Encourage the use of alternative data in credit scoring to extend credit access to underserved populations and SMEs, thus improving financial inclusion and economic participation.

Leverage digital innovations to enhance the usage of financial services and reach previously underserved segments of society.

- Leverage fintech innovations to bypass traditional banking barriers and provide financial services to previously unbanked and underbanked populations.
- Foster the development and adoption of digital financial services, such as mobile money, digital payments and neobanking, to increase financial inclusion.
- Encourage regulatory advancements in open finance to promote competition and innovation in financial services.

Enhance financial literacy programmes and establish robust consumer protection frameworks to ensure the quality of financial services.

- Implement comprehensive financial literacy programmes targeting both adults and youth to improve understanding of basic financial concepts.
- Promote digital financial literacy to enable safe and effective use of digital financial services.
- Strengthen consumer protection frameworks:
    - Develop robust regulatory frameworks to protect consumers from fraud and abusive practices, ensuring transparency and building trust in financial systems.
    - Mandate data sharing among financial institutions to enhance the availability of tailored and accessible financial products.

Towards deepening of capital markets

- Boost the participation of institutional investors in the region's equity markets to foster their development.
- Modernise regulation to facilitate processes, reduce compliance costs, incentivise new issuers in domestic bond and equity markets, and reduce operational barriers for foreign investors.
- Promote policies that lower the cost of issuance in both equity and bond markets.
- Design policies that promote private markets, including domestic venture capital investment.
- Incentivise regional financial integration to increase investment in the region, improve efficiency, reduce transaction costs, improve liquidity, and reduce risks. This includes:
    - In the short run, allowing mutual recognition of deal brokers and interoperability of central counterparty clearing houses to achieve integration.
    - In the medium and long run, consolidating operational and technological integration and homogenising regulatory and tax frameworks across countries.

Notes

[1] Alternative finance encompasses non-traditional capital-raising methods.

[2] A National Financial Literacy Strategy can lower market concentration by enabling consumers to make better choices, reducing provider dominance, and fostering a more dynamic, competitive market.

[3] "DFIs" in this document will always refer only to national and subnational public development finance institutions.

[4] Large companies refer to those companies with market capitalisation greater than USD 1 billion (OECD, 2023[88]).

[5] "A vertical is a more specific dimension of a company's activities that provides a view about niche markets spanning multiple industries. Some examples of verticals are Fintech, healthtech, e-commerce, virtual reality, and advanced manufacturing." (Rudolph, Miguel and Gonzalez-Uribe, 2023[97]).

[6] For most corporate bonds reported on the London Stock Exchange Group database, the governing law was not reported. It is therefore assumed to be local for all bonds when the bonds meet the other three criteria.

[7] For bonds with an original maturity greater than one year and issues greater than USD 1 million.

[8] A CCP takes the role of clearing transactions, meaning it computes the obligations of market participants that result from their trading activities. Therefore, the CCP is an intermediary between buyer and seller, it acts as the buyer to each seller and seller to each buyer (European Central Bank, 2005[131]).

[9] "Supranational entities are organisations or authorities that go beyond the boundaries of a single country, representing a higher level of co-operation and decision making among participating countries which can include regional development banks, international agencies, among others." (Dagnino Contreras et al., 2023[130]).

References

Abuselidze, G. (2021), "The Impact of Banking Competition on Economic Growth and Financial Stability: An Empirical Investigation", *European Journal of Sustainable Development*, Vol. 10/1, https://doi.org/10.14207/ejsd.2021.v10n1p203. [34]

AFD (2023), *"Climate-financial trap: an empirical approach to detecting situations of double vulnerability"*, Agence Française de Développement, https://www.afd.fr/en/ressources/climate-financial-trap-empirical-approach-detecting-situations-double-vulnerability. [85]

AFD/Peking University (2023), *Public Development Banks and Development Financing Institutions Database*, Agence Française de Développement and Institute of New Structural Economics at Peking University, http://www.dfidatabase.pku.edu.cn/. [78]

Aldasoro, I., B. Hardy and N. Tarashev (2021), *What constitutes an international debt security in BIS statistics?*, https://www.bis.org/publ/qtrpdf/r_qt2106z.htm. [103]

ALIDE (2023), *Latin America's Development Banking System : Five Years Later*, Latin American Association of Development Financing Institutions, https://www.alidedatabank.org/1001/plantilla/documentoPublicacionAlide/Book%2055%20Years.pdf. [82]

Almarzoqi, R., S. Naceur and A. Kotak (2015), "What Matters for Financial Development and Stability?", *IMF Working Papers,* No. 15.173, International Monetary Fund, Washington, DC, https://www.imf.org/external/pubs/ft/wp/2015/wp15173.pdf. [11]

Andrade, ,. et al. (2023), *Financing Programs for Women's Financial Inclusion and Access to Finance for Women MSMEs: Results from a Survey of Public Development Banks*, Inter-American Development Bank, Washington, DC, https://doi.org/10.18235/0005104. [58]

Arcand, J., E. Berkes and U. Panizza (2012), "Too Much Finance?", *IMF Working Papers,* No. WP/12/161, International Monetary Fund, Washington, DC, https://www.imf.org/external/pubs/ft/wp/2012/wp12161.pdf. [12]

Arellano, A. et al. (2018), "Policy priorities to promote financial development in the context of the Middle-Income Trap: The cases of Argentina, Colombia, Mexico and Peru", *BBVA Research Working Paper*, No. 18/15, https://www.bbvaresearch.com/wp-content/uploads/2018/12/Financial_development_BBVA_OECD-1-1.pdf. [8]

Atkins, L. et al. (2024), *The cyber clock is ticking: Derisking emerging technologies in financial services*, McKinsey & Company, https://www.mckinsey.com/capabilities/risk-and-resilience/our-insights/the-cyber-clock-is-ticking-derisking-emerging-technologies-in-financial-services. [75]

Aurazo, J. and F. Gasmi (2024), "Financial inclusion transitions in Peru: Does labor informality play a role?", *BIS Working Paper*, No. 1200, Bank of International Settlements, https://www.bis.org/publ/work1200.pdf. [50]

Ayala Pena, D., M. Nedeljkovic and C. Saborowski (2015), "What Slice of the Pie? The Corporate Bond Market Boom in Emerging Economies", *IMF Working Papers*, Vol. 15/148, p. 1, https://doi.org/10.5089/9781513579757.001. [105]

Bakker, B. et al. (2023), *The Rise and Impact of Fintech in Latin America*, International Monetary Fund, Washington, DC, https://www.imf.org/en/Publications/fintech-notes/Issues/2023/03/28/The-Rise-and-Impact-of-Fintech-in-Latin-America-531055. [62]

Banca de las Oportunidades and CAF (2024), *Estudio Experimental de Género*, Banca de las Oportunidades and CAF Banco de Desarrollo de América Latina y el Caribe, https://www.bancadelasoportunidades.gov.co/sites/default/files/2024-03/Estudio%20Esperimental%20de%20g%C3%A9nero.pdf. [54]

Banerjee, A. and E. Duflo (2011), *Poor Economics: A Radical Rethinking of the Way to Fight Global Poverty*, Public Affairs. [43]

Beck, T. (2018), *"Basel III & Unintended Consequences for Emerging Markets and Developing Economies - Part 4: Challenges on Infrastructure and SME lending"*, Center for Global Development, https://www.cgdev.org/blog/basel-iii-unintended-consequences-emerging-markets-developing-economies-part-iv-challenges. [41]

Beck, T. and A. de La Torre (2007), "The basic analytics of access to financial services", *Financial Markets, Institutions and Instruments*, Vol. 16/2, pp. 79-117, https://pure.uvt.nl/ws/files/1023754/The_Basic_Analytics_of_Access_to_Financial_Services..pdf. [46]

Beck, T., A. Demirgüç-Kunt and R. Levine (2007), "Finance, inequality and the poor", *Journal of Economic Growth*, Vol. 12, pp. 27-49, https://doi.org/10.1007/s10887-007-9010-6. [45]

Beck, T. and L. Rojas-Suarez (2019), *Making Basel III Work for Emerging Markets and Developing Economies*, Center for Global Development, https://www.cgdev.org/sites/default/files/making-basel-iii-work-emerging-markets-developing-economies.pdf. [40]

Bejar, P. et al. (2022), "Can Fintech Foster Competition in the Banking System in Latin America and the Caribbean?", *Latin American Journal of Central Banking*, Vol. 3/2, https://doi.org/10.1016/j.latcb.2022.100061. [29]

Berg, R., J. Rubio and N. Lask (2024), *Catalysts of Change: How Entrepreneurs Are Transforming Latin America*, Center for Strategic and International Studies, https://csis-website-prod.s3.amazonaws.com/s3fs-public/2024-03/240308_Berg_Catalysts_Change.pdf?VersionId=WmAhPHJBDXCr7ah9amXNSVSJaG_4a8.f. [101]

BIS (2020), *"Risk-based capital requirements"*, Bank of Intenational Settlements, Basel, https://www.bis.org/basel_framework/chapter/RBC/20.htm. [35]

Boikos, S., T. Panagiotidis and G. Voucharas (2022), "Financial development, reforms and growth", *Economic Modelling*, Vol. 108, https://doi.org/10.1016/j.econmod.2021.105734. [4]

Bonita, D. et al. (2020), "Cross Border Integration of Capital Markets-Lessons from Northern Europe and Emerging Asia for the LAC Region". [112]

Botero-Guzmán, D. et al. (2023), "Stock market integration in member countries of the Latin American Integrated Market (MILA)", *Revista Gestión y Desarrollo Libre*, Vol. 8/16, pp. 1-21. [114]

Bown, C. et al. (2017), *Better Neighbors: Toward a Renewal of Economic Integration in Latin America*, World Bank, Washington, DC, https://openknowledge.worldbank.org/entities/publication/a675c19d-1a46-5e58-9919-788f16c4d7f3 (accessed on 15 March 2024). [111]

Bruhn, M. and I. Love (2013), "The Real Impact of Improved Access to Finance: Evidence from Mexico", *Journal of Finance (forthcoming)*, https://papers.ssrn.com/sol3/papers.cfm?abstract_id=2285013. [23]

CAF (2023), *Encuesta de Capacidades Financieras*, CAF Banco de Desarrollo de América Latina, https://www.caf.com/es/conocimiento/datos/visualizador-encuesta-de-capacidades-financieras/. [69]

Carlson, M., S. Correia and S. Luck (2022), "The Effects of Banking Competition on Growth and Financial Stability: Evidence from the National Banking Era", *Journal of Political Economy*, Vol. 130/2, https://www.journals.uchicago.edu/doi/abs/10.1086/717453. [32]

Cavallo, E. (2023), *Developing Domestic Bond Markets for Growth and Stability*, https://blogs.iadb.org/ideas-matter/en/developing-domestic-bond-markets-for-growth-and-stability/. [110]

Cavallo, E. and E. Pedemonte (2015), *"What is the Relationship between National Saving and Investment in Latin America and the Caribbean?"*, Inter-American Development Bank, https://doi.org/10.18235/0000138. [18]

Christiano Silva, T., B. Miranda Tabak and M. Tetzner Laiz (2021), "The finance-growth nexus: The role of banks", *Economic Systems*, Vol. 45/1, https://doi.org/10.1016/j.ecosys.2020.100762. [7]

Čihák, M. et al. (2012), "Benchmarking financial systems around the world", *Policy Research Working Paper*, No. 6175, World Bank, Washington, DC, https://documents.worldbank.org/en/publication/documents-reports/documentdetail/868131468326381955/benchmarking-financial-systems-around-the-world. [9]

CMF (2022), *Informe de Género en el sistema financiero 2022*, Comisión para el Mercado Financiero (CMF), Santiago, https://www.cmfchile.cl/portal/estadisticas/617/articles-52460_recurso_1.pdf. [55]

Dagnino Contreras, V. et al. (2023), *LAC Sustainable Debt State of the Market 2022*, Climate Bonds Initiative. [130]

David, A., C. Goncalves and A. Werner (2020), "Reexamining the National Savings-Investment Nexus Across Time and Countries", *IMF Working Papers*, No. 2020/124, International Monetary Fund, Washington, DC, https://www.imf.org/en/Publications/WP/Issues/2020/07/10/Reexamining-the-National-Savings-Investment-Nexus-Across-Time-and-Countries-49548. [17]

De La Cruz, A., A. Medina and Y. Tang (2019), "Owners of the World's Listed Companies", *OECD Capital Market Series*, https://www.oecd.org/en/publications/owners-of-the-world-s-listed-companies_ed7ca2f3-en.html. [96]

De la Torre, A. et al. (2011), *Financial Development in Latin America and the Caribbean: The Road Ahead*, World Bank Group, Washington, DC, http://documents.worldbank.org/curated/en/784141468053952645/Financial-development-in-Latin-America-and-the-Caribbean-the-road-ahead. [10]

De Luna-Martínez, J. (2017), "The role of development financial institutions in the new millennium", *World Bank Blogs*, https://blogs.worldbank.org/en/eastasiapacific/the-role-of-development-financial-institutions-in-the-new-millennium. [76]

Demirgüç-Kunt, A., L. Klapper and D. Sin (2013), "Financial Inclusion and Legal Discrimination against Women: Evidence from Developing Countries", *Policy Research Working Papers*, No. 6416, World Bank, Washington, DC, https://doi.org/10.1596/1813-9450-6416. [53]

Demirgüç-Kunt, A. et al. (2022), *Global Findex Database 2021: Financial Inclusion, Digital Payments, and Resilience in the Age of COVID-19*, The World Bank, Washington, DC, https://documents1.worldbank.org/curated/en/099818107072234182/pdf/IDU06a834fe908933040670a6560f44e3f4d35b7.pdf. [64]

Dorodnykh, E. (2014), "Evidences from the Recent History", in *Stock Market Integration*, Palgrave Macmillan UK, London, https://doi.org/10.1057/9781137381705_3. [120]

Easterly, W., R. Islam and J. Stiglitz (2000), *Explaining Growth Volatility*, World Bank, Washington, DC, https://documents1.worldbank.org/curated/pt/447071468761424497/820140748_200404131103725/additional/28159.pdf. [13]

ECLAC (2024), *Capital Flows to Latin America and the Caribbean: 2023 year-in-review*, http://www.issuu.com/publicacionescepal/stacks. [121]

EIB (2023), *Climate risks for Latin America and the Caribbean: Are banks ready for the green transition?*, EIB Economics Department, European Investment Bank, Luxembourg, https://www.eib.org/attachments/lucalli/20230142_climate_risks_for_latin_america_and_the_caribbean_en.pdf. [87]

EIB (2021), *Assessing climate change risks at the country level: the EIB scoring model*, EIB Economics Department, European Investment Bank, Luxembourg, https://www.eib.org/attachments/efs/economics_working_paper_2021_03_en.pdf. [86]

Eichengreen, B., R. Hausmann and U. Panizza (2005), "The pain of original sin", in *Other people's money: Debt denomination and financial instability in emerging market economies*, University of Chicago Press. [107]

European Central Bank (2005), *Central counterparty clearing houses and financial stability*, https://www.ecb.europa.eu/pub/pdf/fsr/art/ecb.fsrart200512_06.en.pdf. [131]

Factris (2023), *What is solvency?*. [122]

Fang, X. et al. (2022), "Bank capital requirements and lending in emerging markets: The role of bank characteristics and economic conditions", *Journal of Banking & Finance*, Vol. 135, https://doi.org/10.1016/j.jbankfin.2020.105806. [37]

Finance in Common (2024), *Finance in Common (website)*, https://financeincommon.org/. [80]

Finance in Common (2024), "G20 - Finance in Common (FiCS) Joint Event 20 & 21 May 2024, Rio de Janeiro", Finance in Common, https://financeincommon.org/g20-finance-in-common-fics-joint-event-20-21-may-2024-rio-de-janeiro-0. [79]

FTC (2023), *Merger Guidelines*, U.S. Department of Justice and the Federal Trade Commission, https://www.justice.gov/d9/2023-12/2023%20Merger%20Guidelines.pdf. [90]

Galindo, A. and A. Izquierdo (2024), *Ready for take-off? Building on Macroeconomic Stability For Growth, 2024 Latin America and Caribbean Macroeconomic Report*, Inter-American Development Bank, https://doi.org/10.18235/0005667. [39]

Gelos, G. (2006), "Banking spreads in Latin America", *IMF Working Paper*, No. 2006/044, International Monetary Fund, Washington, DC, https://www.imf.org/en/Publications/WP/Issues/2016/12/31/Banking-Spreads-in-Latin-America-18792. [31]

Grandes, M. and N. Pinaud (2005), *Reducing Capital Cost in South Africa*, Development Centre Studies, OECD Publishing, Paris, https://doi.org/10.1787/9789264014022-en. [109]

Grifoni, A. et al. (2020), *Estrategias nacionales de inclusión y educación financiera en América Latina y el Caribe: retos de implementación*, https://scioteca.caf.com/handle/123456789/1605. [73]

Haussmann, R. and U. Panizza (2011), "Redemption or abstinence? Original sin, currency mismatches and counter cyclical policies in the new millennium", *Journal of Globalization and Development*, Vol. 2/1. [108]

Herrera, D. (2020), *MSME Financing Instruments in Latin America and the Caribbean During COVID-19*, Inter-American Development Bank, Washington, DC, https://publications.iadb.org/en/msme-financing-instruments-in-latin-america-and-the-caribbean-during-covid-19. [20]

Herrera, D. et al. (2023), *Open finance in Latin America and the Caribbean: Great Opportunities, Large Challenges*, Inter-American Development Bank, Washington, DC, https://publications.iadb.org/en/open-finance-latin-america-and-caribbean-great-opportunities-large-challenges. [49]

IDB/Wilson Center (2016), *Financial Integration in the Pacific Alliance*, Inter-American Development Bank, Washington, DC, https://www.wilsoncenter.org/sites/default/files/media/documents/article/financial-integration-in-the-pacific-alliance_final_report.pdf (accessed on 25 March 2024). [113]

IFC (2017), *MSME Finance Gap: Assessment of the Shortfalls and Opportunities in Financing (database)*, International Finance Corporation, Washington, DC. [25]

ILOSTAT (2024), *Statistics on the informal economy (database)*, International Labour Organization, https://ilostat.ilo.org/es/topics/informality/. [52]

IMF (2023), *Regional Economic Outlook: Western Hemisphere, October 2023*, International Monetary Fund, Washington, DC, https://www.imf.org/en/Publications/REO/WH/Issues/2023/10/13/regional-economic-outlook-western-hemisphere-october-2023. [27]

IMF (2022), *"Financial Soundness Indicators" (database)*, IMF Data, International Monetary Fund, Washington, DC, https://data.imf.org/?sk=51b096fa-2cd2-40c2-8d09-0699cc1764da. [38]

Investing.com (2024), *World ADRs*, https://investing.com/equities/world-adrs. [127]

Joaquim, G., B. Van Doornik and R. Haas (2023), "Bank competition, cost of credit and economic activity: Evidence from Brazil", *BIS Working Papers,* No.1134, Bank of International Settlements, https://www.bis.org/publ/work1134.htm. [33]

Karacadag, C., V. Sundararajan and J. Elliott (2003), "Managing Risks in Financial Market Development: The Role of Sequencing", *IMF Working Paper*. [123]

Lahura, E. and M. Vargas (2021), *Financial development, financial inclusion, and informality: New international evidence*, Banco Central de Reserva del Perú, https://www.bcrp.gob.pe/docs/Publicaciones/Documentos-de-Trabajo/2021/documento-de-trabajo-004-2021.pdf. [51]

LAVCA (2023), *Q3 2023 LAVCA Industry Data & Analysis*, https://www.lavca.org/research/q3-2023-lavca-industry-data-analysis/. [99]

Levine, R. (2018), "Finance, Growth, and Economic Prosperity", *Macroeconomic Review,* Special Feature B, Monetary Authority of Singapore, https://www.mas.gov.sg/publications/economic-essays/2018/finance-growth-and-economic-prosperity. [1]

London Stock Exchange Group (2024), *DataStream (Database)*. [92]

López Marmolejo, A. and M. Ruiz Arranz (eds.) (2024), *Increasing Financial Inclusion to drive development: Economic report on Central America, Mexico, Panama, and the Dominican Republic*, Inter-American Development Bank, Washington, DC. [71]

Maquera Sardon, D. (2022), *Improving the Performance of Female Entrepreneurs in LAC*, World Bank Group, http://documents.worldbank.org/curated/en/856951642746562382/Improving-the-Performance-of-Female-Entrepreneurs-in-LAC. [56]

Mastercard and AMI (2023), *The state of financial inclusion post COVID-19 in Latin America and the Caribbean: New opportunities for the payments ecosystem*, Mastercard and Americas Market Intelligence (AMI), https://www.mastercard.com/news/media/eacheaa4/report_en_ami_mastercard_financial_inclusion_post_covid.pdf?cmp=2025.q2.lac.latam.fis.dir-res.prod.na.eng-regional-press-release.56798.oweb.txt.others.en. [63]

Maudos, J. and L. Solís (2009), "The determinants of net interest income in the Mexican banking system: An integrated model", *Journal of Banking & Finance*, Vol. 33/10, pp. 1920-1931, https://doi.org/10.1016/j.jbankfin.2009.04.012. [30]

Melguizo, A. et al. (2017), "No sympathy for the devil! Policy priorities to overcome the middle-income trap in Latin America", *OECD Development Centre Working Papers*, No. 340, https://doi.org/10.1787/26b78724-en. [91]

Miranda, M. (ed.) (2018), *Latin American local capital markets: challenges and solutions*, CFA Institute Research Foundation. [124]

Morgan, P. and V. Pontines (2014), "Financial Stability and Financial Inclusion", *ADBI Working Paper Series*, Asian Development Bank Institute, Tokyo, http://www.adbi.org/working-paper/2014/07/07/6353.financial.stability.inclusion/. [22]

nuam exchange (2024), *About nuam*, https://www.nuamx.com/en/about-nuam. [115]

nuam exchange (2024), *Invitación para construir un nuevo mercado de capitales*. [117]

nuam exchange (2024), *Regional Stock Report August 2024*. [118]

OECD (2024), *Capital Market Series dataset*. [95]

OECD (2024), *Consumer Finance Risk Monitor*, OECD Publishing, Paris, https://doi.org/10.1787/047b2ea6-en. [74]

OECD (2024), *Financing SMEs and Entrepreneurs 2024: An OECD Scoreboard*, OECD Publishing, Paris, https://doi.org/10.1787/fa521246-en. [26]

OECD (2024), *Global Debt Report 2024: Bond Markets in a High-Debt Environment*, OECD Publishing, Paris, https://doi.org/10.1787/91844ea2-en. [104]

OECD (2024), *OECD Affordable Housing Database - indicator HM1.3 Housing tenures*, OECD Publishing, Paris, https://oe.cd/ahd. [47]

OECD (2024), *PISA 2022 Results (Volume IV). Factsheets. Brazil, Costa Rica and Peru*, OECD Publishing, Paris. [70]

OECD (2023), *Background Note on Capital Market Trends in Latin America*, https://www.oecd.org/corporate/ca/Capital-markets-trends-Latin-America-background-note.pdf (accessed on 19 March 2024). [88]

OECD (2023), *Joining Forces for Gender Equality: What is Holding us Back?*, OECD Publishing, Paris, https://doi.org/10.1787/67d48024-en. [59]

OECD (2023), "OECD/INFE 2023 International Survey of Adult Financial Literacy", *OECD Business and Finance Policy Papers, No. 39, OECD Publishing, Paris*, No. 39, OECD Publishing, Paris, https://doi.org/10.1787/56003a32-en. [67]

OECD (2022), *Recommendation of the Council on High-Level Principles on Financial Consumer Protection*, https://legalinstruments.oecd.org/en/instruments/OECD-LEGAL-0394. [42]

OECD (2021), *G20/OECD-INFE Report on Navigating the Storm: MSMEs' Financial and Digital Competencies in COVID-19 times*, OECD Publishing, Paris, https://doi.org/10.1787/002529a9-en. [66]

OECD (2021), *How's Life in Latin America?: Measuring Well-being for Policy Making*, OECD Publishing, Paris, https://doi.org/10.1787/2965f4fe-en. [129]

OECD (2021), *Key Indicators of Informality based on Individuals and their Household (KIIbIH) database*, OECD Publishing, Paris, https://www.oecd.org/dev/key-indicators-informality-individuals-household-kiibih.htm. [48]

OECD (2020), *Recommendation of the Council on Financial Literacy*, OECD/LEGAL/0461, OECD Publishing, Paris, https://legalinstruments.oecd.org/en/instruments/OECD-LEGAL-0461. [68]

OECD (2020), *The Financial System*, OECD Publishing, Paris, https://doi.org/10.1787/d45f979e-en. [3]

OECD (2019), *Equity Market Development in Latin America Enhancing Access to Corporate Finance*. [94]

OECD (2010), *Latin American Economic Outlook 2011: How Middle-Class Is Latin America?*, OECD Publishing, Paris, https://doi.org/10.1787/leo-2011-en. [36]

OECD et al. (2023), *Latin American Economic Outlook 2023: Investing in Sustainable Development*, OECD Publishing, Paris, https://doi.org/10.1787/8c93ff6e-en. [6]

OECD et al. (2019), *Latin American Economic Outlook 2019: Development in Transition*, OECD Publishing, Paris, https://doi.org/10.1787/g2g9ff18-en. [128]

OECD/CAF/SELA (2024), *SME Policy Index: Latin America and the Caribbean 2024: Towards an Inclusive, Resilient, and Sustainable Recovery*, OECD Publishing, Paris, https://doi.org/10.1787/ba028c1d-en. [21]

Pal, S. and I. Bandyopadhyayv (2022), "Impact of financial inclusion on economic growth, financial development, financial eficiency, fnancial stability, and profitability: international evidence", *SN Business & Economics*, Vol. 2/9, pp. 1-29. [44]

Pirgaip, B., H. Ertuğrul and T. Ulussever (2021), “Is portfolio diversification possible in integrated markets? Evidence from South Eastern Europe”, *Research in International Business and Finance*, Vol. 56, https://doi.org/10.1016/j.ribaf.2021.101384. [119]

Powell, A. and O. Valencia (2023), *Dealing with Debt: Less Risk for More Growth in Latin America and the Caribbean*, Inter-American Development Bank, https://doi.org/10.18235/0004707. [102]

Preqin (2024), *Preqin (Database)*, https://www.preqin.com/. [100]

Preqin (2024), *Preqin Pro glossary of terms*. [98]

Rajan, R. (2006), “Has finance made the world riskier?”, *European financial management*, Vol. 12, pp. 499-533, https://onlinelibrary.wiley.com/doi/abs/10.1111/j.1468-036X.2006.00330. [14]

Red Iberoamericana de Garantías (2023), *Encuesta Sobre la Actividad de los Sistemas de Garantía Iberoamericanos*, https://redegarantias.com/publicacion/encuesta-sobre-la-actividad-de-los-sistemas-de-garantia-iberoamericanos/. [83]

Rodríguez Martínez, H. (2024), *Primera junta de accionistas del mercado integrado nuam exchange*, https://www.portafolio.co/negocios/empresas/primera-junta-de-accionistas-del-mercado-integrado-nuam-exchange-603908. [116]

Rogozinski, N. (2017), *Latin America: The Role of Development Banks*, Global Finance, https://gfmag.com/features/latin-america-development-breathing-room/. [84]

Rudolph, H., F. Miguel and J. Gonzalez-Uribe (2023), *FINANCE Venture Capital in Latin America and the Caribbean*, http://www.worldbank.org. [97]

Sahay, R. et al. (2020), *The promise of fintech : financial inclusion in the post COVID-19 era /*, International Monetary Fund, Washington, DC. [61]

Saona, P. (2016), “Intra- and extra-bank determinants of Latin American Banks’ profitability”, *International Review of Economics & Finance*, Vol. 45, pp. 197-214, https://doi.org/10.1016/j.iref.2016.06.004. [28]

SEC (2012), *Investor Bulletin: American Depositary Receipts*, Securities and Exchange Commission, https://www.sec.gov/investor/alerts/adr-bulletin.pdf. [126]

Statista (2024), *Number of Fintech Users in Latin America in 2023, by Segment*, Statista Research Department, https://www.statista.com/forecasts/1241612/latin-american-caribbean-fintech-users-segment. [65]

Strobbe, F., O. Nie and H. Rab (2023), “Expanding economic growth through a deeper financial sector in Indonesia”, *World Bank Blogs*, https://blogs.worldbank.org/en/eastasiapacific/expanding-economic-growth-through-deeper-financial-sector-indonesia. [5]

Superintendencia Financiera de Colombia (2024), *Resultados FSAP evaluación 2012-2014 principios de valores IOSCO*. [125]

UN Women (2022), *Progress on the Sustainable Development Goals: The Gender Snapshot 2022*, UN Women, New York, https://unstats.un.org/sdgs/gender-snapshot/2022/GenderSnapshot.pdf. [60]

UNCTAD (2024), *Financing for Sustainable Development Report 2024: Financing for Development at a Crossroads*, Inter-agency Task Force on Financing for Development, UNCTAD, New York, https://developmentfinance.un.org/fsdr2024. [57]

UNEP (2023), *Unlocking Circular Economy Finance in Latin America and the Caribbean: The Catalyst for a Positive Change— Findings and recommendations for Policymakers and the Financial Sector*. [89]

Vest (2023), *Latin American Companies on Wall Street: A Path to Global Markets*, https://sproutfi.com/en-US/insights/latin-american-companies-on-wall-street-a-path-to-global-markets/. [93]

Vtyurina, S., A. Robles and B. Sutton (2017), "A License to Issue (Anywhere): Patterns and Drivers of Corporate Bonds in Latin America", *IMF Working Paper*. [106]

World Bank (2024), *The Enterprises Survey*, World Bank, Washington, DC, https://www.enterprisesurveys.org/en/enterprisesurveys. [24]

World Bank (2024), *World Development Indicators (Database)*, World Bank, Washington, DC, https://databank.worldbank.org/source/world-development-indicators. [16]

World Bank (2022), *Global Financial Development (Database)*, World Bank, Washington, DC, https://www.worldbank.org/en/publication/gfdr/data/global-financial-development-database. [15]

World Bank (2021), *The Global Findex Database 2021: Financial Inclusion, Digital Payments, and Resilience in the Age of COVID-19 (database)*, World Bank, Washington, DC, https://www.worldbank.org/en/publication/globalfindex. [19]

World Bank (2008), *Finance for All? Policies and Pitfalls in Expanding Access*, World Bank, Washington, DC, http://hdl.handle.net/10986/6905. [2]

Xu, J. et al. (2021), "What are Public Development Banks and Development Financing Institutions? Qualification criteria, stylized facts and development trends", *China Economic Quarterly International*, Vol. 1/4, pp. 271-294, https://www.nse.pku.edu.cn/docs/2021-10/20211025102148259508.pdf. [81]

Xu, J., X. Ren and X. Wu (2019), *Mapping Development Finance Institutions Wordlwide: Definitions, rationales and varieties*, Institute of New Structural Economics, Pekin University, https://www.researchgate.net/profile/Jiajun-Xu-2/publication/333718771_Mapping_Development_Finance_Institutions_Worldwide_Definitions_Rationales_and_Varieties/links/5d00a58692851c874c5fc9f0/Mapping-Development-Finance-Institutions-Worldwide-Definitions-Ra. [77]

Zuleta, L. (2017), "La Inclusión Financiera de las PyMEs en Colombia", *Revista Coyuntura PyME No 56*, Asociación Nacional de Instituciones Financieras (ANIF), Bogotá, https://www.cepal.org/es/notas/la-inclusion-financiera-pymes-colombia. [72]

4 International finance and partnerships to catalyse international resources

As Latin America and the Caribbean (LAC) prepares for the Fourth International Conference on Financing for Development in 2025, the region must reassess its strategic priorities in light of a challenging international context. A unified agenda is essential for addressing issues such as access to liquidity, risk perceptions, concessional finance, private finance mobilisation and co-ordination among development providers to ensure sustainable financial flows. Aligning private flows with sustainable goals, fostering innovative partnerships, and leveraging the region's attractiveness and investment potential are key to addressing pressing challenges like high debt levels and productive constraints and to increasing climate finance needs. More impactful co-operation, clear investment frameworks, and strategic partnerships are crucial for developing tailored financial tools. These efforts will enable LAC to influence global development financing and partnerships, ensuring that its countries' demands are effectively represented at the 2025 conference.

Infographic 4.1. International financing and partnerships can catalyse more foreign resources in LAC

International finance would have more impact on development with better regulatory frameworks and more ambitious partnerships

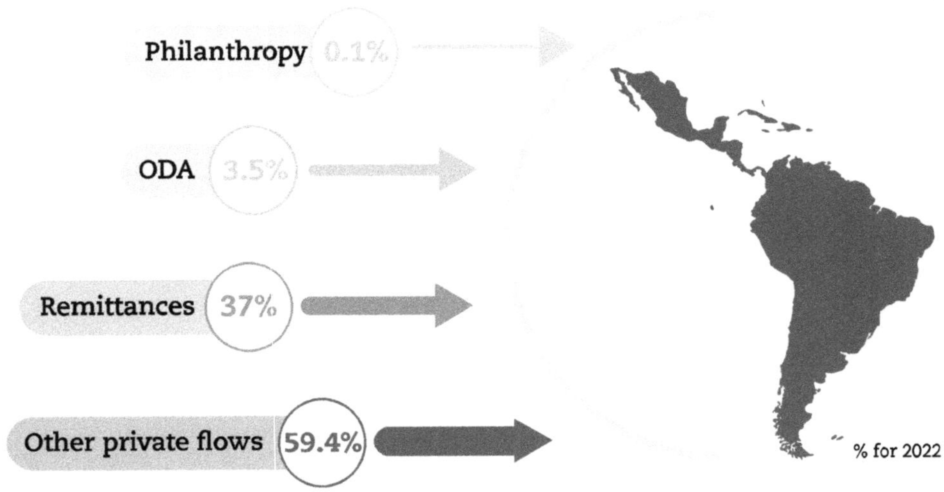

The proper use of debt tools will be key to financing sustainable development

International bond issuance in LAC
GSSS by type and as percentage of total, 2014-23

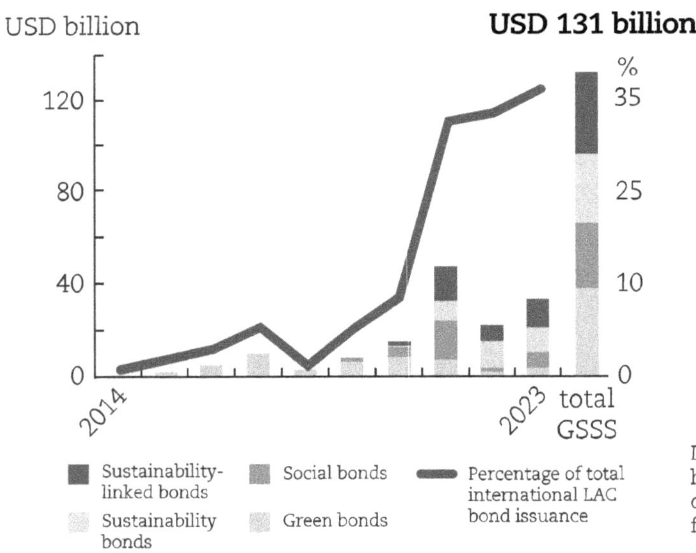

Catastrophe bonds can boost governments' external borrowing by shifting the financial risk of disasters to investors

Debt-for-nature swaps can help countries restructure debt to generate savings for climate action.

Natural disaster clauses can link countries' repayment capacity to their risk exposure

Introduction

The 2015 Addis Ababa Action Agenda (AAAA) on financing for development called for a broader mobilisation of resources, including private funds. It was initially estimated that an additional mobilisation of USD 2.5 trillion annually was needed to meet the sustainable development goals (SDGs) by 2030 (UNCTAD, 2014[1]). This figure was updated in 2022 to USD 3.9 trillion (OECD, 2022[2]). The AAAA intended to provide a new global framework for financing sustainable development by aligning all financing flows and policies with economic, social and environmental priorities, and by providing commitments to develop integrated national frameworks to finance the SDGs at the national level. Nearly a decade later, achievements have fallen short. More than half of the SDGs are off track due to recent crises including the COVID-19 pandemic, which had a considerable effect on Latin America and the Caribbean (LAC), in what ECLAC has called the most lost decade (OECD, 2022[3]).

As the international community prepares for the Fourth International Conference on Financing for Development (FfD4) in 2025, Latin America and the Caribbean is at a crossroads. The region finds itself in a privileged position to support global efforts on energy transition, climate change, biodiversity preservation and the reconfiguration of supply chains. The region also enjoys higher ratios of private finance mobilisation and official development interventions than other developing regions, although unequal among LAC countries, and it continues to be an important destination for private financing flows. LAC is also at the forefront of sustainable debt financing tools, including green, social, sustainability, and sustainability-linked (GSSS) bonds (including blue bonds), catastrophe bonds, natural disaster clauses, debt-for-nature swaps and addressing the financial impacts of loss and damage caused by climate change. Such initiatives have received significant support, showcasing the region's proactive approach to climate resilience. LAC countries have also begun developing and enhancing their sustainable finance frameworks to align with international best practices. At the same time, the region is grappling with longstanding challenges such as low growth, informality, high poverty and inequality rates, significant levels of debt and an unprecedented need to mobilise additional finance to advance the green and digital transitions.

The FfD4 Conference provides a unique opportunity to commit to reforms of financing frameworks at all levels in order to close the financing gap and tap into all sources of funding in an effective and efficient manner. Innovative tools for risk sharing and risk assessment, along with blending instruments and enhanced regulations and standards have great potential to improve LAC's financial landscape in the medium term. This 17th edition of the *Latin American Economic Outlook* contributes to these objectives with a series of policy options to enhance the potential of financing tools, based on co-ordinated actions between policy makers, the private sector and their international partners. The region needs to seize the opportunity of the FfD4 Conference by bringing to the table, in a unified voice, demands to build an enabling international environment that incentivises financing to flow to the region with the aim of boosting the needed development outcomes. Following their initial inputs sent to the FfD4 Elements Paper, LAC countries should continue advocating for a better management of domestic public resources; domestic and international private business and finance; international development co-operation; international trade; debt and debt sustainability; systemic issues of the global financial system; science, technology, innovation and capacity building and data and monitoring.

This chapter begins by analysing the current international financial context. It presents the evolution of multilateral commitments and examines key factors shaping the financing agenda for LAC countries, including debt sustainability and risk assessments. It then presents the potential of key international financial flows that LAC countries could tap into. The chapter then explores novel forms of co-operation between LAC countries, multilateral partners, and the private sector in mobilising new sources of financing towards sustainable development. These include the role of official development assistance (ODA) in mobilising private finance, other official development flows, remittances, and international philanthropy. The chapter next presents the potential of sustainable debt financing tools, including green, social, sustainable and sustainability-linked (GSSS) bonds, as well as new green and sustainable taxonomies. It concludes with key policy messages aiming at boosting the debate ahead of the 2025 conference on financing for development.

Navigating a challenging international financial context

The international financing context has changed considerably over the past few decades. International conferences on financing sustainable development, from the Monterrey Consensus in 2002 to the AAAA in 2015, reflect a shifting global development and financing agenda, with profound consequences for the development of the LAC region. The global landscape presents a complex environment with challenges that include economic disparities between and within countries, financial instability exacerbated by events like the 2008 financial crisis and the COVID-19 pandemic, the need for sustainable development amid environmental concerns like climate change and evolving geopolitical dynamics. The emergence of new players, including emerging economies and non-traditional creditors, adds further complexity to the international financing domain.

The evolution of multilateral commitments in the 21st century

The global development and financing agenda has profoundly evolved since the Monterrey Consensus in 2002. Monterrey declared the need to address the challenges of financing for development globally, particularly in developing countries. It reaffirmed that achieving the internationally agreed development goals demanded a new partnership between developed and developing countries, and therefore gave a prominent role to ODA to complement other sources of financing – especially in those countries with weaker capacity to attract private direct investment (Orliange and Granja e Barros, 2020[4]). It recognised the critical importance of the mobilisation and effective use of financial resources as well as of improving national and international economic conditions to eradicate poverty and achieve sustainable development. It anchored discussions on financing and international financial architecture in the development agenda.

The Second Global Conference on Financing for Development took place in Doha in 2008 with the aim of solidifying the objectives of the Monterrey Consensus into more concrete commitments. In the wake of the 2008 financial crisis, the conference recognised the impacts of such crises on developing countries, and it urged all countries to make the world's global financial system more equitable, sustainable and stable (UNDESA, 2024[5]).

In 2015, the AAAA brought another angle to the global framework for financing sustainable development. This was also the year of major multilateral initiatives, such as Agenda 2030, the Sustainable Development Goals (SDGs) and the Paris Agreement on climate change. The AAAA offered a broader picture of international financing by stating that international public finance and the private sector had an important role to play in complementing the efforts of countries to mobilise public resources domestically. It referred to establishing an enhanced and revitalised partnership for sustainable development. The global nature of the AAAA echoed the SDGs and the Paris Agreement of that same year.

International co-operation has increased since the adoption of the Monterrey Consensus in 2002. But while it has played a critical role in addressing successive crises, it has not kept pace with rising demands. The multilateral finance architecture is under growing pressure to meet today's complex and overlapping challenges more effectively (OECD, 2023[6]). In 2023, France hosted the Summit for a New Global Financing Pact with the aim of laying the groundwork for a renewed financial system suited to the common challenges of the 21st century, such as fighting inequalities, addressing climate change and protecting biodiversity. The summit concluded with the Paris Pact for People and Planet (4P) (France Diplomacy, 2023[7]). In the United Nations General Assembly high-level week in September 2024, world leaders reaffirmed their commitment to the 4P agenda for reforming the international financial architecture and supporting developing countries' enhanced representation in the governance of international financial institutions. More specifically, they supported the Brazilian G20 Presidency's objective of a fairer global governance system, particularly in reforming the international financial architecture (Elysée, 2024[8]).

This historic evolution shows the progression of adapting international financing to a multiplicity of global challenges as well as the rise of new actors, with emerging economies and non-traditional creditors playing a more important role in financing for development. However, this landscape was shaken by the COVID-19 pandemic, which has triggered a renewed and accelerated process of reflection on how best to adapt international financing in an interconnected world with global asymmetries. As LAC prepares for the fourth edition of the conference, the region's countries are putting forward a series of proposals that aim to address the main concerns on financing sustainable development in the region. These proposals show the diversity and variety of positions within LAC (Table 4.1).

Table 4.1. The priorities of selected LAC countries on financing for development

Country	Main proposals
Brazil	Encourage developed countries to increase their ODA commitments with a view to achieving the 0.7% of GDP goal.
	Strengthen tax co-operation within the UN system.
	Combat illicit financial flows and accelerate the repatriation of stolen assets.
	Reduce the cost of remittances.
	Promote the reform of international financial institutions, increasing the representation and participation of developing countries.
	Improve debt treatment mechanisms.
	Promote the mobilisation of new and additional sources of development finance.
	Maintain a balance between public, private, domestic and international sources of financing.
	Mobilise additional financing directly linked to combating hunger and poverty.
	Support the creation of a 2% wealth tax on the wealthiest.
Colombia	Increase financing for the socio-ecological transition.
	Incorporate social inclusion into financing for the green transition.
Guyana	Reform the international financial architecture.
	Adopt a Multidimensional Vulnerability Index, implement the measures in the Bridgetown Initiative and address liquidity support, private capital, development lending, trade and more inclusive governance of international finance institutions.
Jamaica	Give focused attention to the reform of the international financial architecture.
	Consider more inclusive and effective international tax co-operation by addressing the exchange of information.
	Improve mobilisation of domestic resources through tax reforms.
	Give due attention to measuring progress beyond GDP, graduation criteria, allocating official development assistance and facilitating financial access for small island developing states.
Mexico	Search for mechanisms and tools to alleviate the debt of developing countries and middle-income and small island states.
	Reform international financial institutions, particularly multilateral development banks, to open more flexible financing lines for middle-income countries.
	Mobilise international resources that do not generate debt, such as the urgent redistribution of special drawing rights to countries. In this sense, Mexico supports initiatives such as the UN Secretary General's proposal for the SDG Stimulus and Bridgetown 2.0.
Trinidad and Tobago	Boost innovative financing solutions to allow developing countries access to concessional financial resources, increase liquidity and employ effective mechanisms for debt relief.
	Improve international tax co-operation through a more equitable, inclusive and universal approach.
	Work on a Multidimensional Vulnerability Index as a vital tool to assist small island developing states in securing access to concessional financing and improving long-term national planning.

Note: Main proposals were summarised from countries' statements at the High-level Dialogue on Financing for Development on 20 September 2023 at the 78th Session of the United Nations General Assembly and from a questionnaire by the OECD Development Centre to LAC member countries.
Source: (UN, 2023[9]) and responses to the questionnaire on Financing for Development to the delegations of OECD Development Centre LAC member countries.

Factors shaping the financing agenda for LAC

The pursuit of financing for sustainable development of the LAC region takes place in the context of a world with unequal access to resources and asymmetric opportunities for growth. The region faces challenges in the international financing sphere in relation to borrowing costs, debt management, global governance and beyond (Chapters 1 and 2). Identifying these obstacles informs policy solutions and supports the development of strategic positioning on these issues for the LAC region.

Strengthening debt sustainability

There have been some notable international initiatives to address debt management, such as the Debt Service Suspension Initiative (DSSI). In an effort to help developing countries cope with the financial burden of the COVID-19 pandemic, the Group of 20 (G20) and the Paris Club launched the DSSI in May 2020. The initiative suspended USD 12.9 billion in public debt-service payments between May 2020 and December 2021 for 48 participating countries (World Bank, 2022[10]). The DSSI enabled a fast and co-ordinated release of additional resources to beneficiary countries that were severely affected by the pandemic, and the negative net resource transfer – which occurs when countries pay more to their creditors than they receive in fresh funding – did decrease in 2020. However, private creditors did not participate in the initiative (or only on a voluntary basis), and countries feared a credit rating downgrade as domestic credit to the private sector is significant , standing at 56.3% of GDP for the region in 2022 (OSR, 2022[11]; World Bank, 2024[12]).

Another initiative was the Common Framework for debt treatment beyond the DSSI, endorsed by the G20 and the Paris Club, which aims to support low-income countries holding unsustainable debt through a co-ordinated, case-by-case approach involving both official and private creditors, underpinned by International Monetary Fund (IMF) and World Bank (WB) analysis, to ensure long-term debt sustainability (Ministero dell'Economia e delle Finanze, 2021[13]). The new IMF/WB approach to vulnerable countries' financing needs aims at supporting low-income countries and vulnerable emerging economies to address debt vulnerabilities and create fiscal space to finance development and build resilience. The approach includes three pillars: i) structural reforms and domestic resource mobilisation; ii) external financing support, including from IFIS; and iii) country specific actions to reduce the debt burden on a case-by-case basis.

However, so far, the initiatives have proven insufficient to address the need for immediate liquidity in many developing economies, and the negative net resource transfer has continued to deteriorate in LAC. However, there is recognition that repeated cycles of sovereign debt distress over time underline the need for a more effective sovereign debt architecture to help prevent debt crises, support the provision of affordable financing for investment in the SDGs and facilitate more effective and fair restructurings when needed (UN, 2023[14]).

Moreover, global governance asymmetries underlie the significant disparities in countries' access to liquidity during times of crisis, as evidenced by the uneven distribution of special drawing rights (SDRs) allocated to developing nations, as SDRs are allocated to countries in proportion to their quotas in the IMF. SDRs are international reserve assets. SDRs have several advantages over other credit facilities and financing lines, including the fact that they do not generate debt, have a very low cost of use and can reduce the risk premium for highly indebted countries. However, while SDRs are intended to provide liquidity to all IMF member nations, the distribution of SDR allocations favours wealthier countries. Africa, Asia, developing Europe and LAC received respectively 5.2%, 21.5%, 1.1% and 7.9% of the total SDR allocation of August 2021 (ECA/ECLAC, 2022[15]). As a result, developing countries, which may be most in need of liquidity during crises, find themselves at a disadvantage, facing challenges in accessing sufficient SDR resources to address their pressing financial needs.

In its capacity as the current rotating chair of the Heads of Multilateral Development Banks (MDB) group, the Inter-American Development Bank (IDB), in co-operation with the African Development Bank (AfDB), has led a proposal to re-channel SDRs to MDBs building on the issuance of a SDR loan structured as a hybrid capital instrument. Channelling SDRs to MDBs could be explored by countries that are willing and legally able to do so, while respecting the reserve asset status of the resulting SDR-denominated claims and ensuring their liquidity. This could expand the financing options for LAC countries and is projected to leverage up to four times the value of the SDRs, enabling countries to finance social and climate projects that may be challenging through other financial routes (IDB, 2024[16]). This progress comes within the IDB's broader efforts and its key role in increasing co-operation between development actors and in enhancing their mobilisation. Through its position as rotating chair, and as part of the recently approved IDB Impact+ programme, the IDB has led efforts to increase collective effectiveness and a strategic approach to the co-ordination of development partners (IDB, 2024[17]). In the context of limited finance and with an increased number of development actors in the region, the need for greater co-ordination is clear. Increased co-operation by MDBs and the expansion of the use of SDRs increase opportunities for MDBs and necessitate even greater co-ordination of development actors.

Furthermore, 4P leaders at the September 2024 United Nations General Assembly high-level week highlighted the need for solutions to reduce developing countries' debt burdens, including innovative instruments like debt-for-climate, and rechannelling special drawing rights to provide additional fiscal space to emerging economies. They also committed to increasing concessional funding for vulnerable nations and emphasised collaboration to enable multilateral development banks and international financial institutions to achieve a "1 to 1" ratio of private finance mobilised through public resources. Additionally, the leaders recognised the importance of improving the transparency of risk ratings to foster private financial flows and increasing public financing through targeted global levies while supporting domestic resource mobilisation efforts (Elysée, 2024[8]).

Improving risk assessment and enhancing transparency in assets' information

Risk perceptions are more volatile in developing countries and tend to be pro-cyclical, causing economic downturns to develop into even more serious financing issues (ECLAC, 2023[18]; IMF, 2023[19]). This raises the questions of investors' considerations when making investment decisions, and of how these considerations impact development.

The world's few existing credit rating agencies (CRAs) have an important effect on perceptions of risk in the countries in the region. Three CRAs account for more than 90% of the credit rating market (Hung et al., 2022[20]; OECD, 2023[6]). Ratings, which are widely used by all investors in investment decisions, tend to be pro-cyclical, downgrading LAC economies more quickly than developed economies. Downgrade phases tend to be deeper and faster than upgrade phases, and domestic variables could be helpful in smoothing the path of downgrades, whereas this outcome does not hold true during upgrade phases (Broto and Molina, 2016[21]). Negative warnings by CRAs ("reviews", "watches", "outlooks") have a harsher impact on the bond spreads of developing countries than advanced economies (160 basis points vs 100 basis points) and developing countries receive 95% of credit rating downgrades despite milder economic contractions (UNDESA, 2022[22]). When developing countries receive a low credit score, below "investment grade", they have to borrow at greater cost to finance sustainable development (Sachs, 2023[23]). This often leaves LAC countries forced to choose between investing in their long-term sustainable development goals or pursuing short-term credit score improvements (OECD, 2023[6]).

Sovereign credit quality has an important role in determining how costly the access to private external financing will be, with credit rating downgrades having a much bigger impact than upgrades (ECLAC, 2018[24]). This becomes particularly relevant as private financing grows more important in the context of the 2030 Agenda for Sustainable Development and the need to increase the mobilisation of resources for its implementation. Some analyses have highlighted the need to improve the functioning of credit rating agencies through practical measures that could include separating rating from advisory functions, imposing legal liabilities and removing the regulatory reliance on ratings (Portes, 2008[25]).

Improving the availability of information is also crucial. An accurate appraisal of vulnerabilities of developing countries is needed with improved accounting for the compounding impact of climate vulnerability on other structural and economic vulnerabilities. There is the risk of a "climate-financial trap" in which climate disasters or deterioration exacerbate a poor fiscal situation, worsening a country's ability to access international resources to finance sustainable development and prepare for a smooth low-carbon transition (AFD, 2023[26]; AFD, 2023[27]). Efforts such as the Global Emerging Markets (GEMs) risk database consortium attempt to support more accurate risk assessments of LAC countries. The GEMs database offers a comprehensive and transparent repository of risk data, enabling a more holistic view of economic and financial risks. The database, which has put together almost 30 years of anonymised data from around 25 institutions, can help to reduce the gap between perceived and real risks (GEMs, 2024[28]; IFC, 2024[29]). By utilising such tools, investors, policy makers and other stakeholders can access diverse and detailed information, fostering a more informed and resilient financial system. This helps to mitigate the shortcomings of traditional credit rating agencies, promoting better-informed decisions based on a clearer understanding of underlying risks.

Enhancing co-operation across multilateral actors

In the context of constrained financing for sustainable development, the coherence of existing financing is essential, as is co-operation among old and new development actors engaging in the region. Although few actors represent the majority of multilateral financing for the region, an increasing number of development groups have entered LAC in the past two decades. There remains a high concentration in the multilateral financing sphere, with the Inter-American Development Bank, the Development Bank of Latin America and the Caribbean (CAF), the Central American Bank for Economic Integration (CABEI), the World Bank and the European Union (EU) accounting for more than 95% of multilateral finance in 2022 (Figure 4.1). However, the number of multilateral actors in the region has grown from 8 in 2002 to 40 in 2022, while the number of non-development assistance committee countries, regional banks and private philanthropic organisations providing financing for sustainable development has also grown in the region (OECD, 2024[30]).

Figure 4.1. Cumulative share of multilateral financing commitments in LAC, 2022

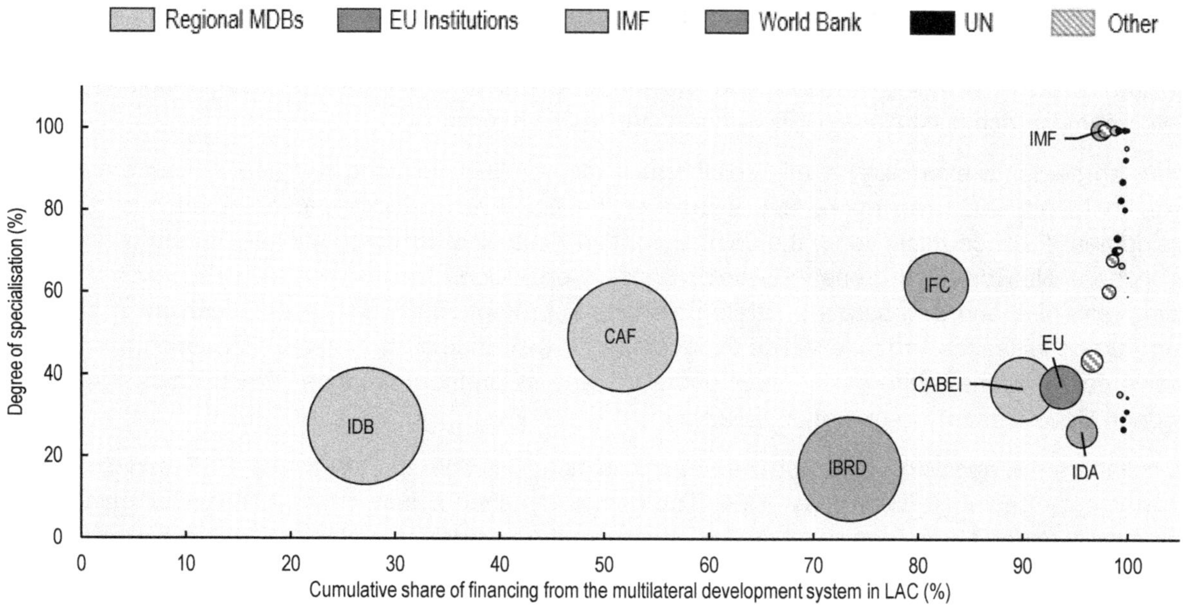

Note: The horizontal axis shows cumulative multilateral financing (as a percentage of total financing to LAC from multilateral institutions and funds). The cumulative share of a given institution is the sum percentage of all commitments up to and including that institution in order of size from left to right on the horizontal axis. For example, CAF and IDB cumulatively represent 51.74% of multilateral financing commitments in 2022. The vertical axis shows the degree of specialisation (the share of each multilateral's total financing of the largest sector in their portfolio). A higher degree of specialisation supposes a higher concentration by sectoral activity. The bubble size represents the financing volume by each multilateral institution or fund, which aggregates ODA and other official flows (OOF) from each institution.
Source: Authors' calculation based on (OECD, 2024[30]; OECD, 2023[6])

StatLink https://stat.link/4lst89

The growth in the number of organisations has arisen from the increase in highly specialised funds, primarily United Nations funds and programmes, as a response to specific crises such as COVID-19. This higher degree of specialisation of smaller funds contrasts with the EU and its Member States, which spreads its financing across a much wider range of sectors. The increased involvement of new actors and funds holds potential to be positive, in particular for large Latin American economies. For example, there has been an increase in the number of specific climate funds active in the LAC region. These funds play an important role in channelling private finance for specific climate goals (see further below for the section on sustainable finance instruments). However, while their activities are relevant, they are not a substitute for governance reform. Efforts are needed to ensure that the increased number of actors enables effective specialisation while maintaining a degree of co-ordination.

More collaboration across development actors could improve the impact of development co-operation. These entities bring different strengths to the table, with MDBs offering financial resources and technical expertise, bilateral agencies providing direct aid, including loans and guarantees, and partners like the EU contributing through grants, loans, guarantees and bonds (Chapter 3). These actors also provide ODA commitments to different sectors, with the United States committed mostly to social infrastructure (42.2%) and humanitarian aid (31.9%). ODA from the EU institutions is more dispersed across sectors (OECD, 2024[31]). More specifically, the EU has made significant commitments to the education, energy, finance and health sectors, which indicates a focus on holistic sustainable development (OECD, 2024[31]).

Collaboration among development actors is crucial for LAC. Collaboration enables pooling resources, leveraging complementary capacities and scaling up financing efforts to meet the diverse development challenges faced by LAC countries. This can ensure a co-ordinated approach to project implementation, maximise the impact of development finance and drive progress towards sustainable development goals. More coherent, co-operative and targeted financing is required by all providers to maximise their respective benefits as, to date, development actions have been too siloed (CGD, 2022[32]). Agreements across financing actors – including national and local development banks as well as global and regional development finance institutions (DFIs) – are a step in this direction.

Recent agreements exemplifying this collaborative approach have been adopted across development banks. In March 2023, an agreement signed at the EU level included the association of European Development Finance Institutions, the Joint European Financiers for International Co-operation and the Practitioners' Network for European Development Co-operation. These groups agreed to build on their existing expertise and collaborate in strategic efforts to promote the EU's Global Gateway strategy and Team Europe initiatives and to leverage their comparative strengths towards transformational impact and valuable contributions to the policy goals of the EU and its partner countries (Practitioners' Network for European Development Co-operation, 2023[33]).

The collaborative approach can also be seen in a financial operation between CAF and the French Development Agency (AFD) in May 2024. The banks launched a new strategic financial instrument to support medium- and long-term collaboration, incorporating non-dedicated funds to achieve green strategy objectives. This mechanism supports CAF's goal to become the region's green bank by addressing climate change and biodiversity, channelling a loan of EUR 200 million to Latin America and the Caribbean combined with technical assistance, alongside expert technical exchanges (CAF, 2024[34]).

By building on existing frameworks – such as those in the Organisation of American States with the Inter-American Council for Integral Development and its Inter-American Agency for Co-operation and Development – the LAC region can work more cohesively to: i) strengthen governance of development co-operation; ii) boost co-operation and policy coherence; and iii) ensure the effective leveraging of national efforts at the regional level. Through improved co-operation, the region can strive to ensure effective collaboration among existing development providers while also establishing new development pathways, leveraging both South-South co-operation and triangular co-operation.

Finally, partnerships between development banks from developed countries and national development banks can provide targeted project financing at lower financial costs. For example, the AFD signed a Tier 2 agreement with the Banco Nacional de Costa Rica (BNCR) in 2021 to finance climate change-related projects, with a particular focus on electric mobility (AFD, 2024[35]). Consisting of two lines of credit, a senior unsecured loan of USD 50 million and a subordinated Tier 2 loan of USD 15 million, the financing programme seeks to provide long-term liquidity while maximising the leveraging effect of the AFD commitment through additional BNCR financial commitments. This is complemented by a four-year EU grant of EUR 3 million for technical assistance to assist the BNCR in aligning its project financing with Costa Rica's climate objectives. This mezzanine operation ensures alignment with the country's sustainable development agenda and helps reduce the cost of financing for the national development bank.

Unlocking the potential of international financial flows

Public and private international financial flows are critical for the development of the LAC region. Even if these flows are relatively small compared to levels in other developing regions, official development assistance remains crucial in LAC as it could be a catalyst to attract and "derisk" the private sector investments to address development needs. Given the lower levels of concessionality, there is a need to further mobilise private finance and other international development flows in an integrated manner to address development needs more effectively.

Official development assistance and other financial flows

Access to grants and concessional loans is essential to support the financing of sustainable development in the region. However, this has come under increasing strain. As a share of gross national income (GNI), ODA for Latin America is the lowest in the world, at close to 1% – and it is declining. This decrease is expected, given that as countries develop, so does ODA as a share of GNI (Piemonté, Kim and Cattaneo, 2024[36]). Indeed, as LAC develops and countries graduate to lower-middle-income status, the ODA share of GNI gradually decreases (Cattaneo, Piemonté and Poensgen, 2020[37]). In contrast, ODA for small island developing countries (SIDS) averaged almost 10% of GNI in 2022, being a crucial means of external financing, as they are mostly still classified as low-income nations (Figure 4.2).

Despite low levels in LAC, ODA remains relevant to addressing the region's critical development needs and plays a crucial role mainly related to capacity building for upper-middle-income countries in the region. Beyond direct financial support, ODA – particularly through technical assistance (TA) and blending finance – can act as a catalyst for mobilising additional resources, such as loans or private sector investments. By providing technical expertise, supporting project preparation, and mitigating risks, TA and blending finance are first steps in unlocking larger funding from international financial institutions and private investors (EIB, 2024[38]; World Bank, 2024[39]). However, recent geopolitical turmoil is impacting international finance and development assistance, as evidenced by announcements of relative decreases in aid from some high-income countries (Gavas and Pleeck, 2024[40]; Bollag, 2024[41]; DEVEX, 2024[42]). ODA has also come under increased demand for specific crises. In 2022, for example, Ukraine received aid of USD 26 billion from Development Assistance Committee (DAC) countries and EU institutions, nearly double the USD 13.52 billion received by LAC in the same year (Carey, Desai and Ahmad, 2023[43]).

Figure 4.2. ODA as a share of GNI, average per region and income group, 2000-22

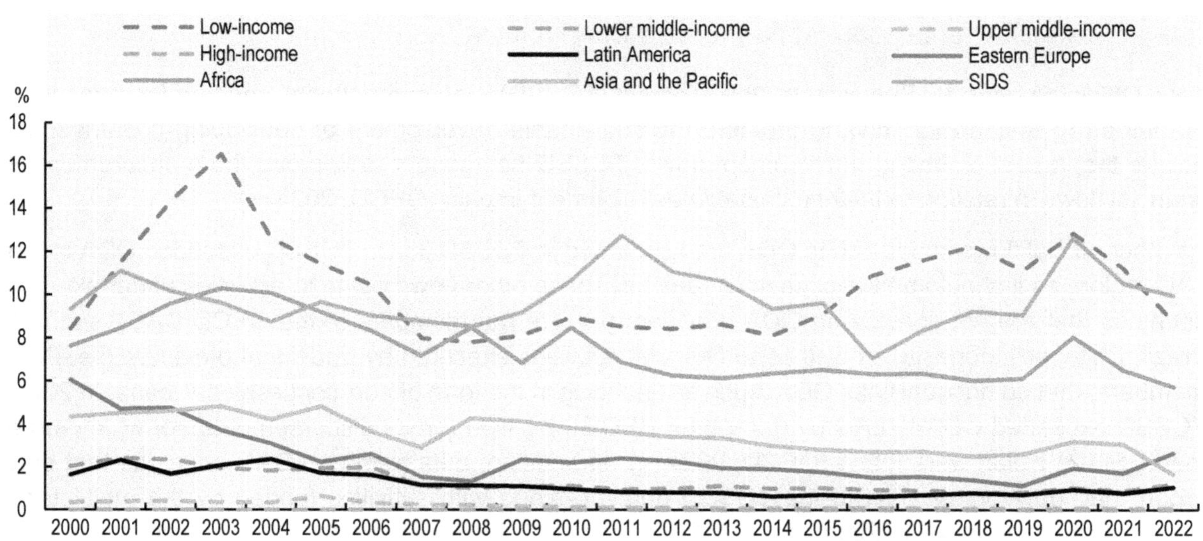

Note: In current prices. Both ODA and GNI are measured in million US dollars. Regions are based on OECD ODA data country groupings and the UN SIDS list. Countries in the SIDS category are excluded from their regional category.
Source: Authors' calculation based on (OECD, 2024[44]; World Bank, 2024[45]).

StatLink https://stat.link/293otw

Even if all commitments were met – including the commitment of dedicating 0.7% of GNI to ODA, or the USD 100 billion dedicated to climate finance per year – most of LAC's financing shortfall would remain, with slight differences across the region. Estimates show that for every dollar of development finance invested, the LAC region would need to mobilise USD 5-6 from other sources to meet an SDG financing gap of USD 650 billion (IDB, 2019[46]). The amount of concessional finance available is therefore very limited relative to the size of the region's economies, and there is no indication that ODA to the region will increase in the years to come. However, the limited ODA received can better used. The United Nations' Multidimensional Vulnerability Index is a tool that can help perform more effective resource allocations and help nations gain access to the concessional financing needed (OECD, 2024[47]).

As more LAC countries continue to graduate as their GNI per capita rises, and as per current ODA eligibility criteria, they will benefit less from ODA inflows. These countries continue to face a steep development financing gap. The limited access to ODA concessional finance creates sustainable development financing issues that can also have an impact on debt. Discussions are ongoing regarding a shift from graduation to "gradation" to enable recently graduated countries to continue to access concessional finance and allow for a balance between ODA and transition finance (ECLAC/OECD, 2018[48]; Cattaneo and Piemonté, 2021[49]).

Further efforts to analyse development finance and how it relates to generating sufficient development flows are taking place. The Total Official Support for Sustainable Development (TOSSD) is an example (Box 4.1). Additional flows accounted relate to activities undertaken by countries that do not consider themselves to be ODA providers, such as Brazil, Chile or Indonesia for instance. Projects tracked within the TOSSD array include, for instance, a standard loan for the multi-dimensional development of popular areas in the city of Guayaquil (Ecuador) provided by the Development Bank of Latin America and the Caribbean (CAF) in 2022. This kind of a cross-cutting project contributes to the achievement of multiple SDGs (3, 9, 11 and 17) by providing access to running water, reducing travel times and transportation costs, reducing the incidence of flooding in certain sectors and the propensity to disease due to exposure to dust and sewage.

Box 4.1. Total Official Support for Sustainable Development

Total Official Support for Sustainable Development (TOSSD) is an international standard for measuring the full array of financial flows to promote the sustainable development of developing countries. To bolster the impact of limited development flows, TOSSD has sought to improve the measurement of financial flows in relation to their sustainable development impact (OECD, 2024[50]).

As other official flows in addition to ODA are accounted in TOSSD flows, TOSSD exceeded ODA in the LAC region, as it should be the case in all regions. These other flows relate to activities undertaken by countries that are not considered ODA providers (i.e. are not members of the OECD DAC), such as Brazil, Chile, or Indonesia, as well as to financial activities executed by traditional providers (i.e. DAC members) that do not qualify as ODA, such as financing in the form of non-concessional loans. In 2022, TOSSD exceeded ODA in LAC by more than USD 28.3 billion (gross disbursements), of which more than USD 21 billion were loans (OECD, 2024[51]). In addition, data from non-DAC countries that only report their development aid to the TOSSD dataset, along with activities funded by the multilateral system through earmarked contributions, totalled over USD 4 billion, including USD 1.7 billion in grants, USD 1.4 billion in loans, USD 488 million in direct provider expenditures, and USD 423 million in other debt securities. TOSSD provides additional granularity on activities funded from earmarked contributions to multilateral institutions, which improves the availability of information on support to developing countries channelled through the multilateral system.

The most recent TOSSD data (support provided in 2022) refer to activities by 121 bilateral and multilateral providers. Of the 19 providers that submitted data on South-South co-operation (SSC) in 2022, 15 supported the LAC region. SCC accounted through TOSSD shows that LAC was the region with the most important co-operation initiatives in 2022, both in terms of gross disbursements and number of activities. Brazil was the country that provided the most SSC activities (1 019), followed by the CAF (296) and Mexico (208). Education-related support represents almost half of the total number of SSC activities. Four Central American countries (Costa Rica, El Salvador, Honduras and Nicaragua) received 80% of the SSC flows to LAC that were reported to TOSSD.

Source: (OECD, 2024[50]).

In 2022, Brazil facilitated, through in-kind technical co-operation experts, the development of a methodology for irrigated rice planting in the Dominican Republic, contributing to three SDGs (2, 6 and 12). The aim of the project is to develop production systems with efficient use of irrigation water, using high-yielding varieties and environmentally friendly technologies for rice cultivation. Rice is one of the main crops in the Dominican Republic, with rice production done mainly under irrigation (98% of the production) by about 30 000 producers (IICA, n.d.[52]).

In 2023, the Chilean Government and the EU launched the Global Gateway Renewable Hydrogen Funding Platform in Chile worth EUR 225 million. With a grant component of EUR 16 million provided by the EU (LACIF), KfW and EIB mobilised together EUR 200 million of investments. The fund will be managed by CORFO and will focus on the development of concrete renewable hydrogen production and application projects in Chile. This support contributes to Chile's plan to become the most competitive green hydrogen producer on the planet by 2030". Concrete projects will build local capacity and knowledge for Chile and the world.

In 2018, EIB provided a loan to Fonplata, a multilateral financial institution owned by Argentina, Bolivia, Brazil, Paraguay and Uruguay. Fonplata's portfolio comprises projects in urban development, renewable energy, drinking water provision, social infrastructure, cultural heritage and rural accessibility in remote areas. This project has already facilitated access to basic services for 1 500 vulnerable homes in rural communities in Bolivia. This pilot project facilitates access to public equipment and services and improves social inclusion through the financing of urban infrastructure, housing, recreational services and transport in the Municipality of Corumbá, Brazil. 107 000 inhabitants benefit now from new paved roads, the development of Parque Jaguatiricas, the restoration of ten historic buildings, improvements in the coastal area of the Paraguay River, the construction of a citizen centre and the revitalisation of Eco Parque Cacimba da Saúde.

Beyond these examples, discussions are ongoing on measuring the full array of development finance. Development banks, including the AFD, and recipient countries have called to go yet one step further to improve the tracking of the impact of development flows. This call reflects the need to better evaluate the development impact of ODA and to increase its integration with other investment flows to align with the SDGs (AFD, 2022[53]). Other analyses suggest that a simplified dual measure of international public financing, reflecting both solidarity efforts and financial impacts, could effectively gauge the contributions of international development institutions to the SDGs, as a complement to ODA and TOSSD (AFD, forthcoming[54]).

More comprehensive and harmonised measures of development finance could contribute not only to provide a clearer picture of the full array of finance devoted to development but also of the partners in the region. For instance, development finance in LAC has diversified beyond DAC donors, with China emerging as a significant player in past decades. The number of projects and amount of China's loans to LAC countries have decreased in recent years. Between 2019-23, the LAC region received an average of just over USD 1.3 billion per year, as compared to peak lending in 2010, when the China Development Bank (CDB) alone issued nearly USD 25 billion to the region (Figure 4.3). Chinese finance to LAC remains concentrated in a few countries. Brazil continues to feature as an occasional recipient of recent Chinese DFI loans (Mayers and Ray, 2024[55]). However, despite being an important player that do not consider themselves to be ODA provider, China is not yet reporting to TOSSD.

Figure 4.3. China's development finance to LAC, 2005-23

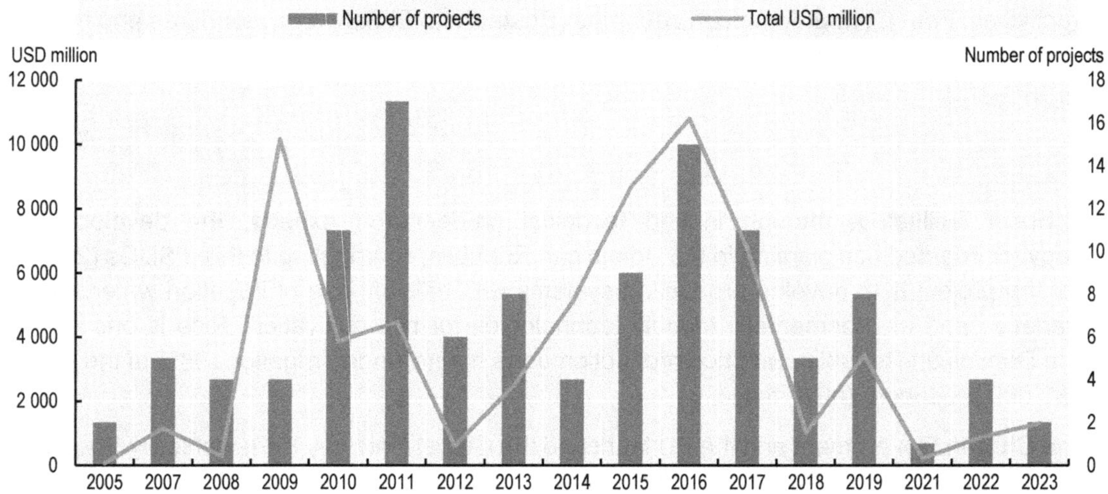

Note: The years 2006 and 2020 are blank because no Chinese loans to the region were identified. Only public and publicly guaranteed (PPG) loans that are made via the two development finance institutions, namely CHEXIM (the Export-Import Bank of the Republic of China) and CDB (China Development Bank), are counted in the dataset.
Source: Authors' elaboration based on (The Dialogue, 2023[56]).

StatLink https://stat.link/06oc4v

LAC requires partnerships to access private finance and ensure its development impact

Private finance is by far the largest external financial flow to LAC. Private investors are the most important external creditor for Latin American governments, and this share has grown over time (ECLAC, 2023[18]) (Figure 4.4). This points to the increasing economic development of the region and a relative decrease in the size of public financing. With ODA flows below the levels observed at the beginning of the 2000s, and the expected continued decreasing trend, other flows need to be better integrated through a sustainable development framework to ensure quality investment and to enable a more coherent development environment.

Figure 4.4. Components of external financing flows to the LAC region, 2011-22

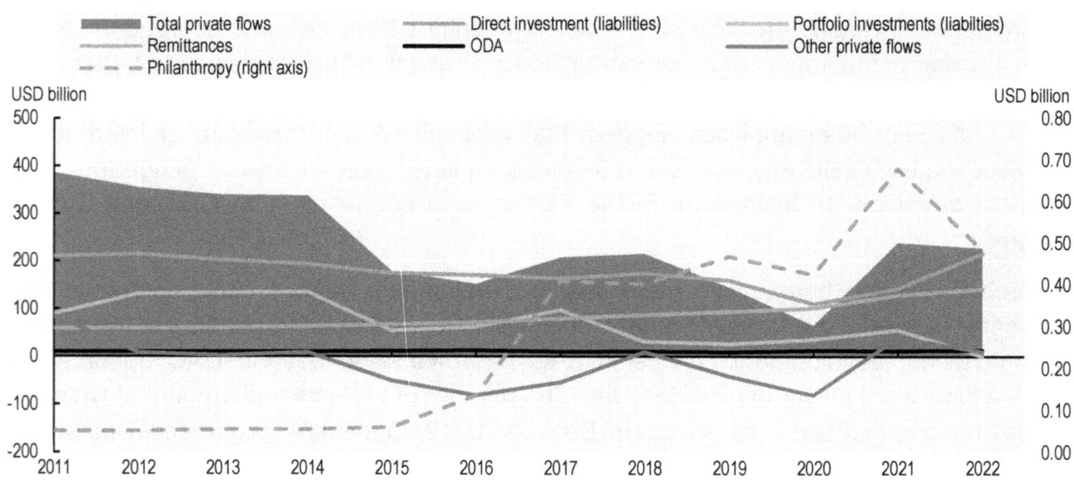

Note: Total private flows include direct investments (liabilities), portfolio investments, and other private flows such as capital accounts, financial derivatives, and other investments (liabilities).
Source: Authors' elaboration based on (OECD, 2024[44]; IMF, 2024[57]).

StatLink https://stat.link/6bhg1p

Enhanced regulatory frameworks contribute to attracting private financing

Stronger FDI regulatory frameworks are needed to ensure that foreign direct investment can better flow towards production transformation and sustainable development in LAC, including into renewable energy, green technologies, and digital innovation, which have great potential in LAC (ECLAC, 2023[58]). Currently, FDI primarily targets larger economies like Brazil and Mexico (OECD, 2023[59]).

Establishing favourable conditions and frameworks can encourage both domestic and foreign investors to allocate their resources to a particular country or region. This includes adopting policies and regulations that promote transparency, predictability and legal protection for investors. It also entails adhering to international standards and best practices in areas such as governance, environmental protection and labour rights (OECD et al., 2023[60]) (Chapter 1).

International co-operation – through initiatives such as the Common Framework of Sustainable Finance Taxonomies and the OECD Blue Dot Network – supports the region in developing and integrating new policies to channel private finance towards achieving the SDGs.

Private finance mobilisation through official flows is increasing in LAC

Mobilising private-sector finance for sustainable development is increasingly seen as a key instrument to meet the SDG financing gap. Mobilisation of private capital could involve the use of official development interventions to reduce the risks for the operation and bring in private-sector finance. The LAC region is better positioned than other regions to trigger private investors for several reasons. First, approximately 87% of private finance mobilised in 2018-20 went to middle-income countries, which is the categorisation of most countries in LAC (OECD, 2023[61]; World Bank, 2024[62]). In addition, the region's increasing institutional capacity, growing capital markets and relative socio-economic similarities position LAC to benefit from innovative sustainable financing tools (IDB, 2019[46]).

In 2022, LAC registered the highest level of private mobilised finance for development at the global level. It totalled USD 21.2 billion, a sharp increase since 2017 (the year that mobilised private finance was introduced to the regular Credit Reporting System) (Figure 4.5) (OECD, 2024[63]). Similar to FDI trends, this was mainly driven by large increases in the largest economies in the region, including Colombia, Brazil, Mexico and Peru (OECD, 2024[63]). The transport sector drove significant increases in Colombia and Peru; the industrial and energy sectors boosted the increase in Brazil, and the communications sector accounted for most of the growth in Mexico (OECD, 2024[63]). This marks a significant improvement since the start of the 2010s, when the region received the least amount of mobilised private finance across regions. It also indicates increased engagement with public-private partnerships within LAC. Furthermore, LAC has the highest private capital mobilisation rate for infrastructure, at an average of USD 4.7 per dollar of public money compared to USD 1.9 per dollar in Asia and the Pacific (Global Infrastructure Hub, 2023[64]). These figures demonstrate the strong position that LAC is holding and a great momentum for even greater mobilisation rates.

Figure 4.5. Mobilised private finance by official development interventions per region, 2012-22

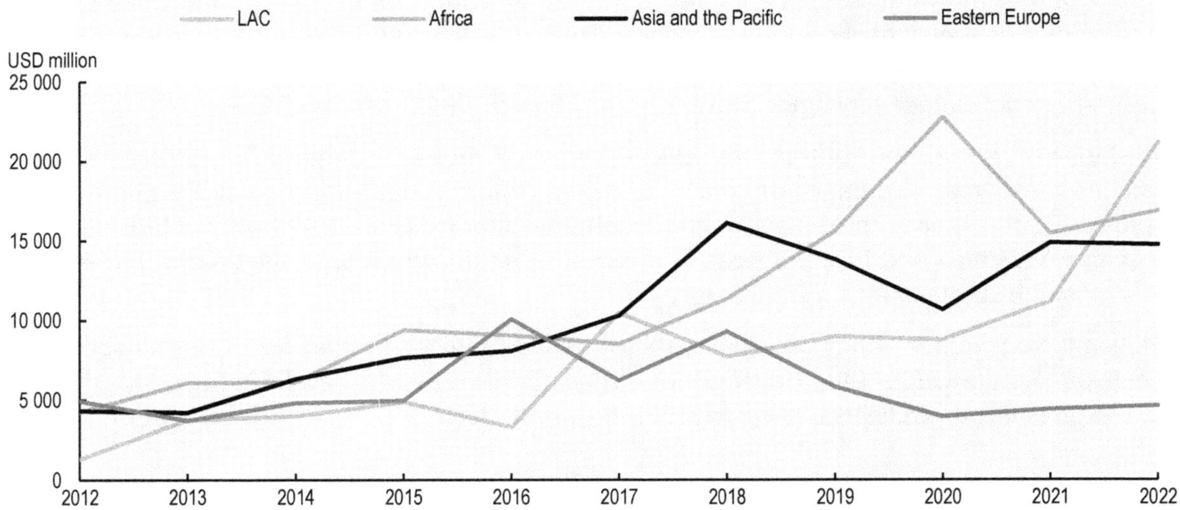

Note: "Asia and the Pacific" includes Asia and Oceania. Only ODA-eligible countries are included. In current prices. "Mobilised private finance by official development interventions" refers to private-sector finance that has been leveraged by specific mechanisms to stimulate additional financial resources for development objectives. It requires a causal link between the finance made available for a specific project and the leveraging instrument involved. The OECD considers the following leveraging mechanisms used by development co-operation providers in its database: syndicated loans, guarantees, shares in collective investment vehicles, direct investment in companies, credit lines, project finance and simple co-financing arrangements.
Source: Authors' elaboration based on (OECD, 2024[63]).

StatLink https://stat.link/mhwab2

International co-operation can have a strategic role in incentivising the flow of private finance to key development sectors that yield profits in the longer term. Development co-operation can help lower economic barriers but also perceived risks, by offering access to "de-risking instruments" that aim to share risks among multilateral, public and private actors, such as blended finance or guarantees offered at concessional or competitive terms to unlock private finance (OECD et al., 2023[60]).

The sectoral distribution of the private finance mobilised to the region by official development interventions shows that there are many opportunities to be explored. In 2022, mobilised private finance was primarily directed towards traditional, economically relevant sectors, with 77.2% allocated to economic infrastructure and services, and 16.4% to production sectors (Figure 4.6). The former includes banking and financial services, transport and storage, energy, and communications. Meanwhile, social infrastructure sectors only received around 4.9% of total mobilised finance in 2022, of which only 0.5% was devoted to education and health. International co-operation can be better focused by providing public financing and by crowding in private financing for sectors that generate significant social and environmental gains but do not attract sufficient private flows.

Figure 4.6. Mobilised private finance by official development interventions to LAC by sector, 2022

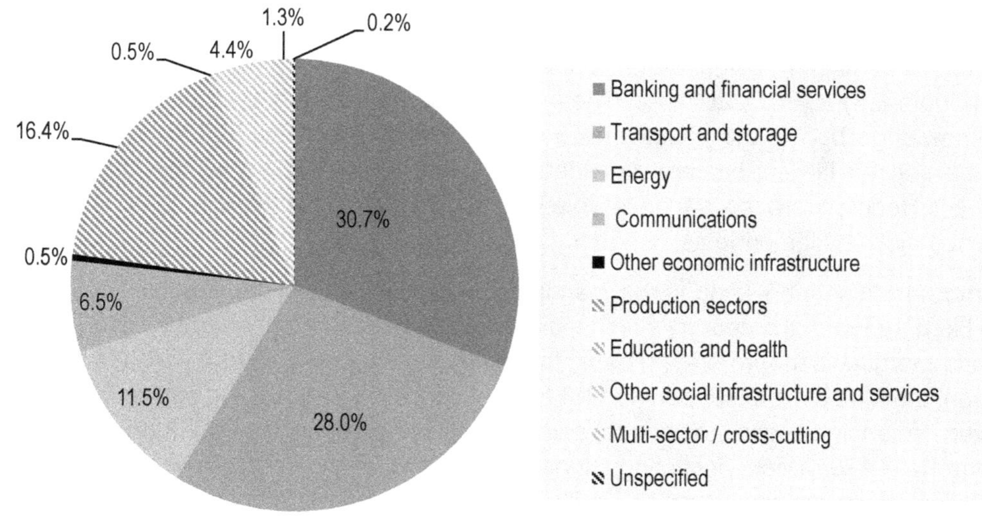

Note: Economic infrastructure and services received 77.2% of total mobilised private finance, where banking and financial services receive 30.7%, transport and storage 28%, energy 11.5%, and communications 6.5%. Next, production sectors receive 16.4% of the total, with industry, mining, and construction accounting for 14.7% and agriculture, forestry, and fishing for 1.5%. Social infrastructure and services only receive 4.9% of the total, of which education and health together account for 0.5% and the other 4.4% relates to water supply and sanitation, government, and civil society. Next, the multi-sector and cross-cutting industry received 1.3% of the total mobilised private finance. Lastly, 0.2% of the total mobilised finance was allocated to unspecified sectors.
Source: Authors' elaboration based on (OECD, 2024[63]).

StatLink https://stat.link/0iu12o

Multilateral development providers are the LAC's largest source of mobilised private finance and therefore have a key role in improving mobilisation outcomes. In the period 2020-22, multilateral providers accounted for almost 83% of mobilised finance, with bilateral providers accounting for just over 17% (OECD, 2024[63]). Multilateral providers include MDBs as well as EU institutions and other funds. Beyond their large share of mobilisation, multilaterals, and particularly MDBs, also mobilise additional bilateral participation (Avellán et al., 2024[65]). MDBs therefore act as a key investor for sustainable development (OECD, 2024[63]).

MDBs have made concerted efforts to boost co-operation and collective lending. In 2023, the largest MDBs made a commitment to increase collaboration towards an acceleration in inclusive sustainable development through improved private-sector mobilisation (World Bank, 2023[66]). This commitment includes a capital adequacy framework measure that could potentially increase their collective lending capacity by around USD 300-400 billion over the next decade. However, without the required large scaling up of financing, these alterations will be insufficient to address the pressing financing needs of developing economies. MDBs will need to provide an annual increment of USD 260 billion in lending to respond to the mounting development challenges (CGD, 2023[67]).

Lending by MDBs has grown significantly in LAC. Annual disbursements increased from USD 30 billion in 2000 to USD 96 billion in 2022, with MDBs providing vital countercyclical support during crises, sharply increasing disbursements in 2009 and after the COVID-19 pandemic. Development banks are in a unique position to accelerate investments in sustainable development, but the size of the paid-in capital bases of MDBs has not increased in line with the expansion of the global economy or with growing investment needs. Scaling up MDB resources has become a key priority for the international community, and the MDBs have begun to undertake a range of reforms to expand their financial capacity.

Bilateral providers can fulfil distinct and complementary development needs. The primary vehicles for bilateral mobilisation are development finance institutions, mostly national and subnational public development banks (PDBs), which play a key role in expanding access to financial markets for micro, small and medium-sized enterprises (MSMEs) by providing technical support and innovative financial services that drive employment (OECD et al., 2023[60]) (Chapter 3). This can be seen in part by the distinct financing tools they offer, with higher usage rates of credit lines (22%) and simple co-financing (11%) than multilaterals (Figure 4.7) (OECD, 2024[63]). These more tailored services are essential at the local level, where local knowledge boosts the effectiveness of mobilisation. Between 2020 and 2022, EU member states were the second largest bilateral providers of mobilisation (35%) after the United States (54%) (OECD, 2024[63]). Hence, there is a particular role here for the EU and its Member States in the promotion of private finance mobilisation projects.

Bilateral partners are also innovating in the mechanisms to mobilise private finance. Spain, for instance, launched the Huruma Fund, the country's first social impact fund, aiming at addressing the funding gap for smallholder and marginalised farmers, primarily in Latin America, sub-Saharan Africa, and Asia. Over its 10-year lifespan, the fund aims to support 45 000 farmers globally by increasing cultivation areas, boosting farmer turnover, enhancing access to finance, and creating sustainable jobs. The fund, which successfully mobilised over EUR 120 million, including significant private investments, highlights the potential of combining public and private resources to achieve large-scale poverty reduction and development goals in high-risk areas (OECD, 2022[68]).

Multilaterals provide more financing to governments, play a key role in climate agenda-related development projects and lead in promoting private-sector financing in infrastructure development (OECD, 2018[69]). This large-scale infrastructure focus is evidenced by the fact that multilaterals utilise syndicated loans (33,7%) and direct investment in companies and special purpose vehicles (30,4%) at a much higher level than bilateral providers (8,8% and 22,3% respectively) (Figure 4.7) (OECD, 2024[63]). Multilaterals are also found to promote investments in global public goods (GPGs) impacting positively on poverty alleviation through developing regional infrastructure and improving sustainable development conditions, though these GPGs remains undervalued and undersupplied (Gulrajani, 2016[70]).

Figure 4.7. Mobilised private finance by official development interventions to LAC, 2020-22

Tools of bilateral and multilateral providers

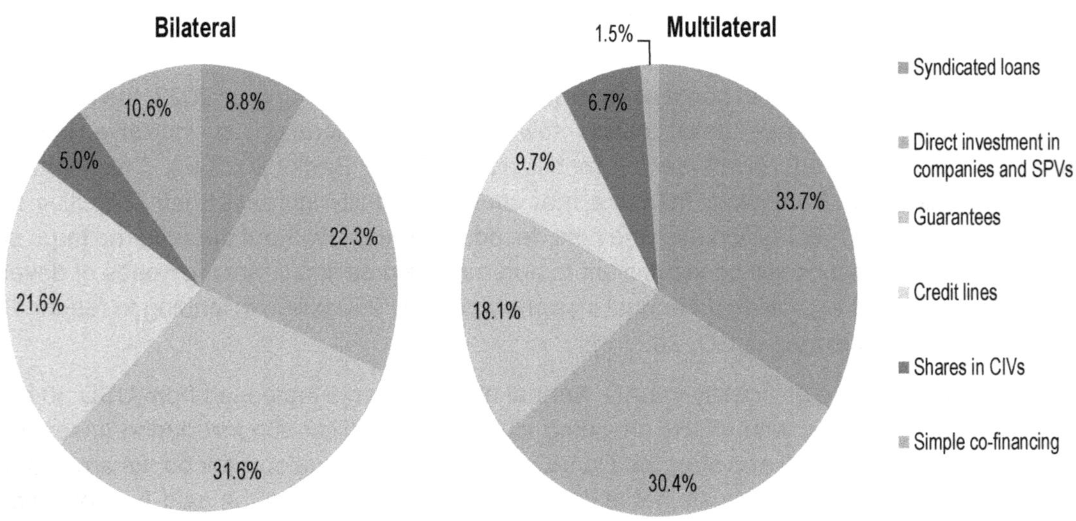

Note: Bilateral data includes only DAC countries. SPVs = special purpose vehicles. CIVs = collective investment vehicles.
Source: Authors' calculation based on (OECD, 2024[63]).

StatLink https://stat.link/ozpi2b

Innovative public-private partnerships include funds with several multilateral institutions as investors. For instance, the Central American Mezzanine Infrastructure Fund II LP (CAMIF II) is a 12-year mezzanine Fund that invested in existing and new (brownfield and greenfield) medium-sized companies or projects in infrastructure and related sectors in Central America, Colombia, the Caribbean, and Mexico. Investors include the IDB, the CABEI, Finnfund, Obviam, and Proparco. The fund aimed at reducing infrastructure bottlenecks, improving private sector development, strengthening investees from a financial and governance perspective and helping them scale up their operations It also helped to demonstrate the business case for private infrastructure projects and encouraged more private investors to enter the sector in the target region (IFC, 2024[71]). There are many examples as well for purely private funds that aim to attract private capital for sustainable development in LAC.

Closer co-operation and innovative financing mechanisms can facilitate resource mobilisation where needs are greatest

Greater co-operation between multilateral and bilateral providers is necessary to ensure their complementarity. Bilateral providers are found to have clearer chains of accountability, while multilaterals have greater financial capacities (Gulrajani, 2016[70]). By combining co-operation across the respective investment sectors and by increasing the level of project co-operation between providers, there are opportunities for increasing the overall mobilisation rate and improving sustainable development outcomes. Bilateral co-operation partners and providers of aid are increasingly focusing efforts on mobilising the private sector through diverse types of initiatives. Recent efforts have been undertaken to innovatively mobilise private sector financing and deepen international partnerships.

LAC partners such as the EU have developed innovative partnership schemes as part of its development strategy for the region. With the Global Gateway Strategy, the EU has put forward a holistic approach to international partnerships and sustainable development with integrated financing structures that bring together investment, trade and co-operation actors aiming to raise environmental, social, governance (ESG) standards. Under the EU-LAC Global Gateway Investment Agenda (GGIA), the EU pledged to mobilise EUR 45 billion in LAC by 2027 through an agenda which is composed of more than 130 projects. This agenda, developed jointly with the region, and presented during the III EU-CELAC Summit in 2023 aims to exemplify how to narrow the global investment gap and support economic recovery while advancing the twin green and digital transitions (European Commission, 2023[72]). The monitoring of the Global Gateway development finance flows will follow, to the extent possible, the TOSSD measure.

Disbursements of TOSSD from EU institutions (and not individual EU countries) to LAC have increased from a total of USD 766 million in 2019 to USD 1 841 million in 2022 (Figure 4.8). The reduction in standard grants throughout this period confirms the decrease in share of concessionality, as grants do not need to be repaid. While grants accounted for 98% of TOSSD in 2019, they only accounted for 34% of it in 2022, the rest being standard loans (65% of the TOSSD received) and shares in collective investment vehicles (1%). The COVID-19 pandemic partly explains the larger share of standard grants in the 2019/20 period, as the EU disbursed more grants to support LAC countries to address the crisis, these being atypical years. However, standard loan disbursements, both concessional and non-concessional, have increased from USD 551 million in 2020 to USD 1 192 million in 2022. Further, TOSSD from the EU institutions benefit most of the LAC countries. In terms of volumes, Brazil the highest recipient.

Figure 4.8. TOSSD disbursements from the EU institutions to LAC 2019-22

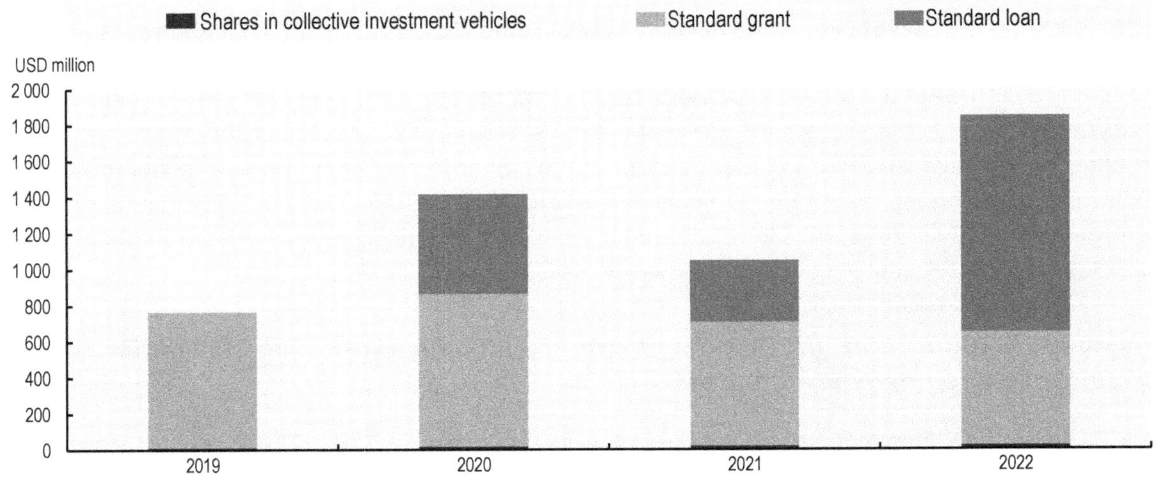

Note: TOSSD from EU institutions to LAC is measured using three financial instruments. First, shares in collective investment vehicles refer to collective undertakings through which investors pool funds for investment in financial or nonfinancial assets or both. These vehicles issue shares (if a corporate structure is used) or units (if a trust structure is used). Second, standard grants are transfers in cash or in kind for which no legal debt is incurred by the recipient. Third, standard loans are transfers in cash or in kind for which the recipient incurs legal debt (and the resulting claim is not intended to be traded). This includes loans repayable in the borrower's currency whether the lender intends to repatriate the repayments or to use them in the borrowing country. Loans also include "instalment sale" and "istisna'a" of Islamic finance. Further, no data is available for standard loans in 2019, as although the EU executed six projects involving standard loans for LAC (Brazil, Colombia, and the Dominican Republic), data is only available for "committed" amounts but not "disbursed". For this reason, they are not included in the dataset, as the dataset only reflects disbursed amounts.
Source: Authors' elaboration based on (OECD, 2024[50]).

StatLink https://stat.link/zv2sfn

The GGIA thereby fosters the mobilisation of quality investments that create local added value and promote growth, jobs, and social cohesion. The EU's offer includes not only capital but also proven technology, regulation, and environmental and social standards. Implemented in a Team Europe Approach, the GGIA provides a platform that brings together the LAC partners, the EU and its Member States, development finance institutions, export credit agencies and the private sector.

The main financial tool to mobilise investments under the GGIA is the European Fund for Sustainable Development Plus (EFSD+). The EFSD+ Guarantee programme provides financing on favourable competitive terms and is implemented through two main paths aiming to mobilise private investments in support of achieving the SDGs. Firstly, the EU provides a EUR 26.7 billion guarantee cover at the global level in a partnership with the European Investment Bank (EIB) to support investments in partner countries where sovereign and other public sector risks are still a major bottleneck. Concretely, EIB signed in 2023 a total of EUR 969 million in loans for LAC, of which 71% relate to climate action and environmental sustainability (EIB, 2024[73]).

Secondly, the EU will provide a guarantee cover of up to EUR 13 billion until 2027 globally under the EFSD+ open architecture. The open architecture window targets private sector investments and is deployed by a range of implementing partners, including international financial institutions and European Development Finance Institutions. These guarantees are often supported by additional tools such as technical assistance and grants through blending (European Commission, 2023[74]) (Box 4.2).

The EU is also undertaking consultations on the integration of export credits to enhance co-ordination of its external development finance tools as part of the GGIA (European Commission, 2024[75]). Between 2016 and 2020, EUR 14.1 billion of export credits were provided to LAC, compared to EUR 32.3 billion of other EU development flows (Council of the EU, 2023[76]). Incorporating sustainable development taxonomy into export credits as planned would improve alignment of financial flows with the development agenda of LAC.

Beyond these private flows, there are other significant financial flows, such as remittances and philanthropy, that can help to support the financing of sustainable development by improving the investment environment and through additional facilitatory roles.

Box 4.2. Unlocking strategic investments: The example of the Latin America and the Caribbean Investment Facility (LACIF)

Blending mechanisms have proven to be a notable transformative tool in the LAC region. Since 2010, the Latin America Investment Facility (LAIF) and the Caribbean Investment Facility (CIF) have together contributed almost EUR 720 million in EU-LACIF contributions for 86 investment projects supporting sustainable development (LACIF, 2024[77]). The now integrated Latin America and Caribbean Investment Facility (LACIF) contributes on average EUR 56 million annually, with financing matched by development finance institutions at a 1:24 ratio (LACIF, 2024[77]).

LACIF focuses on key areas for sustainable development such as renewable energy, climate change adaptation, health, transport, and MSME support (LACIF, 2024[77]). LACIF has thereby targeted countries with lower levels of per capita income that struggle to mobilise private finance, such as Bolivia and Paraguay, representing 25% of LACIF funds contracted. More recently, LACIF contributed to unlocking a EUR 205 million digital connectivity project in Colombia and a EUR 85 million small cities water and sanitation project in Bolivia (EFSD+, 2024[78])

Beyond the above-mentioned country-specific examples, LACIF also promotes private equity investments in the region. An example is the Ecobusiness Fund for Latin America and the Caribbean (EBF LAC), which is an impact investment fund that seeks to promote business and consumption practices contributing to biodiversity conservation, the sustainable use of natural resources, and climate change mitigation and adaptation. The EBF LAC Sub-Fund closed in 2023 with a loan portfolio of USD 644 million, distributed across 12 countries (Colombia, Costa Rica, Dominican Republic, Ecuador, El Salvador, Guatemala, Honduras, Mexico, Nicaragua, Panama, Paraguay, and Peru) and 37 partner institutions (Eco Business Fund, 2024[79]).

Source: (European Commission, 2022[80]); (Council of the EU, 2023[76]).

Remittances can play a significant role in financing for sustainable development

Remittances are a major and stable financial flow for LAC given the region's high outward migration level. (IMF, 2017[81]). However, there is disparity in remittance inflows as the majority are concentrated in a few LAC countries, with the top six recipients – El Salvador, Guatemala, Haiti, Honduras, Jamaica and Nicaragua – receiving significantly higher amounts than the rest (Figure 4.9). Remittances are a key source of finance for those households at the lower end of the income scale (IDB, 2023[82]). Remittances have been found to have a positive influence on growth and poverty reduction in the destination country through increased finance for private households, which can spend the money in the local economy and increase bank deposits, which in turn can boost business lending (Fajnzylber and López, 2008[83]).

Turning to the diaspora in Latin America can be a source of much sought after green finance. After years of emigration, many Latin American countries have established large diasporas. Countries like El Salvador (12.7%), Paraguay (5.8%), Nicaragua (5.2%), and Mexico (4.7%) have substantial diaspora populations as a percentage of their home population (UNDESA, 2020[84]; UNDESA, 2024[85]). Diaspora bonds have been developed to target diasporas to raise funds for specific sectors and infrastructural projects. These are financial instruments issued by a country seeking collaboration with its diaspora, based on the premise of a patriotic dividend, thus offering financing at a lower cost than borrowing from institutional investors.

Diaspora bonds date back to 1951 when Israel first issued them. To date, few diaspora bond projects have been successful, although India and Israel have raised a combined USD 35 billion, and projects in Kenya, Nigeria, Pakistan and the Philippines have yielded positive results (World Bank, 2023[86]; CABEI, 2021[87]; Gevorkyan, 2021[88]). Years of trial and error on diaspora bonds reveal that challenges stem from scarce knowledge about the financial instrument, a lack of knowledge of preferences of the diaspora, and limited planning when issued. For these bonds to be successful, trust between diaspora and diaspora-emitting countries must be firm (OECD, 2007[89]). One way to achieve this is through a dedicated institutional framework for issuing and managing the bonds, while maintaining open dialogue between diasporas and authorities back home (World Bank, 2020[90]).

Figure 4.9. Remittances to LAC countries as a share of GDP, 2003-22

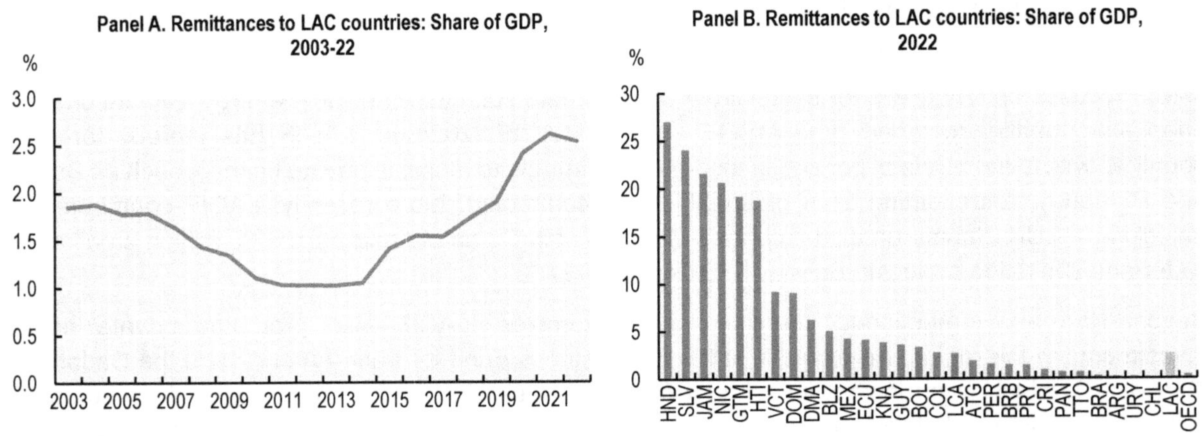

Source: Authors' elaboration based on (World Bank, 2024[91]).

StatLink https://stat.link/9z34v0

At the regional level, remittances as a share of GDP have remained steady over recent years, at 2.5% in 2023 (IDB, 2023[82]). However, when looking at subregions, the relative size of remittances varies considerably. In Central America, remittances accounted for 12.7% of GDP, compared to 9.4% in the Caribbean and only 0.7% in South America. There has been significant growth in absolute terms per subregion, with 13.2% growth in Central America, 7.9% in South America and 2.6% in the Caribbean in 2023 (IDB, 2023[82]). This has been driven by several countries in particular, with high growth in Nicaragua (45%), Argentina (26%), and Peru (14%) (KNOMAD-World Bank, 2023[92]).

These flows can better support some areas of development needs than other flows such as private mobilisation. First, remittances lower income volatility in the LAC region and therefore provide a barrier against poverty (IMF, 2017[81]). Second, remittances can be an important source of financing for MSMEs, although evidence is still limited for LAC (Catrinescu et al., 2009[93]). Between 70% and 80% of remittances are spent on household expenses associated with food, health, housing, and education, among others, and the remaining 20% to 30% are dedicated to business development or savings (OECD, 2024[47]; ECLAC, 2020[94]).

However, the benefits of remittances for the economy can only be fully realised with adequate institutional structures and specific policies that facilitate their complementary development role. For instance, reducing transaction costs could incentivise the flow of remittances to LAC countries. Currently, transaction costs in

LAC are higher than in regions such as East Asia and the Pacific, South Asia, and the Middle East and North Africa. On average, sending USD 200 in remittances costs 6.1% in LAC, compared to 4.3% in South Asia (KNOMAD-World Bank, 2023[92]). Under SDG 10, the United Nations aims to reduce transaction costs to below 3% and eliminate corridors with costs exceeding 5% by 2030 (UN, 2015[95]). Reducing these costs, through digitalisation and other improvements, could bolster financial flows.

Next, improvements could be made to ensure that especially lower-income households have easier access to digital banking for receiving remittances, as a significant share of remittances are transferred via cash transactions (IMF, 2017[81]). Financial policy as well as health and stability of the financial sector will ultimately determine the impact of remittances in the country of origin (OECD, 2017[96]). Finally, the regulatory environment significantly impacts the benefits of remittances. Stable formalised remittance channels can be facilitated by: i) enhancing anti-money-laundering and combating the financing of terrorism (AML/CFT) frameworks; ii) integrating the OECD's Illicit Financial Flows toolkit; and iii) engaging in regional-based regulatory environment solutions (IMF, 2017[81]; OECD, 2016[97]). In addition, financial regulations could provide greater recognition for remittances as collateral for small business loans (CABEI, 2021[87]).

International philanthropy in LAC focuses on civil society and the environment

International philanthropy provides LAC with substantive funding for sectors often overlooked by the private sector. Since 2017, 40 large international donors based in OECD countries have disbursed USD 71.5 billion in philanthropy for development, or about USD 12 billion a year, of which only around 6% (USD 700 million) went to LAC countries (OECD, 2021[98]; OECD, 2023[99]). Domestic foundations based in the region also provide significant capital for development objectives, for example providing more private capital than international organisations to Mexico as of 2019 (OECD, 2021[98]).

While international philanthropic flows are highly concentrated by donor and destination, this has begun to diversify. Close to 75% of funding received from large donors in LAC comes from the top ten international philanthropic donors (OECD, 2023[99]). Yet, other donors are stepping in. Geographically, a few countries benefit from the bulk of the international philanthropic financing. There are two groups of countries: Brazil, Colombia, El Salvador and Mexico, which each received USD 90-100 million per year from philanthropic foundations, and Ecuador, Guatemala, Haiti and Peru, which each received USD 10-20 million per year.

Unlike philanthropy for development at the global level, which focuses predominately on health and education, philanthropic funding for LAC is heavily concentrated in financing civil society (close to USD 2 billion), in particular non-governmental organisations (NGOs), followed by environmental protection (USD 500 000) (Figure 4.10). For some of these large donors, most of their programmatic work related to the environment and climate change is focused on the LAC region. For instance, the focus of the Ford Foundation in the Andean region is mostly on natural resource conservation and the inclusion of marginalised communities (Ford Foundation, 2024[100]).

Figure 4.10. Sectors receiving philanthropic financing in LAC vs. other regions, 2017-22

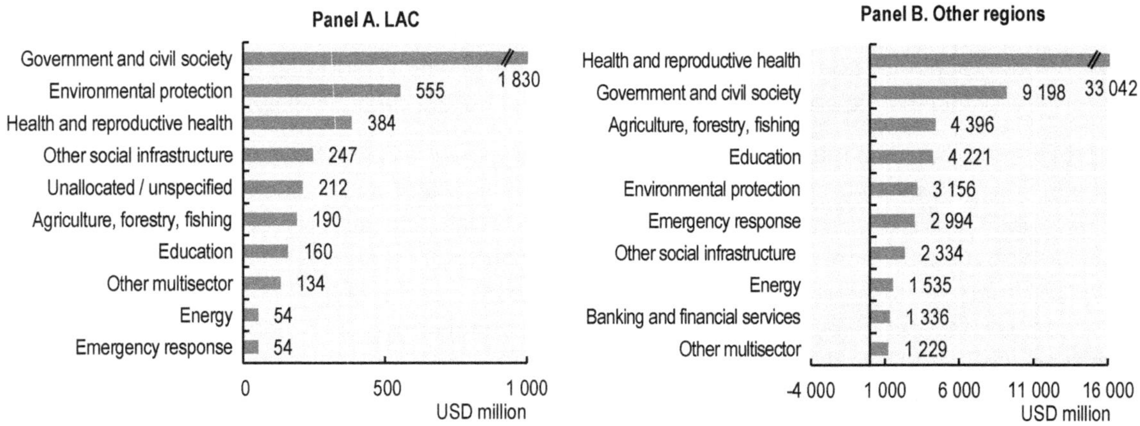

Note: Other regions include developing countries in Europe, Africa, Asia, and Oceania. Data for 2022 do not include Open Society foundations.
Source: Authors' elaboration based on (OECD, 2023[99]).

StatLink https://stat.link/p0r5sw

Philanthropic foundations can also play a role in boosting collaboration across providers of international co-operation, given their unique convening power as a non-state actor and their focused mission objectives. Taking a neutral stance, they can collaborate with different government administrations, private-sector players, NGOs and local communities to address specific challenges. Foundations often provide resources for promising pilot projects that can later be scaled and expanded through collaboration. By leveraging both financial assets and in-house expertise, philanthropic organisations can nudge the co-operation needed to tackle problems that other actors cannot solve independently. The operating flexibility of foundations often allows them to seed investors in new initiatives or innovations, which can solve collective action problems in international collaboration.

This sort of partnership can serve as a model for how philanthropic foundations based in LAC can work in tandem with international organisations to foster sustainable development, highlighting the critical role of regional actors in addressing local challenges.

Scaling up debt tools for financing the sustainable development agenda

Improving and scaling up debt tools such as green, social, sustainability, and sustainability-linked (GSSS) bonds (including blue bonds), catastrophe (CAT) bonds, climate or nature swaps, and natural disaster clauses are key to financing the sustainable development agenda. GSSS bonds can mobilise direct investment into sustainable activities while supporting the development of sustainable capital markets. CAT bonds can increase the external borrowing capacity of governments by transferring the financial risk of catastrophic events to investors, while natural disaster clauses can help to align debt servicing obligations with a country's ability to manage and recover from catastrophic events. For biodiverse and highly indebted countries, climate or nature swaps can serve as important sustainable financing instruments. As these instruments take hold in the region, enhanced regulation and oversight are essential to ensure their effectiveness and mitigate risks.

GSSS bonds can mobilise investment into sustainable activities

The GSSS bond market represents only a small fraction of the global bond market to date. It is still considered a niche sector, representing only 1% of total assets outstanding and around 2% of new issuances globally (OECD, 2022[101]; OECD, 2024[102]). In the LAC region, however, GSSS bonds are proving to be an attractive financing mechanism, increasing from 9.3% of total LAC bond issuance in international markets in 2020 to almost 35% in 2023 (ECLAC, 2024[103]; OECD, 2024[102]). For issuers in LAC, raising funds through these assets instead of traditional bonds has become an attractive option for increasing returns on liquid global capital, diversifying the investor base, mobilising direct capital into sustainable activities and acquiring financial support for creating sustainable capital markets. Between 2014 and 2023, the GSSS international bond market in LAC reached a cumulative value of USD 131 billion (Box 4.3). Total green bond issuance in LAC nearly doubled over four years, from USD 18.8 billion in 2019 to USD 36 billion in 2023. This includes funds such as the Green Climate Fund (GCF) with funding for projects involving LAC countries at USD 3.4 billion (GCF, 2024[104]).

Figure 4.11. International bond issuance in LAC: GSSS by type and as percentage of total, 2014-23

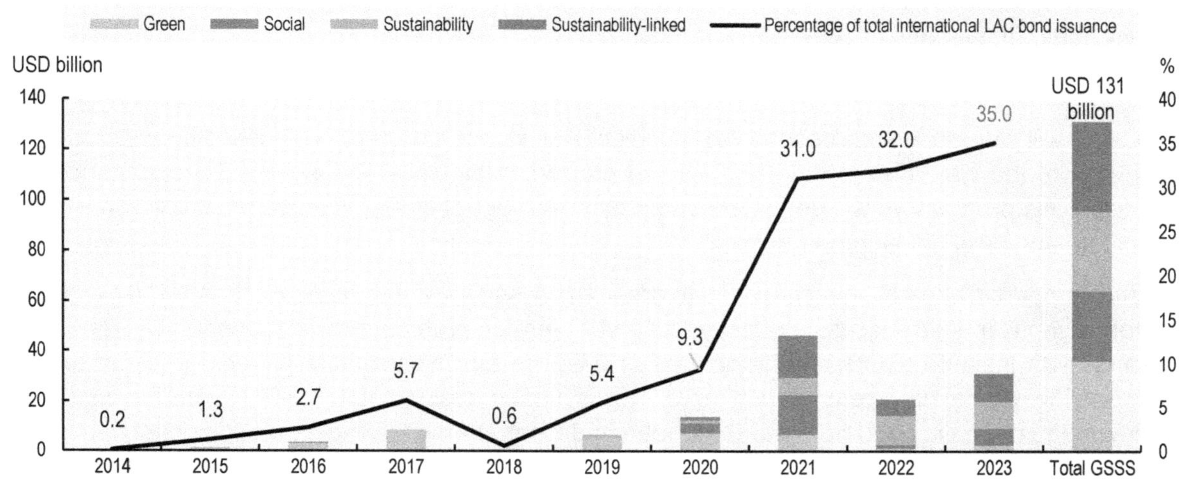

Note: GSSS refers to green, social, sustainability and sustainability-linked bonds. Total sustainability bonds include blue bond issuance.
Source: Authors' calculation based on (OECD et al., 2023[60]; ECLAC, 2024[103]; OECD, 2024[102]).

StatLink https://stat.link/iv5cd9

Building on the success of green bond issuance in Europe, the EU is preparing to launch its Global Green Bond Initiative (GGBI), an investment vehicle aimed at promoting the development of green bond markets in LMICs (Box 4.3). The GGBI aims to mobilise EUR 15-20 billion for sustainable investments (Présidence de la République, 2023[105]). Another example is the LAGreen Fund, which was the first green bonds fund in the region established in 2021 with support from the LACIF blending facility. By investing in green bonds and supporting new issuers with technical assistance, LAGreen facilitates access to this innovative instrument for financing green initiatives in the region. The fund promotes best practices and high impact standards, with the aim of consolidating green bonds as an instrument to mobilise funding from international capital markets, financing the transition to more sustainable economic models. At end-2023, LA Green had already subscribed to nine GSSS bonds across seven countries, having mobilised a total investment of EUR 620 million for green investments (LAGreen, 2023[106]).

Box 4.3. The EU's Global Green Bond Initiative (GGBI)

The GGBI is the EU's initiative to scale up green bond markets in low- and middle-income countries under the Global Gateway strategy. It proposes a holistic approach with three pillars to develop local green bond markets and facilitate the flow of EU capital into green projects in low- and middle-income countries.

Pillar 1: The set-up of an investment fund in the EU – the GGBI fund

The GGBI fund will purchase – as anchor investor – a portion of green bonds issued by sovereign, sub-sovereign, and private entities in low- and middle-income countries, thus sending a strong signal about the quality of the green bond issuance, which will in turn attract other local or international investors to the transaction. The GGBI fund will pool resources from public entities (including European Development Finance Institutions, multilateral and regional development banks, and the UN's Green Climate Fund) and private investors.

Pillar 2: Supporting potential green bond issuers through capacity building and technical assistance

The GGBI will rely on a comprehensive Technical Assistance programme to accompany issuers at every step of the way in designing and issuing green bonds, while sharing the EU experience and expertise. This programme will be implemented by a network of strategic implementing partners such as regional and local development banks.

Targeted support is already being provided to green bond issuers under the GGBI. In 2024, for example, the Dominican Republic successfully issued its first sovereign green bond with support from the Global Green Growth Institute (GGGI) in the context of GGBI to fund sustainable projects in clean energy, transportation, waste management, and more. This issuance, amounting to USD 750 million, marks the first sovereign thematic bond from the Caribbean and Central America region (GGGI, 2024[107]).

Pillar 3: The Green Coupon Facility

To address the high costs of servicing bonds (i.e. the coupons) for some potential green bond issuers, the Green Coupon Facility will compensate issuers for part of the bond servicing costs, through a coupon subsidy in certain specific cases.

Social, sustainability and sustainability-linked bonds have also grown significantly, reaching a cumulative issuance of USD 95.1 billion in 2023 since the inception of this market segment in 2016. This growth highlights the potential of these diverse financial instruments to tackle the region's multi-dimensional structural challenges, which can involve both social and environmental dimensions.

Within the broader category of GSSS bonds, blue bonds are emerging as a powerful tool in the region for financing initiatives aimed at safeguarding oceans and fostering sustainable "blue economies" – economic activities that depend on or impact the use of coastal and marine resources (OECD/IDB, 2024[108]). Blue bonds present a promising opportunity to unlock the financial potential of blue economies in the LAC region, especially in the Caribbean, by providing avenues for substantial and long-term investment (OECD/IDB, 2024[108]). In 2021, BB Blue, a special purpose vehicle (SPV) created to manage Barbados' debt-for-nature swap, issued two blue bonds worth USD 71.6 million. This allowed Barbados to buy back USD 77.6 million in Eurobonds due in 2029 at a discount. Backed by Credit Suisse and guaranteed by the IDB and The Nature Conservancy (TNC), these bonds received better credit ratings than conventional sovereign bonds issued by Barbados (OECD/IDB, 2024[108]). This deal showcased a blended finance approach, facilitated by financial institutions like CIBC FirstCaribbean and Credit Suisse (The Nature Conservancy, 2023[109]). In the same year, a subsidiary of The Nature Conservancy, Belize Blue Investment Company, LLC (BZBIC), backed by Credit Suisse, arranged blue bonds that funded a USD 364 million loan to Belize to repurchase a USD 553 million "superbond" (OECD/IDB, 2024[108]). This superbond represented the government's entire external commercial debt, equivalent to 30% of GDP (Owen, 2022[110]). In 2022, the Bahamas issued two blue bonds totalling USD 385 million, which attracted high demand in the international debt market (ECLAC, 2023[111]).

International financial co-operation will be essential to prevent fragmentation of the GSSS bond market in LAC. It will help harmonise bond standards, taxonomies, and regulatory frameworks across countries while also building capacity in LAC countries that need support for issuance, certification, monitoring, and framework development (see below on sustainable finance frameworks). Aligning bond standards and taxonomies to international standards is important to further boost investors' confidence and streamline the different reporting requirements.

The gradual shift towards sustainable debt securities over conventional bonds indicates a growing investor appetite in sustainable projects. This trend can support both private and public issuers in meeting their sustainability goals. The share of GSSS bond issuance as a proportion of total bond issuance in international markets has risen in the LAC region, reducing the market share of conventional bonds (OECD, 2024[102]) (Figure 4.12, Panel A). Specifically, the share of GSSS sovereign bonds in total sovereign bond issuance in international markets has significantly increased, from 36% in 2022 to 50% by 2023. Consequently, the proportion of conventional sovereign bonds dropped from 64% in 2022 to just 50% in 2023. In the corporate sector, the peak share of GSSS bonds reached 39% of total corporate bond issuance in 2022. However, this share experienced a notable decline in 2023, attributed mainly to increased risk aversion among investors and rising borrowing costs. Similarly, for supranational and quasi-sovereign issuers, the percentage of GSSS bonds in total bond issuance saw a sharp decrease, from 40% in 2022 to 15% in 2023. In 2023, sovereign issuances accounted for the largest share of GSSS issuances, at 74%, followed by corporate issuances at 18% and supranational and quasi-sovereign issuances at 9% (Figure 4.12, Panel B). An example of how green bonds support sustainable development in LAC is their use in advancing the circular economy. Corporate green bond issuances in countries such as Brazil, Colombia, Chile, and Mexico have primarily targeted the pulp and paper industry (UNEP, 2023[112]). In addition to green bonds, other financial instruments—such as hybrid tools like mezzanine and convertible structures, and non-reimbursable funds, including grants and blended finance schemes—have been used in recent years to promote the circular transition in LAC (Chapter 3).

Figure 4.12. LAC's GSSS and conventional bond issuance, by type of issuer, 2020-23

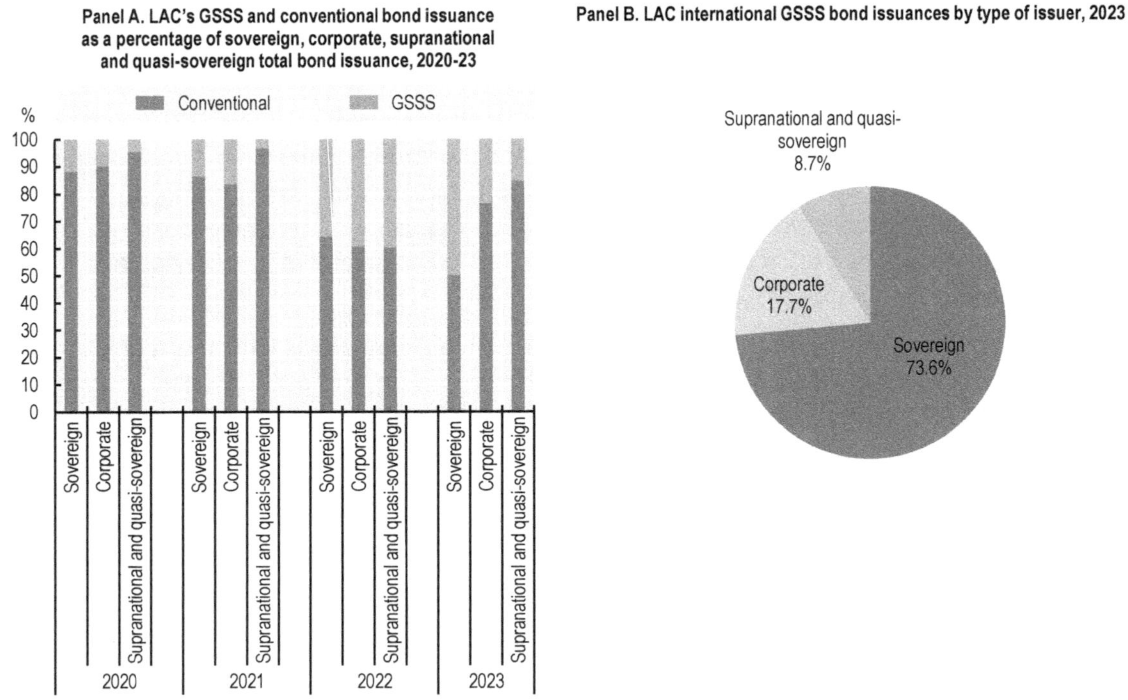

Note: Quasi-sovereign issuers are defined as companies with full or partial government ownership or control. Supranational issuers are defined as entities formed by two or more central governments to promote economic development for the member countries.
Source: Authors' elaboration based on (ECLAC, 2021[113]; ECLAC, 2022[114]; ECLAC, 2023[111]; ECLAC, 2024[103]).

StatLink https://stat.link/r6lzty

Compared to green, social and sustainability (GSS) bonds, sustainability-linked bonds (SLBs) are distinguished by financial characteristics that are contingent on the issuers' meeting pre-determined key performance indicators (KPIs) and sustainability performance targets (SPTs). These are linked, for instance, to the issuer's commitment to reducing greenhouse gas (GHG) emissions or adopting cleaner technologies (OECD, 2024[115]; OECD et al., 2023[60]). SLBs can feature an innovative structure, offering potential rewards in the form of lower coupon rates for issuers if they achieve all sustainability objectives, or imposing penalties if these targets are not met. As such, these types of bonds hold considerable promise for financing initiatives in areas like biodiversity, climate change adaptation and social development – sectors that often lack the large, bankable asset pipelines necessary for issuing traditional GSS bonds. Additionally, unlike GSS bonds, which require underlying assets, SLBs can be backed by an issuer's entire balance sheet, allowing them to be issued in higher values and with longer maturities (OECD, 2024[115]).

SLBs innovative structures in LAC are financing key development areas with multiple sustainable objectives. In 2023, the share of SLBs in total GSSS bond issuance in international markets in LAC stood at 36%, with sovereigns leading the issuance. Despite high volatility in recent years, SLB issuance in developing countries grew significantly following the first issuance in 2019 (OECD, 2024[115]).

Sovereign SLBs can be linked to existing sustainability commitments, enhancing their credibility and relevance. In addition to domestic resource mobilisation, primarily through taxes (see Chapter 2) and green budgeting – which integrates environmental and sustainability considerations into government budgeting and financial planning – these instruments can also help the national government meet its obligations under its nationally determined contributions (NDCs) and the Paris Agreement. Chile and Uruguay became pioneers in 2022 as the world's first nations to issue sovereign sustainability-linked bonds; as of April 2024, they remained the sole issuers in the LAC region (OECD et al., 2023[60]). In March 2022, Chile issued a USD 2 billion sovereign bond tied to two key performance indicators: reducing GHG emissions and boosting energy production. With this issuance, Chile became the first government to link its official NDC commitment on climate change to a bond issuance. Since then, Chile has continued to lead in sovereign SLB issuances, with six issuances in 2023 totalling USD 8 billion. In November 2022, Uruguay issued its first Climate Change-Indexed Bond (BIICC). The country issued another SLB in 2023 totalling USD 700 million (OECD et al., 2023[60]). In 2023, sovereign SLBs had an average value of USD 1.2 billion, higher than other thematic bonds. In 2023, they also had a longer maturity average of 16 years, and lower average coupons of 5%. SLB yields are linked to the achievement or non-fulfilment of KPIs/targets, with adjustments ranging from 5 basis points up to 100 basis points if multiple targets are not met (OECD, 2024[102]).

To scale up SLBs in the region, international financial co-operation is crucial for overcoming barriers hindering market development, particularly in establishing and aligning monitoring and supervision mechanisms to international standards to boost investors' confidence by preventing green/SDG washing. At present, SLBs are at risk of such washing in countries with limited frameworks/taxonomies. International best practices exist (such as the EU Taxonomy) however some countries lack capacity to align their national frameworks to international best practices. Immaterial or not so ambitious KPIs and SPTs, insufficient data quality, and a shortage of skilled analysts to assess SLB KPIs are other risks for greenwashing. International co-operation can build the capacity of regulatory authorities to ensure enhanced quality and availability of data and indicators to track sustainability progress. Regulation and monitoring need improvement, and definitions should be harmonised regionally and internationally to enhance market transparency (see below on sustainable finance frameworks). Additionally, international capacity-building partnerships are essential to bridge regulatory and co-ordination gaps. Developing and utilising locally adapted SLB guidelines that prioritise sustainability will be crucial for developing local-currency bond markets, mitigating currency risk and enhancing financial resilience (OECD, 2024[115]).

Catastrophe bonds can enable governments to increase their external borrowing

Catastrophe bonds have the potential to significantly increase governments' external borrowing capacity by transferring the financial risk of catastrophic events to investors, who are attracted by the potential for higher yields and portfolio diversification (OECD et al., 2022[116]). In 2009, Mexico became the first country to issue a multi-peril multi-region CAT bond, for USD 290 million, using the World Bank's MultiCat Program. The CAT bond provided insurance against earthquake risk in three regions around Mexico City and against hurricanes on the Atlantic and Pacific coasts (World Bank, 2013[117]). Eight years later, in 2017, Mexico received a USD 150 million payout from the World Bank-supported CAT bond (Artemis, 2017[118]) In 2021, Jamaica issued a CAT bond of USD 185 million with the support of the World Bank that is helping the country to address its financing gap by providing coverage for three hurricane seasons. Through this insurance-like risk transfer agreement, Jamaica stands to receive the necessary funds if future storms surpass pre-defined intensity thresholds. Jamaica's experience underscores the importance of collaborating with international financial institutions throughout the pre-issuance and issuance phases of a CAT bond transaction. The World Bank helped Jamaica to secure bilateral financial support in the form of grants from donor countries to finance CAT bond premium and transaction costs related to the design, structure and placement of the CAT bond (OECD, 2024[119]). Although limited, implementation of sovereign CAT bonds by developing countries, such as the ones in Jamaica and Mexico, demonstrates that there is market appetite for this sophisticated financial instrument when it is deployed by highly exposed and vulnerable countries (OECD, 2024[119]).

Multi-country CAT bonds offer a solution for nations unable to issue CAT bonds independently. Such bonds allow several countries to pool resources for regional benefits. The example of the Pacific Alliance, which groups Chile, Colombia, Mexico and Peru, demonstrates how such initiatives can reduce transaction costs and attract a wider investor base, ultimately leading to lower premium rates. These CAT bonds total USD 1.36 billion, representing the largest sovereign risk insurance transaction and the largest CAT bond issuance ever facilitated by the World Bank (OECD, 2024[119]). They enable multiple sovereign nations to enter the CAT bond markets independently, without the need for a risk pooling facility. For Chile, Colombia and Peru, this transaction provides a gateway to capital markets for obtaining disaster risk insurance for the first time. The transaction involved five classes of bonds: one each for Chile, Colombia and Peru, and two totalling USD 260 million for Mexico (OECD, 2024[119]). Efforts are currently underway, with World Bank support, to develop a regional CAT bond for the Caribbean.

To advance the use of catastrophe bonds in LAC, it is crucial to overcome a number of challenges, such as developing robust legal frameworks that support risk transfer effectively. International co-operation is key to establishing clear regulations and procedures governing the issuance and management of CAT bonds that ensure transparency and compliance with international standards. There is also a critical need to define and clarify the roles and responsibilities of all stakeholders involved in the CAT bond ecosystem. This includes issuers, investors, reinsurers, regulatory bodies and government agencies, among others. Establishing clear guidelines and protocols for each stakeholder's involvement will help to streamline processes, mitigate risks and enhance market confidence (OECD et al., 2022[116]; OECD, 2024[119]).

Natural disaster clauses can help mitigate the financial impact of catastrophic events

Natural disaster clauses can link countries' repayment capacity to their risk exposure. By accounting for the financial impact of disasters, these clauses help align debt servicing obligations with a country's ability to manage and recover from catastrophic events. A natural disaster clause was incorporated into Grenada's debt restructuring efforts in 2016, enabling the country to capitalise interest and defer principal maturities on bonds in the event of significant natural disasters, subject to specific conditions. In 2018, Barbados introduced the Barbados Economic Recovery and Transformation programme. This reform initiative, which included debt restructuring for both domestic and external debt, was the basis for the IMF's Extended Fund Facility support programme. An agreement with domestic creditors was reached in late 2018, and natural disaster clauses were added to restructured government bonds. For example, the new bond, maturing in 2029, allows interest capitalisation and payment deferral for two years after a major natural disaster (ECLAC, 2021[120]).

Disaster clauses may lead to higher borrowing costs by encouraging governments to take on more debt at higher yields, potentially delaying repayments for investors. However, recent analyses suggest that these clauses improve borrowing terms overall. Governments tend to increase borrowing until their default risk mirrors that of economies without disaster clauses, with the expectation of delaying repayments. This reduces their expected debt servicing costs, despite higher spreads. Thus, governments accept the higher spreads with minimal impact on their overall borrowing costs (OECD et al., 2022[116]).

Climate or nature swaps can also serve as important sustainable financing instruments

A debt-for-nature swap (DFNS) is a liability management exercise where the country issues a guaranteed instrument (loan or bond) on more favourable terms and then uses the proceeds to buy back outstanding more expensive sovereign debt, generating savings on the interest rate coupon and/or the principal. These savings will be used to finance nature conservation and/or climate change mitigation/adaptation activities. DFNS have already been employed in the region, and new proposals are under development, particularly among biodiverse but highly indebted Caribbean countries with low credit ratings and limited access to markets (OECD/IDB, 2024[108]). These nations can leverage climate or nature swaps to confront their escalating financial challenges. In May 2023, Ecuador executed the largest DFNS to date, replacing a USD 1.65 billion debt with a USD 656 million loan funded by a blue bond. This swap resulted in an average discount of 60% and was financed by a loan granted to the country by an SPV. The loan was enhanced by a USD 85 million guarantee from the IDB and USD 656 million in political risk insurance from the US Development Finance Corporation. The SPV financed the loan through the issuance of the Galapagos Marine Bond, a USD 656 million marine conservation-linked bond with maturity in 2041. Credit Suisse arranged and structured the issuance, with support from 11 private-sector insurers that provided more than 50% in reinsurance, enhancing Ecuador's conservation efforts (West, 2023[121]).

Other LAC countries have also implemented DFNS to manage debt sustainability. In 2021, The Nature Conservancy and the government of Belize finalised a USD 364 million debt conversion aimed at marine conservation (the protection of 30% of Belize's ocean) (Green Finance Institute, 2021[122]). This initiative not only reduced Belize's debt by 12% of GDP but also generated an estimated USD 180 million for conservation efforts (Green Finance Institute, 2021[122]). As in Ecuador's DFNS, the US Development Finance Corporation played a crucial role by providing political risk insurance, which enhanced the credit profile of the bonds to Aa2 – significantly higher than Belize's Caa2 rating (US International Development Finance Corporation, 2023[123]). The transaction represents the largest debt refinancing for ocean conservation worldwide (Green Finance Institute, 2021[122]). In 2022, Barbados conducted a debt-for-nature swap involving USD 150 million of international bonds, resulting in USD 50 million allocated to marine conservation initiatives. This swap holds particular significance for an island nation heavily dependent on its pristine waters and beaches for tourism (Savage, 2023[124]). In July 2024, the EIB and IDB approved guarantees for Barbados totalling USD 300 million to support an innovative debt-for-climate swap, unlocking resources for investing in critical climate adaptation infrastructure projects (European Investment Bank, 2024[125]). In November 2024, supported by the IDB, The Nature Conservancy (TNC), and others, the Bahamas launched a debt conversion project to save USD 124 million over 15 years for ocean conservation and managing its Protected Areas System. The project facilitated a USD 300 million debt buyback using proceeds from a new loan arranged by Standard Chartered Bank (IDB, 2024[126]).

Caribbean islands are also preparing to negotiate with creditors for debt swaps, given their needs for sustainable financing (OECD/IDB, 2024[108]). In 2018, Antigua and Barbuda, Saint Lucia, and Saint Vincent and the Grenadines commenced negotiations with creditors for debt swaps aimed at achieving a reduction in their debt-to-GDP ratio of at least 12.2%. This could result in generating approximately 1% of GDP of resilient growth, which could elevate the weighted average growth rate of these three nations to levels seen before the global financial crisis (ECLAC, 2018[127]). The total value of debt reduction needed to achieve a one percentage point increase in growth across the three countries is estimated at approximately USD 525.9 million, with the total value of the debt haircut ranging from USD 105.2 million for a 20% haircut scenario to USD 263.3 million for a 50% haircut scenario (ECLAC, 2018[127])

Countries in the region must carefully assess the downsides of DFNS before engaging in them. Financial studies on the three DFNS transactions in the region indicate that these swaps alone cannot structurally reduce debt or improve sovereign creditworthiness (Caballero, Gonzalez and Nieto, 2024[128]). While they have reduced debt burdens and slightly improved the gross external financing needs metric, overall sovereign financing needs have remained high, exceeding 100% of current account receipts, with little material improvement in external metrics. From a fiscal perspective, DFNS may be less efficient than similar mechanisms such as conditional grants and broad debt restructuring. This is why these instruments can be useful tools but complementary to debt restructurings (Lazard, 2021[129]). The latter are more effective in ensuring that transferred resources reach their intended targets, whether for financing climate investments or reducing debt burdens, rather than benefiting other creditors (Chamon et al., 2022[130]). From a sustainability perspective, the ability of governments to fulfil long-term conservation commitments is uncertain. DFNS transactions often lack clarity on the green or blue projects they support, with some "blue" bonds having no specified use-of-proceeds. This raises the risk of green/blue washing. Additionally, the extended duration of environmental commitments makes them vulnerable to political changes. Effective enforcement of climate contracts will be crucial in the coming years, as failure to meet commitments may impact the future of debt-for-nature swaps (Caballero, Gonzalez and Nieto, 2024[128]).

Looking ahead, it is crucial to ensure that DFNSs in the region serve two primary objectives: first, to increase fiscal resources for debtor countries unable to fully fund climate investments through loans alone, and second, to prioritise benefits for the debtor. To achieve this, reducing current transaction and agency costs is essential. DFNSs should guarantee that funds saved from reduced debt service are directed towards specific investments rather than general debt obligations, as demonstrated by Belize's recent marine conservation swap (Chamon et al., 2022[130]). When involving buybacks of commercial debt, these transactions should be managed by third-party donors or creditors to potentially secure lower prices than debtor countries. Policies scaling up DFNSs should align with broader climate finance objectives by linking swaps to budget allocations, establishing standardised climate performance indicators for debt instruments and using carbon credits to incentivise swaps from private and public sources. Implementing efficient monitoring and oversight mechanisms will enhance transparency and strengthen institutional frameworks. International partnerships involving multilateral organisations, civil society, NGOs and the private sector can enhance collaboration, monitoring and standardisation (Fuller et al., 2018[131]). International organisations can help standardise the instrument to reduce structuring costs by implementing specific DFNS templates that offer debtor country practitioners clear guidelines and best practices (Lazard, 2021[129]). All these efforts could reduce transaction costs, promote effective emissions reductions and enhance fiscal benefits from DFNS and other climate finance mechanisms (Chamon et al., 2022[130]).

Strong regulation and oversight are needed to ensure effectiveness and mitigate risks

Countries in LAC are focusing on expanding, improving and harmonising sustainable finance frameworks, which are essential to regulating, monitoring and verifying the issuance of GSSS bonds and other sustainable financial instruments. Conceptual frameworks for measurement and decision making are also key to reorienting external flows to recalibrate for social risks and promote quality investment. Frameworks that are more consolidated or interoperable have the potential to reduce transaction costs for investors, making capital markets in the region more attractive. Such frameworks may include disclosures, principles, standards and/or taxonomies that serve two main purposes: i) reducing and managing the environmental, social and governance (ESG) risks of financial activities; and ii) encouraging the flow of capital to assets, projects, sectors and companies that have environmental, climate and social benefits. Sustainable finance frameworks guide the issuance of GSSS bonds at the international, regional and national levels (OECD, 2024[102]).

At the international level, the principles of the International Capital Market Association (ICMA) and the Helsinki Principles are often used as overarching guiding frameworks for the issuance of GSSS bonds at the regional and national levels (OECD et al., 2023[60]). ICMA's suite of instruments – Green Bond Principles, Social Bond Principles, Sustainability Bond Guidelines and Sustainability-Linked Bond Principles – have become increasingly important in international markets. Several countries and corporates around the world now use them as a reference to develop their own frameworks for the issuance of GSSS bonds and other sustainable financial instruments (OECD et al., 2023[60]). Other international frameworks aimed at improving ESG risk management for corporates are also being widely adopted, as demand for corporate sustainability disclosure is increasing from asset managers investing not only in GSSS bonds but also in all types of securities, including equity (OECD, 2023[132]). Such frameworks include, for instance, the OECD's framework on measuring the non-financial performance of firms and the UN's Principles for Responsible Investment, as well as more robust ESG metrics that account for the broader social performance of firms (OECD, 2022[133]).

While overarching principles and guidelines provide valuable advice, it is essential for issuers at the national level to establish clearer, more binding standards and taxonomies. By the end of December 2023, 14 countries in LAC had launched initiatives aimed at developing their sustainable finance frameworks, including protocols, standards, guidelines and/or taxonomies totalling 221 actions (OECD, 2024[102]). These initiatives include actions led by governments (e.g. ministries, central/development banks, and regulatory bodies), private sector entities (e.g. industry associations, capital market entities, stock exchanges, insurance companies and consulting firms), as well as joint efforts, including international co-operation (OECD, 2024[102]).

When examining sustainable finance frameworks in LAC countries, green and sustainable taxonomies stand out. These initiatives have increasingly been adopted throughout the region since 2022. As of May 2024, they had been published in Argentina, Chile, Colombia, the Dominican Republic, Mexico and Panama, and were under development in countries such as Brazil, Costa Rica and Peru (Table 4.2).

Table 4.2. Overview of taxonomy initiatives in selected LAC countries

Country	Stage of taxonomy development	Name	Date	Participants	Taxonomy priority
Argentina	Published	Sustainable Finance Framework	May 2023	Government ministries through the Technical Committee on Sustainable Finance	Economic and social objectives within the context of the UN Sustainable Development Agenda
Brazil	Under development: Action plan published	Sustainable Taxonomy	December 2023	Ministry of Finance, GIZ	Climate change adaptation and mitigation in sectors such as agriculture, extractive activities, electricity and gas, water supply and wastewater management and transportation
Chile	Published	Green taxonomy	August 2023	CBI, IDB, CAF, GIZ, Ministry of Finance	Climate change mitigation and adaptation, water and marine resources, circular economy, pollution, ecosystems and biodiversity
Colombia	Published	Green Taxonomy	April 2022	Government ministries	Land-use sectors (forestry, agriculture and livestock)
Costa Rica	Initial documents proposed	Sustainable Finance Taxonomy	April 2023	The Green Climate Fund, UNEP, European Commission, government ministries, superintendencies, the central bank	Creation of a framework to map, quantify and disclose climate-related financial risks. These methodologies will be tested in the portfolios of banks and insurers to assess their exposure to these risks and define mitigation strategies
Dominican Republic	Published	Green Taxonomy	June 2024	IFC, government ministries	Energy, transport, construction, information and communication technologies (ICT), industry, water and waste
Mexico	Published	Sustainable Taxonomy	March 2023	GIZ, AFD, ECLAC, IFC, GGGI, UK Pact, Bank of Mexico, World Bank, Ministry of Finance	Climate change, gender equality and access to basic services in municipalities
Panama	Published	Sustainable Finance Taxonomy	March 2024	Ministry of Environment, Superintendency of Banks and of Insurance, UNEP	Climate change mitigation and adaptation, water resources, land use, circular economy, pollution and biodiversity
Peru	Under development: Roadmap published	Green Finance Taxonomy	June 2023	Ministry of Environment, GIZ	Climate change, biodiversity and ecosystem services, natural infrastructure, eco and bio-businesses, circular economy and clean production

Note: CBI = Climate Bonds Initiative. GGGI = Global Green Growth Institute. GIZ = German International Co-operation Agency (Deutsche Gesells chaft für Internationale Zusammenarbeit). AFD = Agence Française de Développement. UNEP = United Nations Environment Programme.

Source: Authors' elaboration based on (OECD et al., 2022[116]); (Green Finance for Latin America and the Caribbean, 2023[134]); (Presidencia Argentina, 2023[135]); (Ministry of Economy of Argentina, 2023[136]); (Ministry of Finance of Brazil, 2023[137]); (Government of Mexico, 2023[138]); (Ministry of Finance of Chile, 2023[139]); (UNEP FI, 2024[140]); (Ministry of Finance of Peru, 2023[141]).

These taxonomies establish technical assessment criteria and define green, social, sustainability or sustainability-linked activities based on prioritised sectors and sustainable development goals. In April 2022, the Colombian government published the region's first green taxonomy, with a focus on land-use sectors. Since then, seven more countries have published or made significant progress in developing sustainable or green taxonomies, focusing on climate change mitigation and adaptation, the circular economy, biodiversity protection and sectors such as land use, electricity and water. Interoperability and harmonisation remain crucial, as each taxonomy determines environmental priorities based on its unique context. This is essential for international investors seeking a transparent set of criteria to track the environmental impact of the projects in which they invest. One way to standardise is by following the EU's green taxonomy and classification criteria. Moving forward, it is crucial to ensure that national taxonomies are comprehensive, encompassing all essential production sectors for sustainability, climate change mitigation and digital inclusion (OECD, 2024[102]).

At the EU regional level, the EU Sustainable Finance Framework is employed as a guiding reference for the issuance of GSSS and other sustainable finance mechanisms. This framework encompasses the EU Taxonomy, disclosure regulations, and standards, which help support companies and the financial sector, particularly by facilitating private financing for transition projects and technologies. Established in 2020, the taxonomy lays the groundwork for identifying and labelling environmentally sustainable activities with clear conditions and technical criteria (European Commission, 2020[142]). In 2023, the European Commission expanded the EU Taxonomy's scope by including additional activities and proposed new regulations for environmental, social, and governance (ESG) rating providers. These measures aim to enhance market transparency in sustainable investments and to facilitate the identification of activities eligible for sustainable financing (European Commission, 2023[143]).

The EU Taxonomy exemplifies a harmonised regional framework that enhances market confidence and transparency to facilitate investment in sustainable activities. Ensuring interoperability and clarity between LAC national taxonomies and the EU Taxonomy is crucial. Interoperability involves using similar guiding principles and core elements, such as objectives, sector classifications and science-based criteria with comparable metrics and thresholds (Climate Bonds Initiative/Ambire Global, 2023[144]). Taxonomy comparative studies, like the EU-funded ones for Colombia and Mexico, can enhance transparency for EU and international investors and stakeholders. Such studies can foster market clarity, reduce transaction and research costs, and aid in cross-border capital mobilisation for sustainable investments.

The first Common Framework of Sustainable Finance Taxonomies in LAC marks the initial step towards establishing a harmonised framework akin to that of the EU. Launched in June 2023 by the UN system in LAC, the regional framework was developed by the Working Group on Taxonomies of Sustainable Finance in Latin America and the Caribbean and funded by the EU through the EUROCLIMA Programme (UNDP, 2023[145]). The framework serves as a voluntary guidance tool for entities in the region engaged in or planning to develop taxonomies. It also offers direction for achieving interoperability of taxonomies within LAC and globally. Aligning the methodologies of various taxonomies will enhance investor confidence and minimise transaction costs (OECD et al., 2023[60]).

Policy recommendations

As Latin America and the Caribbean prepares for the Fourth International Conference on Financing for Development in 2025, there are opportunities to assess the region's strategic priorities in a challenging international context. The development of a shared agenda will help the region to pursue sustainable development and present solutions to current challenges at a global level. A shared and integrating agenda would contribute to realise the region's development opportunities and ensure greater sustainable development financial flows. This agenda should address challenges in the international financing context, such as access to liquidity, risk perceptions and access to concessional finance, as well as fragmentation and the need for co-ordination among development providers.

To bring concrete solutions and proposals to the conference, a more unified approach would allow for greater coherence and ensure that that the region's interests are properly represented, being able to influence final negotiations. First, private flows need to be aligned with sustainable and development goals. This entails improving and harmonising regulatory frameworks; better channelling of public policy and foreign investment into areas of productive transformation, including financing from the EU through the GGIA; and equipping the region to reach its 2030 goals. Second, greater collaboration is needed among development actors, including MDBs and DFIs from developed and emerging economies, in order to maximise the coherence and effectiveness of constrained financial resources. This entails using both official and private flows by leveraging the strengths of different actors and providing integrated financing options for the region. LAC can improve its financing outlook by fostering innovative development partnerships with private actors, such as philanthropic providers, and leveraging development flows across developing countries. To make sure that that these private and public flows go towards quality investment, a strong enabling environment with clear frameworks for investment is needed. Strategic partnerships, such as with the EU, offer opportunities to use sustainable taxonomies and mobilisation tools to deliver more sustainable development.

In addition, international partnerships need to contribute towards financing solutions that harness the strengths of the region, such as its rich natural environment and renewable energy potential. Debt tools for financing the sustainable development agenda can address some of the region's most pressing challenges, such as debt distress, climate catastrophes and the risk of biodiversity loss. Effective co-operation to develop these tools and gear them towards the needs of the region can overcome some of the shortcomings of pre-existing financial instruments. The effective implementation of these tools requires enhanced regulation and oversight to improve governance and capacity building.

These solutions can help to build consensus and enable the more effective representation of LAC's interests next year at the Fourth International Conference on Financing for Development. The region has the potential to drive global changes in development financing and partnerships. It therefore would benefit from improved co-ordination and from engaging in constructive development solutions to navigate the challenging environment, both regionally and around the world.

Box 4.4. Key policy messages

Rethinking the international financial architecture

- Enhance multilateral dialogue mechanisms and policy dialogue as the region prepares for the Fourth International Conference on Financing Sustainable Development.
- Boost international dialogue and co-operation within the region to align proposals and look for a unified voice on the challenges facing LAC and middle-income countries.
- Enhance co-ordination mechanisms across development actors (MDBs, DFIs from developed, emerging and developing economies, and bilateral donors) to facilitate the implementation of co-operation projects with the objective of promoting further private investments.
- Engage with international financial institutions, particularly MDBs, to further increase flexible financing lines for middle-income countries.
- Advance the debate on improving risk assessments, including credit ratings, and increase information sharing and transparency among financial actors.
- Call for mobilising international resources that do not impact negatively on debt, such as SDRs, and seek increasing concessional financing for the most needed and for sectors in which purely private investment is difficult to carry out.

Fostering international official and private financial flows

- Foster integrated financing solutions that combine concessional, non-concessional and private financing, promoting the co-ordination of different actors and leveraging their distinct capacities.
- Promote quality sustainable investment, with high standards and adherence to ESG criteria.

- Promote a whole-of-government approach to ensure co-ordination and effectiveness in the mobilisation of international official flows.
- Establish regulatory frameworks that improve the business enabling environment and boost foreign direct investment and technology transfer.
- Support initiatives that increase transparency and facilitate information sharing on risk perception for investors. This will help reduce the gap between perceived and real risks. Promote further risk-sharing instruments between MDBs, DFIs and private institutions.
- Enhance targeted project financing mechanisms, including guarantees and mezzanine operations, between MDBs, DFIs from developed and developing countries to reduce financial costs.
- Promote the use of international development finance measures, such as TOSSD, to map all resources received by LAC, and to inform external financing strategies.
- Measure the impact of increasing official financing flows for attracting private-sector investment through mechanisms such as blended finance operations and other mechanisms of private resource mobilisation.
- Identify the limitations of countries to fully use blended finance and other risk mitigation instruments and provide capacity building for a better use of these instruments.
- Promote private and public partnerships, including with DFIs and multilateral actors as investors, that help the region address global challenges, like the green and digital transitions.
- Establish regulations to lower the cost of remittances and facilitate innovative instruments to increase financial transfers.
- Scale up promising pilots funded by philanthropic donors by partnering with foundations and ensuring mechanisms that guarantee both impact and scalability.

Developing sustainable debt instruments

- Scale up GSSS bonds by enhancing the domestic debt market and developing international capacity-building partnerships that align regulatory frameworks to international best practices and co-ordination gaps between stakeholders.
- Educate and engage investors and issuers of all sizes about GSSS bonds across LAC, focusing on countries that lack capacity building for issuance, certification, monitoring, and framework development.
- Support the expansion and adjustment of SLBs with innovative structures, redirecting capital flows towards projects that promote climate-change mitigation and adaptation while strengthening the social and sustainable dimensions.
- Improve the use of CAT bonds by developing robust legal frameworks that support risk transfer effectively. Establish clear guidelines and protocols for each stakeholder's involvement to streamline processes, mitigate risks and enhance market confidence.
- Evaluate the impacts of debt-for-nature swaps and enhance governance structures through improved transparency, monitoring and oversight mechanisms to foster better engagement with creditors. Bolster co-operation in crafting more transparent debt-for-nature swap frameworks through international collaborations with governments, civil society, NGOs and the private sector.
- Develop well-designed and regulated natural disaster clauses in debt contracts to link the country's repayment capacity to its risk exposure. Allowing countries to defer either interest or principal payments (or both) for a defined period, these key instruments enhance financial resilience in the face of disasters.

- Enhance sustainable financing frameworks and foster co-ordination and harmonisation across countries on sustainable debt instruments, such as GSSS bonds, to boost investors' confidence. Build on established regional frameworks like the EU Sustainable Finance Framework and EU Taxonomy. Establish robust monitoring and verification systems to uphold market transparency and prevent green/SDG washing.

References

AFD (2024), *Supporting the financing of Costa Rica's climate targets alongside BNCR*, Agence Française de Développement, Paris, https://www.afd.fr/en/carte-des-projets/costa-rica-supporting-financing-climate-targets-bncr (accessed on 1 July 2024). [35]

AFD (2023), *Climate-financial trap: an empirical approach to detecting situations of double vulnerability*, Agence Française de Développement, Paris, https://www.afd.fr/en/ressources/climate-financial-trap-empirical-approach-detecting-situations-double-vulnerability (accessed on 30 August 2024). [26]

AFD (2023), *Low-carbon transition and macroeconomic vulnerabilities: A multidimensional approach in tracing vulnerabilities and its application in the case of Colombia*, Agence Française de Développement, Paris, https://www.afd.fr/en/ressources/low-carbon-transition-and-macroeconomic-vulnerabilities-multidimensional-approach-tracing-vulnerabilities-and-its-application-case-colombia (accessed on 30 August 2024). [27]

AFD (2022), "Official Development Assistance at the age of consequences", *Policy Paper*, No. 11, Agence Française de Développement, Paris, https://www.afd.fr/en/ressources/official-development-assistance-age-consequences. [53]

AFD (forthcoming), *Double standards in financing for development*, Agence Française de Développement, Paris. [54]

Artemis (2017), *Mexico confirms $150m cat bond payout for quake*, https://www.artemis.bm/news/mexico-confirms-150m-cat-bond-payout-for-quake/. [118]

Avellán, L. et al. (2024), "Bridging the gap: Mobilization of multilateral development banks in infrastructure", *IDB Working Paper Series*, No. 1299, Inter-American Development Bank, https://doi.org/10.18235/0004006. [65]

Bollag, B. (2024), *French government criticized over $806M cut to aid*, Devex, https://www.devex.com/news/french-government-criticized-over-806m-cut-to-aid-107193. [41]

Broto, C. and L. Molina (2016), "Sovereign ratings and their asymmetric response to fundamentals", *Journal of Economic Behavior & Organization*, Vol. 130, pp. 206-224, https://www.sciencedirect.com/science/article/abs/pii/S0167268116301524. [21]

Caballero, C., K. Gonzalez and F. Nieto (2024), *Debt-For-Nature Swaps Are Gaining Traction Among Lower-Rated Sovereigns*, S&P Global, https://www.spglobal.com/ratings/en/research/articles/240227-debt-for-nature-swaps-are-gaining-traction-among-lower-rated-sovereigns-13010020 (accessed on 30 August 2024). [128]

CABEI (2021), *Remittances in Central America: The role of CABEI*, https://www.bcie.org/fileadmin/user_upload/Remittances_in_Central_America_the_Role_of_CABEI.pdf. [87]

CAF (2024), *CAF receives AFD's support with an innovative financial mechanism to consolidate its position as the green bank of Latin America and the Caribbean*, Development Bank of Latin America and the Caribbean, https://www.caf.com/en/currently/news/2024/05/caf-receives-afds-support-with-an-innovative-financial-mechanism-to-consolidate-its-position-as-the-green-bank-of-latin-america-and-the-caribbean/ (accessed on 15 July 2024). [34]

Carey, E., H. Desai and Y. Ahmad (2023), "Tracing the impacts of Russia's war of aggression against Ukraine on official development assistance (ODA)", in *Development Co-operation Profiles*, OECD Publishing, Paris, https://doi.org/10.1787/5096b978-en. [43]

Catrinescu, N. et al. (2009), "Remittances, institutions, and economic growth", *World Development*, Vol. 37/1, pp. 81-92, https://www.sciencedirect.com/science/article/pii/S0305750X08001344. [93]

Cattaneo, O. and C. Piemonté (2021), "Transition Finance Compendium: Challenges and recommendations for the Development Assistance Committee", *OECD Development Co-operation Working Papers*, No. 94, OECD Publishing, Paris, https://doi.org/10.1787/90f219b1-en. [49]

Cattaneo, O., C. Piemonté and K. Poensgen (2020), "Transition finance country study of Chile: Better managing graduation from ODA eligibility", *OECD Development Co-operation Working Papers*, No. 70, OECD Publishing, Paris, https://doi.org/10.1787/608cbf6d-en. [37]

CGD (2023), *Strengthening Multilateral Development Banks: The triple agenda*, Report of the Independent Experts Working Group, No. 1, Centre for Global Development, https://www.cgdev.org/sites/default/files/The_Triple_Agenda_G20-IEG_Report_Volume1_2023.pdf. [67]

CGD (2022), *Global Cooperation for Development: Current Failures and the Case for Collaboration*, Centre for Global Development, https://www.cgdev.org/blog/global-cooperation-development-current-failures-and-case-collaboration (accessed on 12 March 2024). [32]

Chamon, M. et al. (2022), "Debt-for-climate Swaps: Analysis, design, and implementation", *IMF Working Papers*, No. 162, International Monetary Fund, https://www.imf.org/en/Publications/WP/Issues/2022/08/11/Debt-for-Climate-Swaps-Analysis-Design-and-Implementation-522184. [130]

Climate Bonds Initiative/Ambire Global (2023), *Comparison Study Between the Colombian and EU Taxonomies*, Climate Bonds Initiative, https://www.climatebonds.net/files/reports/cbi_col_eu_taxonomy_01e.pdf. [144]

Council of the EU (2023), *Joint Staff Working Document : Main outcomes of the mapping of external tools of the EU*, Council of the European Union, Brussels, https://data.consilium.europa.eu/doc/document/ST-8157-2023-INIT/en/pdf. [76]

DEVEX (2024), *How Germany is cutting billions from foreign aid*, https://www.devex.com/news/how-germany-is-cutting-billions-from-foreign-aid-107055 (accessed on 3 April 2024). [42]

ECA/ECLAC (2022), *Special Drawing Rights (SDRs) and the COVID-19 crisis*, United Nations Economic Commision for Africa/United Nations Economic Commission for Latin America and the Caribbean, https://repositorio.cepal.org/server/api/core/bitstreams/a4d76467-4802-421e-bb51-207cdb91bccf/content. [15]

ECLAC (2024), *Capital Flows to Latin America and the Caribbean: 2023 year-in-review and early 2024 developments*, United Nations Economic Commission for Latin America and the Caribbean, https://repositorio.cepal.org/server/api/core/bitstreams/ce02481f-b84e-409d-8ccd-30ae1c14efb1/content. [103]

ECLAC (2023), *Capital Flows to Latin America and the Caribbean: 2022 year-in-review and early 2023 developments*, United Nations Economic Commission for Latin America and the Caribbean, https://repositorio.cepal.org/server/api/core/bitstreams/7e7681e0-0855-45f3-9bbe-38ad9feedd63/content. [111]

ECLAC (2023), *Foreign Direct Investment in Latin American and the Caribbean*, United Nations Economic Commission for Latin America and the Caribbean, https://repositorio.cepal.org/server/api/core/bitstreams/fd2ce029-2846-4900-a0e6-14818f6191b3/content. [58]

ECLAC (2023), *Public debt and development distress in Latin America and the Caribbean*, United Nations Economic Commission for Latin America and the Caribbean, https://repositorio.cepal.org/server/api/core/bitstreams/d84a5041-0a2c-4b8e-9b01-d91b187477ce/content. [18]

ECLAC (2022), *Capital Flows to Latin America and the Caribbean: 2021 year-in-review and the first four months of 2022*, United Nations Economic Commission for Latin America and the Caribbean, https://www.cepal.org/en/notes/capital-flows-latin-america-and-caribbean-2021-year-review-and-first-four-months-2022. [114]

ECLAC (2021), "An innovative financing for development agenda for the recovery in Latin America and the Caribbean", *Special Report Covid-19*, No. 12, United Nations Economic Commission for Latin America and the Caribbean, Santiago, https://www.cepal.org/en/publications/47490-innovative-financing-development-agenda-recovery-latin-america-and-caribbean. [120]

ECLAC (2021), *Capital flows to Latin America and the Caribbean: 2020 year-in-review in times of COVID-19*, United Nations Economic Commission for Latin America and the Caribbean, https://www.cepal.org/sites/default/files/news/files/kflowsfinal_web_0.pdf. [113]

ECLAC (2020), *Designing Strategies to Promote Investment of Family Remittances in Value Chains: A toolkit*, https://repositorio.cepal.org/server/api/core/bitstreams/610da794-bea9-4058-9ee9-3eba4db05dad/content. [94]

ECLAC (2018), *Debt for climate adaptation: swap initiative for Caribbean SIDS*, United Nations Economic Commission for Latin America and the Caribbean, https://www.cepal.org/sites/default/files/news/files/19-00814-debt_initiative_flyer-web.pdf. [127]

ECLAC (2018), "Sovereign credit ratings in Latin America and the Caribbean: Trends and impact on debt spreads", *Studies and Perspective Series*, No. 18, United Nations Economic Commission for Latin America and the Caribbean, Washington, DC, https://repositorio.cepal.org/server/api/core/bitstreams/d18622fb-d743-4512-971c-b1d2c61c0f87/content. [24]

ECLAC/OECD (2018), *Emerging challenges and shifting paradigms: New perspectives on international cooperation for development*, United Nations Economic Commission for Latin America and the Caribbean/OECD Development Centre, https://repositorio.cepal.org/server/api/core/bitstreams/414911fd-ec99-4ae8-8e0a-dd3c5a2478e0/content. [48]

Eco Business Fund (2024), *New Horizons - Impact Report 2023*, https://www.ecobusiness.fund/en/impact#:~:text=New%20Horizons%20%2D%20Impact%20Report%202023&text=The%20report%20looks%20back%20at,farmers%20and%20value%20chain%20actors (accessed on 30 August 2024). [79]

EFSD+ (2024), "Board approved INTPA blending operations as of 2021", in *European Fund for Sustainable Development Plus: International partnerships*, European Commission, Brussels, https://international-partnerships.ec.europa.eu/funding-and-technical-assistance/funding-instruments/european-fund-sustainable-development-plus_en#paragraph_5400 (accessed on 29 August 2024). [78]

EIB (2024), *EIB 2023/2024 Global Impact Report*, https://www.eib.org/attachments/lucalli/20240125_eib_global_impact_report_2023_2024_en.pdf. [73]

EIB (2024), *European Investment Bank*, https://www.eib.org/en/products/mandates-partnerships/eu-blending-facilities/index (accessed on 16 October 2024). [38]

Elysée (2024), *4P Leaders working lunch - United Nations General Assembly.*, https://www.elysee.fr/en/emmanuel-macron/2024/09/26/4p-leaders-working-lunch-united-nations-general-assembly (accessed on 3 October 2024). [8]

European Commission (2024), *Civil society dialogue regarding the EU's strategy on export credits*, Brussels, https://policy.trade.ec.europa.eu/eu-trade-meetings-civil-society/civil-society-dialogue-regarding-eus-strategy-export-credits-2024-04-10_en (accessed on 26 June 2024). [75]

European Commission (2023), *Joint Communication to the European Parliament and the Council: A New Agenda for Relations between the EU and Latin America and the Caribbean*, https://www.eeas.europa.eu/sites/default/files/documents/2023/JOIN_2023_17_1_EN_ACT_part1_v7.pdf. [72]

European Commission (2023), *Neighbourhood, Development and International Cooperation instrument – Global Europe*, https://commission.europa.eu/strategy-and-policy/eu-budget/performance-and-reporting/programme-performance-statements/neighbourhood-development-and-international-cooperation-instrument-global-europe-performance_en#:~:text=NDICI%20%E2%80%93%20Global%20Euro. [74]

European Commission (2023), "Sustainable finance package", European Commission, https://finance.ec.europa.eu/publications/sustainable-finance-package-2023_en. [143]

European Commission (2022), *Global Gateway: EU greenlights 40 new guarantee programmes under the European Fund for Sustainable Development plus*, https://ec.europa.eu/commission/presscorner/detail/en/ip_22_7799. [80]

European Commission (2020), *EU taxonomy for sustainable activities*, European Commission, https://finance.ec.europa.eu/sustainable-finance/tools-and-standards/eu-taxonomy-sustainable-activities_en. [142]

European Investment Bank (2024), *Barbados: EIB and Inter-American Development Bank approve guarantees to support climate and fiscal resilience*, European Investment Bank, https://www.eib.org/en/press/all/2024-300-inter-american-development-bank-and-european-investment-bank-approve-guarantees-to-support-climate-and-fiscal-resilience-in-barbados. [125]

Fajnzylber, P. and J. López (eds.) (2008), *Remittances and Development: Lessons from Latin America*, World Bank, Washington, DC, https://publications.iadb.org/en/remittances-and-development-lessons-latin-america. [83]

Ford Foundation (2024), *Our work around the world: Andean Region*, https://www.fordfoundation.org/our-work-around-the-world/andean-region/ (accessed on 5 April 2024). [100]

France Diplomacy (2023), *The Paris Pact for People and the Planet (4P)*, https://pactedeparis.org/pdf/the-paris-pact-for-people-and-the-planet.pdf (accessed on 27 March 2024). [7]

Fuller, F. et al. (2018), *Debt for Climate Swaps: Caribbean Outlook*, IMPACT, https://ca1-clm.edcdn.com/assets/debt_for_climate_swap_impact_briefing.pdf?v=1679478182#:~:text=There%20is%20existing%20experience%20with,climate%20swaps%20in%20the%20region. [131]

Gavas, M. and S. Pleeck (2024), “Maximising EU Concessional Finance for Greater Leverage and Impact”*, CGD Blog post*, Centre for Global Development, https://www.cgdev.org/blog/maximising-eu-concessional-finance-greater-leverage-and-impact. (accessed on 3 April 2024). [40]

GCF (2024), *GCF Spotlight: Latin America and the Caribbean*, Green Climate Fund, https://www.greenclimate.fund/document/gcf-latin-america-and-caribbean-factsheet. [104]

GEMs (2024), *Global Emerging Markets: Risk Database Consortium*, GEMs, Luxembourg, https://www.gemsriskdatabase.org/. [28]

Gevorkyan, A. (2021), *Can Diaspora Bonds Supercharge Development Investment?*, https://www.migrationpolicy.org/article/diaspora-bonds-supercharge-development-investment. [88]

GGGI (2024), *Dominican Republic's Green Bond Debut (USD 750 Million) after Publication of Green, Social, Sustainable Bonds Framework*, https://gggi.org/dominican-republics-green-bond-debut-usd-750-million-after-publication-of-green-social-sustainable-bonds-framework/. [107]

Global Infrastructure Hub (2023), *Infrastructure Monitor 2023: Global trends in private investment in infrastructure*, GI Hub, Sydney, https://cdn.gihub.org/umbraco/media/5462/gihub_infrastructuremonitor_2023-02.pdf. [64]

Government of Mexico (2023), *Taxonomía Sostenible de México*, Secretariat of Finance and Public Credit, Mexico, https://www.gob.mx/cms/uploads/attachment/file/809773/Taxonom_a_Sostenible_de_M_xico_.pdf. [138]

Green Finance for Latin America and the Caribbean (2023), “Avances hacia una taxonomía verde en Latinoamérica”, https://greenfinancelac.org/es/recursos/articulos/avances-hacia-una-taxonomia-verde-en-latinoamerica/. [134]

Green Finance Institute (2021), *“Government of Belize debt conversion for marine conservation”*, GFI Hive, https://www.greenfinanceinstitute.com/gfihive/case-studies/government-of-belize-debt-conversion-for-marine-conservation/. [122]

Gulrajani, N. (2016), “Bilateral versus multilateral aid channels: Strategic choices for donors, ODI Report”, *Overseas Development Institute*, https://odi.cdn.ngo/media/documents/10492.pdf. [70]

Hung, M. et al. (2022), *Market Power and Credit Rating Standards: Global Evidence*, Journal of Accounting and Economics, Vol. 73/2-3, https://doi.org/10.1016/j.jacceco.2021.101474. [20]

IDB (2024), *IDB and AfDB Welcome IMF Executive Board’s Decision Approving Use of SDRs for Hybrid Capital Instruments*, Inter-American Development Bank, Washington, DC, https://www.iadb.org/en/news/idb-and-afdb-welcome-imf-executive-boards-decision-approving-use-sdrs-hybrid-capital. [16]

IDB (2024), *IDB IMpact +*, Inter-American Development Bank, Washington, DC, https://www.iadb.org/en/home/idbimpact. [17]

IDB (2024), *The Bahamas Launches Debt for Ocean Conservation Swap with the support of IDB*, Inter-American Development Bank, Washington D.C., https://www.iadb.org/en/news/bahamas-launches-debt-ocean-conservation-swap-support-idb. [126]

IDB (2023), “Remittances to Latin America and the Caribbean in 2023: Consolidating long-term trends”, *IDB Technical Note*, No. 2845, Inter-American Development Bank, Washington, DC, https://publications.iadb.org/en/publications/english/viewer/Remittances-to-Latin-America-and-the-Caribbean-in-2023pdf. [82]

IDB (2019), *The road to SDG Financing: A new destination for private investment*, Inter-American Development Bank, Washington, DC, https://www.iadb.org/en/news/road-sdg-financing-new-destination-private-investment (accessed on 19 March 2024). [46]

IFC (2024), *Central America Mezzanine Infrastructure Fund II*, IFC Project Information and Data Portal, International Finance Corporation, https://disclosures.ifc.org/project-detail/SII/32338/central-america-mezzanine-infrastructure-fund-ii (accessed on 10 April 2024). [71]

IFC (2024), *Global Emerging Markets Risk Database (GEMs) Consortium*, International Finance Corporation, https://www.ifc.org/en/what-we-do/sector-expertise/syndicated-loans-and-mobilization/global-emerging-markets-risk-database-consortium (accessed on 10 April 2024). [29]

IICA (n.d.), “El cultivo del arroz en República Dominicana”, *Interamerican Institute for Cooperation on Agriculture*, https://iica.int/es/prensa/noticias/el-cultivo-del-arroz-en-republica-dominicana. [52]

IMF (2024), *Balance of Payments and International Investment Position Statistics (BOP/IIP)*, International Monetary Fund, Washington, DC, https://data.imf.org/?sk=7a51304b-6426-40c0-83dd-ca473ca1fd52. [57]

IMF (2023), "Sub-Saharan Africa's risk perception premium: in the search of missing factors", *IMF Working Papers*, No. 2023/130, International Monetary Fund, Washington, DC, https://www.imf.org/en/Publications/WP/Issues/2023/06/23/Sub-Saharan-Africas-Risk-Perception-Premium-In-the-Search-of-Missing-Factors-534885. [19]

IMF (2017), "Migration and remittances in Latin America and the Caribbean: Engines of growth and macroeconomic stabilizers?", *IMF Working Papers*, No. 2017/144, International Monetary Fund, Washington, DC, https://www.imf.org/en/Publications/REO/WH/Issues/2017/05/10/wreo0517?intcid=OBanner. [81]

KNOMAD-World Bank (2023), "Migration and Development Brief 39", in *Leveraging diaspora finances for private capital mobilization*, The Global Knowledge Partnership on Migration and Development, World Bank, Washington, DC, https://knomad.org/publication/migration-and-development-brief-39. [92]

LACIF (2024), *Facts & figures LACIF*, Latin American and Caribbean Investment Facility, Brussels, https://www.eulaif.eu/en/facts-figures. [77]

LAGreen (2023), *Impact Report 2023*, https://lagreen.lu/wp-content/uploads/2023/04/LAGreen-Impact-Report-2023-1.pdf. [106]

Lazard (2021), *Debt-for-SDGs swaps in indebted countries: The right instrument to meet the funding gap? A review of past implementation and challenges lying ahead*, Lazard, https://capacity4dev.europa.eu/discussions/debt-sdgs-swaps-indebted-countries-right-instrument-meet-funding-gap_en. [129]

Mayers, M. and R. Ray (2024), *Feeling the stones: Chinese Development Finance to Latin America and the Caribbean 2023*, The Dialogue, Global Development Policy Centre, https://www.bu.edu/gdp/files/2024/06/GCI-CLLAC-Report-2024-FIN.pdf. [55]

Ministero dell'Economia e delle Finanze (2021), *The Common Framework for debt treatment beyond the DSSI, G20 Italy*, https://www.mef.gov.it/en/G20-Italy/common-framework.html (accessed on 3 June 2024). [13]

Ministry of Economy of Argentina (2023), *Argentina's Sustainable Finance Framework*, https://www.argentina.gob.ar/sites/default/files/argentinas-sustainable-finance-framework-2023.pdf. [136]

Ministry of Finance of Brazil (2023), *Sustainable Taxonomy of Brazil: Action Plan*, https://www.gov.br/fazenda/pt-br/orgaos/spe/taxonomia-sustentavel-brasileira/arquivos-taxonomia/sustainable-taxonomy-of-brazil-december-v2.pdf. [137]

Ministry of Finance of Chile (2023), *Estructura del Sistema de Clasificación o Taxonomía de Actividades Económicas Medioambientalmente Sostenibles para Chile*, https://www.hacienda.cl/areas-de-trabajo/finanzas-internacionales/finanzas-verdes/taxonomia-para-actividades-economicas-medioambientales-sostenibles/documentos/estructura-del-sistema-de-clasificacion-o-taxonomia-de-actividades-economicas. [139]

Ministry of Finance of Peru (2023), *Hoja de Ruta de Finanzas Verdes para el Perú*, https://www.scribd.com/document/654498117/DECRETO-SUPREMO-N%C2%BA-007-2023-MINAM. [141]

OECD (2024), *Aid (ODA) by sector and donor - Bilateral ODA commitments by donor and recipient*, OECD Publishing, Paris, https://data-explorer.oecd.org/vis?tm=ODA%20by%20sector%20bilateral%20commitments&pg=0&snb=5&df[ds]=dsDisseminateFinalDMZ&df[id]=DSD_DAC1%40DF_DAC5&df[ag]=OECD.DCD.FSD&df[vs]=1.1&dq=ALLD.528....Q.&lom=LASTNPERIODS&lo=5&to[TIME_PERIOD]=false (accessed on 2024 August 30). [31]

OECD (2024), *Creditor Reporting System (CRS)*, OECD Publishing, Paris, https://stats.oecd.org/Index.aspx?DataSetCode=crs1#. [30]

OECD (2024), *Fostering Catastrophe Bond Markets in Asia and the Pacific*, The Development Dimension, OECD Publishing, Paris, https://doi.org/10.1787/ab1e49ef-en. [119]

OECD (2024), *Mobilised private finance for development (database)*, OECD Publishing, Paris, https://data-explorer.oecd.org/vis?tm=mobilised%20private%20finance%20for%20development&pg=0&snb=8&vw=tb&df[ds]=dsDisseminateFinalDMZ&df[id]=DSD_MOB%40DF_MOBILISATION&df[ag]=OECD.DCD.FSD&df[vs]=1.0&dq=ALLD.A.100%2B110%2B120%2B130%2B140%2B150%2B200%2B210%2 (accessed on 9 July 2024). [63]

OECD (2024), *ODA Official development assistance: disbursements*, OECD Publishing, Paris, https://data-explorer.oecd.org/vis?tm=ODA%20Official%20development%20assistance%3A%20disbursements&pg=0&snb=11&df[ds]=dsDisseminateFinalDMZ&df[id]=DSD_DAC2%40DF_DAC2A&df[ag]=OECD.DCD.FSD&df[vs]=1.1&dq=.DPGC.206.USD.Q&lom=LASTNPERIODS&lo=5&to[TIME_PERIOD]=. [44]

OECD (2024), "Sustainability-Linked Bonds: How to make them work in developing countries, and how donors can help", *OECD Development Perspectives*, No. 44, OECD Publishing, Paris, https://doi.org/10.1787/7ca58c00-en. [115]

OECD (2024), "The surge of green, social, sustainability and sustainability-linked (GSSS) bonds in Latin America and the Caribbean: Facts and policy implications", *OECD Development Policy Papers*, No. 56, OECD Publishing, Paris, https://doi.org/10.1787/f1c893a3-en. [102]

OECD (2024), *TOSSD Data Visualisation Tool (online dataset)*, Total Official Support for Sustainable Development, https://tossd.online/app (accessed on 2024 July 19). [51]

OECD (2024), *Total Official Support for Sustainable Development (TOSSD) website*, https://www.tossd.org/ (accessed on 1 July 2024). [50]

OECD (2024), *Using the new UN MVI to identify and fill in vulnerability financing gaps in SIDS*, OECD Publishing, Paris, https://one.oecd.org/document/DCD(2024)16/en/pdf. [47]

OECD (2023), *Bottlenecks to Access SDG Finance for Developing Countries*, OECD Publishing, Paris, https://www.oecd.org/g20/oecd-g20-bottlenecks-sdg-finance-developing-countries.pdf. [6]

OECD (2023), "Creditor Reporting System: Private philanthropy for development (Edition 2023)", *OECD International Development Statistics* (database), https://doi.org/10.1787/dd620077-en (accessed on 26 November 2024). [99]

OECD (2023), *Foreign Direct Investment (FDI)*, OECD, Paris, https://www.oecd.org/investment/statistics.htm. [59]

OECD (2023), "Private finance mobilised by official development finance interventions", *OECD Development Perspectives*, No. 29, OECD Publishing, Paris, https://doi.org/10.1787/c5fb4a6c-en. [61]

OECD (2023), *Sustainability Policies and Practices for Corporate Governance in Latin America*, Corporate Governance, OECD Publishing, Paris, https://doi.org/10.1787/76df2285-en. [132]

OECD (2022), *Global Outlook on Financing Sustainable Development 2023: No Sustainability Without Equity*, OECD Publishing, Paris, https://doi.org/10.1787/fcbe6ce9-en. [2]

OECD (2022), *Green, Social, Sustainability and Sustainability-Linked Bonds in Developing Countries: How Can Donors Support Public Sector Issuances?*, OECD Publishing, Paris, https://web-archive.oecd.org/2023-03-17/641975-green-social-sustainability-and-sustainability-linked-bonds.pdf. [101]

OECD (2022), "Measuring the social performance of firms through the lens of the OECD Well-being Framework", *OECD Policy Insights on Well-being, Inclusion and Equal Opportunity*, No. 3, OECD Publishing, Paris, https://doi.org/10.1787/41f3823b-en. [133]

OECD (2022), "Spain's Huruma Fund: attracting private investment for smallholder agriculture", *OECD Case Study*, OECD Publishing, Paris, https://www.oecd.org/en/publications/2021/03/development-co-operation-tips-tools-insights-practices_d307b396/spain-s-huruma-fund-attracting-private-investment-for-smallholder-agriculture_ad085d01.html. [68]

OECD (2022), *The Short and Winding Road to 2030: Measuring Distance to the SDG Targets*, OECD Publishing, Paris, https://doi.org/10.1787/af4b630d-en. [3]

OECD (2021), *Private Philanthropy for Development – Second Edition: Data for Action*, The Development Dimension, OECD Publishing, Paris, https://doi.org/10.1787/cdf37f1e-en. [98]

OECD (2018), *Multilateral Development Finance: Towards a New Pact on Multilateralism to Achieve the 2030 Agenda Together*, OECD Publishing, Paris, https://doi.org/10.1787/9789264308831-en. [69]

OECD (2017), *Interrelations between Public Policies, Migration and Development*, OECD Publishing, Paris, https://doi.org/10.1787/9789264265615-en. [96]

OECD (2016), *Better Policies for Sustainable Development 2016: A New Framework for Policy Coherence*, OECD Publishing, Paris, https://doi.org/10.1787/9789264256996-en. [97]

OECD (2007), *Policy Coherence for Development 2007: Migration and Developing Countries*, OECD Publishing, Paris, https://doi.org/10.1787/9789264026100-en. [89]

OECD et al. (2022), *Latin American Economic Outlook 2022: Towards a Green And Just Transition*, OECD Publishing, Paris, https://doi.org/10.1787/3d5554fc-en. [116]

OECD et al. (2023), *Latin American Economic Outlook 2023: Investing in Sustainable Development*, OECD Publishing, Paris, https://doi.org/10.1787/8c93ff6e-en. [60]

OECD/IDB (2024), *Caribbean Development Dynamics 2025*, OECD Publishing, Paris, https://doi.org/10.1787/a8e79405-en. [108]

Orliange, P. and A. Granja e Barros (2020), "From Monterrey to Addis Ababa and beyond: A new global framework for public finance for sustainable development?", *Carta International*, Vol. 15/3, https://doi.org/10.21530/ci.v15n3.2020.1046. [4]

OSR (2022), *G20's Debt Service Suspension Initiative: A historical comparison*, Observer Research Foundation, https://www.orfonline.org/expert-speak/g20s-debt-service-suspension-initiative (accessed on 27 March 2024). [11]

Owen, N. (2022), "Belize: Swapping debt for nature", *IMF Country Focus*, 4 May, International Monetary Fund, Washington, DC, https://www.imf.org/en/News/Articles/2022/05/03/CF-Belize-swapping-debt-for-nature. [110]

Piemonté, C., J. Kim and O. Cattaneo (2024), "Financing sustainable development in the Organisation of Eastern Caribbean States: A transition finance diagnostic", *OECD Development Co-operation Working Papers*, No. 115, OECD Publishing, Paris. [36]

Portes, R. (2008), *Ratings agency reform*, VoxEU Column, Centre for Economic Policy Research (CEPR), https://cepr.org/voxeu/columns/ratings-agency-reform (accessed on 15 July 2024). [25]

Practitioners' Network for European Development Co-operation (2023), *EDFI, JEFIC and PN Statement of intent on enhanced collaboration of the three networks*, https://www.dev-practitioners.eu/media/documents/EDFI-JEFIC-PN_Statement_of_Intent_-_Final_Version_-_Updated_13-03-2023.pdf. [33]

Présidence de la République (2023), *Chair's summary of discussions at the Summit on a New Global Financing Pact*, https://www.elysee.fr/admin/upload/default/0001/15/4748a23641c5b2d55a47d63d7ed2e16963c11195.pdf. [105]

Presidencia Argentina (2023), *Ministerio de Economía: Resolucion 696/2023*, Ministerio de Economía, Argentina, https://www.boletinoficial.gob.ar/detalleAviso/primera/287232/20230529. [135]

Sachs, J. (2023), "Money makes the world go round – and development succeed", JDS, https://www.jeffsachs.org/newspaper-articles/money-makes-the-world-go-round. [23]

Savage, R. (2023), "Barbados 'debt-for-climate' swap backed by $300 mln EIB, IADB guarantee statement", Reuters, https://www.reuters.com/sustainability/sustainable-finance-reporting/barbados-debt-for-climate-swap-backed-by-300-mln-eib-iadb-guarantee-statement-2023-11-10/#:~:text=In%20September%202022%2C%20Barbados%20carried,vital%20for%20the%20tourism%20sector. [124]

The Dialogue (2023), *China-Latin America Finance Databases*, https://www.thedialogue.org/map_list/ (accessed on 17 September 2024). [56]

The Nature Conservancy (2023), *Case Study: Barbados Blue Bond for Ocean Conservation*, The Nature Conservancy, Arlington, Virginia, https://www.nature.org/content/dam/tnc/nature/en/documents/TNC-Barbados-Blue-Bonds_Case-Study.pdf. [109]

UN (2023), *Financing the 2030 Agenda for Sustainable Development, High-level Dialogue on Financing for Development*, United Nations, New York, https://www.un.org/esa/ffd/ffddialogue2023/#home (accessed on 4 June 2024). [9]

UN (2023), "Reforms to the International Financial Architecture", *Our Common Agenda Policy Brief*, No. 6, United Nations, New York, https://sdgs.un.org/sites/default/files/2023-08/our-common-agenda-policy-brief-international-finance-architecture-en.pdf. [14]

UN (2015), *Transforming our World: The 2030 Agenda for Sustainable Development*, United Nations, New York, https://sustainabledevelopment.un.org/content/documents/21252030%20Agenda%20for%20Sustainable%20Development%20web.pdf. [95]

UNCTAD (2014), *World Investment Report 2014: Investing in the SDGs: An Action Plan*, United Nations Conference on Trade and Development, https://unctad.org/system/files/official-document/wir2014_en.pdf. [1]

UNDESA (2024), *Financing for development*, United Nations Department of Economic and Social Affairs, New York, https://www.un.org/en/development/desa/financial-crisis/financing-for-development.html (accessed on 27 March 2024). [5]

UNDESA (2024), *World Population Prospects (website)*, United Nations Deparment of Economic and Social Affairs, Population Division, https://population.un.org/wpp/. [85]

UNDESA (2022), "Credit rating agencies and sovereign debt: Four proposals to support achievement of the SDGs", *UN DESA Policy Brief*, No. 131, United Nations Department of Economic and Social Affairs, New York, https://www.un.org/development/desa/dpad/publication/un-desa-policy-brief-no-131-credit-rating-agencies-and-sovereign-debt-four-proposals-to-support-achievement-of-the-sdgs/. [22]

UNDESA (2020), *International Migrant Stock (website)*, United Nations Department of Economic and Social Affairs, Population Division, https://www.un.org/development/desa/pd/content/international-migrant-stock. [84]

UNDP (2023), *Common Framework of Sustainable Finance Taxonomies for Latin America and the Caribbean*, United Nations Development Programme, https://climatepromise.undp.org/sites/default/files/research_report_document/common-framework-of-sustainable-finance-taxonomies-lac.pdf. [145]

UNEP (2023), *Unlocking Circular Economy Finance in Latin America and the Caribbean: The Catalyst for a Positive Change— Findings and recommendations for Policymakers and the Financial Sector*. [112]

UNEP FI (2024), *Taxonomía de Finanzas Sostenibles de Panamá*, UN Environment Programme Finance Initiative, United Nations, https://www.unepfi.org/wordpress/wp-content/uploads/2024/03/Taxonomia-de-Finanzas-Sostenibles-de-Panama.pdf. [140]

US International Development Finance Corporation (2023), *In Belize, innovative debt-for-nature swap yields tangible progress in conservation*, https://dfcgov.medium.com/in-belize-innovative-debt-for-nature-swap-yields-tangible-progress-in-conservation-c4518344a25d. [123]

West, O. (2023), "Ecuador pushes through turmoil to pull off largest ever debt-for-nature swap", *GlobalCapital*, https://www.globalcapital.com/article/2bnfn5ca2hpix3y11m9s0/emerging-markets/em-latam/ecuador-pushes-through-turmoil-to-pull-off-largest-ever-debt-for-nature-swap. [121]

World Bank (2024), *Domestic credit to the private sector (% of GDP), World Bank Development Indicators (database)*, World Bank, Washington, DC, https://databank.worldbank.org/reports.aspx?source=2&series=FS.AST.PRVT.GD.ZS&country=LAC. [12]

World Bank (2024), *GNI (current US$), World Development Indicators (database)*, World Bank, Washington, DC, https://databank.worldbank.org/reports.aspx?source=2&series=NY.GNP.MKTP.CD&country=#. [45]

World Bank (2024), *Personal remittances, received (% of GDP) - Latin America & Caribbean, World Bank Group Data (database)*, World Bank, Washington, DC, https://data.worldbank.org/indicator/BX.TRF.PWKR.DT.GD.ZS?end=2022&locations=ZJ&start=2003. [91]

World Bank (2024), *Technical assistance*, Lessons and Practices, https://documents.worldbank.org/en/publication/documents-reports/documentdetail/264181468156582056/technical-assistance. [39]

World Bank (2024), *World Bank Country and Lending Groups (database)*, World Bank, Washington, DC, https://datahelpdesk.worldbank.org/knowledgebase/articles/906519-world-bank-country-and-lending-groups. [62]

World Bank (2023), *Leveraging Diaspora Finances for Private Capital Mobilization*, https://documents1.worldbank.org/curated/en/099740408142422676/pdf/IDU184dfd61b1e135142421a20213728b2e8fa86.pdf. [86]

World Bank (2023), *Statement of the Heads of Multilateral Development Banks group: Strengthening our collaboration for greater impact.*, World Bank, Washington, DC, https://www.worldbank.org/en/news/statement/2023/10/13/statement-of-the-heads-of-multilateral-development-banks-group-strengthening-our-collaboration-for-greater-impact (accessed on 18 March 2024). [66]

World Bank (2022), *Debt Service Suspension Initiative*, World Bank Group, Washington, DC, https://www.worldbank.org/en/topic/debt/brief/covid-19-debt-service-suspension-initiative. [10]

World Bank (2020), *Measuring Policy Coherence for Migration and Development : A New Set of Tested Tools*, World Bank, https://documents1.worldbank.org/curated/en/099435008192425541/pdf/IDU1fa80cd2f18a5b14f621b70214919676c2856.pdf. [90]

World Bank (2013), *Mexico MultiCat Bond: Transferring catastrophe risk to the capital markets*, Global Facility for Disaster Reduction and Recovery, World Bank Group, Washington, DC, https://openknowledge.worldbank.org/server/api/core/bitstreams/42f4a9ed-6f3d-5bbb-bb5b-e5c2cc6703ae/content. [117]

5 Country notes

Reader's guide

The statistical tables follow key areas identified in the *Latin American Economic Outlook (LEO)*: 1) social development; 2) productivity and innovation; 3) investment and private financing; 4) citizens' perceptions and institutions; 5) digital and green transition; and 6) fiscal position.

Latin America and the Caribbean (LAC) average is a simple average of the largest set of LAC countries for which latest data were available as of July 2024.

Organisation for Economic Co-operation and Development (OECD) average is a simple average of the largest set of all OECD member countries for which latest data were available as of July 2024.

To ensure comparability between years, countries for which data are not available for both years of comparison have been excluded from the averages. Exceptions to this are mentioned in the notes.

Applying the same criteria as in previous LEO editions, data selection from international sources prioritises comparability across LAC countries and shows the latest comparable data available at the report's publication date. For this reason, discrepancies with national data may also occur.

Social development

Extreme poverty:[1] refers to the share (%) of the population whose average per-capita income is below the extreme poverty line, as specified by the United Nations Economic Commission for Latin America and the Caribbean. Method of computation: "n" is defined as the total number of persons and "i" is the number of people whose per-capita income is below the extreme poverty line; the percentage of people living in extreme poverty is expressed as I=(i/n)x100 (known as "headcount index"). The average per-capita income is calculated by dividing the total income of each household by the number of people forming it. Data from (ECLAC, 2024[1]), *CEPALSTAT. Statistical Databases and Publications*, https://statistics.cepal.org/portal/cepalstat/.

Poverty:[1] refers to the share (%) of the population whose average per-capita income is below the poverty line, as specified by the United Nations Economic Commission for Latin America and the Caribbean. Method of computation: "n" is the total number of people and "p" is the number of people whose per-capita income is below the poverty line; the percentage of people living in poverty is expressed as P=(p/n)x100. This indicator includes people under the extreme poverty line, by definition. The average per-capita income is calculated by dividing the total income of each household by the number of people forming it. Data from (ECLAC, 2024[1]), *CEPALSTAT. Statistical Databases and Publications*, https://statistics.cepal.org/portal/cepalstat/.

Gini index:[2] measures the extent to which the distribution of income (or, in some cases, consumption expenditure) among individuals or households within an economy deviates from a perfectly equal distribution. A Gini index of zero represents perfect equality; an index of 100 represents perfect inequality. Data from (World Bank, 2024[2]), *World Bank Open Data*, https://data.worldbank.org/indicator/SI.POV.GINI.

Share of total population in informal households:[3] provides the distribution of the total population living in informal households. An informal household has all its workers in informal work. Data from (OECD, 2023[3]), *Key Indicators of Informality based on Individuals and their Households (KIIbIH) database*, www.oecd.org/dev/key-indicators-informality-individuals-household-kiibih.htm.

Share of total population in mixed households: provides the distribution of the total population living in mixed households. A mixed household has both formal and informal workers. Data from (OECD, 2023),

Key Indicators of Informality based on Individuals and their Households (KIIbIH) database, www.oecd.org/dev/key-indicators-informality-individuals-household-kiibih.htm.

Social Institutions and Gender Index (SIGI): measures discrimination against women in social institutions (e.g. formal and informal laws, social norms, and practices). Lower values indicate lower levels of discrimination in social institutions: the SIGI ranges from 0% for no discrimination to 100% for very high discrimination. Data from (OECD, 2023[4]), *Social Institutions and Gender Index (SIGI)*, https://data-explorer.oecd.org/.

PISA score in science:[4] indicates the mean score in science performance as measured by the Programme for International Student Assessment (PISA) for each country. Scientific performance measures the scientific literacy of a 15-year-old in the use of scientific knowledge to identify questions, acquire new knowledge, explain scientific phenomena, and draw evidence-based conclusions about science-related issues. Data from (OECD, 2024[5]), *Science performance (PISA) indicator*, https://data.oecd.org/pisa/science-performance-pisa.htm#indicator-chart.

Productivity and innovation

Labour productivity: estimation that measures output per hour worked as a percentage of OECD output per hour worked (in 2022 international dollars, converted using Purchasing Power Parities). Data from (The Conference Board, 2024[6]), *Total Economy Database*, www.conference-board.org/data/economydatabase/totaleconomy-database-productivity.

High-technology exports:[5] measures exports of products with high research and development (R&D) intensity as a percentage of total manufactured exports. Data from (World Bank, 2024[2]), *World Bank Open Data*, https://data.worldbank.org/indicator/TX.VAL.TECH.MF.ZS.

Patent applications per million people: measures worldwide patent applications filed through the Patent Cooperation Treaty procedure or with a national patent office for exclusive rights for an invention, expressed per million people. Authors' calculations are based on data from (World Bank, 2024[2]), *World Bank Open Data*, https://data.worldbank.org/indicator/IP.PAT.RESD.

Research and development expenditure (R&D):[6] measures capital and current expenditures as a percentage of GDP in four main sectors: business enterprise, government, higher education, and private non-profit. R&D covers basic research, applied research and experimental development. Data from (World Bank, 2024[2]), *World Bank Open Data*, https://data.worldbank.org/indicator/GB.XPD.RSDV.GD.ZS.

Investment and private financing

Total investment:[7] measures the gross fixed capital formation (GFCF) as a percentage of GDP. GFCF includes land improvements; plants, machinery, and equipment purchases; and the construction of roads, railways, and the like (including schools, offices, hospitals, private residential dwellings, and commercial and industrial buildings). According to the 1993 SNA, net acquisitions of valuables are also considered capital formation. Data from (World Bank, 2024[2]), *World Bank Open Data*, https://data.worldbank.org/indicator/NE.GDI.FTOT.ZS.

Foreign direct investment (FDI) net inflows as a % of GDP: measures the net inflows of investment to acquire a lasting management interest (10% or more of voting stock) in an enterprise operating in an economy other than that of the investor as a percentage of GDP. It is the sum of equity capital, reinvestment of earnings, other long-term capital, and short-term capital as shown in the balance of payments. This series shows net inflows (new investment inflows less disinvestment) in the reporting economy from foreign investors and is divided by GDP. Data from (World Bank, 2024[2]), *World Bank Open Data*, https://data.worldbank.org/indicator/BX.KLT.DINV.WD.GD.ZS.

Domestic credit to private sector by banks (% of GDP): measures financial resource, as a percentage of GDP, provided to the private sector by other depository corporations (deposit taking corporations except central banks), such as through loans, purchases of nonequity securities, and trade credits and other accounts receivable, that establish a claim for repayment. For some countries these claims include credit to public enterprises. Data from (World Bank, 2024[2]), *World Bank Open Data*, https://data.worldbank.org/indicator/FD.AST.PRVT.GD.ZS.

Savings: measures gross national income less total consumption, plus net transfers, as a percentage of GDP. Data from (World Bank, 2024[2]), *World Bank Open Data*, https://data.worldbank.org/indicator/NY.GNS.ICTR.ZS.

Market capitalisation: measures the share price times the number of shares outstanding (including their several classes) for listed domestic companies, as a percentage of GDP. Investment funds, unit trusts, and companies whose only business goal is to hold shares of other listed companies are excluded. Data from (World Bank, 2024[2]), *World Bank Open Data*, https://data.worldbank.org/indicator/CM.MKT.LCAP.GD.ZS.

Citizens' perceptions and institutions

Satisfaction with educational system: measures the percentage of the population in the city or area where they live who are satisfied with the educational system or schools. This metric responds to the question: "Are you satisfied or dissatisfied with the educational system or the schools in the city or area where you live?". Data from (Gallup, 2024[7]), *Educational System,* https://ga.gallup.com/Charts/.

Satisfaction with healthcare system: measures the percentage of the population in the city or area where they live who are satisfied with the availability of quality healthcare. This metric responds to the question: "Are you satisfied or dissatisfied with the availability of quality healthcare in the city or area where you live?". Data from (Gallup, 2024[7]), *Healthcare System,* https://ga.gallup.com/Charts/.

Satisfaction with standard of living: measures the percentage of people satisfied with their standard of living. This metric responds to the question: "Are you satisfied or dissatisfied with your standard of living, all the things you can buy and do?". Data from (Gallup, 2024[7]), *Standard of Living,* https://ga.gallup.com/Charts/.

Confidence in judicial system: measures the percentage of the population that expresses confidence in the judicial system and courts within their country. This metric responds to the survey question: "In this country, do you have confidence in each of the following, or not? How about the judicial system and courts?". Data from (Gallup, 2024[7]), *Confidence in Judicial System,* https://ga.gallup.com/Charts/.

Corruption Perception Index: measures citizens' perceptions of the levels of local corruption in their country, where 0 is completely corrupt and 100 is totally clean. Data from (Transparency International, 2024[8]), *Corruption Perception Index*, http://www.transparency.org/en/cpi/2023.

Security risks Indicator: considers the security threats to a state, such as bombings, attacks and battle-related deaths, rebel movements, mutinies, coups, or terrorism. The Security Apparatus Index also considers serious criminal factors, such as organised crime and homicides, and the perceived trust of citizens in domestic security. 0 means low security risks and 10 means high security risks. Data from (The Fund for Peace, 2024[9]), *Fragile States Index*, https://fragilestatesindex.org/global-data/.

Digital and green transition

Share of internet users:[8] measures individuals who have used the Internet (from any location) in the last 3 months. The Internet can be used via a computer, mobile phone, personal digital assistant, games machine, digital TV etc. Data from (World Bank, 2024[2]), *World Bank Open Data*, https://data.worldbank.org/indicator/IT.NET.USER.ZS.

Fixed broadband subscriptions:[9] measures fixed subscriptions to high-speed access to the public Internet (a TCP/IP connection), at downstream speeds equal to, or greater than, 256 kbit/s. This includes cable modem, DSL, fiber-to-the-home/building, other fixed (wired)-broadband subscriptions, satellite broadband and terrestrial fixed wireless broadband. This total is measured irrespective of the method of payment. It excludes subscriptions that have access to data communications (including the Internet) via mobile-cellular networks. It should include fixed WiMAX and any other fixed wireless technologies. It includes both residential subscriptions and subscriptions for organisations. Data from (World Bank, 2024[2]), *World Bank Open Data*, https://data.worldbank.org/indicator/IT.NET.BBND.P2.

Environmentally related tax revenue:[10] measures the revenues from environmentally related taxes as a percentage of GDP. It includes taxes on greenhouse gas (GHG) emissions, fuel taxes, taxes on road use, forestry taxes and revenue from auctioned permits of emission trading systems for GHGs. Data from (OECD et al., 2024[10]), *Environmentally related tax revenue*, https://stats.oecd.org/Index.aspx?DataSetCode=ERTR.

Per Capita Greenhouse Gas Emissions (excluding land use changes) (t CO2e/capita): measures the total annual emissions of six greenhouse gases (CO2, CH4, N2O, HFCs, PFCs, SF6) from energy, industry, waste, and agriculture, adjusted to carbon dioxide equivalents and divided by the population. It excludes emissions from land use changes and forestry due to higher uncertainties. Data from (World Bank, 2024[2]), *World Bank Open Data*, https://data.worldbank.org/indicator/EN.GHG.ALL.PC.CE.AR5.

Renewable energy consumption: measures the share of renewable energy sources within total final energy consumption, expressed as a percentage. Data from (World Bank, 2023), *World Bank Open Data*, https://data.worldbank.org/indicator/EG.FEC.RNEW.ZS.

Fiscal position

Total tax revenues:[11] measures total tax revenues as a percentage of GDP. Data from (OECD et al., 2024[10]), *Revenue Statistics in Latin America and the Caribbean 2024*, https://stats.oecd.org/Index.aspx?DataSetCode=RS_GBL.

Share of VAT (value added tax):[10] measures VAT as a percentage of GDP. Data from (OECD et al., 2024[10]), *Revenue Statistics in Latin America and the Caribbean 2024*, https://stats.oecd.org/Index.aspx?DataSetCode=RS_GBL.

Share of PIT (personal income tax):[10] measures taxes on the income, profits, and capital gains of individuals as a percentage of GDP. Data from (OECD et al., 2024[10]), *Revenue Statistics in Latin America and the Caribbean 2024*, https://stats.oecd.org/Index.aspx?DataSetCode=RS_GBL.

Share of CIT (corporate income tax):[10] measures taxes on the income, profits, and capital gains of corporations as a percentage of GDP. Data from (OECD et al., 2024[10]), *Revenue Statistics in Latin America and the Caribbean 2024*, https://stats.oecd.org/Index.aspx?DataSetCode=RS_GBL.

Tax morale: measures the share (%) of the adult population who find some degree of justification in evading taxes, excluding those who believe tax evasion is not justifiable at all. Data from (Latinobarómetro, 2023[11]), *Opinión Pública Latinoamericana*, www.latinobarometro.org/latOnline.jsp.

Public debt service: measures public debt service as a percentage of tax revenue. Public debt service is calculated as general government primary lending/borrowing minus general government net lending/borrowing. Authors' calculations are based on data from (International Monetary Fund, 2023[12]), *World Economic Outlook Database*, www.imf.org/en/Publications/WEO/weo-database/2023/April and (OECD et al., 2024[10]), *Revenue Statistics in Latin America and the Caribbean 2024*, https://stats.oecd.org/Index.aspx?DataSetCode=RS_GBL.

Social expenditure:[12] measures public social spending as a percentage of GDP. The main social policy areas are old age, survivors, incapacity-related benefits, health, family, active labour market programmes, unemployment, housing, and other social policy areas. For OECD countries, data refer to *Social expenditure* from (OECD, 2023[13]), *OECDStat*, https://stats.oecd.org/Index.aspx?DataSetCode=SOCX_AGG or LAC countries, data refer to *Social public expenditure* from (ECLAC, 2024[1]), *CEPALSTAT. Statistical Databases and Publications*, https://statistics.cepal.org/portal/cepalstat/.

Notes

[1] Poverty and extreme poverty: All data are national-level data, except for Argentina, for which only urban-level data are available (as such, Argentina is excluded from the LAC averages). For the LAC average in 2016, data for Chile is from 2015. For the LAC average in 2023, data for Chile and Mexico is from 2022. Weighted LAC averages for poverty and extreme poverty can be consulted in Chapter 1.

[2] Gini index: For the OECD and LAC averages in 2016, data for Chile is from 2015. For the LAC average in 2022, data for Bolivia is from 2021, and for Panama is from 2023. For the OECD average in 2022: data for Iceland are from 2017; data for Australia, Canada and Switzerland are from 2018; data for Germany and Norway are from 2019; data for Austria, Belgium, Czech Republic, Denmark, Estonia, Finland, France, Greece, Hungary, Ireland, Israel, Italy, Korea, Latvia, Lithuania, Luxembourg, Netherlands, Poland, Portugal, Serbia, Slovenia, Spain, Sweden, Türkiye, United Kingdom and United States, are from 2021.

[3] Informality indicators: For the averages of informality: in 2009, data for Argentina, Costa Rica, Colombia, Mexico and Peru are from 2010; data for El Salvador and Honduras are from 2014; and data for Uruguay is from 2008. For the averages in 2021, data for Chile is from 2017; data for Argentina, Bolivia, Dominican Republic, Paraguay and Uruguay are from 2018; data for Brazil, Honduras and Peru are from 2019; and data for Costa Rica and Mexico are from 2020. Countries for which data are not available for both years of comparison have not been excluded from the averages for the indicators on the share of total population in informal households.

[4] PISA score in science: average for LAC and OECD countries is simple and not weighted following the scheme of replicated weights as in www.oecd.org/pisa/sitedocument/PISA-2015-Technical-Report-Chapter-8-Survey-Weighting.pdf.

[5] High-technology exports: For the LAC average in 2016, data for Belize are from 2017. For the LAC average in 2022, data for St. Kitts and Nevis are from 2017; data for Bahamas and St. Lucia are from 2020, data for Honduras and St. Vincent and the Grenadines are from 2021.

[6] Research and development expenditure: For the OECD average in 2016, data for Australia, Switzerland and New Zealand are from 2017. For the OECD average in 2022, data for Australia are from 2019; data for Chile and Colombia are from 2020, and data for Austria, Belgium, Costa Rica, Czech Republic, Denmark, Estonia, Finland, France, Germany, Greece, Hungary, Iceland, Ireland, Israel, Italy, Japan,

Korea, Latvia, Lithuania, Luxembourg, Netherlands, New Zealand, Norway, Poland, Slovak Republic, Slovenia, Spain, Sweden, Switzerland, Türkiye, United Kingdom and United States are from 2021. For the LAC average in 2022, data for Brazil, Chile and Colombia are from 2020, and data for Argentina, Costa Rica, Cuba, El Salvador, Guatemala, Paraguay, Trinidad and Tobago, and Uruguay are from 2021.

[7] Total investment: For the LAC average in 2022, data for Panama are from 2017 and data for Jamaica are from 2019.

[8] Share of internet users: For the OECD and LAC averages in 2016, data for Chile is from 2015. For the LAC average in 2022, data for Bahamas, Belize, Bolivia, Chile, Cuba, Dominican Republic, El Salvador, Grenada, Guatemala, Haiti, Mexico, Panama, and St. Lucia are from 2021. For the OECD average in 2022: data for United Kingdom, United States, Switzerland, Slovak Republic, New Zealand, Mexico, Japan, Iceland, Ireland, Israel, Canada, Chile, and Australia are from 2021.

[9] Fixed broadband subscriptions: For the LAC average in 2022, data for Antigua and Barbuda, Belize, Bermuda, Bolivia, Dominica, Grenada, Guyana, Haiti, St. Kitts and Nevis and St. Lucia are from 2021.

[10] Environmental tax revenue: For the LAC average, data for Colombia are from 2020. For the OECD average, data for Colombia, Greece and Switzerland are from 2020.

[11] Tax revenues: For the OECD average of total tax revenues in 2021, data for Australia and Japan are from 2020. For the OECD averages of the shares of VAT/PIT/CIT in 2021, data for Australia, Greece and Japan are from 2019.

[12] Social expenditure: For the LAC average in 2021, data for Bolivia, Cuba and Panama are from 2020. For the OECD average in 2021, data for Australia, Mexico and Türkiye are from 2019, and data for Canada, Costa Rica and Japan are from 2020.

References

ECLAC (2024), *CEPALSTAT. Statistical Databases and Publications*, https://statistics.cepal.org/portal/cepalstat/dashboard.html. [1]

Gallup (2024), *Gallup Analytics (database)*, https://ga.gallup.com/Charts/. [7]

International Monetary Fund (2023), *World Economic Outlook Database*, https://www.imf.org/en/Publications/WEO/weo-database/2023/April. [12]

Latinobarómetro (2023), *Latinobarómetro: Opinión Pública Latinoamericana*, https://www.latinobarometro.org/latOnline.jsp. [11]

OECD (2024), *Science performance (PISA)* (indicator), https://doi.org/10.1787/91952204-en (accessed on 2 December 2024). [5]

OECD (2023), *Key Indicators of Informality based on Individuals and their Household (KIIbIH)*, https://www.oecd.org/dev/key-indicators-informality-individuals-household-kiibih.htm. [3]

OECD (2023), *OECDStat Social Expenditure*, https://stats.oecd.org/Index.aspx?DataSetCode=SOCX_AGG. [13]

OECD (2023), *Social Institutions and Gender Index*, https://stats.oecd.org/Index.aspx?DataSetCode=SIGI2023. [4]

OECD et al. (2024), *Revenue Statistics in Latin America and the Caribbean 2024*, https://doi.org/10.1787/33e226ae-en. [10]

The Conference Board (2024), *The Conference Board Total Economy Database™*, http://www.conference-board.org/data/economydatabase/total-economy-database-productivity. [6]

The Fund for Peace (2024), *Fragile States Index*, https://fragilestatesindex.org/global-data/. [9]

Transparency International (2024), *Corruption Perception Index*, http://www.transparency.org/en/cpi/2022. [8]

World Bank (2024), *World Bank Open Data*, https://data.worldbank.org/. [2]

Argentina

Policies to promote financing for development

Regarding policies **to mobilise domestic resources for development and improve fiscal conditions**, Argentina has adopted several fiscal measures. Key legislative initiatives in 2024, such as the *Ley de Medidas Fiscales Paliativas y Relevantes* and the *Ley de Bases y Puntos de Partida para la Libertad de los Argentinos* aim to improve transparency, and reinforce fiscal governance. These reforms include special regimes for asset regularisation and personal property taxes and are designed to alleviate tax burdens on small taxpayers through incentives for electronic payments. Concurrently, Argentina has strengthened its budgetary assessment practices by intensifying monthly monitoring of physical targets, integrating outcome indicators into National Budget oversight, and enhancing the evaluation of 20 to 30 key programmes as outlined in the 2025 budget bill submitted to Congress for approval.

Regarding policies to promote robust, inclusive, and sustainable financial markets, Argentina has implemented a series of public policy measures. General Resolution 788/2019 has streamlined the issuance of social, green, and sustainable bonds since 2019, aligning with global standards to support environmentally and socially beneficial projects. This initiative was updated by General Resolution 963/2023, which revised the "Guidelines for the Issuance of Thematic Negotiable Securities in Argentina", introducing new thematic labels like "blue" and "sustainability-linked" to expand financing options for sustainability projects. Moreover, the establishment of sustainable investment collective funds under General Resolution 885/2021 highlights Argentina's commitment to integrating sustainability into its financial sector. Additionally, Resolution 963/2023 allows Environment Social Governance (ESG) funds to allocate up to 75% of their equity to ESG assets. Furthering these initiatives, General Resolution 940/2022 simplifies the process for issuing social impact bonds, providing crucial financing opportunities for social enterprises and nonprofits. These reforms are complemented with the Corporate Governance Code, which promotes transparency and best practices among listed companies, collectively enhancing market accessibility, regulatory efficiency, and investor confidence. Further, General Resolution 896/2021 on Sustainable Guidelines created educational materials to develop the sustainable debt market and raise awareness among capital market participants about Thematic Bonds as a financing alternative, highlighting the role of external reviewers in ensuring project quality and the significance of socially responsible investors. Finally, to promote private investment, General Resolution 1006/2024 encourages private investment in public infrastructure projects, aiming to diversify funding sources and stimulate economic development across the country.

In terms of **regional and international finance and partnerships to catalyse international resources**, Argentina has pursued collaboration aiming to attract foreign investment. Notably, Argentina is partnering with the European Union under the Global Gateway Investment Agenda, which includes commitments on infrastructure development, waste, and water management, and strengthening electricity transmission capabilities. Additionally, Argentina engages in regional initiatives with Brazil, Chile, and Uruguay, leveraging shared expertise for cross-border business ventures across Latin America. Partnerships with the Inter-American Institute for Cooperation on Agriculture or the Voluntary Carbon Market Integrity Initiative aim to promote sustainable agriculture practices and access carbon market finance.

Argentina: Key indicators

	Argentina		LAC		OECD	
Social development	**2016**	**2023**	**2016**	**2023**	**2016**	**2022**
Poverty (Extreme poverty)	21.5 (2.9)	30.1 (4)	25.8 (8.0)	22.5 (7.4)	N/A	N/A
Gini index	42.3	40.7 (2022)	46.3	44.4 (2022)	33.9	33.4 (2021)
Share of total population in informal households (%)	34.5 (2010)	36.8 (2018)	47.9 (2009)	46 (2021)	N/A	N/A
Share of total population in mixed households (%)	26.1 (2010)	23.5 (2018)	23.2 (2009)	21.3 (2021)	N/A	N/A
Social Institutions & Gender Index (SIGI)	N/A	17.7	25.4 (2019)	21.6	17.5 (2019)	15.3 (2023)
PISA score in science	406 (2012)	406 (2022)	411 (2015)	408 (2022)	489 (2015)	485
Productivity and innovation	**2016**	**2023**	**2016**	**2023**	**2016**	**2023**
Labour productivity (% of OECD)	58	49	36	33	100	100
High-tech exports (% of manufactured exports)	9	5.4	8.5	8	16.5	18.1
Patent applications per million people	20.3	8.9 (2021)	13.8	12.8 (2021)	631.2	572.8 (2021)
R&D expenditures (% of GDP)	0.6	0.5 (2021)	0.3	0.3 (2022)	1.8	2.1 (2022)
Investment and private financing	**2016**	**2023**	**2016**	**2023**	**2016**	**2023**
Total investment, gross fixed capital formation (% of GDP)	14.3	19.1	20.7	20.9	21.9	23
Foreign direct investment (FDI), net capital inflow (% of GDP)	0.6	3.7	4.3	4.6	N/A	N/A
Dom. credit private sector by banks (% of GDP)	13.5	12	45.2	44.4	86.8	76.8
Savings (% of GDP)	14.6	15.1	18.8	20.6	23.8	24.6
Market capitalisation (% of GDP)	8.8 (2019)	8.4 (2022)	50.2 (2019)	35.9 (2022)	69.5 (2019)	64.7 (2022)
Citizens' perceptions and institutions	**2011**	**2023**	**2011**	**2023**	**2011**	**2023**
Satisfaction with educational system (% of population)	66	57	67	65	66	67
Satisfaction with healthcare system (% of population)	65	52	55	52	70	66
Share of people satisfied with their standard of living (%)	75	63	70	73	73	77
Confidence in judicial system (% of population)	40	28	33	40	50	57
Corruption Perception Index (score on a scale of 0 [highly corrupt] to 100 [totally clean])	36 (2016)	37	41.2 (2016)	40.2	67.3 (2016)	66.1
Security risks indicator (score from 0 [low security risks] to 10 [high security risks])	4 (2016)	4.6 (2022)	5.9 (2016)	5.6 (2022)	2.8 (2016)	2.6 (2022)
Digital and green transition	**2016**	**2023**	**2016**	**2022**	**2016**	**2022**
Share of internet users (% of population)	71	89.2	54.5	75.4	81.8	90.7
Fixed broadband subscriptions (per 100 inhabitants)	16.5	25.4	11.2	17 (2023)	30.6	36 (2023)
Environmentally related tax revenue (% of GDP)	1.2	0.8 (2022)	1.0	0.8	1.6	1.8
Per capita greenhouse gas emissions (excluding land use changes) (t CO_2e/capita)	8.6	8.3 (2022)	5.3	5.1	10.7	9.5
Renewable energy consumption (% of total final energy consumption)	9.4	9.2 (2021)	28.9	33.9 (2021)	12.5	14.9 (2021)
Fiscal position	**2016**	**2022**	**2016**	**2022**	**2016**	**2022**
Total tax revenues (% of GDP)	30.7	29.6	21.9	21.5	33.6	34.0
Share of VAT I PIT I CIT	7.1 2.1 2.9	7.1 2.5 2.9	5.9 2 3.2	6.1 2 3.4	6.6 7.8 2.9	7.0 8.2 3.9
Tax morale (% tax evasion justification)	36.1	55.2 (2023)	53.4	58.0 (2023)	N/A	N/A
Public debt service (% of total tax revenue)	6.2	6.9	11.3	12.2	5.4	4.8
Social expenditure (% of GDP)	14.2	13.5	11.3	11.5	20.1	21.4

Note: See the Reader's Guide for definitions and sources.

StatLink https://stat.link/6j1ami

Brazil

Policies to promote financing for development

Regarding policies **to mobilise domestic resources for development and promote investment**, Brazil has adopted measures focusing on taxation and aligning the strategies of development banks with National Development Plans. The New PAC (Growth Acceleration Plan) was launched in 2023 to generate jobs and income, and to reduce social and regional inequalities. Brazil also launched the "Mais Produção" Plan to boost national industry through increased autonomy, ecological transition and modernisation of the Brazilian industrial park. These initiatives prioritise infrastructure, digital inclusion and sustainable development, with significant investments from the Brazilian Development Bank, totalling BRA 270 billion (Brazilian reals) for the New PAC and BRA 250 billion for the "Mais Produção" Plan. Finally, the Ecologic Transition Plan further underscores Brazil's commitment to sustainable development through targeted funding aimed at reducing emissions and promoting green industries. On taxation measures, Brazil is converging its transfer pricing system with OECD standards. It became effective in January 2024 and aimed to reduce double taxation, preventing base erosion and profit shifting. In addition, Law No. 14.754/23 introduced controlled foreign corporation rules for individuals to enforce the annual tax on offshore profits. Furthermore, the government has allowed the updating of the base value of assets abroad, resulting in significant revenue collection. A key reform in consumption taxation that seeks to simplify the system by combining state and municipal taxes was sent to the congress.

Regarding policies to **promote robust, inclusive and sustainable financial markets**, Brazil has focused on its Instant Payment System, Pix, which aims to increase access to electronic payments. Launched by the Central Bank of Brazil, it provides a low-friction, cost-effective payment solution that fosters innovation and new business models. Since 2020, Pix played a pivotal role in digitalising and enhancing the efficiency of Brazil's financial system. Pix quickly became the country's primary payment method, with around 5.5 billion transactions in September 2024. By engaging the financial and payment industries, Pix had 160.5 million people and 17.6 million companies as users by September 2024, thereby fostering financial inclusion and supporting economic growth.

In terms of **regional and international finance and partnerships to catalyse international resources**, Brazil has implemented initiatives to enhance the co-ordination of financing received from external partners. The Authorisation for the Preparation of Programmes and Projects within the scope of the External Financing Commission (Cofiex) oversees and approves public-sector projects or programmes supported by multilateral development banks and foreign government agencies, ensuring that projects are guaranteed by the federal administration. This initiative engages multilateral banks such as the the Development Bank of Latin America and the Caribbean, the Inter-American Development Bank and the International Bank for Reconstruction and Development, alongside government agencies from France, Germany, Japan and Spain. By enhancing transparency and predictability and providing training for public entities in managing credit operations, Cofiex has facilitated various projects across Brazil, benefiting the infrastructure, health, education and environmental sectors.

Brazil: Key indicators

	Brazil		LAC		OECD	
Social development	**2016**	**2023**	**2016**	**2023**	**2016**	**2022**
Poverty (Extreme poverty)	20.9 (5.3)	16.1 (3.6)	25.8 (8.0)	22.5 (7.4)	N/A	N/A
Gini index	53.4	52 (2022)	46.3	44.4 (2022)	33.9	33.4 (2021)
Share of total population in informal households (%)	37.7 (2009)	29.8 (2019)	47.9 (2009)	46 (2021)	N/A	N/A
Share of total population in mixed households (%)	28.3 (2009)	22.3 (2019)	23.2 (2009)	21.3 (2021)	N/A	N/A
Social Institutions & Gender Index (SIGI)	21.2 (2019)	21.6	25.4 (2019)	21.6	17.5 (2019)	15.3 (2023)
PISA score in science	401 (2015)	403 (2022)	411 (2015)	408 (2022)	489 (2015)	485
Productivity and innovation	**2016**	**2023**	**2016**	**2023**	**2016**	**2023**
Labour productivity (% of OECD)	31	30	36	33	100	100
High-tech exports (% of manufactured exports)	16	9.8	8.5	8	16.5	18.1
Patent applications per million people	25.1	21.8 (2021)	13.8	12.8 (2021)	631.2	572.8 (2021)
R&D expenditures (% of GDP)	1.3	1.1 (2020)	0.3	0.3 (2022)	1.8	2.1 (2022)
Investment and private financing	**2016**	**2023**	**2016**	**2023**	**2016**	**2023**
Total investment, gross fixed capital formation (% of GDP)	15.5	16.5	20.7	20.9	21.9	23
Foreign direct investment (FDI), net capital inflow (% of GDP)	4.1	3	4.3	4.6	N/A	N/A
Dom. credit private sector by banks (% of GDP)	62.2	71.6	45.2	44.4	86.8	76.8
Savings (% of GDP)	13.4	15.6	18.8	20.6	23.8	24.6
Market capitalisation (% of GDP)	63.4 (2019)	40.7 (2022)	50.2 (2019)	35.9 (2022)	69.5 (2019)	64.7 (2022)
Citizens' perceptions and institutions	**2011**	**2023**	**2011**	**2023**	**2011**	**2023**
Satisfaction with educational system (% of population)	55	67	67	65	66	67
Satisfaction with healthcare system (% of population)	36	51	55	52	70	66
Share of people satisfied with their standard of living (%)	77	76	70	73	73	77
Confidence in judicial system (% of population)	46	49	33	40	50	57
Corruption Perception Index (score on a scale of 0 [highly corrupt] to 100 [totally clean])	40 (2016)	36	41.2 (2016)	40.2	67.3 (2016)	66.1
Security risks indicator (score from 0 [low security risks] to 10 [high security risks])	6.4 (2016)	6.5 (2022)	5.9 (2016)	5.6 (2022)	2.8 (2016)	2.6 (2022)
Digital and green transition	**2016**	**2023**	**2016**	**2022**	**2016**	**2022**
Share of internet users (% of population)	60.9	84.2	54.5	75.4	81.8	90.7
Fixed broadband subscriptions (per 100 inhabitants)	13.2	22.9	11.2	17 (2023)	30.6	36 (2023)
Environmentally related tax revenue (% of GDP)	0.9	0.7 (2022)	1.0	0.8	1.6	1.8
Per capita greenhouse gas emissions (excluding land use changes) (t CO_2e/capita)	6.2	6.1 (2022)	5.3	5.1	10.7	9.5
Renewable energy consumption (% of total final energy consumption)	45.4	46.5 (2021)	28.9	33.9 (2021)	12.5	14.9 (2021)
Fiscal position	**2016**	**2022**	**2016**	**2022**	**2016**	**2022**
Total tax revenues (% of GDP)	31.6	33.3	21.9	21.5	33.6	34.0
Share of VAT I PIT I CIT	6.6 2.6 3.2	7 3.1 4.4	5.9 2 3.2	6.1 2 3.4	6.6 7.8 2.9	7.0 8.2 3.9
Tax morale (% tax evasion justification)	45.4	44.8 (2023)	53.4	58.0 (2023)	N/A	N/A
Public debt service (% of total tax revenue)	20.5	15.8	11.3	12.2	5.4	4.8
Social expenditure (% of GDP)	16.7	16.4	11.3	11.5	20.1	21.4

Note: See the Reader's Guide for definitions and sources.

StatLink https://stat.link/a3lrvd

Chile

Policies to promote financing for development

Regarding policies to **mobilise domestic resources for development and improve fiscal conditions**, Chile has implemented significant policies focusing on tax reforms and strategic partnerships with development banks. A new tax reform bill, introduced in January 2024, aims to increase tax revenue through measures enhancing tax compliance, adjusting corporate tax rates, increasing taxes on stock gains, and introducing a new wealth tax for high-net-worth individuals. This measure is part of a broader fiscal pact that includes principles for a modern tax system, public spending priorities and commitments to transparency and efficiency. Additionally, the government has proposed new value-added tax liabilities for certain imported goods and marketplace transactions. The Development Bank of Latin America (CAF) has aligned its 2023-26 Country Strategy with Chile's national development plans. This strategy focuses on regional support initiatives, environmental protection, energy transition and digitalisation. The goals are to decentralise development across Chile's regions, support environmental and climate goals, contribute to decarbonising the energy matrix and improve digital connectivity.

Regarding policies **to advance a robust, inclusive, and sustainable financial market**, Chile has implemented significant policies to foster financial inclusion and deepen the banking sector. The introduction of Chile's Fintech Law aims to enhance transparency and resilience within the sector, facilitating an open finance system that reduces information asymmetry and fosters innovation in financial services. State-owned Banco Estado has been instrumental in improving financial inclusion through initiatives like the Cuenta RUT, which provides simplified banking access for a large segment of the population. Additionally, the European Investment Bank has provided a EUR 200 million (Euros) loan to Banco del Estado de Chile to finance mortgages for new housing units with improved energy efficiency standards under the Ecovivienda Programme. Chile's financial markets have also been bolstered by its leadership in issuing green, social, sustainability and sustainability-linked bonds, which constitute approximately 30% of the sovereign debt stock. These bonds, including the world's first sovereign sustainability-linked bonds, have significantly broadened the investor base and mobilised resources for projects aimed at climate change adaptation and social initiatives.

In terms of **regional and international finance and partnerships to catalyse international resources**, Chile has strategically engaged in international co-operation through the Chilean International Co-operation Agency. The agency leads efforts to support development initiatives focused on the eradication of poverty, the reduction of inequality and sustainable development. Emphasising South-South co-operation, Chile shares experiences and policies with LAC nations, fostering mutual development. Additionally, Chile collaborates with countries such as Colombia, Mexico, and Germany, and with the Economic Commission for Latin America and the Caribbean, to bolster feminist foreign policies and international co-operation for development. This collaboration aims to enhance the capacities of ministries of foreign affairs and international co-operation agencies. Furthermore, partnerships with international financial institutions like the European Investment Bank and the CAF demonstrate commitments to regional development, environmental protection, energy transition and digital connectivity.

Chile: Key indicators

	Chile		LAC		OECD	
Social development	**2015**	**2022**	**2016**	**2023**	**2016**	**2022**
Poverty (Extreme poverty)	13.2 (1.7)	8.1 (2.1)	25.8 (8.0)	22.5 (7.4)	N/A	N/A
Gini index	45.3	43	46.3	44.4 (2022)	33.9	33.4 (2021)
Share of total population in informal households (%)	24.5 (2009)	20.2 (2017)	47.9 (2009)	46 (2021)	N/A	N/A
Share of total population in mixed households (%)	23.6 (2009)	20.6 (2017)	23.2 (2009)	21.3 (2021)	N/A	N/A
Social Institutions & Gender Index (SIGI)	36.1 (2019)	27.2 (2023)	25.4 (2019)	21.6	17.5 (2019)	15.3 (2023)
PISA score in science	447	444	411 (2015)	408 (2022)	489 (2015)	485
Productivity and innovation	**2016**	**2023**	**2016**	**2023**	**2016**	**2023**
Labour productivity (% of OECD)	49	49	36	33	100	100
High-tech exports (% of manufactured exports)	8.4	10.7	8.5	8	16.5	18.1
Patent applications per million people	21.3	20.6 (2021)	13.8	12.8 (2021)	631.2	572.8 (2021)
R&D expenditures (% of GDP)	0.4	0.3 (2020)	0.3	0.3 (2022)	1.8	2.1 (2022)
Investment and private financing	**2016**	**2023**	**2016**	**2023**	**2016**	**2023**
Total investment, gross fixed capital formation (% of GDP)	24.1	23.8	20.7	20.9	21.9	23
Foreign direct investment (FDI), net capital inflow (% of GDP)	4.6	6.5	4.3	4.6	N/A	N/A
Dom. credit private sector by banks (% of GDP))	80	79.9	45.2	44.4	86.8	76.8
Savings (% of GDP)	21.1	19.3	18.8	20.6	23.8	24.6
Market capitalisation (% of GDP)	146.5 (2019)	94.4 (2022)	50.2 (2019)	35.9 (2022)	69.5 (2019)	64.7 (2022)
Citizens' perceptions and institutions	**2011**	**2023**	**2011**	**2023**	**2011**	**2023**
Satisfaction with educational system (% of population)	44	56	67	65	66	67
Satisfaction with healthcare system (% of population)	39	45	55	52	70	66
Share of people satisfied with their standard of living (%)	69	76	70	73	73	77
Confidence in judicial system (% of population)	24	31	33	40	50	57
Corruption Perception Index (score on a scale of 0 [highly corrupt] to 100 [totally clean])	66 (2016)	66	41.2 (2016)	40.2	67.3 (2016)	66.1
Security risks indicator (score from 0 [low security risks] to 10 [high security risks])	2.9 (2016)	3.9 (2022)	5.9 (2016)	5.6 (2022)	2.8 (2016)	2.6 (2022)
Digital and green transition	**2016**	**2023**	**2016**	**2022**	**2016**	**2022**
Share of internet users (% of population)	83.6	94.1	54.5	75.4	81.8	90.7
Fixed broadband subscriptions (per 100 inhabitants)	15.9	23	11.2	17 (2023)	30.6	36 (2023)
Environmentally related tax revenue (% of GDP)	1.2	0.8 (2022)	1.0	0.8	1.6	1.8
Per capita greenhouse gas emissions (excluding land use changes) (t CO_2e/capita)	7	7 (2022)	5.3	5.1	10.7	9.5
Renewable energy consumption (% of total final energy consumption)	24.6	24.2 (2021)	28.9	33.9 (2021)	12.5	14.9 (2021)
Fiscal position	**2016**	**2022**	**2016**	**2022**	**2016**	**2022**
Total tax revenues (% of GDP)	20.2	23.9	21.9	21.5	33.6	34.0
Share of VAT I PIT I CIT	8.3 1.8 4.2	9.3 2.5 5.7	5.9 2 3.2	6.1 2 3.4	6.6 7.8 2.9	7.0 8.2 3.9
Tax morale (% tax evasion justification)	41.3	40.9 (2023)	53.4	58.0 (2023)	N/A	N/A
Public debt service (% of total tax revenue)	1.4	N/A	11.3	12.2	5.4	4.8
Social expenditure (% of GDP)	16.2	17.9	11.3	11.5	20.1	21.4

Note: See the Reader's Guide for definitions and sources.

StatLink https://stat.link/i9hqum

Colombia

Policies to promote financing for development

Regarding policies **to mobilise domestic resources for development and improve fiscal conditions**, Colombia has aligned its fiscal framework and the strategies of development banks with National Development Plans (NDP). The Integrated National Financing Framework under the United Nations Development Programme ensures that the General Budget of the Nation for 2020-24 integrates seamlessly with Sustainable Development Goals, optimising budget allocations across sectors. Colombia's Institutional Strategic Plan (2023-26) and the NDP (2022-26) co-ordinate efforts to strengthen the fiscal system and foster sustainable economic growth. The fund for financing the agricultural sector (Finagro) democratised credit, promoting financial inclusion and allocating COP 35.6 billion (Colombian pesos) to green credits for sustainable agriculture over the 2022-26 period. Direct credit lines from Financiera de Desarrollo Territorial S.A. (Findeter) to electricity companies, and policies like Decree 263 of 2024 for subsidised housing development, further highlight Colombia's commitment to sectoral growth and resilience against environmental challenges, reinforcing its role in advancing nationwide sustainable development.

To advance a robust, inclusive, and sustainable financial market, Colombia has implemented initiatives led by the Ministry of Finance and Public Credit and entities such as Banca de las Oportunidades, Findeter, and Bancoldex, to deepen financial inclusion, support small businesses, and boost agriculture through programs like "Creo" and Development Credit. Initiatives such as Open Data and Immediate Low Value Payment Systems enhance financial products and expedite transactions, while efforts to promote gender equity, financial education, and capital market development attract investment. Reforms like the Capital Market Financing and Modernisation Law broaden market instruments and reduce operational burdens. Colombia is also integrating COP-denominated derivatives trading by 2025. Efforts like "Colombia, destino de inversión" and the Law 1955 of 2019 expand market accessibility, while regulatory reforms foster a vibrant financial ecosystem. Colombia's agenda in sustainable finance is evident through green, social, and sustainable bond issuances, alongside initiatives like "A2censo Crowdfunding," which diversify funding for local businesses. The Colombian Financial Superintendence drives innovation with the Open Finance and Digital Supervision projects, promoting fintech growth, secure data exchange, and real-time risk assessment.

In terms of regional and international finance and partnerships to catalyse international resources, Colombia's 2023-26 National Strategy for International Co-operation secures USD 96 million for climate action, environmental justice, and the inclusion of the migrant population from bilateral donors and multilateral institutions. Initiatives like "Colombia + Competitiva" promote financial inclusion for micro, small and medium-sized enterprises, complemented by the World Bank Credit Project to drive sustainable transformation in agriculture. Collaboration with the French Development Agency is advancing electric vehicle mobility while ongoing negotiations with the IDB involve a credit facility backed by CIF resources, targeting decarbonisation, and accelerating inclusive energy transition. Preparation for the Fourth International Conference on Financing for Development underscores Colombia's commitment, with its focus on a USD 4.5 billion Socio-ecological Transition Portfolio for biodiversity conservation, climate change mitigation, renewable energy, and sustainable rural development.

Colombia: Key indicators

	Colombia		LAC		OECD	
Social development	**2016**	**2023**	**2016**	**2023**	**2016**	**2022**
Poverty (Extreme poverty)	29.7 (11.4)	32.7 (15.9)	25.8 (8.0)	22.5 (7.4)	N/A	N/A
Gini index	50.6	54.8 (2022)	46.3	44.4 (2022)	33.9	33.4 (2021)
Share of total population in informal households (%)	62.6 (2010)	54.1 (2021)	47.9 (2009)	46 (2021)	N/A	N/A
Share of total population in mixed households (%)	21.1 (2010)	17.2 (2021)	23.2 (2009)	21.3 (2021)	N/A	N/A
Social Institutions & Gender Index (SIGI)	15 (2019)	23.5	25.4 (2019)	21.6	17.5 (2019)	15.3 (2023)
PISA score in science	416 (2015)	411 (2022)	411 (2015)	408 (2022)	489 (2015)	485
Productivity and innovation	**2016**	**2023**	**2016**	**2023**	**2016**	**2023**
Labour productivity (% of OECD)	26	26	36	33	100	100
High-tech exports (% of manufactured exports)	10.2	8.6	8.5	8	16.5	18.1
Patent applications per million people	11.4	8.4 (2021)	13.8	12.8 (2021)	631.2	572.8 (2021)
R&D expenditures (% of GDP)	0.3	0.3 (2020)	0.3	0.3 (2022)	1.8	2.1 (2022)
Investment and private financing	**2016**	**2023**	**2016**	**2023**	**2016**	**2023**
Total investment, gross fixed capital formation (% of GDP)	22.1	17.6	20.7	20.9	21.9	23
Foreign direct investment (FDI), net capital inflow (% of GDP)	4.9	4.7	4.3	4.6	N/A	N/A
Dom. credit private sector by banks (% of GDP)	47	42.5	45.2	44.4	86.8	76.8
Savings (% of GDP)	17.5	10.8	18.8	20.6	23.8	24.6
Market capitalisation (% of GDP)	40.9 (2019)	19.8 (2022)	50.2 (2019)	35.9 (2022)	69.5 (2019)	64.7 (2022)
Citizens' perceptions and institutions	**2011**	**2023**	**2011**	**2023**	**2011**	**2023**
Satisfaction with educational system (% of population)	71	63	67	65	66	67
Satisfaction with healthcare system (% of population)	49	44	55	52	70	66
Share of people satisfied with their standard of living (%)	76	70	70	73	73	77
Confidence in judicial system (% of population)	32	27	33	40	50	57
Corruption Perception Index (score on a scale of 0 [highly corrupt] to 100 [totally clean])	37 (2016)	40	41.2 (2016)	40.2	67.3 (2016)	66.1
Security risks indicator (score from 0 [low security risks] to 10 [high security risks])	7 (2016)	6.6 (2022)	5.9 (2016)	5.6 (2022)	2.8 (2016)	2.6 (2022)
Digital and green transition	**2016**	**2022**	**2016**	**2022**	**2016**	**2022**
Share of internet users (% of population)	58.1	72.8	54.5	75.4	81.8	90.7
Fixed broadband subscriptions (per 100 inhabitants)	12.5	17 (2023)	11.2	17 (2023)	30.6	36 (2023)
Environmentally related tax revenue (% of GDP)	0.8	0.5	1.0	0.8	1.6	1.8
Per capita greenhouse gas emissions (excluding land use changes) (t CO_2e/capita)	4.1	4.2	5.3	5.1	10.7	9.5
Renewable energy consumption (% of total final energy consumption)	30.5	29.7 (2021)	28.9	33.9 (2021)	12.5	14.9 (2021)
Fiscal position	**2016**	**2022**	**2016**	**2022**	**2016**	**2022**
Total tax revenues (% of GDP)	19.1	19.7	21.9	21.5	33.6	34.0
Share of VAT I PIT I CIT	4.8 1.1 4.9	6.3 1.3 5	5.9 2 3.2	6.1 2 3.4	6.6 7.8 2.9	7.0 8.2 3.9
Tax morale (% tax evasion justification)	53	61.1 (2023)	53.4	58.0 (2023)	N/A	N/A
Public debt service (% of total tax revenue)	10.1	19.5	11.3	12.2	5.4	4.8
Social expenditure (% of GDP)	12.5	11.6	11.3	11.5	20.1	21.4

Note: See the Reader's Guide for definitions and sources.

StatLink https://stat.link/162fio

Costa Rica

Policies to promote financing for development

Regarding policies **to mobilise domestic resources for development and improve fiscal conditions**, Costa Rica has made significant efforts to emphasising fiscal system improvements and aligning strategies with national development goals. The Fiscal Rule limits public expenditure growth based on debt levels and GDP growth rates from recent years. Additionally, the Directorate General of Taxation has implemented a collection plan to address tax arrears, resulting in the collection of more than CRC 70 billion (Costa Rican colons) by August 2024. Moreover, Costa Rica's National Development Banking System has facilitated access to financing and guarantees for micro, small and medium-sized enterprises, benefiting 95 000 businesses and promoting inclusive growth across various sectors.

Regarding policies **to advance a sound, inclusive and sustainable financial market**, Costa Rica has prioritised enhancing its retail payment systems, particularly through initiatives such as SINPE-Móvil and SINPE-TP for public transport payments. Operated by the Central Bank, SINPE-Móvil facilitates instant mobile payments, promoting accessibility and reducing transaction costs for users. SINPE-TP enables contactless payments in buses and trains, enhancing convenience and efficiency in public transportation transactions. Costa Rica has also implemented data-driven policies to boost financial literacy and resilience across the population, including the regular publication of gender-specific financial inclusion indicators and strategic surveys like the National Financial Inclusion Demand Survey. The Superintendencies, in collaboration with the Central Bank and the Ministries of Finance and Environment, approved the Sustainable Finance Taxonomy. This framework identifies environmentally sustainable economic activities that contribute to climate change mitigation and prevention, aiming to effectively mobilise capital towards investments deemed strategic. It also promotes greater credibility, integrity, and transparency in financial information disclosure.

In terms of **regional and international finance and partnerships to catalyse international resources**, Costa Rica has actively pursued initiatives aimed at enhancing the co-ordination and effectiveness of external financing. The country has implemented strategies to align concessional and non-concessional financing, aimed at making optimal use of financial resources to meet national development goals. One key example is the authorisation under Law 10332 of the issuance of international securities, Eurobonds, as part of Costa Rica's medium-term debt management strategy. This approach aims to diversify funding sources, reduce dependency on the domestic capital market, extend debt maturities and improve interest rates by leveraging favourable conditions in global markets. To oversee this process from 2023 to 2025, the Ministry of Finance collaborates closely with international placement banks, credit rating agencies and legal advisors. These efforts reflect Costa Rica's commitment to work with the global financial community to support its development objectives.

Costa Rica: Key indicators

	Costa Rica		LAC		OECD	
Social development	**2016**	**2023**	**2016**	**2023**	**2016**	**2022**
Poverty (Extreme poverty)	16.5 (4.2)	15.9 (3.5)	25.8 (8.0)	22.5 (7.4)	N/A	N/A
Gini index	48.7	46.7	46.3	44.4 (2022)	33.9	33.4 (2021)
Share of total population in informal households (%)	26.9 (2010)	26.8 (2020)	47.9 (2009)	46 (2021)	N/A	N/A
Share of total population in mixed households (%)	27.2 (2010)	16.6 (2020)	23.2 (2009)	21.3 (2021)	N/A	N/A
Social Institutions & Gender Index (SIGI)	27.9 (2019)	10.9	25.4 (2019)	21.6	17.5 (2019)	15.3 (2023)
PISA score in science	420 (2015)	411 (2022)	411 (2015)	408 (2022)	489 (2015)	485
Productivity and innovation	**2016**	**2023**	**2016**	**2023**	**2016**	**2023**
Labour productivity (% of OECD)	41	46	36	33	100	100
High-tech exports (% of manufactured exports)	18.4	20.4 (2022)	8.5	8	16.5	18.1
Patent applications per million people	1.8	2.9 (2021)	13.8	12.8 (2021)	631.2	572.8 (2021)
R&D expenditures (% of GDP)	0.4	0.3 (2021)	0.3	0.3 (2022)	1.8	2.1 (2022)
Investment and private financing	**2016**	**2023**	**2016**	**2023**	**2016**	**2023**
Total investment, gross fixed capital formation (% of GDP)	18.8	16.2	20.7	20.9	21.9	23
Foreign direct investment (FDI), net capital inflow (% of GDP)	4.5	5.4	4.3	4.6	N/A	N/A
Dom. credit private sector by banks (% of GDP)	57.8	50.1	45.2	44.4	86.8	76.8
Savings (% of GDP)	15.9	12.6	18.8	20.6	23.8	24.6
Market capitalisation (% of GDP)	3.4 (2019)	3.2 (2022)	50.2 (2019)	35.9 (2022)	69.5 (2019)	64.7 (2022)
Citizens' perceptions and institutions	**2011**	**2023**	**2011**	**2023**	**2011**	**2023**
Satisfaction with educational system (% of population)	79	77	67	65	66	67
Satisfaction with healthcare system (% of population)	63	65	55	52	70	66
Share of people satisfied with their standard of living (%)	79	78	70	73	73	77
Confidence in judicial system (% of population)	32	48	33	40	50	57
Corruption Perception Index (score on a scale of 0 [highly corrupt] to 100 [totally clean])	58 (2016)	55	41.2 (2016)	40.2	67.3 (2016)	66.1
Security risks indicator (score from 0 [low security risks] to 10 [high security risks])	3.3 (2016)	3.2 (2022)	5.9 (2016)	5.6 (2022)	2.8 (2016)	2.6 (2022)
Digital and green transition	**2016**	**2023**	**2016**	**2022**	**2016**	**2022**
Share of internet users (% of population)	65.9	85.1	54.5	75.4	81.8	90.7
Fixed broadband subscriptions (per 100 inhabitants)	13.1	22.5	11.2	17 (2023)	30.6	36 (2023)
Environmentally related tax revenue (% of GDP)	2.4	2 (2022)	1.0	0.8	1.6	1.8
Per capita greenhouse gas emissions (excluding land use changes) (t CO_2e/capita)	3.2	3.3 (2022)	5.3	5.1	10.7	9.5
Renewable energy consumption (% of total final energy consumption)	34.1	34.2 (2021)	28.9	33.9 (2021)	12.5	14.9 (2021)
Fiscal position	**2016**	**2022**	**2016**	**2022**	**2016**	**2022**
Total tax revenues (% of GDP)	23.5	25.5	21.9	21.5	33.6	34.0
Share of VAT I PIT I CIT	4.4 1.3 2.3	5 1.6 2.7	5.9 2 3.2	6.1 2 3.4	6.6 7.8 2.9	7.0 8.2 3.9
Tax morale (% tax evasion justification)	43.7	41.9 (2023)	53.4	58.0 (2023)	N/A	N/A
Public debt service (% of total tax revenue)	11.8	19.4	11.3	12.2	5.4	4.8
Social expenditure (% of GDP)	11.9	10.5	11.3	11.5	20.1	21.4

Note: See the Reader's Guide for definitions and sources.

StatLink https://stat.link/zdynhm

Dominican Republic

Policies to promote financing for development

Regarding policies **to mobilise domestic resources for development and improve fiscal conditions**, the Dominican Republic is focusing on forthcoming tax reforms seeking to minimise fiscal deficits, ensure equitable contributions from all sectors of society, and strengthen overall fiscal management. Key elements include removing exemptions to broaden the tax base, improving tax administration and compliance, and transitioning towards a more progressive tax structure. The Dominican Republic's National Pluriannual Plan for the Public Sector, designed by the Ministry of Economy, Planning and Development, aligns public investment with the National Development Strategy and sets forth government priorities over a four-year horizon. These efforts collectively reinforce the Dominican Republic's commitment to sustainable development and strategic resource allocation, enhancing its capacity to achieve national and international development goals, including those outlined in the 2030 Agenda and partnerships such as with the World Food Programme.

Regarding policies **to advance a robust, inclusive, and sustainable financial market**, the Dominican Republic has implemented significant measures to foster financial inclusion and deepen the banking sector. The National Financial Inclusion Strategy aims to increase access to financial services, especially for underserved populations, through mobile banking, financial literacy programmes and microfinance initiatives. The Fifth National Open Government Action Plan (2022-24) incorporates gender and social inclusion commitments, aiming to bridge inequality gaps. Additionally, the Alliance for Financial Inclusion's Gender Inclusive Finance Mapping project supports women's financial inclusion by identifying barriers and enablers in the financial sector. To promote capital market development, regulatory frameworks have been introduced to enhance transparency and efficiency. Initiatives such as the Inter-American Development Bank Invest's Small and Island Action Plan and the strategic alliances of the Development Bank of Latin America and the Caribbean (CAF) aim to finance sustainable projects and promote a green agenda, diversifying the financial instruments available to investors and providing businesses with alternative funding sources.

In terms of **regional and international finance and partnerships to catalyse international resources**, the Dominican Republic has actively pursued collaboration to attract foreign investment and promote sustainable development. Through the European Union and Dominican Republic partnership, the country engages with Team Europe (the EU, the European Investment Bank, and key European nations) to foster inclusive growth. The government's strategic initiatives include leveraging private capital in the energy sector and establishing public-private partnerships in the aim of attracting more than USD 1 billion in private investments. Additionally, CAF's USD 40 million financing line supports initiatives for women-led enterprises and enhancements to industrial parks. As the Dominican Republic prepares for the Fourth International Conference on Financing for Development in 2025, it is placing a priority on securing resources for climate change resilience, social infrastructure, and sustainable economic growth. This aligns closely with the EU's 2021-27 strategy under the Global Europe: Neighbourhood, Development, and International Co-operation Instrument, which emphasises collaboration and sustainable development.

Dominican Republic: Key indicators

	Dominican Republic		LAC		OECD	
Social development	**2016**	**2023**	**2016**	**2023**	**2016**	**2022**
Poverty (Extreme poverty)	26.7 (7.0)	18.2 (4.9)	25.8 (8.0)	22.5 (7.4)	N/A	N/A
Gini index	45.7	37 (2022)	46.3	44.4 (2022)	33.9	33.4 (2021)
Share of total population in informal households (%)	N/A	42.3 (2018)	47.9 (2009)	46 (2021)	N/A	N/A
Share of total population in mixed households (%)	N/A	25.2 (2018)	23.2 (2009)	21.3 (2021)	N/A	N/A
Social Institutions & Gender Index (SIGI)	18.2 (2019)	14.8	25.4 (2019)	21.6	17.5 (2019)	15.3 (2023)
PISA score in science	332 (2015)	360 (2022)	411 (2015)	408 (2022)	489 (2015)	485
Productivity and innovation	**2016**	**2023**	**2016**	**2023**	**2016**	**2023**
Labour productivity (% of OECD)	32	36	36	33	100	100
High-tech exports (% of manufactured exports)	4.4	6 (2022)	8.5	8	16.5	18.1
Patent applications per million people	2.7	0.6 (2021)	13.8	12.8 (2021)	631.2	572.8 (2021)
R&D expenditures (% of GDP)	N/A	N/A	0.3	0.3 (2022)	1.8	2.1 (2022)
Investment and private financing	**2016**	**2023**	**2016**	**2023**	**2016**	**2023**
Total investment, gross fixed capital formation (% of GDP)	22.9	32.2	20.7	20.9	21.9	23
Foreign direct investment (FDI), net capital inflow (% of GDP)	3.3	3.9	4.3	4.6	N/A	N/A
Dom. credit private sector by banks (% of GDP)	25.6	29.5	45.2	44.4	86.8	76.8
Savings (% of GDP)	21.6	27.5	18.8	20.6	23.8	24.6
Market capitalisation (% of GDP)	N/A	N/A	50.2 (2019)	35.9 (2022)	69.5 (2019)	64.7 (2022)
Citizens' perceptions and institutions	**2011**	**2023**	**2011**	**2023**	**2011**	**2023**
Satisfaction with educational system (% of population)	67	75	67	65	66	67
Satisfaction with healthcare system (% of population)	54	62	55	52	70	66
Share of people satisfied with their standard of living (%)	68	72	70	73	73	77
Confidence in judicial system (% of population)	29	46	33	40	50	57
Corruption Perception Index (score on a scale of 0 [highly corrupt] to 100 [totally clean])	31 (2016)	35	41.2 (2016)	40.2	67.3 (2016)	66.1
Security risks indicator (score from 0 [low security risks] to 10 [high security risks])	5.5 (2016)	5.8 (2022)	5.9 (2016)	5.6 (2022)	2.8 (2016)	2.6 (2022)
Digital and green transition	**2016**	**2022**	**2016**	**2022**	**2016**	**2022**
Share of internet users (% of population)	63.9	84.4	54.5	75.4	81.8	90.7
Fixed broadband subscriptions (per 100 inhabitants)	7.2	11.1 (2023)	11.2	17 (2023)	30.6	36 (2023)
Environmentally related tax revenue (% of GDP)	1.8	1.7	1.0	0.8	1.6	1.8
Per capita greenhouse gas emissions (excluding land use changes) (t CO_2e/capita)	3.9	3.7	5.3	5.1	10.7	9.5
Renewable energy consumption (% of total final energy consumption)	15.3	14.8 (2021)	28.9	33.9 (2021)	12.5	14.9 (2021)
Fiscal position	**2016**	**2022**	**2016**	**2022**	**2016**	**2022**
Total tax revenues (% of GDP)	13	13.9	21.9	21.5	33.6	34.0
Share of VAT I PIT I CIT	4.6 1.2 2	5 1.4 2.2	5.9 2 3.2	6.1 2 3.4	6.6 7.8 2.9	7.0 8.2 3.9
Tax morale (% tax evasion justification)	53.4	62.6 (2023)	53.4	58.0 (2023)	N/A	N/A
Public debt service (% of total tax revenue)	19.5	20.4	11.3	12.2	5.4	4.8
Social expenditure (% of GDP)	7.7	8.6	11.3	11.5	20.1	21.4

Note: See the Reader's Guide for definitions and sources.

StatLink https://stat.link/woxpna

Ecuador

Policies to promote financing for development

Regarding policies **to mobilise domestic resources for development and improve fiscal conditions,** Ecuador has been focusing on promoting redistributive economic policies and equitable tax collection as specified under its 2024-25 National Development Plan (NDP). The NDP also focuses on enhancing customs efficiency and ensuring progressive public spending to foster social mobility. The Development Bank of Ecuador plays a critical role by financing infrastructure projects and public works across the country. For instance, in the first quarter of 2024, the bank facilitated USD 146.7 million across 65 credit operations, benefitting more than 7 million people in various provinces. The bank's strategic objective to support territorial development aligns with national policies that aim to reduce inequality and address chronic child malnutrition through targeted project financing. In its efforts to attract new sources of private investment, the Government of Ecuador promotes the Investment Contract as a legal instrument at both national and international levels. This contract defines the terms, benefits, and incentives available to companies making new investments in the country. It enables investors to secure applicable tax incentives, access national or international arbitration, and benefit from additional advantages. The development of the National System for Investment Attraction and Facilitation focuses on the Single Investment Window, a tool that coordinates efforts between public and private institutions to simplify, facilitate, and optimise processes for supporting and implementing national and foreign investment projects.

Regarding policies **to advance a sound, inclusive and sustainable financial market,** Ecuador has implemented the National Financial Inclusion Strategy to increase access to financial services, particularly for underserved populations in rural areas. This strategy includes deploying mobile banking units and expanding microfinance services.

In terms of **regional and international finance and partnerships to catalyse international resources,** Ecuador achieved a significant milestone in 2023 with a historic USD 1.6 billion debt-for-nature swap, the largest of its kind, reducing Ecuador's debt stock by USD 1 billion and saving USD 1.5 billion in debt service. The initiative aims to allocate substantial funds for the conservation of the Galapagos Islands, solidifying Ecuador's leadership in using financial mechanisms for environmental protection. The European Investment Bank Global contributed USD 125 million to enhance the power interconnection system between Ecuador and Peru as part of the EU-Latin America and the Caribbean Global Gateway Investment Agenda. To combat organised crime and drug trafficking, the European Union funded the Strengthening of Security Co-ordination Mechanisms in Guayaquil project, which also enhances co-ordination among key Ecuadorian security institutions. Additionally, the World Bank Group's Country Partnership Framework for Ecuador has facilitated re-engagement in targeted development areas. Moreover, the Promoting South-South and Triangular Co-operation project, supported by a debt-swap program with Italy and administered by the United Nations Development Programme, aims to boost institutional co-operation. Ecuador also leverages concessional international climate finance to meet its Nationally Determined Contributions targets. With substantial EU support, it promotes strategic private investments, particularly in the mining sector, to align its regulations with international standards.

Ecuador: Key indicators

	Ecuador		LAC		OECD	
Social development	**2016**	**2023**	**2016**	**2023**	**2016**	**2022**
Poverty (Extreme poverty)	24.3 (7.5)	25.3 (7.4)	25.8 (8.0)	22.5 (7.4)	N/A	N/A
Gini index	45	44.6	46.3	44.4 (2022)	33.9	33.4 (2021)
Share of total population in informal households (%)	N/A	N/A	47.9 (2009)	46 (2021)	N/A	N/A
Share of total population in mixed households (%)	N/A	N/A	23.2 (2009)	21.3 (2021)	N/A	N/A
Social Institutions & Gender Index (SIGI)	28.9 (2019)	17	25.4 (2019)	21.6	17.5 (2019)	15.3 (2023)
PISA score in science	N/A	N/A	411 (2015)	408 (2022)	489 (2015)	485
Productivity and innovation	**2016**	**2023**	**2016**	**2023**	**2016**	**2023**
Labour productivity (% of OECD)	31	27	36	33	100	100
High-tech exports (% of manufactured exports)	9.2	6.7 (2022)	8.5	8	16.5	18.1
Patent applications per million people	2.7	2 (2021)	13.8	12.8 (2021)	631.2	572.8 (2021)
R&D expenditures (% of GDP)	N/A	N/A	0.3	0.3 (2022)	1.8	2.1 (2022)
Investment and private financing	**2016**	**2023**	**2016**	**2023**	**2016**	**2023**
Total investment, gross fixed capital formation (% of GDP)	20.7	19.7	20.7	20.9	21.9	23
Foreign direct investment (FDI), net capital inflow (% of GDP)	0.8	0.3	4.3	4.6	N/A	N/A
Dom. credit private sector by banks (% of GDP)	29.4	53.7	45.2	44.4	86.8	76.8
Savings (% of GDP)	21.3	23.5	18.8	20.6	23.8	24.6
Market capitalisation (% of GDP)	N/A	N/A	50.2 (2019)	35.9 (2022)	69.5 (2019)	64.7 (2022)
Citizens' perceptions and institutions	**2011**	**2023**	**2011**	**2023**	**2011**	**2023**
Satisfaction with educational system (% of population)	75	62	67	65	66	67
Satisfaction with healthcare system (% of population)	56	36	55	52	70	66
Share of people satisfied with their standard of living (%)	70	68	70	73	73	77
Confidence in judicial system (% of population)	26	25	33	40	50	57
Corruption Perception Index (score on a scale of 0 [highly corrupt] to 100 [totally clean])	31 (2016)	34	41.2 (2016)	40.2	67.3 (2016)	66.1
Security risks indicator (score from 0 [low security risks] to 10 [high security risks])	6.5 (2016)	5.6 (2022)	5.9 (2016)	5.6 (2022)	2.8 (2016)	2.6 (2022)
Digital and green transition	**2016**	**2023**	**2016**	**2022**	**2016**	**2022**
Share of internet users (% of population)	54.1	72.7	54.5	75.4	81.8	90.7
Fixed broadband subscriptions (per 100 inhabitants)	9.8	16.1	11.2	17 (2023)	30.6	36 (2023)
Environmentally related tax revenue (% of GDP)	0.4	0.3 (2022)	1.0	0.8	1.6	1.8
Per capita greenhouse gas emissions (excluding land use changes) (t CO_2e/capita)	4.4	4.3 (2022)	5.3	5.1	10.7	9.5
Renewable energy consumption (% of total final energy consumption)	14.8	18.9 (2021)	28.9	33.9 (2021)	12.5	14.9 (2021)
Fiscal position	**2016**	**2022**	**2016**	**2022**	**2016**	**2022**
Total tax revenues (% of GDP)	19.9	20.9	21.9	21.5	33.6	34.0
Share of VAT I PIT I CIT	6 N/A N/A	6.8 N/A N/A	5.9 2 3.2	6.1 2 3.4	6.6 7.8 2.9	7.0 8.2 3.9
Tax morale (% tax evasion justification)	53.5	53.6 (2023)	53.4	58.0 (2023)	N/A	N/A
Public debt service (% of total tax revenue)	7.7	2.1	11.3	12.2	5.4	4.8
Social expenditure (% of GDP)	8.8	11	11.3	11.5	20.1	21.4

Note: See the Reader's Guide for definitions and sources.

StatLink https://stat.link/9lhw17

El Salvador

Policies to promote financing for development

Regarding policies **to mobilise domestic resources for development and improve fiscal conditions**, El Salvador has embarked on significant efforts highlighted by recent reforms to its Income Tax Law in March 2024. Reforms such as the exemption from taxation of passive income from foreign sources were designed to attract foreign investment and simplify tax regulations. These initiatives are pivotal in broader efforts aimed at enhancing fiscal transparency, improving the business climate, and aligning with the goals outlined in the National Development Plan (NDP), known as Plan Cuscatlán. The NDP addresses critical challenges such as climate vulnerability, poverty, food insecurity and migration, aiming for inclusive and sustainable growth pathways. These strategies prioritise infrastructure development and economic resilience, reflecting El Salvador's commitment to fostering long-term development.

Regarding policies **to advance a sound, inclusive and sustainable financial market**, El Salvador has implemented robust public policy initiatives to foster financial inclusion and deepen its banking sector. The National Financial Inclusion Policy (NFIP), launched in 2021, is designed to expand financial access and services across marginalised groups. Co-ordinated by the Central Reserve Bank of El Salvador and other stakeholders, NFIP focuses on enhancing digital financial services, promoting financial literacy, and developing innovative financial products. This initiative plays a crucial role in improving access to financial services for low-income individuals and women as well as micro, small and medium-sized enterprises, thereby fostering economic empowerment and resilience. Concurrently, El Salvador is committed to developing its capital markets through initiatives aimed at strengthening equities, bond markets and private equity investments. These measures are pivotal for diversifying funding sources, attracting both domestic and foreign investments, and establishing a robust financial infrastructure essential for sustainable economic growth.

In terms of **regional and international finance and partnerships to catalyse international resources**, El Salvador strategically engages in initiatives aimed at enhancing co-ordination and mobilising external financing. The country prioritises sustainable and inclusive economic growth, focusing on productive inclusion, digital transformation, and the transition to a green economy. Investments in renewable energy and public infrastructure play a crucial role in creating quality jobs, boosting income growth, and fostering environmental sustainability. These investments are supported by institutions like the European Fund for Sustainable Development Plus and the European Investment Bank, as well as by the active engagement of the European Union private sector. Additionally, El Salvador's involvement in the US Agency for International Development's Regional Development Co-operation Strategy aims to address regional challenges such as economic prosperity, governance, security, and environmental resilience. These efforts align with El Salvador's NDP and its commitments to sustainable development frameworks.

El Salvador: Key indicators

	El Salvador		LAC		OECD	
Social development	**2016**	**2023**	**2016**	**2023**	**2016**	**2022**
Poverty (Extreme poverty)	40.4 (10.7)	27.9 (8.6)	25.8 (8.0)	22.5 (7.4)	N/A	N/A
Gini index	40	38.8 (2022)	46.3	44.4 (2022)	33.9	33.4 (2021)
Share of total population in informal households (%)	52.4 (2015)	54.4 (2021)	47.9 (2009)	46 (2021)	N/A	N/A
Share of total population in mixed households (%)	21.6 (2015)	22.2 (2021)	23.2 (2009)	21.3 (2021)	N/A	N/A
Social Institutions & Gender Index (SIGI)	22.9 (2019)	19.6	25.4 (2019)	21.6	17.5 (2019)	15.3 (2023)
PISA score in science	N/A	N/A	411 (2015)	408 (2022)	489 (2015)	485
Productivity and innovation	**2016**	**2023**	**2016**	**2023**	**2016**	**2023**
Labour productivity (% of OECD)	N/A	N/A	36	33	100	100
High-tech exports (% of manufactured exports)	5.4	6.4	8.5	8	16.5	18.1
Patent applications per million people	0.6	0.3 (2021)	13.8	12.8 (2021)	631.2	572.8 (2021)
R&D expenditures (% of GDP)	0.1	0.2 (2021)	0.3	0.3 (2022)	1.8	2.1 (2022)
Investment and private financing	**2016**	**2023**	**2016**	**2023**	**2016**	**2023**
Total investment, gross fixed capital formation (% of GDP)	15.5	22	20.7	20.9	21.9	23
Foreign direct investment (FDI), net capital inflow (% of GDP)	2	1.9	4.3	4.6	N/A	N/A
Dom. credit private sector by banks (% of GDP)	48.7	52.1	45.2	44.4	86.8	76.8
Savings (% of GDP)	13.7	18.1	18.8	20.6	23.8	24.6
Market capitalisation (% of GDP)	N/A	N/A	50.2 (2019)	35.9 (2022)	69.5 (2019)	64.7 (2022)
Citizens' perceptions and institutions	**2011**	**2023**	**2011**	**2023**	**2011**	**2023**
Satisfaction with educational system (% of population)	72	81	67	65	66	67
Satisfaction with healthcare system (% of population)	61	68	55	52	70	66
Share of people satisfied with their standard of living (%)	62	77	70	73	73	77
Confidence in judicial system (% of population)	29	67	33	40	50	57
Corruption Perception Index (score on a scale of 0 [highly corrupt] to 100 [totally clean])	36 (2016)	31	41.2 (2016)	40.2	67.3 (2016)	66.1
Security risks indicator (score from 0 [low security risks] to 10 [high security risks])	7 (2016)	6.3 (2022)	5.9 (2016)	5.6 (2022)	2.8 (2016)	2.6 (2022)
Digital and green transition	**2016**	**2022**	**2016**	**2022**	**2016**	**2022**
Share of internet users (% of population)	29	62.9	54.5	75.4	81.8	90.7
Fixed broadband subscriptions (per 100 inhabitants)	6.4	10.7	11.2	17 (2023)	30.6	36 (2023)
Environmentally related tax revenue (% of GDP)	0.6	0.4	1.0	0.8	1.6	1.8
Per capita greenhouse gas emissions (excluding land use changes) (t CO_2e/capita)	2	2.1	5.3	5.1	10.7	9.5
Renewable energy consumption (% of total final energy consumption)	20.7	21.9 (2021)	28.9	33.9 (2021)	12.5	14.9 (2021)
Fiscal position	**2016**	**2022**	**2016**	**2022**	**2016**	**2022**
Total tax revenues (% of GDP)	20.5	22.9	21.9	21.5	33.6	34.0
Share of VAT I PIT I CIT	7.5 3 3.2	9.1 3.3 4.1	5.9 2 3.2	6.1 2 3.4	6.6 7.8 2.9	7.0 8.2 3.9
Tax morale (% tax evasion justification)	33.7	53.7 (2023)	53.4	58.0 (2023)	N/A	N/A
Public debt service (% of total tax revenue)	14.2	20.1	11.3	12.2	5.4	4.8
Social expenditure (% of GDP)	7.8	10.8	11.3	11.5	20.1	21.4

Note: See the Reader's Guide for definitions and sources.

StatLink https://stat.link/r3p5uy

Guatemala

Policies to promote financing for development

Regarding policies **to mobilise domestic resources for development and improve fiscal conditions**, Guatemala has made significant efforts to improve its fiscal system and aligning the strategies of development banks with National Development Plans. The K'atun National Development Plan 2032 aims to address regulatory and institutional challenges that impede improvements in tax administration, transparency, control, and accountability. The government has prioritised policies to enhance public finance management and domestic revenue mobilisation, and to strengthen the application of fiscal legislation and improve the efficiency of the tax collection system. The "Guatemala No Se Detiene" plan further supports resource mobilisation by focusing on key areas like human capital, infrastructure, and legal certainty.

Regarding policies **to advance a sound, inclusive and sustainable financial market**, Guatemala has focused its National Financial Inclusion Strategy for 2019-23 on thematic areas and cross-cutting lines to enhance financial inclusion nationwide. Prepared by the Bank of Guatemala, the Ministry of Economy of Guatemala (MINECO) and the Superintendency of Banks, this comprehensive strategy aims to co-ordinate the efforts of the public and private sectors. It emphasises modern, safe, and reliable payment methods, expanding access to diverse credit products, developing accessible savings services and broadening insurance coverage. It also includes financial education programmes, legal protections for financial service users, effective communication, support for entrepreneurship and for the development of micro, small and medium-sized enterprises, fostering economic growth and reducing poverty.

In terms of **regional and international finance and partnerships to catalyse international resources,** Guatemala has initiated strategic collaborations to enhance industrial competitiveness and leverage nearshoring. For example, several innovative programmes aimed at financing the reduction of socio-natural disaster risks in Guatemala were successfully implemented through collaboration with partner organisations and private-sector entities. Initiatives led by the World Food Program, Aseguradora Rural, MiCRO, Harvest Plus, Columbia University and the International Centre for Tropical Agriculture resulted in the development of a mobile application to simplify microinsurance registration, financial inclusion, and training. In addition, the National Investment Attraction Strategy aims to reach USD 1.6 billion in FDI by 2024, focusing on sectors like processed foods, pharmaceuticals, and business services. This strategy, overseen by MINECO, involves collaboration with institutions such as the Ministry of Foreign Affair and the Ministry of Agriculture. The objective is to foster long-term economic growth and formal employment creation, focusing on two key strategies: i) enhancing Guatemala's competitiveness in 20 established industrial sectors with the aim of furthering diversification and improving export capabilities; and ii) capitalising on the nearshoring trend to draw investments into four advanced sectors: pharmaceuticals, medical devices, electronic equipment manufacturing and business services. Furthermore, Guatemala is vigorously promoting itself as a prime investment destination with the support of entities like the National Competitiveness Programme and the Guatemalan Association of Exporters. The creation of Invest Guatemala is instrumental in facilitating foreign investments and assisting local businesses in expansion efforts.

Guatemala: Key indicators

	Guatemala		LAC		OECD	
Social development	**2016**	**2023**	**2016**	**2023**	**2016**	**2022**
Poverty (Extreme poverty)	N/A	N/A	25.8 (8.0)	22.5 (7.4)	N/A	N/A
Gini index	N/A	N/A	46.3	44.4 (2022)	33.9	33.4 (2021)
Share of total population in informal households (%)	N/A	N/A	47.9 (2009)	46 (2021)	N/A	N/A
Share of total population in mixed households (%)	N/A	N/A	23.2 (2009)	21.3 (2021)	N/A	N/A
Social Institutions & Gender Index (SIGI)	28.6 (2019)	25.7	25.4 (2019)	21.6	17.5 (2019)	15.3 (2023)
PISA score in science	N/A	N/A	411 (2015)	408 (2022)	489 (2015)	485
Productivity and innovation	**2016**	**2023**	**2016**	**2023**	**2016**	**2023**
Labour productivity (% of OECD)	17	18	36	33	100	100
High-tech exports (% of manufactured exports)	5.8	5.8	8.5	8	16.5	18.1
Patent applications per million people	0.2	0.5 (2021)	13.8	12.8 (2021)	631.2	572.8 (2021)
R&D expenditures (% of GDP)	0.02	0.1 (2021)	0.3	0.3 (2022)	1.8	2.1 (2022)
Investment and private financing	**2016**	**2023**	**2016**	**2023**	**2016**	**2023**
Total investment, gross fixed capital formation (% of GDP)	13.9	16.6	20.7	20.9	21.9	23
Foreign direct investment (FDI), net capital inflow (% of GDP)	1.3	1.5	4.3	4.6	N/A	N/A
Dom. credit private sector by banks (% of GDP)	35.1	37.4	45.2	44.4	86.8	76.8
Savings (% of GDP)	14.8	19.3	18.8	20.6	23.8	24.6
Market capitalisation (% of GDP)	N/A	N/A	50.2 (2019)	35.9 (2022)	69.5 (2019)	64.7 (2022)
Citizens' perceptions and institutions	**2011**	**2023**	**2011**	**2023**	**2011**	**2023**
Satisfaction with educational system (% of population)	72	75	67	65	66	67
Satisfaction with healthcare system (% of population)	55	59	55	52	70	66
Share of people satisfied with their standard of living (%)	70	81	70	73	73	77
Confidence in judicial system (% of population)	38	51	33	40	50	57
Corruption Perception Index (score on a scale of 0 [highly corrupt] to 100 [totally clean])	28 (2016)	23	41.2 (2016)	40.2	67.3 (2016)	66.1
Security risks indicator (score from 0 [low security risks] to 10 [high security risks])	7.3 (2016)	6.5 (2022)	5.9 (2016)	5.6 (2022)	2.8 (2016)	2.6 (2022)
Digital and green transition	**2016**	**2022**	**2016**	**2022**	**2016**	**2022**
Share of internet users (% of population)	34.5	54.4	54.5	75.4	81.8	90.7
Fixed broadband subscriptions (per 100 inhabitants)	3.1	5.1 (2023)	11.2	17 (2023)	30.6	36 (2023)
Environmentally related tax revenue (% of GDP)	0.9	0.8	1.0	0.8	1.6	1.8
Per capita greenhouse gas emissions (excluding land use changes) (t CO_2e/capita)	2.5	2.6	5.3	5.1	10.7	9.5
Renewable energy consumption (% of total final energy consumption)	63.2	62.1 (2021)	28.9	33.9 (2021)	12.5	14.9 (2021)
Fiscal position	**2016**	**2022**	**2016**	**2022**	**2016**	**2022**
Total tax revenues (% of GDP)	13.2	14.4	21.9	21.5	33.6	34.0
Share of VAT I PIT I CIT	4.8 | 0.4 | 2.9	5.9 | 0.5 | 3	5.9 | 2 | 3.2	6.1 | 2 | 3.4	6.6 | 7.8 | 2.9	7.0 | 8.2 | 3.9
Tax morale (% tax evasion justification)	49.9	60.7 (2023)	53.4	58.0 (2023)	N/A	N/A
Public debt service (% of total tax revenue)	11.6	11.6	11.3	12.2	5.4	4.8
Social expenditure (% of GDP)	7.2	7.7	11.3	11.5	20.1	21.4

Note: See the Reader's Guide for definitions and sources.

StatLink https://stat.link/t0cv4j

Mexico

Policies to promote financing for development

Regarding policies **to mobilise domestic resources for development and improve fiscal conditions**, Mexico has made significant efforts to eliminate universal compensation between different types of taxes in the aim of reducing tax evasion and improving transparency and accountability in the tax system. Implemented since 2019, this policy has generated substantial resources and provided greater control over value-added tax (VAT) balances. Another crucial initiative is the adoption of a Base Erosion and Profit Shifting strategy, aligning Mexico's tax system with international standards to curb tax avoidance by multinational corporations. Initiatives like the Zero VAT rate on sanitary pads, tampons and menstrual cups aim to lower economic barriers for women, ensuring equitable access to essential products. Furthermore, the Employment Subsidy introduced in 2024 specifically targets lower-income individuals, boosting their disposable income and promoting fairer tax distribution. The country has also modernised its tax laws to include digital economy transactions, facilitating VAT collection from foreign digital service providers and promoting economic formalisation.

To advance a **sound, inclusive and sustainable financial market**, Mexico has implemented its National Financial Inclusion Policy (PNIF) for 2020-24 to enhance financial inclusion and financial health nationwide. Co-coordinated by several public administration entities, this policy aims to achieve critical purposes, including expanding access to financial products and services, promoting digital payments, and strengthening financial infrastructure to mitigate information asymmetries. The PNIF also places a strong emphasis on improving the economic and financial literacy of citizens, along with ensuring financial protection mechanisms for vulnerable groups such as women, migrants, indigenous, elderly and rural populations. In support of the Sustainable Development Goals (SDGs), Mexico has introduced sovereign bonds linked to the SDGs, mobilising approximately USD 18 billion since 2020. Additionally, the Sustainable Finance Mobilisation Strategy aims to redirect capital flows towards sustainable projects. Furthermore, the Sustainable Mexico's Sustainable Taxonomy, a pioneering financial policy instrument, is an integral part of this Strategy guiding investments into activities with positive environmental and social impacts, with gender equality as a priority objective. The Strategy also includes financial inclusion and literacy programmes and advocates for mainstreaming gender equality within financial institutions and financial inclusion initiatives. These comprehensive efforts involve collaboration among national, subnational, and international institutions, fostering public-private dialogue and supporting the development of a resilient, inclusive and sustainable financial market.

In terms of **regional and international finance and partnerships to catalyse international resources**, Mexico has initiated strategic collaborations to enhance institutional strength and innovation across various sectors. For instance, it implemented a new regulatory process to manage technical co-operation, ensuring transparency, regulation, and co-ordinated support from international financial organisations to their member countries. This co-operation includes information gathering, knowledge transfer, training, courses, certifications, studies, and analyses aimed at supporting the design and implementation of public policies and strategic projects through non-reimbursable resources. It involves collaboration across Mexico's public sector and federal entities, with the goal of fostering sustainable economic growth and development. The Ministry of Finance and Public Credit oversees the allocation of these resources, with progress being made towards the creation of a normative document to guide internal regulations. This initiative underscores Mexico's commitment to leveraging international partnerships for innovation and strengthening institutional capabilities.

Mexico: Key indicators

	Mexico		LAC		OECD	
Social development	**2016**	**2022**	**2016**	**2023**	**2016**	**2022**
Poverty (Extreme poverty)	37.6 (8.4)	28.6 (6.2)	25.8 (8.0)	22.5 (7.4)	N/A	N/A
Gini index	46.9	43.5	46.3	44.4 (2022)	33.9	33.4 (2021)
Share of total population in informal households (%)	41.6 (2010)	36.8 (2020)	47.9 (2009)	46 (2021)	N/A	N/A
Share of total population in mixed households (%)	24.8 (2010)	27.2 (2020)	23.2 (2009)	21.3 (2021)	N/A	N/A
Social Institutions & Gender Index (SIGI)	29 (2019)	21.9 (2023)	25.4 (2019)	21.6	17.5 (2019)	15.3 (2023)
PISA score in science	416 (2015)	410	411 (2015)	408 (2022)	489 (2015)	485
Productivity and innovation	**2016**	**2023**	**2016**	**2023**	**2016**	**2023**
Labour productivity (% of OECD)	57	50	36	33	100	100
High-tech exports (% of manufactured exports)	20.6	17.6	8.5	8	16.5	18.1
Patent applications per million people	10.8	8.8 (2021)	13.8	12.8 (2021)	631.2	572.8 (2021)
R&D expenditures (% of GDP)	0.4	0.3 (2022)	0.3	0.3 (2022)	1.8	2.1 (2022)
Investment and private financing	**2016**	**2023**	**2016**	**2023**	**2016**	**2023**
Total investment, gross fixed capital formation (% of GDP)	23.7	24.4	20.7	20.9	21.9	23
Foreign direct investment (FDI), net capital inflow (% of GDP)	3.5	1.7	4.3	4.6	N/A	N/A
Dom. credit private sector by banks (% of GDP)	25.1	25.4	45.2	44.4	86.8	76.8
Savings (% of GDP)	19.4	19.7	18.8	20.6	23.8	24.6
Market capitalisation (% of GDP)	31.7 (2019)	31.1 (2022)	50.2 (2019)	35.9 (2022)	69.5 (2019)	64.7 (2022)
Citizens' perceptions and institutions	**2011**	**2023**	**2011**	**2023**	**2011**	**2023**
Satisfaction with educational system (% of population)	64	70	67	65	66	67
Satisfaction with healthcare system (% of population)	54	60	55	52	70	66
Share of people satisfied with their standard of living (%)	69	83	70	73	73	77
Confidence in judicial system (% of population)	32	47	33	40	50	57
Corruption Perception Index (score on a scale of 0 [highly corrupt] to 100 [totally clean])	30 (2016)	31	41.2 (2016)	40.2	67.3 (2016)	66.1
Security risks indicator (score from 0 [low security risks] to 10 [high security risks])	8 (2016)	8.6 (2022)	5.9 (2016)	5.6 (2022)	2.8 (2016)	2.6 (2022)
Digital and green transition	**2016**	**2023**	**2016**	**2022**	**2016**	**2022**
Share of internet users (% of population)	59.5	81.2	54.5	75.4	81.8	90.7
Fixed broadband subscriptions (per 100 inhabitants)	13	20.5	11.2	17 (2023)	30.6	36 (2023)
Environmentally related tax revenue (% of GDP)	1.5	1.0 (2022)	1.0	0.8	1.6	1.8
Per capita greenhouse gas emissions (excluding land use changes) (t CO_2e/capita)	6.6	6.4 (2022)	5.3	5.1	10.7	9.5
Renewable energy consumption (% of total final energy consumption)	9.2	13 (2021)	28.9	33.9 (2021)	12.5	14.9 (2021)
Fiscal position	**2016**	**2022**	**2016**	**2022**	**2016**	**2022**
Total tax revenues (% of GDP)	16.6	16.9	21.9	21.5	33.6	34.0
Share of VAT I PIT I CIT	3.9 3.4 3.5	4.3 3.7 4	5.9 2 3.2	6.1 2 3.4	6.6 7.8 2.9	7.0 8.2 3.9
Tax morale (% tax evasion justification)	62.6	66.9 (2023)	53.4	58.0 (2023)	N/A	N/A
Public debt service (% of total tax revenue)	18.8	29.9	11.3	12.2	5.4	4.8
Social expenditure (% of GDP)	9.9	10.2	11.3	11.5	20.1	21.4

Note: See the Reader's Guide for definitions and sources.

StatLink https://stat.link/ie382r

Panama

Policies to promote financing for development

Regarding policies **to mobilise domestic resources for development and improve fiscal conditions**, Panama has made significant efforts to foster an investment-friendly environment characterised by historically low tax rates. This approach aims to attract investments while acknowledging challenges like chronic fiscal deficits and limited fiscal space for social inclusion policies. The country has prioritised economic growth and resilience through partnerships with national development banks, aligning these efforts with Panama's National Development Plan. Investments are strategically directed towards critical sectors including infrastructure, renewable energy, and climate resilience, supported by international funding from entities like the World Bank and the Green Climate Fund. In parallel, Panama has launched initiatives such as the Indigenous Peoples National Development Plan and the National Adaptation Plan, which aim to diversify the economy, promote sustainability, and tackle ongoing social inclusion challenges. With support from the Development Bank of Latin America, Panama is strengthening implementation of the National Financial Literacy Strategy.

Regarding policies **to advance a robust, inclusive, and sustainable financial market,** Panama has strategically implemented several initiatives. A USD 40 million World Bank project is enhancing public financial management systems over five years in the aim of improving fiscal sustainability and expenditure efficiency through the consolidation of the Panama Public Financial Management Information System. The World Bank Group's new Country Partnership Framework (2024-28) emphasises priorities such as job creation, economic diversification, inclusion and resilience to natural shocks and climate change, with a particular focus on finance of small and medium-sized enterprises and public investment management. Panama's banking sector is undergoing digital transformation, driven by fintech innovations that promote financial inclusion. The Digital Agenda, launched in 2020, aims to transform the state administration, reduce inequality, and enhance competitiveness. Panama is also making substantial investments in infrastructure projects such as the Panama Canal water management system, the Gorgas Memorial Institute, the North Panama Hospital, and an electricity interconnection with Colombia. These efforts are geared towards enhancing public infrastructure and fostering national economic growth.

In terms of **regional and international finance and partnerships to catalyse international resources**, Panama actively participates in collaborative efforts aimed at advancing the sustainable development goals and enhancing economic resilience. A United Nations initiative, "The Unpostponable Agenda for the Sustainable Development Goals in Panama", was launched to guide national development plans to address persistent inequalities, particularly in critical sectors such as food systems, energy, digital connectivity, education, jobs, and social protection. Developed with the Electoral Court ahead of the May 2024 elections, this initiative underscores Panama's commitment to accelerating sustainable development through comprehensive policy frameworks aligned with Agenda 2030. Panama has also established partnerships with the European Union under the Global Gateway Investment Agenda. These collaborations prioritise green and digital transitions, health, education, and sustainable economic recovery. They aim to harness international funding and expertise to enhance Panama's climate resilience and achieve climate neutrality by 2050. Initiatives like the Sustainable Finance Taxonomy are instrumental in aligning financial flows with climate objectives, reinforcing Panama's commitment to sustainable development and global climate goals.

Panama: Key indicators

	Panama		LAC		OECD	
Social development	**2016**	**2023**	**2016**	**2023**	**2016**	**2022**
Poverty (Extreme poverty)	16.7 (7.4)	14.3 (6.5)	25.8 (8.0)	22.5 (7.4)	N/A	N/A
Gini index	50.4	48.9	46.3	44.4 (2022)	33.9	33.4 (2021)
Share of total population in informal households (%)	N/A	N/A	47.9 (2009)	46 (2021)	N/A	N/A
Share of total population in mixed households (%)	N/A	N/A	23.2 (2009)	21.3 (2021)	N/A	N/A
Social Institutions & Gender Index (SIGI)	N/A	15.2	25.4 (2019)	21.6	17.5 (2019)	15.3 (2023)
PISA score in science	365 (2018)	388 (2022)	411 (2015)	408 (2022)	489 (2015)	485
Productivity and innovation	**2016**	**2023**	**2016**	**2023**	**2016**	**2023**
Labour productivity (% of OECD)	N/A	N/A	36	33	100	100
High-tech exports (% of manufactured exports)	1.2	1	8.5	8	16.5	18.1
Patent applications per million people	16.9	8 (2021)	13.8	12.8 (2021)	631.2	572.8 (2021)
R&D expenditures (% of GDP)	0.1	0.2 (2022)	0.3	0.3 (2022)	1.8	2.1 (2022)
Investment and private financing	**2016**	**2023**	**2016**	**2023**	**2016**	**2023**
Total investment, gross fixed capital formation (% of GDP)	38.4	29.5 (2022)	20.7	20.9	21.9	23
Foreign direct investment (FDI), net capital inflow (% of GDP)	9.1	2.8	4.3	4.6	N/A	N/A
Dom. credit private sector by banks (% of GDP)	79.1	68.3	45.2	44.4	86.8	76.8
Savings (% of GDP)	29.7	37.2 (2022)	18.8	20.6	23.8	24.6
Market capitalisation (% of GDP)	24.8 (2019)	20.4 (2022)	50.2 (2019)	35.9 (2022)	69.5 (2019)	64.7 (2022)
Citizens' perceptions and institutions	**2011**	**2023**	**2011**	**2023**	**2011**	**2023**
Satisfaction with educational system (% of population)	73	57	67	65	66	67
Satisfaction with healthcare system (% of population)	65	50	55	52	70	66
Share of people satisfied with their standard of living (%)	77	74	70	73	73	77
Confidence in judicial system (% of population)	32	42	33	40	50	57
Corruption Perception Index (score on a scale of 0 [highly corrupt] to 100 [totally clean])	38 (2016)	35	41.2 (2016)	40.2	67.3 (2016)	66.1
Security risks indicator (score from 0 [low security risks] to 10 [high security risks])	5.4 (2016)	4.9 (2022)	5.9 (2016)	5.6 (2022)	2.8 (2016)	2.6 (2022)
Digital and green transition	**2016**	**2022**	**2016**	**2022**	**2016**	**2022**
Share of internet users (% of population)	54	73.6	54.5	75.4	81.8	90.7
Fixed broadband subscriptions (per 100 inhabitants)	10.7	18.1 (2023)	11.2	17 (2023)	30.6	36 (2023)
Environmentally related tax revenue (% of GDP)	0.7	0.4	1.0	0.8	1.6	1.8
Per capita greenhouse gas emissions (excluding land use changes) (t CO_2e/capita)	4.3	4.2	5.3	5.1	10.7	9.5
Renewable energy consumption (% of total final energy consumption)	22.1	28 (2021)	28.9	33.9 (2021)	12.5	14.9 (2021)
Fiscal position	**2016**	**2022**	**2016**	**2022**	**2016**	**2022**
Total tax revenues (% of GDP)	15.5	13.1	21.9	21.5	33.6	34.0
Share of VAT I PIT I CIT	2.6 1.5 1.8	1.8 1.9 1.2	5.9 2 3.2	6.1 2 3.4	6.6 7.8 2.9	7.0 8.2 3.9
Tax morale (% tax evasion justification)	46.7	52.4 (2023)	53.4	58.0 (2023)	N/A	N/A
Public debt service (% of total tax revenue)	10.5	13.1	11.3	12.2	5.4	4.8
Social expenditure (% of GDP)	8.5	10	11.3	11.5	20.1	21.4

Note: See the Reader's Guide for definitions and sources.

StatLink https://stat.link/q6in8p

Paraguay

Policies to promote financing for development

Regarding policies to **mobilise domestic resources for development and improve fiscal conditions**, Paraguay has implemented significant measures focusing on tax system modernisation and strategic reforms. The introduction and enforcement of a 2019 law on modernising and simplifying the national tax system has played a crucial role in expanding Paraguay's tax base and increasing revenue. This reform unified previous taxes, such as the Income Tax on Commercial and Industrial Activities and Services and the Income Tax on Agricultural Activities, while introducing new measures such as extended tax bases, allowance for tax losses carried forward and transfer pricing regulations. These initiatives are pivotal in enhancing fiscal transparency, improving the business climate, and aligning with the goals of the National Development Plan (NDP). The NDP outlines Paraguay's development vision for 2030 and focuses on four strategic axes: i) reducing poverty and promoting social development; ii) achieving inclusive economic growth; and iii) improving Paraguay's global integration; and iv) political-institutional strengthening.

Regarding policies to **advance a robust, inclusive, and sustainable financial market,** Paraguay has implemented comprehensive strategies. Efforts include initiatives to improve financial literacy, expand internet access and reduce transaction costs. These efforts are critical for achieving full financial inclusion by 2030 under the NDP. Notably, Paraguay launched an Instant Payment System in 2022, enabling real-time transactions and improving efficiency and transparency in the payment system. Legislative initiatives, such as the proposed Financial Inclusion Law, aim to formalise the economy by promoting the widespread adoption of payment methods —primarily electronic— that accurately identify the parties involved and enhance transaction traceability. Likewise, in 2022, the Law on Trust Services for Electronic Transactions came into force, which provides a safe and reliable framework for electronic transactions, promoting greater participation in the formal economy and encouraging innovation in the financial sector. Furthermore, Paraguay has been at the forefront of integrating of Sustainable Development Goals bonds into national regulations, demonstrating its commitment to sustainable financing and economic resilience. This commitment was evidenced by the issuance of a sustainable bond by the Development Finance Agency through the Asunción Stock Exchange in December 2023. These initiatives collectively highlight Paraguay's proactive approach to fostering a resilient financial ecosystem aligned with global sustainability goals.

In terms of **regional and international finance and partnerships to catalyse international resources**, Paraguay has embarked on strategic collaborations aimed at promoting sustainable economic development and enhancing its role in global markets. These collaborations emphasise integrating sustainable practices such as green financing and the building of resilience against socionatural risks. Key partnerships include ongoing support from the World Bank for infrastructure projects, Inter-American Development Bank investments in energy efficiency and collaborations with the Global Green Growth Institute to foster green investments. Paraguay's NDP, prioritises sustainable growth, green investments, and social inclusion, reinforcing Paraguay's commitment to fostering economic resilience. In 2024, Paraguay's role as host of the Organisation of American States General Assembly and the Mercosur Summit underscores its commitment to regional co-operation and economic integration efforts, aimed at strengthening ties with neighbouring countries and advancing in mutual development goals.

Paraguay: Key indicators

	Paraguay		LAC		OECD	
Social development	**2016**	**2023**	**2016**	**2023**	**2016**	**2022**
Poverty (Extreme poverty)	24 (7.9)	19.6 (7.3)	25.8 (8.0)	22.5 (7.4)	N/A	N/A
Gini index	47.9	45.1 (2022)	46.3	44.4 (2022)	33.9	33.4 (2021)
Share of total population in informal households (%)	66.3 (2009)	57.4 (2018)	47.9 (2009)	46 (2021)	N/A	N/A
Share of total population in mixed households (%)	21.3 (2009)	25.5 (2018)	23.2 (2009)	21.3 (2021)	N/A	N/A
Social Institutions & Gender Index (SIGI)	32.8 (2019)	20.6	25.4 (2019)	21.6	17.5 (2019)	15.3 (2023)
PISA score in science	N/A	N/A	411 (2015)	408 (2022)	489 (2015)	485
Productivity and innovation	**2016**	**2023**	**2016**	**2023**	**2016**	**2023**
Labour productivity (% of OECD)	25	24	36	33	100	100
High-tech exports (% of manufactured exports)	7.6	10	8.5	8	16.5	18.1
Patent applications per million people	5.4 (2018)	1.5 (2021)	13.8	12.8 (2021)	631.2	572.8 (2021)
R&D expenditures (% of GDP)	0.1	0.1 (2021)	0.3	0.3 (2022)	1.8	2.1 (2022)
Investment and private financing	**2016**	**2023**	**2016**	**2023**	**2016**	**2023**
Total investment, gross fixed capital formation (% of GDP)	19.1	20.6	20.7	20.9	21.9	23
Foreign direct investment (FDI), net capital inflow (% of GDP)	2.1	0.6	4.3	4.6	N/A	N/A
Dom. credit private sector by banks (% of GDP)	41.3	52.5	45.2	44.4	86.8	76.8
Savings (% of GDP)	24.4	20.1	18.8	20.6	23.8	24.6
Market capitalisation (% of GDP)	N/A	N/A	50.2 (2019)	35.9 (2022)	69.5 (2019)	64.7 (2022)
Citizens' perceptions and institutions	**2011**	**2023**	**2011**	**2023**	**2011**	**2023**
Satisfaction with educational system (% of population)	67	71	67	65	66	67
Satisfaction with healthcare system (% of population)	63	51	55	52	70	66
Share of people satisfied with their standard of living (%)	61	79	70	73	73	77
Confidence in judicial system (% of population)	32	37	33	40	50	57
Corruption Perception Index (score on a scale of 0 [highly corrupt] to 100 [totally clean])	30 (2016)	28	41.2 (2016)	40.2	67.3 (2016)	66.1
Security risks indicator (score from 0 [low security risks] to 10 [high security risks])	6.8 (2016)	6 (2022)	5.9 (2016)	5.6 (2022)	2.8 (2016)	2.6 (2022)
Digital and green transition	**2016**	**2023**	**2016**	**2022**	**2016**	**2022**
Share of internet users (% of population)	53.4	78.1	54.5	75.4	81.8	90.7
Fixed broadband subscriptions (per 100 inhabitants)	3.9	12.8	11.2	17 (2023)	30.6	36 (2023)
Environmentally related tax revenue (% of GDP)	1.0	0.8 (2022)	1.0	0.8	1.6	1.8
Per capita greenhouse gas emissions (excluding land use changes) (t CO_2e/capita)	6.7	6.7 (2022)	5.3	5.1	10.7	9.5
Renewable energy consumption (% of total final energy consumption)	62.5	58.8 (2021)	28.9	33.9 (2021)	12.5	14.9 (2021)
Fiscal position	**2016**	**2022**	**2016**	**2022**	**2016**	**2022**
Total tax revenues (% of GDP)	13.4	14.7	21.9	21.5	33.6	34.0
Share of VAT I PIT I CIT	5.1 0.2 2	5.1 0.2 2.8	5.9 2 3.2	6.1 2 3.4	6.6 7.8 2.9	7.0 8.2 3.9
Tax morale (% tax evasion justification))	67.8	57.2 (2023)	53.4	58.0 (2023)	N/A	N/A
Public debt service (% of total tax revenue)	6.6	12.4	11.3	12.2	5.4	4.8
Social expenditure (% of GDP)	8.5	9.7	11.3	11.5	20.1	21.4

Note: See the Reader's Guide for definitions and sources.

StatLink https://stat.link/eyvdh3

Peru

Policies to promote financing for development

Regarding policies **to mobilise domestic resources for development and improve fiscal conditions**, Peru has prioritised the complete implementation of the General Anti-Avoidance Rule to address tax avoidance. Law 31110 aims to strengthen Peru's agricultural, irrigation, agro-export and agro-industrial sectors while upholding labour rights in line with national and international standards. It establishes a gradual increase over time of the income tax rate based on the taxpayer's annual net income, to ultimately reach the standard rate of 29.5%. This measure is intended to boost sector competitiveness and overall development. Peru enacted Legislative Decree 1488 and Law 31652 to encourage private investment through special depreciation regimes and temporary measures for buildings, construction, and electric vehicles. Law 30309 promotes scientific research and technological innovation by providing additional tax deductions for related expenses. Additionally, Peru has enhanced tax administration and compliance by implementing Mutual Administrative Assistance for Exchange of Information and lifting banking secrecy for audit purposes, aiming to reduce tax evasion effectively. Legislative Decree 1424 limits interest deductions to prevent profit shifting, while Legislative Decree 1381 targets tax avoidance by addressing non-co-operative jurisdictions.

Regarding policies **to promote a sound, inclusive and sustainable financial market**, Peru has implemented a National Financial Inclusion Policy (PNIF), approved by Supreme Decree No. 255-2019-EF, set to run until 2030. Led by the Ministry of Economy and Finance and supported by other key institutions, the PNIF has five primary objectives: i) building trust in the financial system across all population segments; ii) expanding access to suitable financial services; iii) reducing market frictions; iv) developing telecommunications infrastructure and digital platforms; and v) strengthening institutional co-ordination mechanisms. Significant achievements include training more than 360 000 people on financial inclusion topics, expanding digital payment training for micro and small enterprises, extending internet service to more than 2 000 new locations and launching the DNI-Account, which has facilitated the opening of 24 million accounts to improve financial accessibility. Additionally, Peru has issued social, green, and sustainable bonds and prioritised local-currency fixed-rate sovereign bonds to boost the share of local currency in the public debt portfolio and strengthen capital markets.

In terms of **regional and international finance and partnerships to catalyse international resources**, financing from the IDB Invest and the International Finance Corporation plays a crucial role in promoting private-sector investment across diverse sectors, such as social infrastructure, tourism, manufacturing, and the digital economy. Additionally, the National Sustainable Infrastructure Plan for Competitiveness prioritises large-scale projects worth nearly USD 40 billion, focusing on sustainable infrastructure in sectors such as health, education, transportation, and energy. The National Policy for the Promotion of Private Investment in Public-Private Partnerships and Asset Projects seeks to close public infrastructure gaps and boost economic growth by encouraging private-sector participation. This policy, supported by the World Bank, emphasises the importance of transparent regulatory frameworks and efficient project management.

Peru: Key indicators

	Peru		LAC		OECD	
Social development	**2016**	**2023**	**2016**	**2023**	**2016**	**2022**
Poverty (Extreme poverty)	19.1 (5.2)	18.3 (4.2)	25.8 (8.0)	22.5 (7.4)	N/A	N/A
Gini index	43.6	40.3 (2022)	46.3	44.4 (2022)	33.9	33.4 (2021)
Share of total population in informal households (%)	67.2 (2010)	60.6 (2019)	47.9 (2009)	46 (2021)	N/A	N/A
Share of total population in mixed households (%)	24.2 (2010)	26.5 (2019)	23.2 (2009)	21.3 (2021)	N/A	N/A
Social Institutions & Gender Index (SIGI)	24.5 (2019)	18.6	25.4 (2019)	21.6	17.5 (2019)	15.3 (2023)
PISA score in science	397 (2015)	408 (2022)	411 (2015)	408 (2022)	489 (2015)	485
Productivity and innovation	**2016**	**2023**	**2016**	**2023**	**2016**	**2023**
Labour productivity (% of OECD)	21	20	36	33	100	100
High-tech exports (% of manufactured exports)	4.8	4.6 (2022)	8.5	8	16.5	18.1
Patent applications per million people	2.3	2.8 (2021)	13.8	12.8 (2021)	631.2	572.8 (2021)
R&D expenditures (% of GDP)	0.1	0.2 (2022)	0.3	0.3 (2022)	1.8	2.1 (2022)
Investment and private financing	**2016**	**2023**	**2016**	**2023**	**2016**	**2023**
Total investment, gross fixed capital formation (% of GDP)	21.4	21.3	20.7	20.9	21.9	23
Foreign direct investment (FDI), net capital inflow (% of GDP)	3.5	1.5	4.3	4.6	N/A	N/A
Dom. credit private sector by banks (% of GDP)	42.8	45.6 (2022)	45.2	44.4	86.8	76.8
Savings (% of GDP)	20.4	19.5	18.8	20.6	23.8	24.6
Market capitalisation (% of GDP)	43.3 (2019)	28.9 (2022)	50.2 (2019)	35.9 (2022)	69.5 (2019)	64.7 (2022)
Citizens' perceptions and institutions	**2011**	**2023**	**2011**	**2023**	**2011**	**2023**
Satisfaction with educational system (% of population)	50	51	67	65	66	67
Satisfaction with healthcare system (% of population)	41	38	55	52	70	66
Share of people satisfied with their standard of living (%)	62	65	70	73	73	77
Confidence in judicial system (% of population)	15	17	33	40	50	57
Corruption Perception Index (score on a scale of 0 [highly corrupt] to 100 [totally clean])	35 (2016)	33	41.2 (2016)	40.2	67.3 (2016)	66.1
Security risks indicator (score from 0 [low security risks] to 10 [high security risks])	7.3 (2016)	5.8 (2022)	5.9 (2016)	5.6 (2022)	2.8 (2016)	2.6 (2022)
Digital and green transition	**2016**	**2022**	**2016**	**2022**	**2016**	**2022**
Share of internet users (% of population)	45.5	74.7	54.5	75.4	81.8	90.7
Fixed broadband subscriptions (per 100 inhabitants)	6.9	10.4 (2023)	11.2	17 (2023)	30.6	36 (2023)
Environmentally related tax revenue (% of GDP)	0.4	0.4	1.0	0.8	1.6	1.8
Per capita greenhouse gas emissions (excluding land use changes) (t CO_2e/capita)	3.2	3.1	5.3	5.1	10.7	9.5
Renewable energy consumption (% of total final energy consumption)	27.2	30.6 (2021)	28.9	33.9 (2021)	12.5	14.9 (2021)
Fiscal position	**2016**	**2022**	**2016**	**2022**	**2016**	**2022**
Total tax revenues (% of GDP)	16.1	19.2	21.9	21.5	33.6	34.0
Share of VAT I PIT I CIT	6 1.8 3.8	7.3 2 5.8	5.9 2 3.2	6.1 2 3.4	6.6 7.8 2.9	7.0 8.2 3.9
Tax morale (% tax evasion justification))	60.8	56.8 (2023)	53.4	58.0 (2023)	N/A	N/A
Public debt service (% of total tax revenue)	5.8	7.1	11.3	12.2	5.4	4.8
Social expenditure (% of GDP)	N/A	N/A	11.3	11.5	20.1	21.4

Note: See the Reader's Guide for definitions and sources.

StatLink https://stat.link/orc084

Uruguay

Policies to promote financing for development

Regarding policies **to mobilise domestic resources for development and improve fiscal conditions**, Uruguay has made significant efforts by introducing the CO_2 Specific Internal Tax on carbon emissions from petrol, alongside reductions or elimination of the IMESI tax on hybrid and electric vehicles. Policies limiting exemptions for rural property and wealth taxes on certain forests further support environmental goals. To alleviate the tax burden on lower-income taxpayers, Uruguay has increased deductions in the Personal Income Tax and raised the non-taxable minimum in the Social Security Assistance Tax. Moreover, adjustments to the progressive scales for the Tax on Income from Economic Activities aim to support micro and small businesses.

Regarding policies **to advance a sound, inclusive and sustainable financial market**, Uruguay has implemented a series of strategic initiatives with a strong emphasis on sustainability and innovation. A key initiative is the issuance of the Climate Change Indicator Indexed Bond (BIICC) in October 2022. This bond directly ties the government's financing strategy to achieving climate and nature-based objectives by 2025, featuring a novel two-way interest rate structure that adjusts based on Uruguay's environmental performance. The BIICC aims to complement the government's funding programme, diversify the investor base, and align sovereign financing with environmental goals. Additionally, the Sustainable Finance Roundtable, established in December 2021, serves as a platform for public and private sector collaboration to promote sustainable finance nationally. Supported by the Inter-American Development Bank and the United Nations system, this roundtable focuses on integrating environmental, social and governance criteria into financial practices. Furthermore, in November 2023, the World Bank approved a Climate Change Indicator-Indexed Loan, offering potential interest rate reductions if Uruguay exceeds its methane emission reduction targets in beef production. These initiatives co-ordinated by the Ministry of Economy and Finance in partnership with other national institutions, underscore Uruguay's commitment to sustainable financial development and environmental stewardship. The government also introduced regulations to simplify the issuance of publicly offered securities, aiming to promote their use and revitalise the stock market. Other related incentives include the SIGA guaranteed loan program.

In terms of **regional and international finance and partnerships to catalyse international resources,** Uruguay has launched several strategic initiatives to bolster industrial competitiveness and leverage sustainable energy transitions. The Green Hydrogen Roadmap, introduced by the Ministry of Industry, Energy and Mining, aims to promote significant changes in energy sources and industrial raw materials and includes the establishment of a Single Investment Window for Green Hydrogen. Looking ahead to 2040, Uruguay aims to consolidate a green hydrogen industry capable of achieving an annual turnover of USD 1.9 billion and generating more than 30 000 quality jobs. This comprehensive strategy aligns Uruguay's industrial development with global sustainability objectives, fostering economic growth and job creation through international private-sector investments in the green energy sector.

Uruguay: Key indicators

	Uruguay		LAC		OECD	
Social development	**2016**	**2023**	**2016**	**2023**	**2016**	**2022**
Poverty (Extreme poverty)	3.6 (0.2)	4.5 (0.2)	25.8 (8.0)	22.5 (7.4)	N/A	N/A
Gini index	39.7	40.6 (2022)	46.3	44.4 (2022)	33.9	33.4 (2021)
Share of total population in informal households (%)	28.5 (2008)	16.3 (2018)	47.9 (2009)	46 (2021)	N/A	N/A
Share of total population in mixed households (%)	27.7 (2008)	18.3 (2018)	23.2 (2009)	21.3 (2021)	N/A	N/A
Social Institutions & Gender Index (SIGI)	22.2 (2019)	19.4	25.4 (2019)	21.6	17.5 (2019)	15.3 (2023)
PISA score in science	435 (2015)	435 (2022)	411 (2015)	408 (2022)	489 (2015)	485
Productivity and innovation	**2016**	**2023**	**2016**	**2023**	**2016**	**2023**
Labour productivity (% of OECD)	60	62	36	33	100	100
High-tech exports (% of manufactured exports)	10.6	10.7	8.5	8	16.5	18.1
Patent applications per million people	7.6	6.7 (2017)	13.8	12.8 (2021)	631.2	572.8 (2021)
R&D expenditures (% of GDP)	0.4	0.4 (2021)	0.3	0.3 (2022)	1.8	2.1 (2022)
Investment and private financing	**2016**	**2023**	**2016**	**2023**	**2016**	**2023**
Total investment, gross fixed capital formation (% of GDP)	16.9	17.4	20.7	20.9	21.9	23
Foreign direct investment (FDI), net capital inflow (% of GDP)	-0.9	-0.6	4.3	4.6	N/A	N/A
Dom. credit private sector by banks (% of GDP)	25.6	28.8	45.2	44.4	86.8	76.8
Savings (% of GDP)	18.3	13.8	18.8	20.6	23.8	24.6
Market capitalisation (% of GDP)	N/A	N/A	50.2 (2019)	35.9 (2022)	69.5 (2019)	64.7 (2022)
Citizens' perceptions and institutions	**2011**	**2023**	**2011**	**2023**	**2011**	**2023**
Satisfaction with educational system (% of population)	62	60	67	65	66	67
Satisfaction with healthcare system (% of population)	75	62	55	52	70	66
Share of people satisfied with their standard of living (%)	74	74	70	73	73	77
Confidence in judicial system (% of population)	50	48	33	40	50	57
Corruption Perception Index (score on a scale of 0 [highly corrupt] to 100 [totally clean])	71 (2016)	73	41.2 (2016)	40.2	67.3 (2016)	66.1
Security risks indicator (score from 0 [low security risks] to 10 [high security risks])	3.5 (2016)	3.9 (2022)	5.9 (2016)	5.6 (2022)	2.8 (2016)	2.6 (2022)
Digital and green transition	**2016**	**2022**	**2016**	**2022**	**2016**	**2022**
Share of internet users (% of population)	66.4	89.9	54.5	75.4	81.8	90.7
Fixed broadband subscriptions (per 100 inhabitants)	27.3	32.4 (2023)	11.2	17 (2023)	30.6	36 (2023)
Environmentally related tax revenue (% of GDP)	1.6	1.4	1.0	0.8	1.6	1.8
Per capita greenhouse gas emissions (excluding land use changes) (t CO_2e/capita)	12.3	12.2	5.3	5.1	10.7	9.5
Renewable energy consumption (% of total final energy consumption)	60.3	57.8 (2021)	28.9	33.9 (2021)	12.5	14.9 (2021)
Fiscal position	**2016**	**2022**	**2016**	**2022**	**2016**	**2022**
Total tax revenues (% of GDP)	25.5	26.6	21.9	21.5	33.6	34.0
Share of VAT I PIT I CIT	7.1 3 2.6	6.8 3.9 2.8	5.9 2 3.2	6.1 2 3.4	6.6 7.8 2.9	7.0 8.2 3.9
Tax morale (% tax evasion justification)	39.8	47.1 (2023)	53.4	58.0 (2023)	N/A	N/A
Public debt service (% of total tax revenue)	9.5	7.5	11.3	12.2	5.4	4.8
Social expenditure (% of GDP)	14.7	12.9	11.3	11.5	20.1	21.4

Note: See the Reader's Guide for definitions and sources.

StatLink https://stat.link/89na75

www.ingramcontent.com/pod-product-compliance
Lightning Source LLC
Chambersburg PA
CBHW061206240926
51846CB00006B/1124
9789264812130